Louis Tracy

An American Emperor

The Story of the Fourth Empire of France

Louis Tracy

An American Emperor
The Story of the Fourth Empire of France

ISBN/EAN: 9783337170547

Printed in Europe, USA, Canada, Australia, Japan

Cover: Foto ©ninafisch / pixelio.de

More available books at **www.hansebooks.com**

"The American at last threw him off, maimed and cursing, but it was too late."

(See page 222.)

An American Emperor

THE STORY OF THE FOURTH EMPIRE OF FRANCE

BY

LOUIS TRACY

Author of "The Wings of the Morning," "The Wheel o' Fortune"
"The Pillar of Light," etc.

ILLUSTRATED

G. W. DILLINGHAM COMPANY
PUBLISHERS   NEW YORK

COPYRIGHT, 1897
BY
G. P. PUTNAM'S SONS

THIS BOOK IS DEDICATED
TO ONE WHO TOOK THE KEENEST INTEREST
IN ITS PROGRESS
AND READ EACH PAGE
AS IT WAS WRITTEN—
MY WIFE

CONTENTS.

CHAPTER	PAGE
I.—A Box at the Opera	1
II.—Monsieur et Mademoiselle	11
III.—The Refusal and the Resolve	21
IV.—Munitions of War	32
V.—An Invasion of Paris	43
VI.—Jerome is Puzzled	52
VII.—A Challenge	61
VIII.—A Startling Scheme	71
IX.—How Vansittart Became a Frenchman	82
X.—Vansittart's Proposal	93
XI.—On the Verge of the Desert	104
XII.—The Battle of El Hegef	117
XIII.—The Tomb in the Wilderness	127
XIV.—Vansittart Rides for a Fall	138
XV.—A Storm Brewing	148
XVI.—A Rival Prince	157
XVII.—The Storm Bursts	168
XVIII.—How Jerome Enjoyed his Holiday	180
XIX.—De Tournon's Downfall	188
XX.—Some Royalties—and Others	198
XXI.—The Rivals	208
XXII.—A Captured Lion	219
XXIII.—Murder as a Fine Art—with Illustrations	231
XXIV.—The Meeting of Directors	240
XXV.—How the Sahara was Flooded	251
XXVI.—A Combat of Monarchs	263
XXVII.—Introspective	271
XXVIII.—Adumbrations	278

Contents.

CHAPTER	PAGE
XXIX.—INTRIGUE	287
XXX.—TWO WOMEN	297
XXXI.—THE SOIRÉE	307
XXXII.—A MINISTERIAL PANIC	316
XXXIII.—THE PRESIDENT TAKES ACTION	326
XXXIV.—VANSITTART MEETS THE CABINET	337
XXXV.—A BLOODLESS REVOLUTION	347
XXXVI.—THE PRINCESS MARCHESI	356
XXXVII.—THE CONSPIRATORS	366
XXXVIII.—THE SIEGE OF ST. CLOUD	374
XXXIX.—THE CONSPIRACY ENDS	386
XL.—ARIZONA JIM SPEAKS HIS MIND	398
XLI.—THE CORONATION	408
XLII.—"SAHARA, LIMITED," WOUND UP	418

ILLUSTRATIONS

	PAGE
"The American at last threw him off, maimed and cursing, but it was too late" . . . . . . *Frontispiece*	
"It was otherwise with Arizona Jim"	144
"It was monstrous. It was the betrayal of France" . .	316
"Utterly disheartened, cowed, brow-beaten, disgusted, and disappointed, the ex-ministers of the Republic passed out into the night"	346

AN AMERICAN EMPEROR

CHAPTER I

A BOX AT THE OPERA

JEROME K. VANSITTART was the richest man in the world.

He owned vast territories; he controlled railways and fleets; cities paid him tribute, and myriads of workers toiled, that his wealth might magnify unceasingly.

In a word, he was a State rather than an individual.

Computations of the amount of his fortune differed by hundreds of millions, and the public estimate of his riches was based more upon cubical measurements than the common standard of dollars and cents.

Thus, when the Sunday edition of the *New York Clarion* sought to enlighten its readers as to the financial calibre of their most remarkable fellow-citizen, it summed him up as follows :—

"If Vansittart wished to build his Fifth Avenue residence of solid gold, he could do so, and then pave with silver the avenue and West 57th Street in front of his house."

The *Universe*, which was nominally opposed to him, stuck to the illustration.

"Vansittart is going to lay out 58th Street in copper," it said. "He has just added a cent per ton to freight rates on the New York Central."

Of course the democratic *Record* must develop the phrase.

"There is trouble on Wall Street," wrote the city editor. "Vansittart shook up Lake Shores yesterday, and knocked diamond sparks out of every bear on 'Change."

Strange circumstances had conspired to produce this man, the economic phenomenon of the United States.

He was the heir of the princes of American industry. A weird medley of marriage and death had added here a fair domain, there a huge section of some populous commune. Two transcontinental railroads had scarce fallen to his lot before the chief river-way of the Eastern States was added to the inheritance, to be quickly succeeded by three magnificent lines of Atlantic steamers.

He was conscious only of the power of his money. Its extent could merely be approximately gauged by annual valuation.

It was possible, therefore, for him to suddenly carry out strange resolves which shook the financial world by their magnitude and thoroughness. On one occasion, whilst travelling to St. Louis from Chicago, his train narrowly escaped being wrecked in a collision caused by two jealously competing companies' tracks crossing each other. By telegraph he promptly instructed his agents to buy up both systems. The marvellous sequel to the story came when within twelve months the receipts were quadrupled by judicious management and economical administration. For the first time in their history the lines paid a dividend.

Again, he was but ill served in a hotel by a careless waiter. Vansittart stepped out to the office, exchanged a few words with the proprietor, wrote a check, and returned. "I now own this place," he said to the waiter, "and if you don't look after the comfort of the guests, including myself, you will be discharged."

Of course, the tale was told, with its inevitable result,—the hotel soon required to be enlarged to accommodate the crowds that flocked to it.

Demagogues who thundered fierce philippics against the unprecedented aggregation of riches in the lap of this one individual, invariably added, as though grudgingly, and deprecating the fact, "Personally, Vansittart is an uncommonly nice fellow."

And this was but the bare truth. He might best be described as a splendid example of the cultured American gentleman, which means that he was clever, polished, strong in principle, and weak only in his affections, generous to the utmost limit of common sense, courteous and considerate to all who came within reach of his magnetic personality.

He was young, but twenty-six years of age, when this strange and eventful history opened; athletic, as his school record at Winchester and his college triumphs at Yale clearly showed; somewhat inclined to be studious, but in unexpected directions, of which his ordinary scholastic course gave slight signs. Languages and engineering were his professed hobbies, and in these he excelled.

Only his few intimate friends realized that some day he might perhaps write an introspective book that would astonish the world; and its title would be *Influences that Mould Character*, for no other man of his years had read so much or thought so deeply concerning this his favorite subject for speculation and comparative analysis.

Had Vansittart's own wishes been consulted in the ordering of his destiny, he would have gone through life in the leisured ease of a man whose pleasant patrimony is doled out to him by quarterly payments from Government stocks.

But in his case this was impossible. Inheriting more ample revenues and more real power than any crowned king, and finding, when he came to man's estate, that anything like personal supervision of the manifold interests he controlled was out of the question, he nevertheless firmly established an all-pervading sense of fairness and justice in the conduct of his affairs.

Himself a miracle of individualism, he was an ardent

advocate of the collective principle. One remarkable outcome of the spirit and practice of comradeship which he had engendered among his subordinates was, that at the end of five years after he had attained his majority his wealth had consolidated to a degree that astounded men of narrow intellectual calibre, whilst it gratified his own utilitarian theories.

Although in manner and conversation a versatile and well-informed man of the world, his tastes were simple. A high-tempered horse, a readable book, a perfect gun, a well-balanced salmon-rod,—these were his chief desires. For the rest, the potentiality of money had ceased, or it had not yet begun.

And he had never been in love.

A vulgar attachment had no charms for him, and he drew back nervously from the social environments which must inevitably surround him when he at last contracted a union suitable to his rank and condition.

As this, at any rate, was the explanation he offered to his friends when they rallied him on the question of matrimony, the experienced reader will quickly perceive that the one woman in the world for whom he would risk far more than the thraldom of married life had not yet flitted forth from the chaos of humanity into his existence.

Yet on the night when this story opens he was preoccupied to an unusual degree, and the inspiring cause was a woman.

The magnificent Opera House on Broadway was crowded with fashionable New York. A good opera by a French company was produced that evening for the first time, and expectation rose high concerning the work.

Seats were at a premium, and had steadily advanced in price during weeks past. When New York society returns to the city from Newport or Saratoga, it travels in a groove, and woe betide the fashionable dame who is unable to see and be seen at this *première*,—the culminating point of a brilliant season.

Even Vansittart, lounging easily in his comfortable box on the first tier, felt glad that he was spared the crush and bustle of the stalls and circle; and he seldom congratulated himself upon the immunity from worry conferred by wealth, for he knew too well what nonsense it was to think that money could buy freedom from care.

But he had dined well, with his greatest friend, Dick Harland, an Englishman with a sound heart, a healthy appetite, and a poorly lined pocket, who had left him for the moment to drive to his hotel for a forgotten overcoat.

The two were classmates at Winchester, and had remained faithful to their boyish liking for each other.

Harland was now visiting New York; but he refused to stay at Vansittart's mansion, nor would he allow his all-powerful comrade to put him in the way of developing his scanty resources.

His explanation was characteristic. "I regard you always as Jerry Vansittart," he wrote, "the chap who used to go shares with me in sixpennyworth of gingerbread and oranges, when either of us was broke at the end of the term; and I feel that if I met you now as a social equal, or took your help in forwarding my career" (Dick's career threatened to develop into that useful but unremunerative calling, a gentleman jockey), "we would not be quite the same to each other. Give me a quiet hour during my visit to New York, when we can have a quiet jaw about old times, and I shall be more than pleased."

Vansittart humored his wish; but the hour had spread into a whole afternoon, and Harland could not decline the subsequent dinner and a vacant chair in the millionnaire's box at the opera.

Whilst awaiting the arrival of his friend, Vansittart, who was effectively screened from observation by a curtain, leisurely surveyed the occupants of the other boxes.

Most of the people were known to him; and those who were not were uninteresting, until his eye lit upon the form of a lady who sat in lonely state directly opposite to him.

True, she was not unaccompanied, as an older woman sat near her, but in a manner suggesting an attendant rather than a chaperon.

In repose, the face of the fair unknown had the clearly cut outline and delicate grace of a beautiful statue; but when she turned to speak to her companion it manifestly brightened with rare animation, and when she smiled, Vansittart thought he had never before seen so lovely a woman.

She was simply, almost poorly dressed, yet in her dark hair sparkled a tiara that a queen might have worn; and Vansittart felt that under ordinary circumstances none but persons of considerable means could afford to rent a box at the Metropolitan Opera House on these occasions.

Who was she? Not a New-Yorker, as no such woman could be in the front rank of society and yet remain outside his circle of acquaintances. She must be a foreigner, a Frenchwoman, or an Italian; for her alternating moods of stateliness and vivacity, the elegance of her manner, and the dark color of her eyes and hair, gave reasonable suggestion of either nationality.

Vansittart was first puzzled, then interested, then absurdly annoyed.

What did it possibly matter to him who the lady was? So he settled himself back in his box to listen to the first strains of the overture, and in the next moment found himself hesitating whether or not to ring for an attendant, and try to solve the mystery.

Now, he was a man who never allowed himself to waver in a resolution. The very fact that he detected a momentary disinclination to pursue the inquiry further was sufficient to impel him forthwith to press the button of the electric bell; and in that simple act he committed himself to the greatest task ever yet undertaken by one man.

The message spasmodically jarred into life on the indicator

was destined to fill the civilized world with its clamor, but the obsequious attendant who came in answer to the bell little knew that he was the first of a countless host of men and women who would bow before that imperious summons.

"Ask the acting manager to be good enough to see me at his convenience," said Vansittart; and in a little while the gentleman thus designated entered, for in such a matter the millionnaire's wish was law.

"Mr. Gutman," explained Vansittart, "I wish to know something of the lady in the opposite box. Can you tell me her name and any facts connected with her?"

"She is something of an enigma, sir," was the answer. "The name in which she engages her box is 'Mademoiselle Honorine de Montpensier.' She occupies a suite of apartments in the Netherlands Hotel, and her companion is the Comtesse de Fontainebleau. Notwithstanding her unassuming name, the younger lady is obviously a woman of considerable distinction."

Both men were now looking straight at the persons they were discussing, and Mademoiselle de Montpensier noticed them. She slightly withdrew from observation; and the Comtesse at the same moment moved her chair, not from necessity, but seemingly by force of habit.

Vansittart regretted his involuntary rudeness when too late.

"The Comtesse de Fontainebleau treats her as though she were a reigning monarch," he said with a smile.

"There are kingdoms of all sizes, sir," replied Mr. Gutman. "Some are no larger than an ordinary room."

"Why do you say that?"

"Because this young lady puzzles me. I am certain that she is not rich, yet she invariably orders our most expensive box, and will accept no other. She is very gracious and pleasant in manner, but extremely reserved. She wears finer diamonds than any woman in America,—diamonds that cannot be bought nowadays,—but her dress is plain and not costly. There are many contradictions in her speech and habits, and I am only certain of one thing in regard to her,— she is undoubtedly a well-born and most charming woman."

"How is it I have not seen her before?"

"She has only lived in New York for about a month, sir, and I am afraid that we are now honored by your presence for the first time this season."

Vansittart smiled. "You are right, Mr. Gutman," he said. "I must really mend my ways."

At this moment Harland entered.

"Sorry for being late, old chap!" he exclaimed. "I mislaid my check, and the scoundrel in charge of the cloakroom treated me like a thief until I found it. By Jove, what a stunning woman!"

His eyes were riveted on Mademoiselle de Montpensier, who had leaned forward in her absorption with the beautiful strains of the *adagio* movement.

The others laughed at his words, and the official left the two friends together.

"What has amused you?" said Harland.

Vansittart told him of the preceding conversation, and the subject dropped.

As the night progressed, the American repeatedly found himself covertly looking at the fair unknown, and speculating upon her identity. He was so ill at ease that even the unobservant Harland could not help commenting on it.

"What is the matter, Jerry?" he said at last; "you don't seem up to the mark. Had you dined at my hotel, I should have blamed the cook; but I suppose that such an explanation can hardly apply to that palace of yours in Fifth Avenue."

Not often was Vansittart cornered for a phrase. But this time he could offer no valid excuse for his preoccupation; and without troubling to analyze his motives, he replied,—

"The fact is, Dick, that I feel something of the terrible isolation which, we are told, surrounds a powerful king. I suffer the infliction of being regarded as a great potentate in the world of finance and commerce ; and I often shudder at the thought that I have no real friend, no hearty chum, as you used to be, old fellow."

The unwonted bitterness in his tone surprised both speaker and listener, and neither uttered a word for some moments.

"So you even suspect me," said Harland at length, coloring deeply.

"Suspect ! No. But why do you pretend that our lives must practically remain apart ? Why do you insist upon the difference between our stations ? Why do you regard the payment of a hotel bill as marking your independence ?"

Vansittart was personally amazed at this outburst. He had harbored no such thoughts. He was the last man in the world to give voice to them even if felt. Whence did they spring, and what semi-hysterical state caused them to blurt forth unbidden and uncontrolled ?

Harland was astounded.

"Well, this is a rum go," he said after another pause. "Here am I, a poor devil buying race-horses on commission, accused of spurning the friendship of my greatest pal, who unfortunately happens to be the boss millionnaire on earth. I'll tell you what, Jerry. I can't write a letter worth a cent, and I am a frightful duffer at saying ' no ' when I want the other chap to think I would like to say ' yes ' ; but if you will call me your secretary, and give me an attic and five hundred a year, I'll stick to you till you tell me to quit."

"Call it five thousand, and it's a bargain!" cried Vansittart eagerly.

Harland hesitated. "Honestly, Jerry, I am not worth it," he said, adding with hesitation, "unless you let me look after your stable, too. I might save the money there."

Vansittart laughed heartily. "You have hit the nail on the head first time, Dick," he said. "You shall not be my secretary, but my Master of the Horse !"

The two men shook hands on the contract, whilst Mademoiselle Honorine de Montpensier, attracted by their unusual behavior, gazed at them steadily for a little while through her lorgnette.

And she had the faculty which is invaluable to a monarch, —she never forgot a face.

CHAPTER II

MONSIEUR ET MADEMOISELLE

"I DID n't think you were so fond of music, Jerry. As for me, I am just getting the hang of it. Hitherto I believed that the *Post-Horn Galop* knocked everything; but Signor What's-his-name knows a bit, does n't he?"

Vansittart chuckled as he listened to Harland's remarks. Five successive nights had they followed the dulcet strains of French and Italian romantic opera, until Dick, in despair, seriously endeavored to grasp the meaning of that which enthusiasts raved about.

It was not the voice of a Plançon, nor the baton of a Mancinelli, that brought Vansittart to the theatre. But with reference to the lady he had been mute, and he heard with apparent nonchalance Harland's frequent and highly laudatory comments upon her appearance and style.

"What a figure for the box seat in a spin down to Hurlingham!" he had said. "How she would paralyze 'em on the Row! She 's not unlike Evelyn. You remember my sister, don't you?—little thing with flaxen hair and blue eyes. You sold a new bat at half price so as to raise the price of some chocolates when mother brought her to school one day. Evelyn looks smart now, I can assure you, but this one is on the dark and tragic side. Would n't you like to see her in war-paint?"

"What on earth are you talking about?" laughed Vansittart.

"I mean that she must be killing when dressed for dinner

or a dance, and not in everlasting black. She ought to wear a coronet and a fur cloak."

Harland had an ermine robe in his mind, but he was happily oblivious of conventionality in phrase or thought.

Nevertheless, Vansittart was still separated from the lady by the width of the theatre, and he had ascertained by judicious inquiry that she had not evinced the slightest curiosity concerning him.

He felt intuitively that to seek an introduction in the ordinary way was hopeless. Such a woman was beyond the reach of society, and to gain her friendship or regard he must adopt some unusual method. Why he was so anxious to meet her, or what the result might be, he resolutely declined to ask himself.

Whilst Dick was puzzling his brains to find out why the writer of the "argument" should call upon him to admire the consecutive fifths in the intermezzo, Vansittart was working out a plan of action.

"Dick," he said suddenly, "my trainer in Virginia writes to say that he wants me to inspect some brood mares before they join my stud. I am somewhat pressed for time just now. Will you go for me, starting to-morrow, and returning towards the close of the week?"

"Like a bird!" cried the unconscious Dick. "I know more about that game than I do about 'themes for the French horn' and 'symphonic diapasons.'"

Next day, as the result of a conference with Mr. Gutman, Vansittart rented every available box in the theatre for a month. He found that Mademoiselle de Montpensier paid daily for her accommodation.

The clerk in the box-office also had his instructions; and when the Comtesse de Fontainebleau presented herself, he explained that Mr. Jerome K. Vansittart had acquired all the boxes for the use of his friends, but had instructed him to say that the Comtesse and Mademoiselle would gratify him were they to use their box exactly when they chose.

"Am I to understand that we can pay Mr. Vansittart instead of the management of the theatre?" demanded the lady coldly.

"No, madam: the boxes are reserved for his guests."

"We are not Mr. Vansittart's guests," said the Comtesse with increasing asperity, and she swept out of the theatre.

As the result, neither lady was seen again; and Vansittart had not only the trouble of issuing invitations to fill his ill-advised purchase, but also the mortification of knowing that he figured as an ill-mannered plutocrat in the eyes of her whom he wished to conciliate.

One day he met her at the door of a fashionable shop in West 23d Street. He was so surprised that he looked at her too earnestly, and she quickened her pace to regain her carriage. A crevice in the pavement caught the point of her parasol and jerked it from her hand. A newspaper boy darted forward, returned the article, and was rewarded with a quarter and a sweet smile.

Vansittart quietly swore at himself, ordered six dozen parasols from an astounded store-clerk, and discovered when they arrived that he had meant silk ties.

The incident put him in good humor again.

"I cannot for the life of me tell why I am making such an ass of myself," he reflected; "but I will speak to that woman somehow, even if she lives ever afterwards in the belief that I am a frightful cad. In such a case one longs for the easy pertness of the youth of Broadway."

He tried a visit to the Netherlands Hotel, and charmed the manager by his interest in the affairs of that flourishing institution.

"Yes, sir, we have a good many people who stay here for long periods," he said in reply to a question. "We have one pair of ladies here who are very distinguished. They give no trouble; but the younger one, who carries herself like an empress, actually wanted Louis Quatorze furniture in her sitting-room. Why, sir, it costs a small fortune to import it."

The cue was sufficient. Within two hours Vansittart owned the hotel, and a Louis Quatorze suite was forwarded the same afternoon.

What would happen next he did n't trouble to inquire, but events marched as rapidly as the fifth act of a transpontine melodrama.

That evening he received a delicately perfumed note, with a silver " H " and a fleur-de-lys stamped thereon, and it read as follows:—

" Mademoiselle Honorine de Montpensier desires to see Mr. Jerome K. Vansittart. Mademoiselle de Montpensier will await him at the Netherlands Hotel, to-morrow at four P.M."

This message utterly nonplussed him. It was, in the first instance, quite inexplicable that there should be a communication of any sort from the lady, and this unusual circumstance was only made more complex by the emphatic phraseology employed.

Once, when in London, he had been " commanded " to visit the Queen at Windsor ; but with the exception of the, to an American, unaccustomed word, the rest of the invitation was couched in language of dignified courtesy.

Here, on the other hand, he detected a hostile, almost menacing tone, coupled with an imperative " fail not herein, or——!" Why, the thing sounded like a *lettre de cachet*. And how came it that the name of the older lady was wholly omitted ?

Abandoning speculation as futile, he surprised Dick after dinner by taking an unexpected interest in the development and prospects of the Virginian stud farm, and, strange to relate, only slept the more soundly because of the confused state into which his ideas had become entangled whilst pursuing his strange quest.

Precisely at the appointed time he presented himself at the Netherlands Hotel. At the entrance to the ladies' suite he was received by a solemn porter, who inspected his card and ushered him at once into a spacious chamber, announcing his name with the painful precision of a Frenchman speaking English.

His first impression was that he had chosen the Louis Quatorze furniture with a singularly happy eye for effect ; and then, in a somewhat dim light, he became aware that Mademoiselle Honorine de Montpensier rose when he entered the room, whilst the Comtesse de Fontainebleau, who was present, remained seated, and completely ignored him.

He would have spoken, but the younger lady anticipated him.

In a singularly sweet voice, which rendered her foreign accent delightfully piquant, and but ill accorded with her frigid politeness, she said,—

" We have sent for you, Mr. Vansittart, to request an explanation of your attitude towards us. Whilst we cannot complain of any direct rudeness or incivility on your part, we cannot fail to notice that you are, for some reason best known to yourself, striving to thrust your personality upon us. That which was merely an inconvenience with regard to the opera has now become somewhat distressing, as it perhaps compels us to leave a quiet and suitable abode. May we ask in what way we have earned these disagreeable attentions ? "

During this address the lady looked at him steadily. She made no attempt to relieve the situation by asking him to be seated, and although she used the plural form of speech, the other woman gave no sign of acquiescence or even of interest. Her attitude was one of complete indifference.

Vansittart would have been confused had not a strong sense of resentment come to his aid. All the ridiculousness of his present position, and the folly of his previous actions, vanished before the fact that a woman, younger than himself and delicately beautiful, was treating him as though he were an ill-bred clown.

He looked her straight in the eyes as he replied, without a trace of nervousness or diffidence in his voice,—

"There is little need in asking for an explanation, mademoiselle, when you have already condemned me as an officious and even offensive cad."

"We have not said so," she said, her eyebrows slightly elevated, and the ghost of a politely deprecating smile flitting across her features.

"No, but your manner is even more eloquent than your words. I have only to apologize for an apparent rudeness on my part, to promise that no further cause for misapprehension shall arise, and to withdraw."

For an instant the lady paused before she spoke, and Vansittart knew that he was now fighting in the enemy's territory.

"My words were carefully considered," she said, "and do not bear the extreme interpretation you place upon them."

"I am glad to think that you are now speaking for yourself, mademoiselle." This with a quiet glance towards the Comtesse.

The remark momentarily puzzled Mademoiselle de Montpensier. Then, with a bright smile of comprehension, she explained,—

"I have throughout uttered only my own sentiments, and any fault of expression or an ill choice of words arises solely from the fact that I am translating my thoughts into that which is to me a foreign language."

"You leave me nothing but apologies," he said with a touch of sadness.

"I would prefer an explanation." There was an easy return to her attitude of frigid politeness in the remark.

The American now became amused, and, had the lady but known it, her case was already lost.

He looked around the room, and inquired, simply but unexpectedly,—

"May I sit down?"

The request annoyed her by its directness, but she could not refuse. Motioning him to a chair, she seated herself at some distance, and for the first time the Comtesse de Fontainebleau showed that she was other than an automaton by glancing covertly at Vansittart.

He found himself gazing fixedly at a finely modelled bust of Louis Philippe, which occupied the centre of the mantelpiece; but, as neither of the ladies helped him by word or sign, he had no option but to renew the attack.

"Do you know anything of me?" he said.

"I know that you are reputed to be the most wealthy man in the world," replied Honorine.

"That is my chief characteristic, I fear."

"I also have not failed to notice that you are very fond of the opera, but I really am unable to see how your many doubtless excellent qualities can affect this interview, Mr. Vansittart."

"They are most important, mademoiselle," he said gravely, "as evidence of motive. I at once plead guilty to the charge of seeking your acquaintance. I suppose my chief object in so doing was to gratify an idle curiosity. We were *vis-à-vis* at the opera, and you were strangers to New York society. At the same time, if I may say it without offence, you were obviously people of consequence, and it seemed odd to me that I had never met you. Personally, I rather avoid than court new acquaintances; but for some indefinable reason, which I have utterly failed to analyze, I was impelled to seek an introduction to you. When every other method failed, I tried what could be done with money. Being a novice in the art, I suppose I went awkwardly to work, with the result that I am forced to make this unconvincing but quite true explanation of my presence here to-day."

Mademoiselle de Montpensier settled herself more comfortably in her chair before she answered,—

"You interest me, Mr. Vansittart."

"I am delighted to find out that you can travel so far along my line of thought," was the quick reply. "Will you permit me to ask my aunt, the Princess Marchesi, to call upon you?"

"The Princess Marchesi!" she cried in astonishment, turning to her companion as though to seek an explanation.

"Yes," said the Comtesse, speaking for the first time, and in French, "a second marriage. The lady was known as 'la belle Americaine' of the American colony in Rome."

"Oh! I understand. I shall be most pleased to receive —to be honored by the company of the Princess," she went on, addressing Vansittart. "And I suppose that as you are my landlord, I had better be civil to you." This with a very pleasant laugh. "Will you take tea with us? Let me introduce you to the Comtesse de Fontainebleau."

Vansittart was now more bewildered than ever. Nothing in the manner of either lady betrayed the slightest embarrassment at the queer turn taken by events. And who was the younger woman, a girl seemingly of twenty, who could thus juggle with a difficult situation, and dispense so easily with the *convenances* that necessarily govern social intercourse?

The Comtesse was evidently a *grande dame*, yet she treated the other with marked deference, notwithstanding the disparity in their ages and apparent rank.

Of one thing he was certain,—he was dealing with no mere adventuress, who maintained an absurd masquerade to cloak her designs. The affair was more mixed than ever: so he ceased any attempts to unravel it, trusting to the future to elucidate what was now puzzling in the extreme.

During the tea, the mere suggestion of which was an innovation upon American customs, he chatted pleasantly with the two ladies on commonplace topics, earning the kindly regard of the Comtesse by gliding off into French as fluently as though it were his mother tongue.

The sound of her native language tended considerably to raise the spirits of Mademoiselle de Montpensier. She was naturally a volatile and lively girl, and she now astonished and delighted Vansittart by her brightness and vivacity.

"Will you tell us," she said with a meaning smile, "how much this cup of tea has cost you?"

"Nearly three million dollars," he replied promptly, responding to her humor, whilst he joined in the laughter at the extravagant conceit.

"And a lot of bad temper on my part at being kept from my favorite operas," she added.

"Ah!" he said, "that cost cannot be measured in money. You make me bankrupt by the mere suggestion of it."

"I am pleased to note that you have acquired the French language to the best advantage," she cried. "But tell me, why did you not avoid all the trouble by requesting your aunt, the Princess, to call upon me?"

"Because I am a mere man. In what I shall venture to term affairs of the heart rather than the head, men never take the obvious course."

Honorine was now too much amused to repel this dramatic advance, but she changed the conversation.

"I am much obliged for the new suite of furniture, though I suppose you will raise the rent on account of it? Oh, you need not deny. Capitalist landlords are the worst with their poor tenants. But I really must have my box again."

"The theatre returns to its normal state to-night, mademoiselle, so far as you are concerned, and as the opera is *La Traviata*, I hope you will learn to be merciful to those who have erred."

Vansittart shortly afterwards took his leave, but not without a cordial invitation to come again.

When he had quitted the room, Honorine said, "I find him droll, the American."

"And he is of good address, although so rich, mademoiselle," replied the Comtesse.

"Yes," said the other thoughtfully, "his wealth is a power greater than that of kings. Even I felt afraid to be so severe with him."

Vansittart walked slowly across the avenue to his own residence, trying to piece together scattered impressions from the midst of a medley of incongruities. At the door he met Harland, arrayed in breeches and gaiters, and about to try a new hack in Central Park.

"Where have you been, Jerry?" said his friend.

"I don't know. Having tea with an empress, I think."

"Hullo, a flirtation! What has come over you, old man? This sudden love of Italian opera, joined to worship of the teapot, suggests possibilities. It's not the fat woman who sang last night, I hope?"

"No, not the fat woman. Empresses are never fat."

CHAPTER III

THE REFUSAL AND THE RESOLVE

VANSITTART was not a man to do things by halves. Once he had made up his mind to a course, he followed it with resistless energy, and before a fortnight had passed he was, in his own opinion, irretrievably committed to the task of wooing and winning Mademoiselle Honorine de Montpensier as his wife.

The novelty of the pursuit was in itself a recommendation to his ardent temperament. He did not ask himself whether or not that which men called love had come to him.

As already indicated, he was not one to whom affairs of the heart were matters of every-day occurrence. Marriage, of course, he had frequently contemplated as a distant possibility, and in the main it had presented itself to him as a disagreeable adjunct to his position. The fact that almost any woman in the world might be considered an eligible partner for this multi-millionnaire had directly contributed to his general attitude upon the question. Now that he was faced by an element of mystery and reserve, sympathies which had long lain dormant were awakened into fresh activity.

Repeated visits to the apartments occupied by the two ladies, often with his aunt the Princess Marchesi, and occasionally alone, when he had infrequent opportunities of a *tête-à-tête* with Honorine, had revealed to him more clearly her many excellent qualities of head and heart.

But her history and surroundings were still impenetrably veiled.

True, his aunt had recognized in her a descendant of one of the many branches into which the Bourbon dynasty of France had split up since its dissolution. To her knowledge, the lady had no special claim to consideration in this respect ; and it was, to say the least, incomprehensible to a free-minded American that a really sensible woman like Mademoiselle de Montpensier, and a born leader of society such as the distinguished and pleasant-mannered Comtesse de Fontainebleau, should lend themselves to what seemed to him to be, if not trivial, at least unconvincing and inadequate devices, in the conduct of their relations to each other and to the ordinary affairs of life.

Vansittart, however, believed himself to be in love.

He also cherished the delusion that when a man is in love he fails to apply to his affairs the calm and equable mind which he would devote to mere matters of business.

In a word, he abandoned himself unquestioningly and utterly to his ideal, and definitely decided to contract an alliance with the beautiful and fascinating Frenchwoman.

Knowing something of her straightforwardness in action and disregard for conventionality, he determined to declare his views to her without delay or circumlocution. He put to her the question in so many words to be favored with a private interview, and the request was granted with prompt brevity. As he neared her apartments at the appointed hour, he tried hard to imagine himself to be an earnest and impassioned lover.

He almost found himself smiling at the nonchalance with which he approached his task. But as he had already crushed into nothingness so many doubtful circumstances, he resolved almost fiercely not to allow any self-questioning now, but to go straight through with the business on the lines he had determined upon.

The two young people were by this time upon such terms of friendly intimacy, that, under other conditions, their meeting would have admitted of an agreeable chat on mutually interesting topics. The manner of this *rencontre*, however, did not permit of ease.

Mademoiselle de Montpensier would not have been a woman had she failed to recognize that Vansittart had some powerful motive in so formally demanding an interview. There was therefore a silent constraint in her unaffected reception of him, and both found it difficult to maintain a conversation on commonplace lines.

Curiously enough, neither the man nor the woman seemed to be in sympathetic mood. Both knew that there was something hidden between them; and Vansittart, less tactful than the beautiful Frenchwoman, soon felt the situation to be intolerable.

He at once rose from the chair in which he had been seated at some distance from Honorine, walked over towards her, and, looking her straight in the face, said,—

"I fear, Mademoiselle, that I may shock, and perhaps even pain you, by the bluntness of what I am about to say; but it is impossible for me, where you are concerned, to adopt subterfuge or pretence. I feel, therefore, that the only course open to me is, to put in the fewest and plainest words the object of my visit here to-day. I have come to ask you to be my wife."

He paused, being himself utterly unable to add a word in furtherance or extenuation of his strange avowal.

He had of course, early that day, planned many speeches and methods of declaring himself. They were all excellent to his thinking at the time, but they had all vanished into nothingness; and at least it might be urged that the lady could make no mistake as to what he meant, whilst he was inwardly amazed to find that his first lucid thought after the words had left his lips was that he was now irretrievably committed to the supreme step of his career.

For once Mademoiselle de Montpensier was at a loss to frame an adequate reply. She blushed deeply, cast down her eyes, and Vansittart, in strange altruistic mood, found himself calmly reviewing the possibilities of her decision, and deciding quite judicially that the chances were apparently in his favor.

Nothing but an every-day proverb came uppermost. "The woman who hesitates is lost," he thought; and Mademoiselle de Montpensier undoubtedly hesitated.

At last she spoke, and her words came slowly but distinctly.

"I cannot deny, Mr. Vansittart," she said, "that your unlooked-for proposal is flattering to me. I will even go so far as to say that under other conditions, and with perhaps more mature reflection on the part of both of us, it might even have been agreeable to me; but I must tell you, with the same openness and candor that you have displayed towards me, that our marriage is quite impossible."

Again Vansittart experienced the almost maddening emotion that it was his logical faculty rather than his heart which was disturbed by her answer.

What reason could such a woman find so completely convincing in her decision? He was fully conscious of the fact that no living man, whatever his title or position, could offer a woman higher prospects than himself.

From her manner it was unreasonable to suppose that a prior affection controlled her resolve. During their brief acquaintance they had discovered many mutual sympathies, and, for his part, he thought he had never encountered in either sex a nature so closely allied to his own. Yet she had refused him, and he knew, without further questioning, that his case was hopeless.

The situation was too dramatic for other than simplicity.

"If it is painful to you," he said, "to pursue the subject, I will forthwith drop it forever, expressing the hope in the same breath that my momentary presumption will in no wise disturb our friendly relations. But I cannot help adding that I am surprised and grieved at your decision, and it will perhaps tend to mitigate my sorrow if you deem fit to give me some brief explanation of your evidently fixed purpose."

Honorine had now somewhat recovered her composure. She rose quite frankly, taking his hand in hers, and said,—

"Even had you not asked me, I had already resolved to explain fully all that I feel must now be mysterious to you. And let me say, in the first instance, that I deeply regret that any inadvertence on my part should have led you to believe that any other outcome of the friendship between us was possible or probable. I cannot marry you because my life is already pledged to a pursuit which I have no option but to regard as dominating every personal wish and sentiment. You perhaps do not know that I am a lineal descendant of two lines of the kings of France. To me alone this sad heritage is committed by fate, and fate alone can govern my destiny. I am a mere puppet in the hands of an all-wise Providence.

"By the Salic Law a woman may not ascend the throne of France, but by the same law she who inherits that domain cannot marry other than its ruler. Were you the Emperor of France, Mr. Vansittart, though your kingdom did not extend beyond this door, and though you were poorer than the meanest domestic of this hotel, I should be compelled to become your wife, and I hope that in such a consummation fate would have been kind to me. Need I say more to show how impossible is our union, and at the same time how grateful I am for your regard?"

She sighed deeply as she spoke, and the two stood for some little while unable to find further expression for their tumultuous thoughts.

Jerome regarded the beautiful creature before him with a new feeling of reverential awe. His acute mind was quick to grasp all the hopelessness and vastness of the task to which she was pre-ordained. Had he sought through the wide world for a companion suited to the boundless wealth he possessed, he could have found no other woman so richly endowed.

Yet his inheritance was a reality, hers but a shadow—a pity, and the more pitiful because true.

In a sort of numb self-consciousness he thought that the dream of his life was ended.

Yet it was at that moment only commencing, which shows that men can no more interpret the apparently well-ordered events of ordinary existence than the jumbled incoherence of disturbed slumber.

At last Honorine again addressed him, this time with a weak smile, that came through ill-repressed tears as a rainbow in a storm-swept summer sky.

"Do not think me vain or mad," she murmured. "I am sadly happy in my life's work. If I said otherwise, it would not be the Queen of France who spoke, but a wretched actress who strove to convince herself in sublime folly. It is the will of Heaven. I *am* the Queen, and I shall never yield the throne of my fathers."

Her grasp tightened with the concluding phrase, and there came into her eyes an imperious light that went to Jerome's soul.

He bowed and kissed her hand in respectful homage and assent. The act was graceful. It lent gravity to the first words he had uttered since his avowal.

"In order to win you, mademoiselle," he said, "I must first found the Fourth Empire of France."

It was a species of decorous joke, he thought; and Honorine smiled in sympathy with him as she answered,—

"Yes, there is no other solution of the difficulty."

He added, "If I were the Emperor of France, you would marry me?"

With even greater emphasis she replied," Yes," and this time without any qualification.

Each felt that further conversation on the point was impracticable, and even painful; so after a kindly farewell they separated.

Never before had Vansittart been thwarted in any important design.

As he strolled forth into the bright sunshine of a lovely day in autumn, he tried to laugh at his own absurdity, and planned out a snow-shoe expedition after Canadian elk, with Harland as a companion, to fill in the winter months.

But the far distant wastes of pine and prairie were very shadowy and indistinct, whilst there ever recurred to him the vision of the chivalrous woman who preferred the airy nothingness of a fantastic dream to the fair prospect of love and riches that he had offered her.

Rather than seek the majestic seclusion of his home, he turned off into Central Park.

His steps wandered aimlessly like his thoughts, and before long he found himself gazing idly at the animals in the Zoölogical Gardens.

"Here," he said to himself, "the philosopher may find the crude semblance of all the complex passions that shake human nature. One may well wonder which is the happier state. How strange that there should be such development merely because a tailor supplies our garments instead of nature!"

He laughed unmirthfully at the notion, and narrowly escaped being struck by a large foreign bird, flying blindly, with hideous cry and clatter, from the pursuit of another of its species, hot in chase with murderous intent.

The incident alarmed a herd of deer calmly browsing in a neighboring enclosure. They blamed Vansittart for the noise; and at once the does and hinds gathered, implicitly trustful, behind the patriarch of the family,—a many-antlered stag, who boldly faced the intruder, and was forthwith prepared to offer battle should he cross the fence.

The eyes of the two met in steady challenge, but the deer was the more simple-minded. He saw there was not to be a struggle, and resumed his interrupted dinner.

"You are right, my fine warrior," said Vansittart aloud. "It is the man's place to fight, not the woman's."

"Where is the fight, stranger?" came a strong, hearty voice close to him. "Because if there's trouble, I'm on.

I live on it. I love it. I go foolin' round lookin' for it, an' I find it every time."

Vansittart wheeled about suddenly, and confronted a splendidly built man, taller even and more powerful than himself, with a bold and handsome face, and honest blue eyes,—a stalwart vagrant, whose ragged state argued that in his encounters with trouble his fortunes if not his person had been scarred.

The millionnaire, in his pre-occupied mood, had not heard his approach ; and the two men stood silent for a moment, whilst each measured the points of the other. Approval was seemingly mutual.

" Do you tell me that you like a row for the mere sake of it ? " said Vansittart with an amused look.

" That 's what it has come to," was the answer. " I was raised among Arizona blizzards, and they 've chased me right round the globe. I had a nice little ranch in Texas, an' a whirlwind lifted house an' cattle into the next location. I built a sawmill on the Red River, an' a cyclone not only took the fixtures out by the roots, but shifted the bed of the river. I struck a mine in South Africa, an' nearly got hanged by the Boers after they had gobbled up the claim. Since then I 've changed my occupation. I 'm now hunting blizzards."

" You 're a curiosity," exclaimed Vansittart.

" Not a bit. But I 've got my back up. I 'm naturally a peaceable man, but just now I 'm agin' things generally."

" Indeed, I sympathize with you fully," said the millionnaire.

" And I 've sort of cottoned on to you, stranger," replied the other. " Now, who do you want licked ? You seem a handy sort of fellow yourself, but I suppose you don't want to spoil your clothes. It don't matter about mine. I 'm hard up, so we 'll call it five dollars for a square lay-out."

Vansittart laughed. " I have no personal animosities," he said, " but let me help you, all the same."

He felt for his pocket-book; but the new-comer's face flushed deeply, and an angry gleam came into his eyes. " I did n't figure to have trouble with you," he growled, " but I 'm not aware that I begged from you."

" Nor am I aware that to offer help is to give offence," said Vansittart hotly. " However, you can take your change either in dollars or blows. I can hand on either with ease." He was clearly in no humor to be misunderstood.

" Draw poker!" shouted the other with delight, as he jammed his hat down upon his head as a preliminary. " But I like you, allee same. Tell me who you are while you can speak."

Jerome quietly approached him, saying: " While you can listen, I will tell you. My name is Vansittart; and when you are presentable again, you can come and see me at my house there. I will then try and give you a fresh start. Meanwhile you had better get your hands up, as I am going to knock you down."

But the stranger backed away from him, not cowed, but amazed.

" Say," he gasped, " air you Vansittart the millionnaire?"

" Yes. What of that? I can nevertheless use my fists."

" So you kin, but not on me, *if* you please. I can't knock up agin' so much bullion. It 's a million to a hayseed, and I 'm the seed. No, sir. Let me quit and ruminate on the queer side of things."

" Come," said Jerome, whose variable mood was now attracted by the man's oddity. " Take something as a loan. Fix yourself up a bit, and call upon me to-morrow at three o'clock. I am sure you will be able to repay me. No, I will not be refused. Give me your name, so that my servants may readily admit you."

" Jim Bates—' A-ri-zo-na Jim ' they generally call me," was the other's slow response, whilst he hesitatingly took the " wad " of notes which Vansittart thrust into his hands.

The gentleman from Arizona watched Jerome's retreating

figure until it was lost among the trees. He then, with characteristic caution, counted the money. "Ninety dollars," he said at last. "Ninety gol-fired dollars. Three months' solid keep from a man I 'd just offered to lick. All right, Mr. Vansittart, sir. You will get 'em back if each dollar draws blood!"

When Jerome reached his home it was time to dress for dinner; but he strode rapidly to Harland's room, and suggested that a simple meal and a bottle of wine might meet their necessities, as he was anxious for a long and undisturbed talk afterwards.

"That will suit me down to the ground, old fellow," said Dick, "particularly as you seem to have something on your chest. I am cuter than you think, and I don't like to see you moping after some ballet-dancer at the opera."

Vansittart laughed at Dick's penetration, and the latter knew the cause of his mirth when he heard Jerome's story later.

The American told his friend the whole of the circumstances, and Dick's eyes became saucer-like in their wideness at the *dénouement* of that afternoon.

"I always said she was a stunner, but I never thought she was an empress," he said reflectively at the close of the recital.

"And yet she is a true woman," mused Vansittart, "tender-hearted and kindly,—one who would cling to the man she loved, whether he was prince or peasant, had it not been for some dying injunction from a crack-brained father, I suppose."

"Yes," said Dick, "that 's it. And it 's not fair. It is n't a woman's game to fight for an empire."

Jerome started from his chair, and paced the room with hasty strides.

The curious manner in which Harland had echoed his own reflections in the Park had set a mad notion jostling with every reasoning faculty he possessed. For a while his brain was on fire ; and when he had calmed down somewhat, his face was pale, and set in firm resolve.

Stopping in front of Harland, he said quietly as he lit a cigar,—

" I 'll do it ! "

" Do what ? "

" Conquer France ! "

" Conquer fiddlesticks ! " cried the other. " You must be going cracked. Rich as you are, you can't buy an army and a fleet big enough for the job."

The millionnaire smiled. " I don't want either—yet," he said. " The day has gone by since men were able to carve out kingdoms by those means."

" Then what *will* you do ? "

" I will form a company which will be called ' France, Limited,' and I will hold the founders' shares myself ! "

CHAPTER IV

MUNITIONS OF WAR

WHEN Vansittart expressed his intention to turn France into a limited liability company, he was of course speaking figuratively.

In plain language, he had resolved to pit his brains and his money against a prospective French monarchy; and his sudden declaration to Harland only meant that he had discovered the means rather than the idea, for this had been slowly evolving itself for some hours.

Late into the night they talked. Although the Englishman thought it was his duty to try and dissuade his friend from a quixotic enterprise, he soon abandoned the attempt, and threw himself heart and soul into the undertaking.

Jerome had the rare faculty of sleeping soundly, no matter how exciting the events of the day might be, so he awoke next morning refreshed and unagitated.

His project was now stronger and clearer in his mind, and he lost no time in taking the first steps towards realizing it.

He could not start operations without the sinews of war, so after breakfast he drove to his central estate office to consult with his chief financial agent, Mr. Peter Studevant.

As a rule this old and trusted servant of the family inclined towards conservatism, and some of the operations entered into by his young master had made him gasp by their Napoleonic boldness, but he had long since ceased to advise him on such points.

Every speculation which Vansittart had entered into on a

tremendous scale had yielded equally extravagant profits, and the old gentleman felt that Jerome's grasp of principle was vastly more important and potential than the Studevant knowledge of detail.

Still, had the white-haired General Manager of the Vansittart Estate known the nature of the scheme to which Jerome was now committed, he would not have breakfasted so peacefully, nor read the Wall Street records so calmly, as he approached his office by the Elevated Railroad.

When the millionnaire entered Mr. Studevant's room, he closed the door and bolted it, to avoid interruption.

"Surely not the Grand Trunk again, Mr. Jerome!" cried the old gentleman. "You can see further into things than I can, but there surely is no money in that?"

"No," said Vansittart, "not the Grand Trunk. But I want a lot of money, all the same. Now, Mr. Studevant, I want you to give me as careful an approximate estimate as is possible. By using every possible source, and without disturbing the markets too greatly, how much money can I have at immediate call within three weeks?"

Mr. Studevant wrinkled his brows, and made some calculations on a blotting-pad. "One hundred and twenty-five millions," he answered.

"From your reply, I take it that the money would be lodged mostly in the Banks of England and France?" said Jerome.

"Yes. Any such movement in dollars would depreciate silver."

"And in six months how much?"

More and longer calculation, some thought, and there came the words, "About five hundred millions, with careful realizations."

"Twelve months later how much?"

"If plans were laid now with any such gigantic object in view, perhaps another five hundred millions."

"Eleven hundred and twenty-five millions," mused Vansittart. "It staggered France before, but I question if it is enough. Is that all I am worth, Mr. Studevant?"

The older man began to perspire. Some new and terrible scheme had fascinated his master. This time he was surely mad. "By selling your New York and Chicago estates and mortgaging your property in London," he stammered feebly, "no doubt a further vast sum could be raised; but surely, sir, you are amusing yourself at my expense?"

"No, indeed!" laughed the other: "the joke will cost me a bit perhaps, but I am quite serious with you."

"May I ask, sir," said the General Manager, with a great effort at regaining his wonted air of dignified composure, "if you really have some definite idea of committing yourself and your splendid fortune to some tremendous operation which requires all this money?"

"Yes," replied Jerome shortly, too occupied with his own all-absorbing thoughts to notice the saddened emphasis of the question.

"Then, sir," said Mr. Studevant, rising from his chair, and speaking with difficulty, for his voice trembled with emotion, "I will be party to no such lunacy. I have served your grandfather, your father, and yourself for fifty long years, but you must seek some other agent for your great interests. I resign forthwith."

Vansittart now perceived that his faithful adherent was much perturbed. He approached Mr. Studevant, laid his hand upon his shoulder, and said,—

"What, old Peter, as I used to call you when I was a little chap, are you the first to desert the ship when she plunges into a gale?"

"But there is no gale, Jerry," whimpered the old gentleman. "Things were never better. It is only the captain who is becoming crazy. Why, everything is going wonderfully well. There is a clear gain of one hundred and fifty millions in that last amalgamation with the Baltimore and Ohio. And your Telegraph Consolidation Scheme brought in seventy millions. You could set back London, Paris, and Berlin, if you chose."

Mr. Studevant paused for want of breath, and a smile on Jerome's face warned him that he was hardly using the best line of argument.

"Come, come, Peter!" cried the millionnaire. "You shall not condemn me unheard. Sit down. Let us get in some whiskey and soda and cigars, and fairly talk the matter out."

Mr. Studevant afterwards said that it was the spirits, but Jerome held that it was his warm old heart, that grew enthusiastic. Anyhow, before an hour had passed, he was plunged into Vansittart's campaign up to the neck.

He could do no more business that day.

He hurried off to his house, and alarmed his daughter, when she told him that dinner would be served in ten minutes, by saying cheerfully, "Ten minutes! One hundred and twenty-five millions in ten minutes! It absolutely cannot be done in a second less than ten clear days, and Sunday is a *dies non!*"

At last he woke up to actualities, and hastened away to dress, murmuring as he went, "One thing I can do, I can save five or ten out of the wreck for him, and he will never know!"

That afternoon, as Vansittart was passing from the dining-room to the library in his house, he heard a fierce altercation in the hall between the footman at the door and some person who appeared to be forcibly demanding admission.

He instantly recognized the voice of his friend from Central Park, Arizona Jim; but he was too late in hurrying to the rescue to prevent the latter from holding up the terrified servant in the most approved Western manner.

The footman was backing across the hall and up the stairs, with his hands held high above his head, and the cold muzzle of a six-shooter pressed against his forehead, whilst Mr. James Bates was apostrophizing him as follows :—

"You call me a tramp, you white-headed idiot! You tell

me to get out, when your boss asks me to come and see him! If it was n't that I 'm afraid to spoil those rich duds of yours that your boss paid for, I would n't trouble to rush you with a good honest gun, but I 'd simply plug you until you were sick. You just skip up them stairs and tell him I 'm here, or I 'll make you strip first, and whip you afterwards!"

Vansittart speedily rescued the amazed footman, and puzzled the poor man still more by telling him sharply that he ought to have brought in Mr. Bates's message, without venturing to decide for himself whether or not he should be admitted.

Arizona Jim soon calmed down in the presence of the millionnaire.

He had, it is true, effectively changed for the better in his costume, but he still smacked far too much of the prairies for the quiet respectability of Fifth Avenue.

"I told you yesterday," said Vansittart, "that I might be able to do something for you, and, since we met, an opening for your services has presented itself to my mind. Have you any family ties or other distractions that prevent you from devoting yourself absolutely to my orders?"

"Not one, boss," was the reply. "Until you gave me that wad yesterday, it did n't seem as though there was a darned soul in creation that cared whether I was alive or dead."

"Then," said Vansittart, "are you prepared to accompany me anywhere, to do anything in an honorable sense that I may ask you, and to risk your life, if necessary, in any undertaking in which I risk my own?"

"Governor," said Arizona Jim heartily, "I 'm on. What you sez, goes. But," he added deprecatingly, "I ain't much of a valet, if that 's what you mean."

"Thank you," said Vansittart with a laugh, "I don't expect services of that sort. Strict obedience to orders, and a straight punch with the right, will be your chief qualifications."

"Bully for me!" roared Mr. Bates with an air of vast relief. "There ain't a man in New York better qualified for the job than myself."

"I think," said Vansittart, entering into his humor, "I shall call you 'The Captain of the Guard.'"

"Holy poker!" shouted Arizona Jim, slapping his thigh with increased animation. "That's my hand to a spot."

.   .   .   .

In his first conversation with Mr. Studevant, Jerome had barely outlined the magnificent scheme to which he had intended to devote the whole of his resources, and, if necessary, his life. Many an hour of long and anxious consultation was needed before the financial situation alone became sufficiently clear to permit of other aspects of the project being attended to.

At last it was definitely settled that if no European war or severe financial crisis paralyzed the money-markets of the world during the next eighteen months, there could not be the slightest doubt that Mr. Vansittart was in possession of liquid assets worth at least twelve hundred and fifty millions.

When the long and tedious calculations necessary to achieve this purpose were ended, Jerome turned himself with renewed ardor to the more exacting actualities of his campaign.

The leading firm of lithographers in New York executed for him a huge chart of northern Africa, which bore upon its surface not only the latest approved records from European and American geographical institutions, but also collated the information given by all recent travellers through the arid wastes that are traversed alone by the great caravan routes running from Algiers and Morocco to the centre of the Dark Continent.

Armed with this portentous document, the millionnaire sought the assistance and advice of his own engineers, who deputed the junior member of their firm, Mr. Walter C.

Maclaren, to devote himself wholly to the researches required to be made by Vansittart.

Mr. Maclaren was also commissioned to associate with himself, in the enterprise committed to his charge, two of the best-known younger members of the engineering profession in London and Paris; and the trio, with several competent assistants and an ample supply of scientific instruments, were to proceed with the utmost possible despatch to the French colony on the southern shores of the Mediterranean.

What they did there during the winter and early spring months of the following year will be shown in due course.

Another curious preparation made by Vansittart was to give instructions in New York, a city renowned for the excellence of its woodwork, for the practical construction of a huge palace in iron, wood, glass, and papier maché, made in sections which would render it easy of shipment, and yet so designed as to bear, when put together, a semblance of great strength, durability, and beauty.

Special pains were taken that this structure should be completed rapidly. The business house intrusted with its ultimate construction was enjoined to give out the work in many sections to different contractors.

There was no limit of money or expense—only of time; and it was a condition precedent to the final signing of the specifications, that the entire building should be ready to be loaded on shipboard, for transport to and immediate erection in any part of the world, by the following May.

Weeks and even months elapsed whilst Vansittart was planning and perfecting the preliminaries of his gigantic scheme. Not only did he devote attention to what might be termed the purely mechanical side of his venture, but he gave many hours of careful thought to the principles which should regulate his own conduct.

It must not be forgotten that for this inquiry he was already well equipped by reading and reflection. He subjected every phase of the undertaking that presented itself to him to searching and merciless scrutiny by the philosophical light of his earlier studies.

Thus it was that in the exact mapping-out of his future actions he accepted propositions which were apparently wildly impracticable, whilst he rejected others which had fair seeming at first glance, but which in their ultimate outcome threatened to depart from the rigid principles he had laid down for his own guidance.

Told in a sentence, he depended upon the sympathies of what may be termed the genuine artisan class, controlled and directed by means of his vast wealth, to achieve the purpose to which he was devoted.

He knew that a power even greater than that of money was the people's will, and he also knew that no man could hope to lead any popular movement unless he succeeded in causing the multitude to believe that his scheme was theirs, and that they governed rather than were subject to the course of events. This, briefly put, was his philosophy : its application in detail will be made manifest hereafter.

During these busy days he did not often see Mademoiselle Honorine de Montpensier.

When they met, it was rather with the courtesy of a prince and princess in treaty diplomatically for an alliance, than with the unrestrained freedom of young people who thought themselves to be in love with each other.

Of course, before he had taken any definite steps towards the realization of his project, Vansittart had confided it in general terms to the lady in whose monarchical pretensions it had found its birth. She was at first astounded, then alarmed, and finally convinced.

" You are already a king, Mr. Vansittart," she said, " for a crown alone does not make a man worthy to rule. The boldness of your imagination is so closely allied with attention to practical details, that you remind me of no one in history more than Napoleon the Great."

" It is flattering," he said with a smile, " to have you say so, particularly as there may be some little foundation in fact for the hereditary instincts you claim to have discovered in me."

"What!" cried Honorine, "have I during all this time been harboring a rival pretender?"

"Hardly that," he said, "for I fear that my claims would not stand the scrutiny of the *Almanach de Gotha*. But as a matter of fact there can be no doubt that among my ancestors was Prince Jerome Bonaparte, a cousin of the Emperor, who emigrated to the United States when the Napoleonic dynasty crumbled into ruins after Waterloo. It is surely by some lingering trait of heredity that a free-born American like myself can devote himself so thoroughly to the fortunes of even so fascinating a queen."

Honorine looked at him for a moment in deep thought, and then blushed somewhat as she said, "I hoped there was a cause more recent and more tangible for your devotion, as you term it, than such a far-fetched one as that."

Vansittart started a little at the words. Had he, then, become so merged in the struggle for empire, that love was wholly out of court? But he was not at a loss for an answer.

"You forget," he said, "that you yourself have placed a limit on my words in other directions."

It was now Honorine's turn to be confused. She had unwittingly opened the door for a flirtation, and it was not yet time for tender passages between them.

"I can only say," she replied, "that I commit myself implicitly to your care. I will do what you ask me without question or comment, for I feel deep down in my heart a conviction that you will succeed; and it is not for a weak woman to imagine that she can control or direct a brain like yours."

This gave Vansittart an opportunity to prefer a request he had long contemplated. It was necessary for the development of his undertaking that Mademoiselle Honorine de Montpensier should accompany him to France; and he now explained his desire to her in a few direct words, without the slightest attempt to hint at possible developments in case his plan succeeded, for it was tacitly admitted between them that if Vansittart's mad project were successful, and he really could seize the throne of France, their marriage was a foregone conclusion.

The lady raised no scruples about yielding to his wishes.

"We shall be ready to accompany you," she said, "whenever you are prepared, but I hope you have not forgotten that my presence in Paris might be a serious hindrance to your designs. I am known to the authorities, and would certainly be regarded as a dangerous personage in the royalist interest. Any member of the Government might recognize me immediately, and order my prompt expulsion from France. Have you considered these features of the case?"

"Fully," replied Vansittart, "and in my judgment they constitute a most favorable condition."

"In that case," she said, "my consent is unqualified, only please give me a few hours to pack."

These words were uttered with a pleasant smile; for she already had some experience of Vansittart's methods, and would not have been surprised if he had proposed to hurry her off without her hat.

At last he decided to cross the Atlantic quietly in his own magnificent yacht, the *Seafarer*. His arrangements were made ostensibly for an extended tour in Europe, and no one outside the chief personages already known to the reader was acquainted in the slightest degree with the fantastic project to which the *Seafarer* was about to bear her owner and his companions.

On the evening before the date of their departure—which took place, by the way, early in March—Vansittart found Harland awaiting him in their common sanctum, and apparently immersed in a brown-study.

"What is the matter, Dick?" said the millionnaire cheerily.

"Well, I have been thinking," said Harland.

"The unusual operation seems to have distressed you."

"Don't laugh at me, old chap. Don't you see, to-morrow you will be almost irrevocably committed to this business, and it is such a terrible affair that I cannot help asking myself what is to be the outcome of it all?"

"To my thinking, it will result in my becoming an emperor, and you a duke of some place or another."

"That is all very well," said Dick. "I care as little about being a duke as you do about the other thing. But suppose it all goes wrong, and you lose your life, or get into jail, or some such miserable business as that? Have you really allowed for such a possibility?"

"No," replied Vansittart with a laugh. "I may lose my life. That eventuality is always with a man; but I shall not get into jail, and I shall not be disgraced."

"Then," said Harland, springing to his feet, "I am with you in the deal right through. There is only one thing more, old fellow. During this empire business, am I to call you 'Jerry' or 'your Majesty'?"

"'Jerry' always," said Vansittart, "and 'your Majesty' when I am crowned and there are other people about."

"I think I understand," said Harland. "By the way, is it at all a part of the scheme that I should flirt with the Comtesse de Fontainebleau?"

"No," laughed Vansittart, "I would not test even your constancy so far."

CHAPTER V

AN INVASION OF PARIS

PARIS was in a turmoil.

Rumors had reached her amiable citizens of an American visitor whose wealth exceeded that of Solomon, and whose generosity was at once magnificent and indiscriminate. A correspondent of the *Figaro* had announced that the new-comer, in addition to the enormous current account he had opened at the Credit Lyonnais, had brought with him, secured in several stout Gladstone bags, the sum of $2,500,000.

"When asked what his purpose was with so big a sum," went on the vivacious scribe, "he replied that he knew it was the habit to tip waiters in Europe!"

That he not only understood the art of tipping, but had also carried it to a supreme point of excellence, soon became clear. Jerome Vansittart did not display indecent speed on his journey to the French capital. For two days he rested at Havre, whence came the most extraordinary stories of his munificence. His route through Normandy was marked by a golden stream which vied in brilliance with its silver rival the Seine, along whose banks the leisurely express of the Chemin de Fer de l'Ouest carried him.

At Rouen he was awaited by a crowd of curious spectators, who cheered him as he stepped upon the platform to take the five-minutes' stroll which fortunately varies the journey. The American smiled and took off his hat ; then (so ran the report which paralyzed Paris) he mounted upon a chair in the refreshment buffet, which offers its diminutive grapes and stale rolls to famished travellers, and in a tone of voice whose irony only his companions recognized, exclaimed in excellent French,—

"Gentlemen, I regard this kind welcome as a greeting between two nations. We each offer of our best and dearest. France gives to me her noble enthusiasm, America gives to you—a more vulgar, but alas! her only valuable offering—her wealth. I have observed the spire of your superb cathedral. It is not well that so noble an inspiration of art should exhaust itself, as if by inanition, in a pinnacle of wood. Gentlemen, if your excellent municipal authority should grant me the permission, I will build for your cathedral the finest spire of stone in Europe."

Curiosity gave way to excitement, and excitement to an outburst of acclamation. So carried away was the meagre porter who helped the American down from his perch, that he scarcely noticed the hundred-franc note that the millionnaire pressed into his hand in return for his service. And thus, through dense volumes of smoke and cheering (for Rouen station is prettily situated between two noisome tunnels), the train rolled off on its thoughtful passage to Paris.

In the capital nothing had occurred for some time, and therein Vansittart was fortunate. The report that the British Ambassador had tried to poison the President was quite a month old, and, besides, had been fully proved to be a *canard;* and the second visit of the Czar was already a thing of the past. Paris was hungry for excitement; and when Paris is really hungry, it is amazing what excellent fare she can make out of the most meagre materials. The visit of the American came just in time, and everyone was awaiting his arrival with impatience.

One man alone, M. Loubet, the manager of the Grand Hotel, was suffering agonies of apprehension. All the morning he had paced the *entresol* with restless footsteps, now pausing to send wild and contradictory messages to his *chef*, now despatching waiters to the floor above with desperate instructions to the corps of servants who had been placed there at an absurdly early hour with strict injunctions not to budge.

"*Mon Dieu!*" exclaimed the poor man to his assistant. "What am I to make of this madman? I tremble for my life. To talk to him—*c'est impossible!* He has ordered the whole first floor. The whole first floor, mark you!"

"But why does he take the whole floor?" asked the under manager. "*Parbleu!* Does he, then, sleep in forty beds? Does he recline himself in thirty sitting-rooms?"

"That is not all," continued the perplexed M. Loubet. "He has demanded everything perfect, and yet how am I to satisfy his extraordinary taste? American millionnaire! What to give him?"

"Yes, yes!" murmured the other sympathetically.

"But I was not to be beaten. I! But no, certainly not. I studied our great writers. They have travelled in America. They are great observers. There is the excellent Paul Bourget, for instance; and M. Blouet, he named Max O'Rell. I bought their works and read them through. And I had arranged a *menu* for our guest which would have astounded him."

"You *had* arranged it?" questioned his assistant.

"Yes, that is where I am unlucky. I discovered from those admirable authors that American princes eat molasses, clam chowder, cream soda, and many vicious things. Ah, the infinite labor of getting these remarkable dishes! I had drawn up a *menu* which would have brought tears into the eyes of the wanderer. And will you believe! My *chef* sends up a point-blank refusal to cook it! And this terrible guest, who threatens to buy up the hotel and turn me out if I do not manage things well, will find no clam chowder and not a single molass! It is terrible! Yet what am I to do? I have to obey my cook, and there is only the *dîner à la*

Parisien, so pleasing to us, so trivial to the strong, ferocious taste of the American."

How much longer the afflicted manager would have continued his lamentations it is impossible to say; but at that moment there was a noise in the Boulevard des Capucines as of shouting, and both men started to their feet, realizing that at last the dreaded visitor had arrived, and that their period of purgatory had commenced.

An extraordinary cavalcade was making its way at a fast gallop through the Place de l'Opéra. At the Gare St. Lazare, Jerome K. Vansittart had found waiting for him the exquisite open carriage and the four beautiful bays that he had especially ordered from London; and in attendance two broughams, each with a pair of jet-black horses, in which his secretary and his personal attendant were to follow him.

As he handed Mlle. de Montpensier into the landau, one of the crowd sagely observed,—

"That is not a private citizen arriving from Havre. It is more like an emperor with his suite!"

Vansittart overheard the remark and smiled, then, turning round to the man, remarked,—

"If I look like an emperor, let me have the satisfaction also of acting like one."

And with this he pushed into his hand a brilliant diamond ring.

The astonished Frenchman fell back for a moment, then, as if struck by a swift, apprehensive thought, darted forward to the carriage.

"If you should want me, monsieur"—and he paused; but his look was singularly significant.

The American gazed hard into the man's eyes. Then slowly he said,—

"To-morrow at twelve."

The horses were whipped up, and with a fine dash the cavalcade swept down the Rue du Havre and along the Rue Auber, till the noble Place de l'Opéra and the Grand Hotel were reached.

At the entrance a vast crowd had assembled, and porters and policemen alike were powerless to keep a free passage. The mob struggled into the courtyard, surrounded the carriage, occupied every square inch of space, and to the troubled manager it looked as if the Parisians themselves had come to his rescue, and had decided for him the vexed questions of cook and clam chowder alike.

Vansittart was not in the least perturbed. A close observer might have noticed that there was a faint smile of gratification upon his face ; and when he turned to his companion, she looked upon him with a troubled expression, which seemed to combine fear and wonder.

Bending low, he whispered in her ear,—

" Behold the beginning of an empire ! "

A faint smile brightened her face. But to her this abject flattery of the Paris crowd, such as would become a king, paid to an alien who brought unbounded wealth, was a strange, almost terrible thing. This man ! what enormous power was his that brought whole peoples to his feet ! Loyalty, the slow growth of years ; self-interest, that sprang with difficulty from social necessity,—these could doubtless invest with power and dignity a chosen prince; but what was this new and cunning witchcraft that could in a moment, like a miracle, stupefy the brains of men, and exalt the individual in the twinkling of an eye ?

She had never clearly grasped Jerome's quixotic scheme, could scarcely believe in it, or understand by what method it was to succeed. It was now only that she began to comprehend, and she shuddered as she did so.

Meanwhile Jerome had stepped from the carriage. He saw beyond the excited throng the form of the landlord, waving his hands with despair, as he stood in the covered courtyard. He noticed, too, that a gendarme near him had cuffed an over-zealous enthusiast on the ear, and was struggling hopelessly to beat back the crowd.

" Stay, my friend ! " he called to the officer. " There are only two forces that can disband a mob quickly and quietly.

One is to ask them for money, the other is to give it to them."

As he spoke, he opened a large wallet that he carried with him, and, taking out handful after handful of gold, he flung it to the right and left with a pleasant invitation to his admirers to partake of his *largesse*.

In a moment the crowd had parted, and was swaying and surging over the spots where the bright Napoleons lay. Between, in the fallow and barren ground that bore no treasure, lay a broad avenue, along which the American and Mademoiselle de Montpensier quickly passed. They were greeted with demonstrations of delight by M. Loubet.

"Welcome, monsieur!" he cried. "You have managed well; but there are few men who could have afforded so costly a passage."

"M. Loubet," returned Jerome gravely, "it has cost me 5000 francs to cross your courtyard. I hope that we may now mount to our apartments free of charge."

M. Loubet bowed, perplexed. Without more ado, however, he ushered his visitors to the first floor.

"Mademoiselle's suite, monsieur, is to the left, as you directed. It is entirely re-furnished and re-decorated. I was also fortunate enough to secure the recently discovered paintings of Jean François Millet for her boudoir. It was a matter of a little difficulty. Would you believe it, I had to bid against the Government of France!—I, the manager of the Grand Hotel, and an honest patriot! Still the Government is not rich, like you, monsieur; and I secured the six at a cost of 200,000 francs apiece. They are very beautiful, and the Minister of Fine Art had already prepared a place for them in the Louvre."

"You have done well, M. Loubet," was Vansittart's response. "You will see that mademoiselle's maids are properly housed. The French attendants I ordered for her are here?"

"Yes, monsieur."

"Then you can go, sir; and when dinner is ready, you will be good enough to ask mademoiselle whether she will do me the honor of joining me. Ah! and, by the way, the wines,—you have them, of course? I will examine them myself,—the 1834 port, the 1880 Cliquot, and, above all, the 1862 Chateau Lafitte."

M. Loubet trembled slightly, and a perspiration broke out upon his brow.

"There are the twenty dozen of the port, monsieur," he stammered, "and the two hundred dozen of the Veuve Cliquot, just as you ordered."

Vansittart's brow gathered.

"Go on, sir. What of the claret?"

"It was a miracle that we got it, monsieur," replied Loubet, his pallor increasing. "There were only forty dozen bottles in Europe, and they were distributed in the most perplexing way. I sent out my agents. They bribed and cajoled—yes, monsieur, and, I regret to say, lied also. In the end they obtained thirty-eight dozen at an enormous cost. I have spent twelve thousand francs. But monsieur knows that to bribe the butlers of our chief clubs, and to ransack the cellars of princes—it is a terrible task."

"Well, well!" interrupted Jerome angrily. "That matters not. You have thirty-eight dozen?"

M. Loubet wiped his brow.

"To tell you the truth, monsieur, the number is short by a half a dozen."

"How?" exclaimed the American sternly. "You scoundrel, what have you been doing?"

"I owe you a million apologies, monsieur," returned the unhappy Loubet. "But what could I do? You know that the Czar of Russia visited Paris last week. Everything was well prepared,—crowds, decorations, banquets, receptions,—all was there but Chateau Lafitte of 1862. Not a bottle, monsieur, could M. le Président obtain! France was disgraced. Paris was threatened with eternal shame. They searched the clubs, they came here. They discovered all! Ah, pardon me, monsieur, but I am a patriot. The honor of the country is dear to me. Besides, they threatened me. I might have been sent to the galleys. In the end I sold the Republic six bottles at two hundred francs the bottle. France was saved. The President smiled. Paris was once more gay. The Czar drank Chateau Lafitte of 1862, and next day he signed the treaty!"

And a faint glow of pious exaltation gleamed in Loubet's eye.

Inwardly Vansittart shook with laughter. But assuming a look of frightful menace, he exclaimed,—

"You have done this, sir. Remember a second time that I yield precedence to no emperor and to no president. I do not give my wine to cement unholy alliances. Go, sir! and take care the dinner is beyond reproach."

And he turned swiftly into his apartments.

"These poor children!" he exclaimed to himself as he flung himself upon his couch. "I must imitate the methods of a wise parent. Now we must frighten them, and now we must stuff them with sweetmeats. Oh, Paris, Paris! you are in truth the cradle of the French people, only unfortunately they seem never to get out of long-clothes!"

Next day a new officer was added to his staff. Punctual to the hour he had named, the Frenchman of the St. Lazare arrived, and had a remarkable interview with the American.

"I think we understand each other without undue explanation," Jerome had said. "I gather you are a royalist, M. Folliet?"

"I am devoted to the cause, monsieur; and it was by reason of that that I lost my distinguished post."

"And that was?"

"Monsieur, I was Prefect of the Police!"

Jerome started. This was good fortune indeed.

"And you know Paris?"

"Every nook and corner, monsieur, and every notable

creature,—man, woman, and child,—together with their private histories. The police here do not leave much for others to glean."

"Enough!" cried Jerome gaily. "We jested yesterday of emperors. Well, I have an appointment to offer you. I will make you my Chief of Police. You shall have double your salary as prefect, and we shall be faithful to each other, M. Folliet. Remember that we both serve the same cause."

And thus it came about that Jerome had three officers of state, a Master of the Horse, a Captain of the Guard, and an up-to-date Lecocq.

CHAPTER VI

JEROME IS PUZZLED

DURING the next day or two Vansittart fully lived up to his reputation. Never had there been such a golden harvest for the gleaners of the Paris streets.

If a workman raised his cap to him, he threw him a Napoleon.

"Frenchmen have been polite for centuries," he explained, "and got nothing by it. Now it is time to reward them."

He did several extraordinary things. Once he saw in the Avenue de la Bourdonnais an *ouvrier* and his wife gazing longingly at the windows of one of those cheap eating-houses with which the street abounds. He stopped to inquire, and found that the poor man could not afford dinner and could get no work. Vansittart immediately bought him the restaurant, and left the new and stupefied landlord engaged on a tremendous meal which threatened to clear the *menu*.

These things made him popular. He was dogged by reporters, and a fabulous history grew around him. It was said he had offered to rebuild the Tuileries; and a furious sensation was caused to north and east by the astounding rumor that he had bought up the whole of Montmartre and Belleville, and was going to let the workmen of Paris occupy their houses free of rent. These stories were absurd inventions.

But many others were quite true, and in particular one of them which ran like wildfire through the city. One morning Jerome was observed to descend from his carriage at the statue of Strasbourg, remove his hat reverently, and stand in deep reverie before the sorrowful image for full ten minutes.

The American felt for France then. He knew her heartaches, and could enter into sympathy with them.

That night, when he appeared at the Opera House, where he had taken six boxes for his friends, he was loudly cheered; and the orchestra, not knowing what national air to play on the occasion, by a sort of vague association of ideas, struck up *The Man that Broke the Bank at Monte Carlo*.

The effort was well meant. No one present, save the British and Americans, knew what the words were, and the tune was taken for the American anthem. It was enthusiastically received.

These extravagances half amused, half saddened Vansittart. He felt he was angling for big fish, and that such bait as he used should not attract as easily as it did. But Paris is a child, ever longing for a new toy, hugging it with rapture when she has got it, and then tossing it impatiently away. Jerome was not deceived. He knew that such popularity as this was essentially ephemeral, and night after night he revolved the scheme that should bring to his feet this wonderful nation. He knew, that, whatever his plan was, it would be one that would sound ridiculous and impossible to the cold ear of man. But such things had been before. It was his lot to make real the wild romances of the past, to combine D'Artagnan and Aramis in the flesh. He had to become, as it were, a Jules Verne of politics.

On the fourth morning he was in his private room,—the Salle du Zodiac of the hotel, which had been converted into a noble library,—when a servant announced a visit from Mademoiselle de Montpensier, who requested the favor of an interview.

Vansittart met her with every manifestation of respect. No salute other than a warm pressure of the hand passed between them. The unexpressed compact between them was faithfully kept. Honorine was the bride of France, and it was only when Jerome should be able to offer her the homage of an Emperor of France that he would speak to her with the warmth of an accepted suitor.

"We have scarcely met since we arrived here!" said Honorine, looking upon the American with mock disapproval. "I could not endure longer not to know what you have been doing for France—and for us both!"

She added these last words with a delicious hesitation. Jerome came nearer her.

"Alas! mademoiselle," he said, "we must remember what a country we are in, where everyone is free to do as he likes and everyone is suspected, where we are all emperors and slaves alike. This separation tries me cruelly, but it is some consolation to know each day that I am something, if only an inch, nearer our goal."

"And by what queer doings!" exclaimed Honorine with a merry laugh. "I have been reading the papers, and I can scarcely credit them. What! have you really promised to fête all the children of Paris?"

"And why not?" demanded Jerome with a smile. "I shall also invite the mothers, and surfeit them with soup, salad, and sirup. After all, what does it mean?—a mere trifle, and so many poor folk made happy, and so many—"

"Poor folk thanking the American!" put in the other mischievously.

Jerome bowed.

"Exactly. You are becoming a politician, mademoiselle. If I bought a restaurant for a couple of starving beggars, what of that? It cost me no more than a thousand dollars for good-will, furniture, and food. The old proprietors are quite happy, for I saw them next day dining outside their quondam house, calling insolently for *déjeûner*, and cursing their successors bitterly because they had put black bread in the *croûte au pot!* It will gladden them for a month merely to come back to the old place and sneer at the new ways."

"And can it be that you have promised at your own

expense to get the fountains played at Versailles next Sunday?"

"A mere bagatelle. Do you know what it means? Ten thousand francs. Why, I give as much for a scarf-pin."

"Yes," retorted Honorine. "And do you know what *La Lanterne* calls it?"

"I have n't the honor of reading *La Lanterne*."

"Well, the fountains are only played on saint days, so *La Lanterne* speaks of next Sunday as the *Fête de St. Jonathan*."

The American laughed.

"I am already canonised! That is well!" he declared. "When the people begin to find a nickname for you, it shows that they either love you or—"

"That they hate you!" exclaimed Honorine sadly.

"Ah, no! They do not hate me. At least, they shall not have cause for that. They may wonder at me, or laugh at me; but I am a determined wooer, am I not?" (Honorine turned her head away) "and I shall win this pretty Paris, believe me, yet. But tell me, mademoiselle, I am eager to know. Do you disapprove my methods? Do you wish me to find some other way?"

Jerome paused anxiously. He was not certain how far his bride to be, this proud French girl, would relish her countrymen being thus trifled with and made sport of. Would she rebel against the implied contempt in all this generous patronage? But he had not calculated how strong was the tie that bound the spirited girl to the order that had passed away, and how far she was in real sympathy from this rebellious city and this perjured country.

Republican France was to her not sacred. Her people became dear once more when they returned to the oath they had forsworn.

So Honorine contented herself with thanking Jerome for his brave struggles for her ambitious scheme.

"The reward is so poor, should you succeed!" she declared, looking at him with a little melancholy smile.

"It would be so!" exclaimed Vansittart, "if the mere bubble of a crown were all I should obtain. But you know well how insignificant to me is kingship itself. I wish to succeed; but success, once got, I despise. I am not fighting for the emperor, but for the empress. And then," he concluded a little sadly, "I may or may not get the reward I long for."

"What!" cried the other reproachfully, "do you already accuse me of ingratitude?"

"Ah, mademoiselle! The future alone can disclose our fortunes; but, believe me, if it is ever in my power to bestow upon you a gift worthy of yourself, it shall not be stained or diminished by conditions. It shall be the free offering of a man who loves you, and is content that he has given you your heart's desire."

Tears sprang to Honorine's eyes.

"Jerome," she said, repeating his name for the first time, "I am ashamed and humiliated when I look into the unfathomable depths of your devotion. Such nobleness of heart and such courage of soul I do not deserve. No, the cause alone is worthy of it. Yet I shall know how to appreciate it. I do so now, and besides," she smiled, "what monster are you conjuring up to torment you?"

"Yes," he exclaimed with a sigh of relief, "there is at least no other claimant of royal blood to complicate matters."

As he uttered these words, he was astounded to see that Honorine's color changed into a deadly pallor, and that she sank back with a shudder into a chair.

He sprang towards her.

"Are you ill? Oh, what is it, Honorine?" he cried.

Then, striding towards the bell, he would have rung it, but, recovering with an effort, she begged him to reassure himself.

"Do not be alarmed," she said. "It was a sudden chill. I will retire to my apartments. Let us meet at dinner," she added, as if remorsefully : "I shall not go to the ambassador's reception this afternoon."

Jerome was about to usher the Princess from the room, when the footman, throwing open the door, evidently in ignorance that his master was engaged, announced M. de Tournon, Minister for the Interior.

On hearing the name, Honorine started violently, and, giving her hand to Jerome, hastened as though in eagerness across the floor to the other end of the room, whence a small entrance led to a private corridor. As she reached the threshold, she turned for a moment to the American, and in a low voice, not without a tremor of emotion, murmured,—

"M. de Tournon! Do not trust him! He is our enemy!"

Jerome handed her gravely out. Then, concealing the surprise that her words had caused, he turned with a smile to greet the minister, who, with hat in hand and a beam of ineffable sweetness on his face, was awaiting his host.

M. de Tournon's composure was also not without art; for, as he entered, his eyes had fallen upon the pale face and lithe figure of Mlle. de Montpensier at the very moment when she had turned to give her lover the word of warning. A strange look had for a moment entered his eyes. It might have been gratification, it might have been malice, or perhaps a little of both.

But M. de Tournon's large and sallow face, with its dark-rimmed eyes, its full lips, its ample chin which served to vary a swelling fulness of cheek that spread on both sides to two aggressive ears, had been well disciplined during a quarter of a century of political intrigue amongst the kaleidoscopic factions of the city of Paris; and as he peremptorily dismissed the impertinent glance which had intruded into his eye without bidding, and ordered his features into a sweet semblance of affability, he presented a cheerful appearance to the American as he advanced to meet him.

"I am indeed honored by this unexpected visit, M. de

Tournon," Vansittart declared, as he begged his visitor to be seated.

"Pardon me," replied the minister, "I fear I have offended. I am but a poor exchange for my predecessor."

Jerome waved his hand deprecatingly.

"To so distinguished a statesman," he said, "and to one held so justly high in the esteem of his countrymen, time and place should always yield."

"I am not curious, Mr. Vansittart, but I rejoice that there is one link already between us, as it strikes me. Surely I am not mistaken when I say that I believe I have met the charming lady who has just left you. It was—let me see— surely at Fontainebleau. Yes, it must have been Fontainebleau. What spot more natural for those who are young? You know the place, doubtless,—delightful, well-wooded, romantic,—a spot designed by Heaven for lovers. Ah! the leaves of Fontainebleau have fluttered sadly over many a vow that was destined to be broken.

"Dear me! I used to go there myself, not to love,—for, alas! I am not one who has been favored by the cruel sex,— but merely to catch the inspiration of romance which these dear young people appear to shed around them. For the very atmosphere of Fontainebleau has a magical quality. It makes old hearts young, and stern hearts tender. The very trees there enter into wedlock, and the rocks weep. I must really beg you to go to Fontainebleau; for you, at least, are of an age to love."

"I would not make the leaves of its forest sad for all the world," replied Jerome with a smile; "and as for romance, does not my window look out upon the Boulevard des Capucines?"

"Ah, well!" sighed the tender-hearted minister, "if you are a cynic, it is hopeless; but at least it makes it all the easier for me to broach the very dull, dry business which has brought me here. Perhaps you are aware, Mr. Vansittart, that the French Republic has a very eager solicitude for her guests from other shores. I may say, indeed, that she has a maternal interest in them, and watches over them with a care and exactitude which does honor to the tenderness of her heart. The Republic of France does not wish her visitor to be received without ceremony, and to remain unannounced and unobserved. Therefore it is her habit to make a few respectful inquiries about her guests, so that she may know who they are and where they come from, where they honor her by staying, and when they go,—a mere formality which enables them in a foreign country not to be without identity should harm befall them."

"And also," interrupted Jerome with mock gravity, "enables the tender-hearted mother to lay her hand upon them speedily, should they meditate harm against her."

"Ah!" and M. de Tournon indulged in a fat laugh which lumbered in many creases along his cheeks, "you take a gloomy view. I was anxious that you should not be intruded upon by a mere officer of police, and so I did myself the honor of calling in person to save you from annoyance."

"It is indeed a fortunate visit," replied Vansittart, "for I also had important business to discuss with you. But may I be so rude as to inquire whether you attend the levee at the American Embassy this afternoon?"

"It is my intention."

"Then I may have the honor, perhaps, of offering you a seat in my carriage, and we may discuss my little matter on the way. In the meantime, rest assured, M. de Tournon, that I shall furnish you with the full particulars that you desire. They will not be interesting. The American tourist is undoubtedly the most unromantic and the least dramatic figure in the world. He would never dream of putting a republic to serious inconvenience."

"You will not, of course, misunderstand. Our interest extends to every member of your household; and I need not say how pleased I shall be if I discover in the charming lady of whom I have just had the good fortune of catching a glimpse, an old acquaintance."

Vansittart bowed, then rose and rang for his carriage.

He was not a little puzzled by this visit. What could Honorine mean by her strange warning? What was the meaning of this acquaintance that the French Minister claimed? And why this pointed reference to her when he asked for information about the household? Beyond all, why the continual allusion to Fontainebleau and love? Did de Tournon wish to convey that it was some romance of Honorine's that he had surprised there? That was the only explanation. Jerome fancied that he detected a faint undertone of veiled irony in M. de Tournon's references to her. He felt a sharp pang at his heart which he could scarcely tell to have sprung from jealousy or from fear.

But he turned to the minister, without displaying his emotion, saying,—

"And now, monsieur, I have to ask from you the strangest and most difficult favor that has ever been asked of any French Minister of the Interior."

"Do not fear," replied de Tournon gaily, as he proceeded with his host downstairs, "I will grant you anything you ask for, excepting only my portfolio."

CHAPTER VII

A CHALLENGE

IT is a long way from the Grand Hotel to the Rue Galilee, where the American Embassy is situated. Jerome therefore opened his business with deliberation.

"You are aware, M. de Tournon," he said, "that every civilized man has a longing for a permanent home. He cannot forever wander about purchasing a right to occupy a place in another man's house."

"I, too, am domestic," purred the minister.

"And therefore it is that I require to find some suitable abode. It should be large, certainly historical,—for we Americans, you know, are compelled to dwell upon the historical associations of others,—and it should be both secluded and near Paris. To get such a home is no easy task. And really your houses are so small."

M. de Tournon slightly elevated his eyebrows.

"My dear Mr. Vansittart," he replied, "I should repair without delay to a house-agent, who will be delighted to assist you without any introduction from the Minister of the Interior."

"Ah!" sighed Jerome, "there is my difficulty. The house I am thinking of, I fear, cannot appear in any agent's catalogue ; and what is more, monsieur, its disposal, I am inclined to think, lies entirely in your department."

"In *my* department !" exclaimed the minister with surprise. "I wholly fail to follow you."

"I must ask a thousand pardons, M. de Touruon. You may think me most audacious, I may even be guilty of apparent disrespect towards the Republic; but in my numerous visits to Paris I have observed a large number of noble houses which belong to the state, and have remained unoccupied for ages. Some are turned into picture galleries, others are quite deserted and useless. Now, this spectacle has pained me. As a practical man, I grieve to see such absolutely commodious premises left to their natural decay, or used as lumber-rooms for the scattered rubbish of a nation's art. Monsieur, it is one of these I would purchase and reclaim, and I beg your kind assistance."

"And its name?" demanded the bewildered minister, who had been gaping at the American as if dazed, and not knowing what sacrilegious word would next fall from his lips.

"Monsieur," continued the American with equanimity, "I desire to purchase the Palace of St. Cloud."

If the Minister of the Interior had been shot, he could not have bounced up in his seat with more alacrity. He looked at Vansittart in a dumb and helpless way for a few seconds, and then gasped,—

"St. Cloud! But, monsieur, that has been the residence of kings! St. Cloud, the country-seat of Louis the Great and of our great Napoleon! St. Cloud, the—"

"The home also of Blücher and Von Bismarck," interrupted Jerome. "Yes, I admit its history is striking and varied. It has served as a delightful hunting-box for your kings, and, I understand, is the recognized headquarters for your enemies whenever they besiege your capital."

"You speak lightly, monsieur," responded the minister with a certain dignity; "but you must remember that if France no longer cherishes her kings, yet these memorials of them are cherished as one may treasure up family heirlooms, quaint, old-fashioned jewels which adorned a period with which we are no longer sympathetic. It is in such memorials that the Past writes itself visibly, so that the Future may pause and read."

"Such sentiments are highly honorable," said Jerome. "But it is for you also to remember, M. de Tournon, that of such writing St. Cloud does not form a sentence, not a coherent phrase, not an articulate word, nay, scarcely a syllable. It consists of three dungeons and a couple of walls; and if its ruins be valuable at all as a memorial, it can only be to remind you of the perfect workmanship of the German officers, and of the excellent precision of German cannon-balls."

"If, then, only a ruin—"

"I will rebuild it."

"You are a private citizen, and not even a Frenchman."

"With regard to that, we will speak again. Meanwhile—I offer my price, and will not claim the palace forever. Let us say that the Republic will sell the ruins and the gardens for two million francs. Then—as, of course, if you are good enough to help me, you will need in many little ways to educate opinion on the point—let us add privately, between ourselves, two more millions. Really, if you consider it, the scheme seems feasible."

M. de Tournon was clearly agitated.

"Here we are at the Embassy," he said hurriedly. "I will think over it. Perhaps it may be managed. To-morrow I will call upon you, and we will discuss the matter."

Distinctly pale, he stepped from the carriage, and, together with his companion, mounted the spacious staircase of the Embassy to the grand salon.

The scene was a notable one. Such an assemblage of men as only Paris could produce were gathered together. The splendid diplomatic corps reckoned in its numbers the wittiest and the most skilful representatives of foreign powers. Here, too, were the intellectual and spiritual leaders of a people rich at all times in a poetry, in an art, and in a literature, which, beyond those of other countries, are ever exquisitely tender, nobly original, and animated with living force

The dramatist whose works filled the theatres of Europe; the sculptor whose statues are fought for by connoisseurs, and only with difficulty carried off by a jealous government, to be established in that princely palace of art, the Luxembourg; the novelist, too, whether analytic or symbolic, unfailing offspring of every stray mood that swept over society; critics, who have given to the name a meaning that in England would sound incongruous, and who have turned criticism into creation; men of genius, those true sons of France who, with no distinct mission and no clear predilection for any sphere of labor, yet seem to hold wisdom in solution, and have elevated conversation into a graceful and brilliant form of art; all the richest and rarest of a country of ideals, of willing self-sacrifice, of joyous temperament; and not a few of the select spirits of other lands, who find in the clearer, keener air of intellectual Paris a finer stimulant to their talent,—these, in bright perplexing confusion, formed the circle which was now doing homage to the vivacious wife of the American Ambassador.

But as Vansittart's eyes fell delighted on the scene, they instinctively sought out that other order of men,—an order with which he was so soon to be concerned,—the statesman and the politician.

A fine display they made, it must be confessed; for they possessed more of that mastership, that quickness of eye, that rounded evenness of manner, which spring from long association with affairs. Your poet and your sculptor bear about with them some mark of their profession in a certain dreaminess or a wistfulness of face, or, it may be, not an awkwardness, but an unfamiliarity with the world as there represented. True art develops from a supreme reserve, and this reserve hedges them round even when they fancy they have cast it off.

But the keen-eyed, alert, apprehensive politicians—as Jerome picked them out one by one, he smiled to himself as he thought that he, single-handed, isolated, alone, was to do battle with them all, and challenge to so monstrously unequal a contest the cream and flower of French statesmanship.

"Can my scheme be really chimerical, after all, as it seems?" he mused. "Am I pitting myself against all this splendor of genius? Napoleon once did; but Napoleons are not produced in Fifth Avenue. Well, well!" he said to himself, "Napoleon started with a musket, and I with a check-book. Perhaps the modern Napoleon is better thus."

But, as if to answer his queries, one of the company, who had been making his way towards him, bowed to him and said,—

"You will excuse me, Mr. Vansittart! I have had the honor of being requested by our gracious hostess to introduce myself to you, and render you such assistance as you may require."

Jerome bowed in turn.

"I am delighted, monsieur; and, as a first mark of confidence, may I be bold enough to inquire your name?"

"I am M. Liancourt."

"The statesman!" exclaimed Jerome in surprise.

"That title is too high for me," was the modest reply, "but I devote perhaps too much time to political matters."

Jerome looked at his companion with undisguised admiration and interest. Liancourt had never held office. He was a mysterious party of himself.

Yet his voice was so powerful, and his influence so commanding, that he had wrecked two ministries within a twelvemonth, and practically created their successors. What his own ambition was, or what precisely his convictions were, no one clearly knew. He was always *l'homme inconnu*, sharp in satire, merciless in debate, unerring in retort, yet with a grave, serious eloquence of his own whenever he chose to exercise it. Unfathomable to friend and foe, he seemed to dwell in perpetual ambush. Jerome found him tall and handsome, somewhat advancing to middle age, with dark hair and swift keen eyes, which gave him a striking personality.

"You slight yourself," observed the American after his rapid summary of the man. "You wield a power in the affairs of France such as I venture to think has no equal amongst her ministers."

"Monsieur," replied Liancourt, "you mistake. Elsewhere politicians have power; in France never! Do you want to know where the power in French politics lies? It is there, and there only!"

And he pointed out of the window at the open street, with its ceaseless press of hurrying pedestrians.

Jerome started. It seemed to be a reply to his own misgiving. He smiled as he turned to M. Liancourt.

"Which only means," he said, "that the acknowledged leaders do not lead."

"That is true. We hate to set over us men of ability. Paris fears talent, and is in mortal dread of genius. Do you observe the President over there, talking to Monsieur Sully? Do you imagine he possesses power? It was precisely because he is incapable of it that he was chosen for the office. He is head of the state in everything save essentials. In fact, he has a talent for incapacity. He has made an art of mediocrity. But he is tall, and he rides well, and he happened to have secured the great *chef*, M. Prevost, before we knew he was in the market, and *voilà tout!*"

"But your ministers!"

"Shall I show you a couple of them? You know M. de Tournon, I observe. He is a great patriot, so sacrificing of self that he will waive any conviction he possesses to retain for the country his invaluable services. He has kept his portfolio under three ministries.

"Regard M. Ribou, the Minister of War. He obtained that gallant post because he won a duel with M. Printemps of the *Gaulois*. You will see how narrow his brow is, how deep his eyes, how prominent his nose and chin. He retains some striking features of the chimpanzee. They are indicative of his character. He is narrow, mean, jealous, and vain. But, alas! our countrymen are sometimes a little childish. He jumped into fame, and first became minister because on a certain occasion we were discussing some trivial arrangement with Germany about consular rights.

"He suddenly remembered the date, and sprang up. 'M. le Président!' he shouted, 'have you forgotten that this is the 4th of September? On such a day I refuse to discuss any matter of agreement between perfidious Germany and ourselves!' That was enough. He was the idol of the hour, and a week later he was invited to take up an unimportant portfolio to support a tottering government. He saved it."

Jerome scrutinized M. Ribou with very natural curiosity. The Minister of War had a peculiar interest for him.

M. Liancourt pointed out several other celebrities with much wit and acuteness. Under his examination each minister became vacuous, feeble, and of small account.

"Politics seem to be in no better condition than in my own country," Vansittart said with a laugh, "yet we are both republics dedicated to liberty."

"With a difference," answered Liancourt. "Do you remember what the wise man said? With you, liberty is a wife. You sometimes disregard her, and sometimes are not overkind to her; but still you are married, and you respect the bond. With us, liberty is a mistress. Our affection is more violent, our passion more fierce; but then, we may change and cast her off at any moment. In fact, France is waiting for a master. She is wearing her widow's weeds as coyly as she can, in the hope that her very obduracy may attract a suitor."

The two men advanced into the room, and mingled in the throng. A gay volley of even fire made conversation dangerous and enticing. In these salons still wanders the spirit of the old days of the Fronde and the rule of the immortal Louis.

Vansittart entered with nonchalance into the engagement, and astonished his audience by his readiness and his wit. Smiles rained on him from the women, and envious glances from the men. In half an hour he had made a dozen friends. M. de Tournon watched him closely, and M. Ribou seemed no less interested. But Jerome moved through the assembly, affable and inscrutable.

Later on he joined the men in a lower apartment, where, according to the hospitable habits of the Embassy, cigarettes and refreshments of a stronger character than those above were provided as a *bonne bouche*.

The talk here was more animated and less constrained. Politics, art, philosophy, were in the air, through which epigrams flew like so many witches on their broomsticks. Suddenly M. Ribou, who had been making himself merry with the editor of the *Figaro* on an indiscretion of the President, turned round to Vansittart and said,—

"Come, Mr. Vansittart, we are all a little anxious to know your opinion of us poor Parisians. Am I intrusive in asking you?"

At this question the conversation came to a pause, and all eyes were turned upon the visitor. Vansittart slowly took from his lips a cigarette, and, an extraordinary idea rushing through his mind, thus replied :—

"M. Ribou, Paris is the most delightful city in the world, and her citizens the most charming of all peoples; but there is one defect that I notice with grief. It is a thousand pities that a race otherwise so accomplished should be so deficient in the art of cooking!"

A general cry of amazement greeted this reply.

"Monsieur is jesting, surely," put in M. de Tournon with an incredulous look. "Do you not know that our cooking is the most elegant and the most delicate in the world?"

"Ah! M. de Tournon," responded Jerome languidly, "it has such a reputation; but cooking, after all, is a matter of the material world, and not of the imagination. Your dinners are volatile, airy, deliciously fanciful, what you will, but there is an abstract element about them. They are the dinners of men that dream. They tend to become impalpable and shadowy. There is needed a touch of Eastern opulence, or, shall I say, of Western coarseness. But your people dwell upon the emotional and the transcendental. Things material are to them mere obstacles in the way of ideas. It is so with your cooking."

"Pardon me, monsieur!" interrupted Liancourt with a smile, "if our cooking is a similar obstacle, we manage to clear it away expeditiously."

"No," urged the American. "Take your *menu*, your soup, for instance. Is not three quarters of it a tremendous effort to defy analysis? It abhors clearness and the display of its elements. Your fish loses its character in the effort to die away into the impalpable. As a matter of fact, your fish is only used as a kind of accompaniment to your sauces. As to your *entrées*, they lack substance. I admit they are wonderful, appetizing, fascinating; but they lack the fundamental. Each dish seeks to secure the hollow pretence of not being food, but a mere garnish, a pretty relish for the appetite, which toils unsatisfied, but finds no solid ground. Is it not so with your wines?—wines so light that they seem almost to be liquid in the abstract, the mere primal element resting for a moment on a flavor, and threatening to dissolve in a flash."

"You should not bring the philosopher to table," observed some one.

"Rather," retorted Jerome, "you should not bring the poet to the kitchen. Your cooking is like your character,—brilliant, piquant, superficial, irresistible, lacking in depth and substance, but aglow with a fine sense of taste. You are, as I said, dreamers. Your food is dream-like. It seems to tremble on the threshold of existence, fearing to assume bodily form. Just as you seek to avoid the stern facts of life, so your cooking is a mere turning-aside from reality. It is

all an evasion, a subterfuge. Yes, and it is all in all to you.
Your cooking is a true art ; for all art is at once bewitchingly
beautiful and a lie. French cooking, I maintain, is the
most superb lie that has ever been uttered. You should put
over your cook's apartment the old phrase, *Splendide Mendax*.
That is why, gentlemen, I maintain that in the true
sense you do not know how to cook."

"We are unfortunate, monsieur," said M. Ribou, "or we
might have had the good fortune of some instruction in this
art we know not of. Is it that in a new country some divine
secret has been discovered ? "

"I shall be happy to demonstrate the truth of my theory,"
replied Jerome calmly. "If the company desire proof, may
I be so rash as to offer to provide it ? "

A murmur of assent travelled through the room, half of
them amused, half a trifle perplexed.

"Then, gentlemen," exclaimed Jerome, "I take it as a
challenge ; and I shall insist, in common fairness, that all of
you here shall attend me on the occasion. I need but a
week. Shall we say, then, Wednesday, at the Grand Hotel ?
And let us fix the hour at half-past seven. Is it a bargain ? "

The extraordinary offer, and the curiosity it evoked, attracted
every one. A general acceptance, from the minister
down to the poet was made, and, with hilarious warnings to
the American on the audacious and impious task he had
undertaken, the company separated.

Jerome seemed to be particularly happy as he returned
home.

"Whatever becomes of the theory," he murmured to himself,
"they shall hear a proposal which will unsettle their
equilibrium for a month ! "

CHAPTER VIII

A STARTLING SCHEME

THE guests, on mounting the staircase of the Grand Hotel on the appointed day, and entering the banqueting-room, were struck speechless with amazement. It was as if they had stepped out of Paris and suddenly found themselves in some storied palace of the East ; or as if Aladdin's magic carpet had whisked them to a mysterious nook in fairyland, where every object that the eye rested on was a new marvel, and where wonder grew on wonder till the tired sense refused its office, and accepted the incredible with stupefied acquiescence.

A delicate perfume pervaded the air,—a sweet seductive scent which refused to be distinguished, and haunted one like some pleasant dream half remembered and half forgotten.

The table, arranged as a complete circle, occupied the middle of the room. In the centre was a fountain of the most delicate workmanship in purest porcelain. From this a thousand slender sprays scattered their cooling streams, almost all of them horizontally, that the vision of the *vis-à-vis* should not be interfered with. Two glorious threads of water, however, shot high to the ceiling, and as they turned and became transformed into mist, an ingenious electric arrangement infused them with all the infinite hues of prismatic light, and they fell to earth, dazzling and sparkling like infinitesimal clusters of jewels.

And this marvel was far exceeded by the sight which greeted the astonished eyes of the guests when they regarded the boundaries of the room.

Everything had disappeared. There were no walls—only a wonderful garden such as romancists have never conceived of nor poets dreamed.

For here was the miraculous in all its forms. Spring nodded to Autumn, Summer to Winter. The inexorable law which governs the seasons no more existed. All that the teeming year produced was present in rich profusion. At one end of the room was a stately orange-tree, with its ruddy fruit growing upon the branches. Hard by, the citron, the lime, the apple, the pear, the pomegranate, spread their fragrant foliage, still in full life and in the exotic state, breathing the odorous air of far-off lands, and carrying the mind to countries remote, to barbarous languages and savage manners. Upon the ground sprang the lowlier fruits,—the pine, the melon, and innumerable others which rarely travel from their distant home. Here was, in truth, a paradise for gourmets!

But even this did not equal the wondrous glory of the ceiling. By what sprites or by the genius of what magician had their host torn from its lodgment in some far country this noble vine, which spread its luxuriant branches, alive with a hundred quivering tendrils, above their heads, and formed a verdant roof for them during their repast? Yet here it was, its great trunk springing from its native soil, and its leaves seeming still in the freshness of their delicate bloom. From the branches hung countless clusters of rare black grapes but just above the heads of the company, and it was only necessary to stretch forth the hand to secure the coveted prize. Luckless vine! born to give pleasure unto men for generations, yet yielding up thy life for a single night's wonderment to gratify the tastes of a few Parisian gentlemen.

In fact, the room, with all its splendor of tree, flower, fruit, and foliage, was another of those ever-increasing proofs, now becoming almost tedious to Vansittart, of the irresistible power of wealth. When he had first held conierence with the manager of the hotel, that worthy gentleman had emphatically declared that the American's scheme was mad, impracticable, hopeless. After half an hour's earnest conversation, however, M. Loubet's eyes grew gradually larger, and his tone less emphatic; and it may even be said that his opinions in general did not remain so rigid as at first. This may clearly be gathered from his last remark, made almost reverentially.

"Yes," he said, "as you say, the miraculous can occur. All can be carried out according to orders. As for me, I assure you, monsieur, I will, if necessary, break into the Jardin des Plantes and crown your table with the treasures of the Republic!"

It was in a hushed and almost solemn stillness that the guests took their seats. These they discovered by the napkins of rare Indian silk on which their names were delicately embroidered in threads of gold. The table was covered with silver relieved by the most beautiful blooms, and by the plate of each guest was a nosegay of priceless exotics.

No wonder that even ministers unbent, that philosophers became aroused, that the eyes of poets gleamed, and that an air of refined and intelligent animalism appropriate to good eating passed over the faces of the company!

M. Lesieur, the erotic poet, wagged his great head in delighted anticipation; the eyes of M. Lacontel, the Minister from the Colonies, furtively sought the wine list; M. Legru, the famous journalist of *La Patrie*, tightened his napkin round his throat, and shook himself free in readiness for an encounter; and even Cornelius Van Regen, the American Ambassador, turned approvingly upon his fellow-countryman, and felt a thrill of triumph at this victory.

The dinner was superb. Did it prove Jerome's theory? Who can say, for who can remember? The delicious wines hurried on the appetite, and each course was forgotten in the sweet apparition of its successor.

Vansittart's cook was a supreme genius. He was an Arab

of many languages and an extraordinary palate. He would simply taste a new dish in Russia, India, Spain,—where you will,—retire for an hour, and produce it for you, but invariably improved by some more delicate treatment. All dishes were to him alike. He knew the cuisine of every country.

Silent, phlegmatic, proud, yet faithful, he never cared for money or reward. He had a deep satisfaction in his own unique superiority. Only once had Jerome complained of a dish. Next day the Arab was missing. Jerome waited a week, then packed up a bag, and went off to Cairo. There he found his cook, sitting, as when he first met him, at the door of a tiny house in the bazaar, calmly smoking his hookah. His master approached him gently, administered a severe kick, and ordered him to his hotel. The Arab meekly obeyed, and since then had never threatened to depart.

When dinner was over and even rarer wines were brought on, the conversation became animated and brilliant. During the meal the soft strains of a distant orchestra—for so it seemed—stole through the room, so faint as not to disturb speech, so clear and delicious as to intoxicate the ear whenever there came a pause.

But now even this ceased; and as the waiters handed to each guest a cigarette case of solid gold, with his initials upon it, as a souvenir of the feast, the company abandoned themselves to the charms of rapid and sparkling talk. There was not one who was not excited by the wonderful wines, not one eye that did not glow a little feverishly, and not a tongue that did not wag a trifle more freely than its wont.

"Dinner," observed M. Lefevre of the Academy, "is the poetry of the animal. To blend, to humanize, the material; to refine and chasten it; to secure the perfect cadence which lies in a well-chosen *menu*; to soothe alike and in equal degree every sense,—that is real poetry of a sort."

"Poetry, egad! That's good!" ejaculated an under secretary who was a little tipsy. "Let's have a poem!

Such a dinner deserves it. There 's that lazy Lesieur, who lives on a reputation made ten years ago. Come, let 's have an impromptu!"

" And you shall!" declared M. Lesieur, suddenly rising, his great head scarce steady on his narrow shoulders. "Come! I will toss you a trifle in honor of our host."

And folding his arms, as if in deep thought, he slowly repeated,—

> " Seeds of the East, strewn far,
>   By the breath of the ocean wind,
>   To lands of golden hope that are
>   'Neath the radiance rare of the Western star,
>   And a sky that is clear and kind!

> " Blossoms and buds that spring
>   In the virgin fields of the West,
>   That scatter their bloom in the air, and fling
>   Their odors sweet without reckoning,
>   O'er continents not so blest!

> " Odors that soothe the hot
>   And feverish pulse of the East,
>   Which lies all spent and has quite forgot
>   Whether it ever had youth or not,
>   And scrunches the crusts of its own death feast!"

A murmur of doubtful applause greeted this effusion. Poor Lesieur was born to gloom; but on this occasion his melancholy picture of the East ill accorded with his appearance, which was that of a man who had dined singularly well.

"You did not repeat it exactly as you gave it me this morning for *La Patrie*," whispered M. Legru.

"Alas!" replied the poet, "it is a mistake. No man should go in for impromptus who has not a really good memory."

"America will be a nation when it has won its first European war," M. Liancourt was saying. "We cannot invent glory for a banner, nor truth for a national motto."

"National mottoes," replied the host, "are mere hypocrisies. If you desire to find out the weakness of a country, find its motto, reverse it, and, behold! there it stands revealed."

"But surely," protested M. Ribou, "that cannot apply to France?"

"To France?" exclaimed Jerome in surprise, "more than to any other nation. Take your national motto, *Défense d'afficher*—"

"*Mon Dieu!*" interrupted M. Lacontel. "Do you imagine that to be our national motto?"

"Certainly," replied the American calmly. "What else?"

"*Liberté, Egalité, Fraternité,*" repeated M. Lacontel sententiously.

"Nonsense!" cried Jerome. "True, I have seen those words somewhere—let me see, yes, on the Morgue, where they appeared to me singularly appropriate. Elsewhere, indeed, they could in no wise be correct. On the other hand, I have seen *Défense d'afficher* on every public building, church, school, institution, monument, gallery, museum, palace, cathedral. What must I conclude? It must be your national motto,—*Défense d'afficher* (' Bill-sticking not allowed ').

"Now, gentlemen, how hypocritical, how false! Do the French nation ever engage in any other occupation but advertising? Is not Paris, in herself and in all her parts, a mere advertisement of the things you pique yourselves upon in history? You win a battle. Do you not immediately build a bridge, a monument, a street, and call them all after it? Is not the Seine spanned by advertisements of Napoleon? Are not the Champs Elysées studded with them? Do you not even call your streets after historical dates? If you achieve anything nowadays, do you not immediately plaster the world with advertisements? Do not your papers shriek and your telegraph wires groan? Why, France is nothing but a colossal bill-sticker, and she uses the whole of Europe as a gigantic hoarding."

"M. Liancourt smiled, the Colonial Minister winced. M. Ribou bit his lips, the poet groaned.

"Look at Versailles," continued Jerome. "You have used its walls simply for advertisements. 'Come in here,' you cry, 'and see the fine things we have done!' And there in ceaseless succession, Napoleon at Jena, Napoleon at Austerlitz, Napoleon at Wagram—everywhere Napoleon, and repeated a dozen times! What a mirror to a nation's vanity! There is the bill-sticking genius again. Paris and Versailles are absolutely plastered with these interminable advertisements. Not that I pretend that I have ever seen a picture or a monument of Waterloo."

"Monsieur!" cried the poet, rising in wrath and lurching forward, "let me tell you—"

"Nay, sir!" remarked Jerome pleasantly, "I do not blame you. A tradesman naturally shows his best wares in the window, and his doubtful ones he discreetly keeps in the shop."

"Your philosophy is hard on England," observed Liancourt, laughing.

"Precisely. Imagine! *Honi soit qui mal y pense!* ('Shame to him who thinks ill of it!') And is there a country where they *do* think more ill of it, where they *are* more tied to convention and form and barbarous Puritanic absurdities, than England? And this country of Mrs. Grundy placidly takes *Honi soit* for its motto!"

"Yet a useful motto when you consider England's genius for land-grabbing," murmured M. Lacontel, he of the Colonies.

"Yes," added M. de Tournon, "for you Americans alone have escaped her clutches."

"By England's stupidity," put in the American Ambassador. "She forgot we had gone out of childhood. A boy of eighteen objects to wearing his father's cut-down clothes."

"But did you gain?" interjected M. Liancourt. "You got rid of the second-hand suit and went in for a misfit!"

"Ah!" replied the ambassador, "we are unfortunate. We have had a long succession of tailors to take up the job, but somehow they never succeeded in getting further than the pockets."

"And, besides," snarled the journalist, "American misgovernment is absolutely essential for the Sunday editions of the New York papers."

"Nay," was the sweet response, "if you were ever to try the experiment of a newspaper in Paris, you would find it only an incidental evil."

"America is so vast, so isolated!" said M. Ribou. "You never put forth offshoots such as would bring you into touch with other nations."

"That is so," replied Vansittart. "America is engaged in colonizing her own country."

"You have the instinct from England," remarked M. Lacontel. "With her it is not art, but nature. She is but an animal, and her sons are mere unformed creatures of savagedom. Great Britain flings her barbarians out to other climes and other shores. They are a brood of vegetable brutes, who care not where they fall. They immediately take root in the earth, and are natives in a month."

"Alas! yes," moaned M. Lesieur. "France is too civilized to colonize. The Frenchman is a delicately nurtured flower that needs its native soil. Transplant him, and he fades!"

"In other words," added M. Liancourt, "the Frenchman is always the Boulevardier. He must be within reasonable distance of his café."

"Sentiment governs us, you see, even in politics!" and M. Lesieur looked seraphic.

"Yes," retorted Jerome, "a neurotic sentiment, like that of your poetry. That is why in colonizing you instinctively choose the unhealthy spots."

A laugh went round the table; and Jerome seeing his opportunity, struck in again.

"You need colonies, gentlemen. Who can deny it is the ambition of all nations to have the truest of immortalities, a great colonial empire,—alas! the only immortality that they can look to with certainty. A greater France, a France of the seas, a France that has its arms round the world,—is not that the dream of all true patriots?"

There was a murmur of assent.

"But there are difficulties. What corner of the earth is there left? Where can you plant your children? England is always beforehand. Her step is like that of the giant of fable. Each time she plants her foot on earth, her strength is doubled. What is left, all Europe has struggled for; and if an odd fragment is to be found, do not all the powers sit round it, snarling, and showing their teeth? Then where is France to colonize?"

"There is still force!" muttered the Minister of War.

"An idle hope. No; you need a new continent, some fresh hemisphere, perhaps a region in the centre of the earth. And then your colony, as you say, must be near France. Her sons will not live happily unless they are near their beloved Paris. You observe how you add to other difficulties a final one that seems insuperable?"

"That *seems* insuperable!" exclaimed M. Lacontel with significant emphasis. His eyes were fixed in deep engrossment on the American's face. Jerome went on calmly,—

"I said *seems;* for, gentlemen, I have an idea that if you cannot find a colony close to your elbow, if no habitable spot be left on earth, then"—

"Yes, yes!" cried a dozen eager voices.

"Why, in that case," continued Vansittart imperturbably, "there is nothing left but to create a new continent, to call it from the vasty deep, to construct a colony; in other words, to manufacture what you do not find ready to hand."

A gasp of surprise went round the table at these extraordinary words. The excitement of the evening had done its work. Every one was inflamed and roused from his ordinary calmness of temperament. This incredible utterance, so flattering to French hopes, yet so extravagant, flashed through every mind like the thrill of some sudden but pleasurable shock. A dead hush prevailed, and minister and poet alike gazed earnestly at Vansittart as he continued,—

"I am in earnest, messieurs. I believe in what I say. It rests with you. Do you desire a great, a mighty addition to your empire close at hand, within a day or two's journey from your own country?"

A shout of assent arose. The tension was almost unbearable.

"Then behold!" and at these words Jerome suddenly displayed to the company a map of Europe and northern Africa. All else was colored green. France alone was colored red; and, to the bewilderment of his guests, they observed that this color leapt over the Mediterranean Sea, and spread through the vast territory of the Sahara.

"Impossible!" gasped the Colonial Minister.

M. Ribou trembled. M. de Tournon, in his excitement, swept some glasses off the table. Even the phlegmatic Liancourt became pale.

"No, gentlemen," cried Vansittart, flinging the map away, "it is *not* impossible! That great wilderness, with its burning sands, has been for centuries the blot on the map of civilization. It shall remain so no longer. I tell you that the Sahara can be watered, you can drive canals through it, you can transform it into a smiling country. It shall be a second France, a new dominion of the Republic.

"Do you think I speak at random? I shall prove to you, M. Lacontel, nay, to any one who chooses, that it is merely a matter of money. My engineers have already surveyed the country. They are convinced. They have prepared their plans. In five years the Sahara shall be one of the most fruitful regions of the earth.

"And to whom shall it belong? Gentlemen, I back up my opinion with my whole wealth. I place it at the feet of the Republic. France shall undertake the work, and I will throw in my lot with her. France shall be the pioneer amongst the nations. Gentlemen, the Sahara—you are the flower of the French people—shall the Sahara be left to England, or shall it flourish under the tricolor?"

At this question an extraordinary scene took place. There was no resisting the magnetism, the spirit, the calm assurance, of this powerful American. Every one started to his feet with a cry; and a shout of "France and the Sahara!" was taken up and repeated with wild enthusiasm by all. The flushed faces of the excited statesmen vied with the more mad exuberance of the rest. It was many minutes before there came a lull in the storm.

Then M. Liancourt cried out, raising his glass unsteadily to his lips,—

"To the nuptials of France and the Sahara!"

Jerome stayed his arm.

"Nay," he said gravely, "you are premature. Let me propose a toast more fitting. Gentlemen; 'To their betrothal!'"

And with loud cries the glasses were drained and the stupefied party, unable to restrain their excitement, separated into groups, and the great dinner-party was at an end!

CHAPTER IX

HOW VANSITTART BECAME A FRENCHMAN

A SENSATIONAL item of news appeared in the *Figaro* side by side with the report of the banquet.

It had many headings, and the information it contained was sufficiently startling to occupy the minds of the Parisians for the whole of that day.

It announced to its readers that Jerome K. Vansittart had become naturalized as a citizen of the Republic of France, and a short Act to be forthwith passed through the Chamber would place him in full enjoyment of all the rights and privileges appertaining thereto. This was sufficiently remarkable, but there were many who rubbed their eyes with amazement when they read the statements which followed.

"It is both rare and difficult," said the *Figaro*, "for a foreigner to become a citizen of France unless he has won a right to that distinction by long residence, or by distinguished services to the Republic. M. Vansittart can at present claim neither, and yet there are very potent reasons why this honor should have been conferred upon him.

"In the veins of M. Vansittart flows the blood of one of the royal houses of France. He is not a foreigner. He is a citizen whose circumstances have kept him apart from his native land.

"The story is strange and romantic, but we can vouch for the accuracy of the facts.

"Students of French history—and what honest patriot has not followed the glorious annals of our great country—will be aware that there were several offshoots of the Buonaparte family who were overwhelmed in the ruin of the great empire, and who sought a safe exile on foreign shores.

"One of the most distinguished of these was Prince Jerome,—not the uncle, but the cousin, of Napoleon,—a man whom destiny seemed to have marked out for a noble career, and who certainly would have become the prince of one of the empires of Europe which the great Buonaparte was carving out for himself and for France. This Jerome, upon the fall of his cousin, having sought in vain to accompany him to the accursed island of St. Helena, fled to America, hoping that in that new land of promise bright ideals of freedom and of empire might be realized.

"From that time forth nothing was heard of Prince Jerome, and it was believed that the sorrows of his house had overwhelmed the man, and that he had fallen a victim to his own despair.

"This was not so. Prince Jerome was one who accepted fate with equanimity. He found America to be a country which needed honest labor and civic devotion. He became a citizen of America, took unto himself a large tract of the country, and there followed the habits and pursuits common to those who may be called the pioneers of civilization in that new continent. He married and had a daughter, and it is from this daughter that M. Jerome K. Vansittart is directly descended. It will therefore be seen that M. Vansittart's great-grandfather was the cousin of the greatest of French emperors, and that therefore his claims to citizenship in our country are not those of a foreigner coming from an alien shore.

"We understand that strong representations were made to the Office of the Interior, that, in view of the extraordinary and romantic circumstances surrounding M. Vansittart's birth and descent, the usual tedious preliminaries should be dispensed with, and that he should enter into the full rights of citizenship immediately.

"So long as the French heart beats warmly, so long will the name of our great Napoleon have power to persuade. The argument was successful.

"M. Vansittart we may claim with satisfaction as a fellow-subject of our mighty Republic."

When Jerome read this interesting and fanciful story, he smiled with a satisfied air. But as he took out of his pocket a check-book, and proceeded to write a check for a very large sum made payable to M. de Tournon, the Minister for the Interior, he said to himself,—

"There is something even more persuasive in its effect than the name of 'our great Napoleon!'"

The news excited Paris. Vansittart had made himself popular, not merely by his wit and address amongst the higher classes, but in particular amongst the unknown multitudes that form the populace, by his courtesy, his consideration, and his extreme affability.

Jerome was aware that his chief conquest would be that of the workmen of Paris. It was well enough to secure the good favor of the brilliant members of Paris society who glittered in drawing-rooms, and whose names were on every-one's tongue. But, after all, it was not these who were the serious members of the community. It was not these, as M. Liancourt had observed, who ruled the fortunes of France. Poets, philosophers, statesmen, wits,—these were weathercocks, light-headed creatures, who would bend before circumstances, and who might be expected to be found in the wake of success.

But the truly solid part of the nation—the ballast, as it were, to a ship that would otherwise be dangerously light—was the great multitude of silent workmen who walked of a morning to their manufactory, who sat dreamily at their cafés at *déjeûner*, who spoke little, who seemed to think little, whose lives consisted in the same ceaseless round of common existence,—the workshop, the café, the home.

Yet it was this ponderous mass which, set moving, had

the power to overturn ministries and to throw down empires. The honest *ouvrier*, who loves peace, who cares not for the ceaseless excitement of political fanaticism,—him and his class it was necessary for the ruler of France to convince.

And, curiously, Vansittart had already moved them. His honesty and kindness had been so free from ostentation, his generosity so quiet and so thoughtful, and his manner had so much of that real spirit of good comradeship which is the ideal so sought for and so little found in Republican countries, that he seemed to be a man of the people, and his enormous wealth only added the touch of romance to his figure which made him loom largely in the eyes of those who regarded him.

Jerome was to discover the extraordinary progress he had made in the affections of the people in a very remarkable way. One or two of the more disreputable papers in Paris had already commenced to attack this American. One of them, *Le Soir*, had attempted to jeer at him for his wealth by publishing extravagant stories about him, and by giving him ridiculous names, all of which were not heeded by anybody.

But one morning *Le Soir* made a very unhappy mistake. In a violent article, in which it shrieked forth anathemas against this wealthy stranger who was taking Paris by storm, the writer wound up,—

"Does this man imagine that by his vulgar gold, torn by violent hands from a starving and miserable country by unholy and dastardly methods of financial sharp practice— does he imagine that he can secure for himself thereby an honored position in our stately capital, or be accepted by our distinguished society?

"And yet such is the audacity of the monster, that he comports himself as an emperor!

"We, the mere miserable citizens of our own country, are expected to bow the knee before this new dictator, or, shall we not rather at once call him, Jerome the First!"

The editor was pleased when he had written this, for he had given Vansittart a nick-name, and nick-names in Paris are very dangerous.

He forgot, however, that it is all in the throw of the die. Sometimes a nick-name makes, not mars.

The fact was that in the eyes of the Parisian multitude Vansittart had something of the kingly air, and it pleased their imagination to regard him in the light of a great prince. Since they knew that he was a descendant of their adored Napoleon, they had placed around his head the halo of sentiment; and they considered how possible it was, that, had fortune been more kindly, this fine, noble, dangerous American might have sat upon the throne of France. When, therefore, they read the virulent article in *Le Soir*, they were inflamed, not to wrath, but to enthusiasm, by the new name that the editor had found for the man he hated.

The next time that Vansittart drove in the streets of Paris, he was astonished to find himself greeted by loud cries of " Long live Jerome the First ! "

The name had run through Paris like a fire. Not a street *gamin* but caught it up and repeated it.

Already Vansittart, though he had not found his throne, had received his kingly title.

Who that knows Paris will be surprised?—who that knows the yearning of her people for a fixed and settled government, for the rule of the strong man, for the personal ascendency of the individual? for the French citizen at heart despises the shifting, inconstant statesmanship which knows not where it is going or whence it comes, such as marks its present constitution,—a chamber which is the home of ignorant demagogues or vain-glorious aspirants, where man marks out man, faction fights with faction, and the Republic is forgotten in the mean struggle for personal aggrandizement.

Politics were, in fact, a mere trade, in which men made their money or lost it, on which they staked their reputations and made their fortunes or achieved their ruin ; or perhaps, better still, it was a game in which the only thing of importance was not the state, that tremendous interest always at stake, but the diseased ambitions of reckless gamblers, which put now this and now that party into power. There was no permanence in such policy, no sound principle at the bottom of it. Over and over again the people of France yearned for something nobler, for some fixed and honorable form of government; beyond all things, for some powerful monarch to rule justly and gather round him those who were prudent and wise and statesmanlike.

Of late this feeling had had a curious stimulus from the visit of the Czar of Russia to the capital.

There are words which fall upon French ears with a curious effect,—an effect that has power to heat the blood and overthrow empires. They are words, coming from the past, long since disused, and yet laden with the hopes and emotions of a brave and brilliant nation.

When the Czar had gone through the streets of Paris, and the soldiers and populace alike had shouted in loud tones of acclamation " *Vive l'Empereur !* " there was no doubt of the enthusiasm for their distinguished visitor. But the phrase lingered pleasantly in their memory ; it fired their imagination ; it recalled the past ; its sound, as it swelled forth from ten thousand voices, seemed to bear with it the accents of their own great history, and to recall too vividly those noble passages in the annals of France which fired the emotions and stirred the spirit of the citizen.

Were they, then, to shout " *Vive l'Empereur !* " only to those who came from other countries, and never to one of themselves ? There were some who remembered how they cheered Napoleon the Third before that fatal declaration of war which ruined the Third Empire. There were others whose imaginations carried them back to those wonderful scenes of excitement and national passion, when the great Emperor himself would pass in the streets of Paris, and the name, made nobler by a hundred victories, would burst from the lips of an adoring people.

There are some countries which are phlegmatic and logical and sober. To them names are but symbols; but to others these names have around them an atmosphere of passion. France is the land of emotion. A word can inflame her; and the word, thus early sinking deep in her heart, was already calling forth all her slumbering energies, all her hidden dreams and hopes.

And thus it was that when the Paris mob cried out, at first perhaps carelessly and half with a smile, but afterwards without the smile and half seriously, "*Vive Jerome Premier!*" it was still more natural to go into the café and think. And what those thoughts were, who can tell?

Most of all, the sound was dear to the French soldiery. To have their Emperor restored was dearer still. To them it meant empire, victory, glory.

In fact, there could be no doubt that the worst day's work the editor of *Le Soir* ever did for himself, and the best turn that had ever been done to Vansittart, was when, in contempt, he put into the mouths of the Parisians the name which invested the American with some of the attributes of kingship.

Jerome was sitting in a happy frame of mind in his study two days after the famous banquet, when, with an unceremonious bang and a clatter of feet, his Master of the Horse broke in upon his meditations.

"Hullo, Dick!" he cried. "Why this uproar? Brought your whole blood-stock with you?"

"Look here, old man!" was the reply. "What on earth will you be doing next? If things go on like this, my brain 'll burst, and in that case you won't win the Grand Prix next year. Have you seen the *Telegraph?*"

"No," replied Jerome languidly. "Anything in it?"

"Yes, by George! they've started a column called
"'VANSITTART DAY BY DAY.'"

The American took the paper, glanced at it, and then put it quietly on the table.

"My dear Dick," he said, "they don't quite seem to have grasped me in Fleet Street yet, and I'm not particularly anxious that they should. When English journalism comes into the game, it means cards face-up right way through. The *Telegraph* is smart enough, perhaps; but I tell you, if it wants to keep up with me, it will have to be 'Vansittart hour by hour,' 'minute by minute,' yes, 'second by second.' There's no going slow now, Dick. We're in it."

"Do you really imagine you can make a flourishing colony of the Sahara?"

"Not only do I think it, I know it, and, what is more, I am going to spend every penny I have in the world, if necessary, in doing it!"

"But why, in the name of wonder?"

"Because it's the biggest thing left on earth to do. Do you remember how Alexander cried for new worlds to conquer? Well, I have found what he could n't see. I'm going to conquer a new world, and that new world is the Sahara. I'm going to add a new vast country to civilization. Don't you think that a scheme like that is worthy of a man? Look at my wealth! What am I going to do with it? Fritter it away in benefactions and speculations, in doing odd good turns, building a church or two, and endowing a couple of universities? Not I! Such wealth gives a man boundless power, and I feel that I have similar responsibilities. I intend to confer a service upon mankind. People shall say of Vansittart, not that he was rich, but that he used his riches well. I shall rank," he ended with a merry laugh, "with Sebastian Cabot and Christopher Columbus!"

"But how unpracticable a proposal! It's worse than reaching the North Pole."

Jerome looked grave.

"My dear Dick, the difficulties of the Sahara have seemed

insuperable, simply because the money needed to overcome them was beyond the practical range of finance. There is nothing on earth that money cannot do. Well, we have money, France and I : we will do it together. Shall we say a hundred millions sterling to start with, it shall be there. Is a second hundred millions wanted, a third, a fourth, a fifth, the money shall never be to seek. In a few years' time the Sahara will be exporting fruits, grain, and cattle. Do you smile? But will you believe me when I say that there have been many practicable schemes prepared, and that I have one now which has obtained the approval of the first three engineers in the world?"

Dick looked at his friend admiringly.

"I believe you can do anything you like, Jerry," he said ; "but I did not know you were such a philanthropist."

"Call it ambition, if you like. Mind, I am not doing this simply to call into existence a new continent. I want to find along those vast sandy deserts the smiling tokens of a pleasant and prosperous country. The canals are important, of course, but they are no mere speculation on my part. I am thinking of quite different things, of farms and townships, of the vast wealth to be derived from a willing people, whose charges will be the signs of their prosperity. I am not going to water the Sahara and leave it there to fate. I am going to develop it,—to build great cities and great docks,—to make a second France of it. You see, do you not, that it is a new kingdom that I am thinking of, —a kingdom which will rise by magic from desert and waste, from arid wilderness and burning sands. Will it not be something to have effected it?"

"It is wonderful," admitted Dick pensively. "But you are dragging France into it. You are now a Frenchman. What is your idea there? Why not do the whole thing yourself?"

"Ah, Dick !" smiled Jerome. "I must read you a chapter out of a little book I am preparing, which will show you that more is necessary for a prosperous colony than money and good soil. It must have a sentiment, and a history ready made. It must belong to a great country, it must be colonized by a noble people. You will never be able to found a happy colony by a limited liability company alone. I have chosen France, partly for that reason, partly because of my mission here. Don't you see, Dick, that it is the Sahara that will place me on the throne of France?

"They are always dreaming of the aggrandizement of France, of new colonies, of great deeds, of dazzling victories. Do you remember how the Suez Canal made them frantic with jubilation, that it was *they* who had initiated and carried through an undertaking so stupendous? Was it not so with the Panama scheme? Every Frenchman, rich or poor, subscribed, and subscribed again, not merely because there was hope of profit, but because each one believed he was doing something for the glorification of his country, that he was helping in a cause that would throw new lustre around the head of France. Even when the scheme collapsed, it was not all dishonor. The aged De Lesseps—inculpated as the rest—do you not remember how there remained to the end a feeling of reverence for him, and all because, though it proved a failure, he *had* endeavored to do something to increase the power and splendor of France? They honored him for the mere wish, the mere desire, though they were ruined by it. *That* could never be quite forgotten even amid the public despair.

"This new scheme is by far the vastest, the most extraordinary, the most romantic, the most incredible of all. And it will *succeed*. Remember that. Dick, France will be at my feet in six months. I am giving her a new colony, a new empire. I am letting her achieve the last miracle left to be performed. Her pride, her honor, are concerned as they have never before been concerned in a scheme of empire, science, or finance. What will my position be if I can succeed in all this? Ay, and right through I am the one man who can direct, who can foresee, who can command, who can keep the exchequer ever full. Dick, old fellow," and Jerome got up and paced the room, showing for the first time how deeply he was moved by the extraordinary possibilities of his scheme, " the problem is solved. I set out to conquer a people. I shall do it, ay, and honestly too,—for I shall be a friend to France. She shall never have cause to turn and accuse me."

Then suddenly sinking down in his chair, he said abruptly :

" What about a hand at poker ? "

CHAPTER X

VANSITTART'S PROPOSAL

WHEN Vansittart, early in July, asked France to give him at the outset fifty millions sterling, which he proposed to double out of his own pocket, for the purpose of starting the conquest of the Sahara, he no longer used the language of heated rhetoric, but descended to plain facts and figures.

He was not now dealing with the imaginative poet or the venal politician, but with the shrewd and cautious investor, who had to be convinced, that, at the end of years of frightful struggle against the most potent forces of nature, a fertile province as large as the whole of Europe would be won for France from the wastes of torrid sand.

For the French to embark upon any such wild-cat scheme, it was necessary, in the first instance, to secure Government sanction for the company, which was curiously entitled "Sahara, Limited, and Jerome Vansittart."

This was easily obtained, and carried with it a certain amount of prestige; for, although ministers held aloof from the undertaking, the fact that they had allowed the money to be subscribed was regarded as in some sort an official imprimatur.

But what did Vansittart propose? It will best serve to elucidate this remarkable narrative of events if quotations be liberally made from the original prospectus. The accompanying map will also make clear the chief features of the design.

"My intention," he wrote (and he invariably used pronouns in the first person) "is to rescue from the sleep of ages a rich, fruitful, and bounteous land, which Nature, in her last fierce struggle to remain barbarian, has shrouded from the tents of men.

"There is no room for doubt that in prehistoric days the region now known as the Great Desert of the Sahara consisted of an inland sea whose waters washed the shores of a fertile country stretching from the southern centre of the Mediterranean to the Atlantic Ocean. Its bays and estuaries flooded the depressions that run from the existing desert northwards to Morocco and Algeria, and southwards to Timbuktu and Lake Tchad.

"Your scientists, MM. Desor and Cosson; eminent Englishmen like Sir Charles Lyell, Professors Ramsay and Boyd Dawkins, and Messrs. Wallace, Tristram, and George Maw,—unite with Teuton geographers, represented by Herr Escher von der Linth, in definitely establishing the early submergence of the Sahara below the level of the sea.

"Sir Charles Lyell declares his conviction that the Desert of the Sahara was under water between the twentieth and thirtieth degrees of latitude, 'so that the eastern part of the Mediterranean communicated with that part of the ocean now bounded by the West Coast of Africa'; and Mr. Wallace writes, 'The important fact has now been ascertained that a considerable portion of the Sahara south of Algeria and Morocco was under water at a very recent epoch.'

"I affirm without fear of contradiction, that, aided by the people of France, I can again subjugate this dried-up ocean bed, with the far-reaching difference between its former and its future state, that, whereas salt water once covered the face of the land, its place will now be taken by vivifying fresh water.

"Can this be done? Yes, by men and money spent without stint, and directed and encouraged by the intelligence that an all-wise Providence has given to us.

"The map shows clearly the position of Cape Juby on the Atlantic seaboard opposite to the Canary Islands, and the series of salt lakes, called Shotts, extending from the Gulf of Gabes in the Mediterranean as far as the centre of the Algerian province of Constantine. It also shows two lines of railway running from Algiers to El Aghuat, and from Philippeville to Biskra.

"El Aghuat and Biskra are the two main caravan centres for the Desert,—trading-points selected by the Arabs from the times when the north of Africa was throughout as fertile as Herodotus found Egypt where now the Suez Canal runs through an arid plain, in which the mirage alone conjures up ghostly visions of the glorious past. These railroads will be built forthwith.

"Through a fourteen-mile barrier of sand and rock, at a site already selected at Boca Grande near Cape Juby, an aqueduct will carry daily to the parched wilderness 100,000,000 gallons of distilled water. The sea will be guided into gigantic basins erected on the coast. Here the salt will be extracted, forming in itself a remunerative article of commerce; and the residuum of sweet water will be allowed, under efficient scientific control, to irrigate and fertilize the Great Desert of Igidi up to the base of the mud walls of the city of Timbuktu.

"On the eastern side a number of short canals will connect the Mediterranean Sea with Shott Jerid, Shott Rharsa, Shott Ashishina, and Shott Melrhir, thus enabling ocean-going steamers to reach almost to the outskirts of Biskra. At this terminus of the salt-water system, similar appliances to those proposed to be used on the Atlantic coast will deliver an equal volume of distilled water into the wadys, or valleys, that lead from Biskra to the southwest through the Sandhill region and close to the Muydir Plateau.

"It is impossible to believe that even the enormous quantity of 200,000,000 gallons of distilled water daily, flowing from east and west into a region that contains nearly three and a half millions of square miles, will alone suffice to bring it back under the control of the agriculturist and the stockbreeder.

"But there are throughout this vast territory great mountain ranges, which during the rainy season pour torrents of fresh water down their slopes, to be greedily swallowed by the desert, which has been desiccated by the unchecked heat of the sun throughout the rest of the year.

"What the Boca Grande and Biskra aqueducts will accomplish is the suspension of the process of complete evaporation which now goes on annually.

"The forces of nature will thus co-operate with us in yearly increasing area and power; and it is mathematically certain that within five years after the fresh-water canals have commenced to pour their contents into the interior, the Great Desert of the Sahara will cease to exist as a geographical expression.

"My engineers, who have been making exhaustive surveys during many months past, have issued reports which fully bear out my statements, and the most satisfactory feature of the project is that the world will not be called upon to wait for its completion before ocular proof is given of its success. Each foot won from the desert is an asset for the shareholders, and is an extension of France.

"As to the cost, the two railways, with ample equipment, will require ten millions sterling. That they will at once be remunerative is amply shown by the fact that the French Government and private speculators alike have long entertained their construction.

"In the larger scheme it is difficult to forecast the expenditure. On the salt-reduction works alone, some fifty millions of pounds will be spent; the canals and aqueducts will require another hundred millions; and a similar sum will go toward establishing and consolidating this newly-won empire.

"I am, by the will of the Great Ruler, wealthy enough myself to do this work unaided. But I prefer to be associated with the people of France in the greatest enterprise that has yet been attempted by the human race; and, to give earnest proof of my convictions, I propose to finance the project on the following basis:

"The capital of the company will consist, in the first instance, of £100,000,000 sterling in 1,000,000 shares of £100 each. Of this sum, 500,000 ordinary shares are now offered to the public at par; and I subscribe an equal amount in deferred shares, which will not rank for dividend until six per cent. is paid on the ordinary capital. I also guarantee four per cent. interest out of my own purse during construction; and, if the proposal should prove to be impracticable after this first stage of expenditure is exhausted, I undertake to repay every ordinary shareholder at par.

"If, however, as I believe, it be proved beyond doubt to be successful, further capital will be called for as needed, always bearing four per cent. interest during construction, and issued in the same proportions and under the same conditions as the first amount.

"The sum which I personally expend in interest will be returned to me as a preferential charge upon earnings after the payment of six per cent. on the ordinary capital.

"In a word, people of France, if you believe in me as I trust in you, we will march together triumphantly to the conquest of the richest domain yet wrested by humanity from grudging Nature."

The foregoing is but a digest of Jerome's forcible and convincing appeal, and his remarkable statements were supported in calm and clear terms by the expert reports which he annexed to the main document. He explained, in parenthesis, that the term *pound sterling* had been used throughout as the most convenient unit of value, owing to the predominant position of England in the financial world.

Although this statement was not soothing to French vanity, Jerome knew that the highest possible unit was imperative in the view of the tremendous system of accounts necessary for the careful conduct of the enterprise ; and he cleverly gilded the pill by observing that the shares would in this form be more readily marketable in England when they had risen by force of circumstances to a high premium.

It may be urged that the stock of the company was placed beyond the reach of the small investor by reason of its price ; namely, 2500 francs per share.

But the riches of France are far more evenly divided among the people than in other countries ; and he was able to reach a lower level of the population, even with this maximum price, than would have been possible outside the limits of the Republic.

At a stroke of the pen he settled the unemployed problem in France. Besides asking for and obtaining the money of her wealthier citizens, he announced that in due course there would be unlimited openings for labor and skilled artisans upon the works, and that to every man who passed two complete years in his employment he would personally give one fully-paid deferred share. As it was stipulated that these shares would absorb two thirds of the earnings after the preferential claims of the ordinary shares were met, he suggested that ultimately they would be the more valuable possession of the two.

To say that this marvellous production astounded France, is simply to state a bald fact.

"It is a proclamation, not a prospectus," said a member of the Senate when he had finished reading it.

"Yes," said another, "they are curious phrases,—'I and the people of France,' 'this newly-won empire,' and the rest."

"He is an inspired madman," growled de Tournon. "I must watch him closely, for, if he succeeds, there will be no stopping him."

The French Press, corrupt and venal to the last degree, realized that there was no chance for Panama peculations in this huge project, and with few exceptions, following the bent of public sympathies, eulogized the proposal and its originator to the magnificent extent of the French language.

In England, "Vansittart and his Desert," as *Truth* dubbed the company, were received with some degree of hesitancy. But the *Times* frankly confessed that the vastness of the scheme disarmed criticism. "It is a creation of genius," said the great newspaper, "and it cannot therefore be tested by ordinary standards. All that the average man can do is to reflect upon the wide meaning of M. Vansittart's statement that he is individually rich enough to back the enterprise by the full amount of capital supposed to be required. That he will be strongly supported by the French investor cannot be doubted; and the question naturally occurs to the English mind, 'What cannot be achieved by a sum equal to half the national debt of England?' We wish this bold American, or Frenchman as he now is, luck in his undertaking."

The *Telegraph* contented itself with several leading articles upon the history of the world from the earliest periods, with obvious references to the canalization of Mars and the discovery of Uranus.

It was left for the *Daily Mail* to take a really useful view of the situation. It sent a special commissioner to Boca Grande; and he reported that the gradients were dead in favor of Jerome's plans, "if only the salt could be extracted from a sufficient quantity of water." Upon this finding, the city editor of that enterprising journal advised some one in Brixton not to dabble in the shares, but to invest in brewery debentures.

The British Foreign Office kept an eye upon Vansittart's proceedings; and the Permanent Under Secretary, after a scrutiny of the map and a consultation with the Keeper of Records anent a certain long-forgotten treaty with Spain, solemnly winked at his immediate subordinate as he made a memorandum for the information of his chief.

The meaning of that portentous drooping of the eyelid unfolded itself in later days.

Meanwhile stories of Vansittart's generous magnificence were in the mouths of all men.

People had ceased to marvel at his wealth and his extravagance, for the bounds of wonder had long been reached. But still they talked; and when descriptive columns appeared in the papers concerning the rapid erection of his splendid palace at St. Cloud,—" a dream built of commonplace materials," wrote the *Gil Blas* concerning it,—the omnibus proprietors of Paris began to run special lines of vehicles to enable curious Parisians to inspect the structure for themselves.

Vansittart insisted upon regarding all such visitors as his guests, and light refreshments were dispensed to them with ready hospitality. Thus St. Cloud again became a household word in Paris, and the association was clearly of an imperial character.

The American colony in Paris were greatly puzzled by the proceedings of their apparently eccentric fellow-countryman.

They crowded his receptions, and with characteristic *naïveté* invited him to confide his intentions to them fully and without reserve. But although the American papers had dozens of " interviews " and articles by " well-informed " correspondents, Vansittart and his motives remained a sealed book to them, save in so far as his actions were common property.

The New York journals might guess and surmise to their heart's content, but not one of them was any the wiser; and, curiously enough, none of them thought it necessary to interview the employees at the Netherlands Hotel.

To the Press and the public alike, Vansittart's career seemed to have commenced with his arrival in France.

The only man, outside Vansittart's two chosen confidants, who knew anything more of the business than appeared on the surface, was M. de Tournon, the Minister of the Interior.

By means of his spies he was kept acquainted with the comings and goings of Jerome and his companions; and he was absolutely unable to account for the prolonged presence of Mademoiselle de Montpensier in the hotel, and her complete seclusion.

She was visited by no members of the Royalist party; nor was Vansittart himself a *persona grata* with them, for no man who attracts the respect and obtains the confidence of the French people can be complacently regarded by the Bonapartists, and Orleanists, and Bourbonists, and other opportunists in behalf of royalty, in Paris.

These factions have their only hope, their sole opportunity, in disorder or political turmoil. Obviously the American, with his money-making and empire-building proposals, in no way furthered their cause.

"Then what is the woman doing in the case?" said M. de Tournon. "A thousand thunders! the more this man pays me, the less do I understand him."

And already Vansittart had bribed him handsomely. The naturalization, the granting of the park of St. Cloud for a residence, the mere registration of the company, with its peculiar charter and still more peculiar name, had each added to de Tournon's exchequer.

Nevertheless he felt that he was but a counter in a game which he could not see, and he hated Jerome for the affable grace with which he bent all things to his will.

He had boggled long at the nomenclature of the company. "It suggests," he said to Vansittart, "that whilst the Sahara is limited, Jerome Vansittart is not. The Minister of the Interior, in such a matter, should ask the extent of your designs." This with an unctuous smile of jocose politeness.

"I do not care to have my designs questioned when I pay for their accomplishment," replied Vansittart, and de Tournon winced at the allusion. He offered no further opposition, however. It was not yet time to bite the hand that fed him.

De Tournon would not have felt so content with his personal prospects had he known that M. Liancourt had seen each of the later checks paid to him by the millionnaire, and that ex-Prefect Folliet was watching both him and his agents with lynx-like care.

As it transpired, Vansittart knew not only what was passing in his own mind, but also in that of M. de Tournon: so thus far the game lay with him.

. . . .

On the evening of their last conversation, M. de Tournon was engaged upon an occupation which would have proved deeply interesting to Vansittart could he have been present.

He was writing letters. The last of them was very carefully and clearly worded. It was addressed to M. Contral, Prefect of Police. It ran,—

"I desire you to pick out a couple of your most secret and reliable men, upon whose discretion you can absolutely depend. One of these shall take up his station near the Grand Hotel, and watch carefully all the movements of Mademoiselle de Montpensier, at present staying there. He shall also follow her wherever she goes. The other man shall proceed to Fontainebleau. I desire that he shall look carefully after the thatched cottage where we surprised Prince Henri two years ago, and also keep an eye on the grotto in the wood to which we followed the Prince on the afternoon of his assignation with the lady I have mentioned. Both men will report daily, and you will forward these reports to me. Your close attention to these instructions shall not go unrewarded. I still have the nomination to the Silver Star."

"Curse this American!" growled the minister, when he had sealed this curious document. "His Sahara scheme upsets every calculation I have made. These madmen of

Paris are already making a god of him. However, he has a tender spot, clearly; I, both an excellent memory and a well-drilled staff of officers. We shall see. There will be a struggle to the death between us in six months. And I will then be sitting in the President's chair!"

CHAPTER XI

ON THE VERGE OF THE DESERT.

"THAT is our chief difficulty," said Maclaren to Vansittart, as they stood together on the shore of the Shott Jerid, in the province of Tunis, towards the close of a burning day in August.

The engineer pointed, as he spoke, to a vast expanse of white-brown plain, a crumbling amalgam of sea salt and sand; and it will thus be perceived that the term *shore* was only a relative one when applied to this great inland lake, which is only separated from the Mediterranean by a narrow isthmus some twelve miles in width, but extends for one hundred miles right across Tunis from the Gulf of Gabes.

"The present height," he explained, "is an average of sixty feet above sea-level, but it is only a crust of varying thickness, resting upon islands and shallows, and covering irregularly a huge underground lake, which we have repeatedly sounded to a depth of over a hundred feet below sea-level. The neighboring Shotts, principally Rharsa and Melrhir, are uncovered, and maintain an average depth in the main channels of thirty feet, being themselves some seventy feet below sea-level."

"So I understood," said Vansittart. "In your soundings here through boreholes, have you succeeded in tracing the general position of the deep parts of the lake with any degree of accuracy?"

"Oh, yes! I have a chart which shows this clearly

enough. And jolly dangerous work it was, working on this treacherous stuff. We only lost one camel laden with theodolites, but the Arabs about here tell a blood-curdling story of a caravan with a thousand camels going slap through on one occasion. Not a man or a beast escaped alive, as the subsidence was wholesale. Towards the west there is quite a stretch of clear water, and here we have the prevalent depression below sea-level."

"A Frenchman, Captain Roudaire, proposed to cut a canal through the crust, did he not?" said Jerome.

"That's what we shall have to do, but we won't start cutting operations until we are compelled."

"What then?"

"We will blow the stuff up with dynamite. Do you see that line of posts, with little red flags, extending for nearly a mile, at intervals of fifty yards? Each of those marks a deposit of dynamite and gun-cotton alternately. They are connected electrically, and I suggest that you should blow up the lot to-morrow morning. You will see something fresh in the way of explosions, I can assure you."

Vansittart had only arrived at the Gulf of Gabes in the *Seafarer* that day; and he had at once ridden over to El Fejej, on the borders of the shott, where Maclaren had established his permanent camp.

For a little while, it must be confessed, his heart sank within him as his Arab pony shuffled through the loose sand, or picked his way among scattered heaps of volcanic rock.

It was his first sight of the road towards the Great Desert; and as the silent wastes unfolded their vast solemnity before him, he realized how puny was his power in face of this majestic expanse of a ruined continent.

Science told him that in every rock and in each separate particle of sand lay the open records of the ages. Here were the fossil remains of marine animals and plants; here were gaunt water-courses, which even yet became raging torrents when the too rare rain-clouds burst over the neighboring heights; here was salt water beneath his very feet in gloomy and awesome caverns.

Yet human nature is but weak, and the once sanguine millionnaire was momentarily depressed by the thought that he was committed to an apparently superhuman undertaking.

"Ah, well!" came the reflection of slight comfort, "Columbus believed in the existence of land when others saw nought but the rolling Atlantic. I must be equally steadfast on the opposite quest, and perhaps I shall be equally right."

A long talk with the cheery Maclaren had reassured him. The skilled engineer had faith in nothing that was not verified by his instruments, and they assured him that the first stage of the enterprise was merely a matter of energetic digging and a liberal use of explosives.

Early next day the camp was agog with excitement.

Some vague idea of what was going to occur had caused a great multitude of Arabs, Tuaregs, and negroes to assemble in the locality, and a quaint hum went through this wild-looking crowd as Vansittart moved through their midst towards the tent which shielded the electric battery from the fierce rays of the sun.

Maclaren had already made a personal tour of the whole line of explosives, and assured himself that everything was in order. He was calm and confident.

"Press that button," he said to Vansittart, "and there will be a commotion."

Jerome smiled, for an odd thought came to him at the moment.

A similarly simple movement in the box at the New York Opera House had revealed to him the identity of Honorine de Montpensier, with its bewildering train of consequences.

Now, with equal ease, the pressure of a little ivory knob would reveal to him—what?

He put forth his hand, and, almost before he was conscious

of the contact, a dull roar of overpowering volume came to him from the congealed surface of the lake. The earth shook violently; terrible reverberations caused a series of less forcible earth tremors; a dense cloud of dust slowly spread itself over all things, for a time blotting out even the bright radiance of the sun; and from the crowd of natives came an awful yell of terror and amazement.

"It's all right!" shouted Maclaren through the turmoil. "When the smoke clears off, you will see the first mile of your new waterway."

He was right; but a long and anxious period of suspense had to be borne with such patience as the different onlookers could summon to their aid, before the great dust-cloud had sufficiently dissipated to enable them to glean, by fitful visions through the murky depths, some definite idea of the result of the explosion.

Magnificent and awe-inspiring as the spectacle was in its earlier glimpses, it was not for nearly an hour that its full extent could be ascertained.

A wide and deep rift of irregular proportions had been torn through the overlying crust; and the waters of the lake, flurried into activity after a rest of centuries, were now seen sparkling brightly in the full brilliance of a powerful sun.

The pathway cleft through the mass of salt and sand, although following the general line previously marked by the posts, was highly irregular in its conformation.

In some portions a wholesale subsidence had opened a gap nearly a quarter of a mile in width; in others the greater thickness of the crust, or the fact that it was supported in some manner beneath, narrowed the passage down to a few yards; but the rent made by the explosion would evidently not end for many a long day.

Ever and anon some huge mass of *débris*, varying in size from a few cubic yards to a vast bulk containing many thousands of tons, would break away from the unsupported sides of the excavation, and fall with a tremendous crash into the water.

In some parts the crust filled up the bed of the lake and created small islands, but as a rule it had been swallowed up in the depths; and there could not be the slightest doubt, that with similarly drastic methods, adopted throughout the whole extent of Shott Jerid, it would be a comparatively easy task for a dredger to secure as broad a passage as might be desired for vessels of any tonnage.

And it must not be forgotten that the real surface of the lake was much below sea-level; so that, when the connecting canal was made through the isthmus that separated it from the Gulf of Gabes, the whole of the existing obstructions to navigation would be hidden away far beneath the new level attained by the water.

Vansittart was himself so stirred by the great spectacle— which had suddenly dispelled the doubts and fears of the preceding day, and had made his scheme as plain and definite to his eye as it was to his brain in the quietude of his library at New York—that for a long while he could not find words to express his emotion.

Even Maclaren, who added to the cool and collected demeanor of the unperturbed Yankee no inconsiderable spice of the phlegmatic disposition inherited from his Scottish ancestors, was at first silent whilst he surveyed the superb result of his labors.

But professional instinct soon restored him to a normal frame of mind.

"I never saw or heard of a mile of canal being made as easily as that," he said with a smile, his eyes still fixed upon the glittering waters, which were always becoming more distinct and well defined in their area. "If only we can turn the salt water into fresh, the job is as good as done already."

His words recalled Vansittart to his surroundings, and he said,—

"I must congratulate you, Mr. Maclaren, upon the success of your initial step. I candidly confess that I never dreamt of such progress being made at the outset. A photograph of the fissure will send up the shares of the company twenty points, and they are now at a slight premium on faith alone."

"There is nothing like the combination recommended by the Apostle," said Maclaren. "Faith, hope, and charity go a long way, but they must be supplemented by good works."

"It is obvious," observed Vansittart after a pause, "that there will be much danger attending your operations until the unsupported crust on each side of the water-way has sunk to its new natural level. I hope that you will not needlessly expose your life, nor the lives of your employees, until this risk at least has disappeared."

"There is not the slightest need of it. I shall not even attempt to blow up a passage through the whole length of the lake. I think that our next effort should be on a larger scale, starting from a point about five miles distant. By following out this principle on an ever-extended basis until we reach the open water on the western shore, I feel certain that the rest can be left to natural laws of gravitation. Long before the Gabes Canal is excavated the whole of the crust on this lake will have sunk to such an extent that there will be absolutely no hazard attending the passage of a steamer through the main channel of the lake. Nature herself will be our best engineer, not alone in this portion of the project, but in many others. It is no small thing to throw open these hundreds of square miles of water to evaporation. Even this limited achievement means a very considerable increase of rainfall during years to come."

"I think," said Vansittart thoughtfully, "that when a man has reasoned out a proposition, he ought to tie a towel round his eyes, rather than witness its gradual accomplishment. I must admit that twenty-four hours ago I was more than dubious as to the outcome of our undertaking. Reason told me that I could have made no mistake : every other sense, encouraged no doubt by the appearance of things, rose in rebellion, and for the time completely subjugated my logical faculties."

"Ah, well!" replied Maclaren, "you can afford to have your bad quarter of an hour ; for I am convinced, sir, that in this scheme of yours you have struck the biggest thing that has yet been achieved by mankind. If you were not a rich man, Mr. Vansittart, you would have gained fame as an engineer, and I am personally delighted to have the opportunity of being associated with you in this great work. When it is ended, I think I shall be about used up."

"Not a bit," laughed Vansittart. "My chief engineer, Mr. Maclaren, will, I hope, always remain in that position ; and I think there will be ample scope for your abilities before you begin to have trouble with the gas and water authorities of the big cities which we shall see established in the middle of the Sahara."

A flush of pleasure turned even the bronzed cheek of the engineer to a deeper hue, for Vansittart could have found no better way of conveying his appreciation of the services rendered to him than in the few simple words just uttered.

If ever a man saw his life's work spread out before his feet in ample panorama, Walter Maclaren did so at that moment.

Whilst the two men were thus conversing, they did not notice that amidst the crowd of natives, now slowly recovering from the stupor into which they had been plunged by the events of the preceding hour, a new and unaccountable commotion was gradually making its presence felt.

Strange cries, guttural exclamations in Arabic and the less sonorous tongues of the desert, came from the motley assembly ; and more than one *Moullah*, or Mohammedan priest, was rapidly working himself into a state of perfectly ungovernable rage, whilst he gesticulated wildly, first towards the lake, and anon in the direction of Vansittart and his immediate companions.

At last the attention of both men was enlisted by this curious demonstration.

"What is the matter with those chaps?" said Vansittart; "they seem to have something troubling their minds more than enough."

Maclaren gazed anxiously at the crowd, and then scrutinized the lake.

"I don't like their attitude," he said. "You never know what these cut-throats may be up to. Whenever a *Moullah* starts to harangue them, you may be sure that it means mischief. By Jove! what is that?" he added, sweeping the full length of the excavation with his glasses.

Following his example, Vansittart also scrutinized the scene; and, by the aid of a powerful field telescope, he made out objects that appeared strangely like the inanimate forms of men and laden camels strewn about among the *débris* collected on a small island in the centre of one of the open reaches of water.

"I have seen a few odd things in the course of my life," he said; "but if those are not the bodies of men and animals, I will never trust my eyes again. And how on earth did they get there? I am prepared to swear that there was not a living creature anywhere nearer than this spot to the scene of the explosion before it took place."

"There can be no doubt about that," cried Maclaren, speaking rapidly and excitedly. "Those confounded apparitions down there are well-preserved spooks. They are the relics of that caravan I told you about, which was swallowed up years ago in this lake, and they have been kept nice and fresh by the brine beneath, for the purpose of giving us a tremendous lot of trouble straight away."

"Why," said Vansittart, "how can they affect us?"

"These superstitious idiots of natives," replied Maclaren, dropping his glass and pointing towards the now yelling multitude that swayed and vociferated at some little distance, "will readily imagine that we have disturbed the dead in their graves, and that Allah has taken this means to pronounce a thorough-going curse upon our work. This is the ugliest business that could possibly have happened."

"It really looks as though you were right," said Vansittart, who, although ignorant of the language and customs of the Arabs and their kindred tribes, could not fail to notice the growing frenzy of the crowd of fanatics who had so unfortunately witnessed what they believed to be a miracle.

"Do you really think they mean mischief?" he added; for there was now a definite movement in the crowd, and an aged *Moullah* had advanced alone towards the small group of Europeans.

"Yes, I am sure of it," said Maclaren, whose face now wore an aspect of grim determination. "We shall have to shoot quick and often if we mean to save our lives. Get your revolvers ready," he went on quietly to the few assistants who stood near him. "Form a half circle facing towards the mob, and when I tell you to fire, blaze away at your best pace into the thick of them!"

"Is this really necessary?" said Vansittart, who shrank from thus marking the inauguration of his enterprise with the loss of human life.

"It may be," replied Maclaren, "but we will only act on the defensive. Perhaps this *Moullah* may explain matters a bit. Here, Abdullah Khan!" he cried to the interpreter attached to the party, "come and tell us what this old vagabond says."

The *Moullah*, who was now quite close to them, was a fearsome object. His hair and straggling beard were matted with the dirt of years.

His body, naked but for a loin cloth, and emaciated with long years of religious penance, glistened with oil; and in his hand he brandished a large knife, whose glittering blade well accorded with his fierce and murderous aspect.

He growled something in Arabic, whilst his eyes were fixed with the lambent glare of a tiger upon Vansittart. The interpreter, himself an outcast Arab, shaking with fear, explained in broken English,—

"This is great priest, Sahib," he said. "He very angry at bones of his fathers being profaned. He say you have done an evil thing. You must go away, and never look upon the dead again."

"Tell him," said Maclaren, "that we could not help this thing, and did not know of it, and that we will inter the bones with all respect. Tell him, too, that the great Sahib," indicating Vansittart, "will give plenty of bakshish."

The interpreter held a brief conversation with the *Moullah*, and it was obvious that no progress had been made towards reconciliation.

"The great priest says," again explained Abdullah Khan, whose terror had increased during his animated colloquy with the wretched being who strove to impose his will upon them, "that he will not take bakshish. All the Sahibs must go away at once. It would be well for you to obey him," added the man upon his own account.

"That which he asks is impossible," said Maclaren sternly. "We cannot be interrupted in our work, and we refuse to meet his wishes. We will do anything he asks in reason, but it is impossible for us to leave this place."

Again the interpreter explained; and Vansittart, in the desire to impress the *Moullah* with his kindly intentions, stepped nearer to him, and sought by expression and gesture to tone down the emphasis of their refusal to fall in with the desires of the crowd, of whom the priest was obviously the spokesman.

The act nearly cost him his life. When the aged fanatic understood that there was to be no retrogression by these foreign devils who had disturbed the weird grave found by the caravan during that terrible catastrophe of the half-forgotten past, he sprang towards Vansittart with the clear intention of plunging the knife into his heart.

Jerome was utterly unprepared for this dramatic development of events, and would have fallen a victim to Mohammedan hatred of the dominant race, had not, in that supreme moment, a bullet lodged itself in the *Moullah's* brain.

The wretched man fell back under the force of the blow as though he had been struck by lightning.

The knife dropped from his nerveless grasp, and he crumpled up, a sorry heap of dead humanity, upon the ground.

It was Arizona Jim whose promptitude had thus solved a difficult situation.

Bates had been an amazed spectator of that morning's proceedings; but throughout the whole of the remarkable incidents that had taken place, he never abandoned for a moment the *rôle* which Vansittart had imposed when he humorously dubbed him his " Captain of the Guard."

Had the Day of Judgment suddenly supervened, Jim Bates would still have striven to be faithful to his trust.

Joined to this tenacity of purpose was that natural quickness, " on the draw," which he had imbibed with his mother's milk in the wild and woolly West. None but an *habitué* of the drinking-saloons of Denver in its infancy could have fired that shot with such remarkable promptitude and precision.

Vansittart hardly realized what had occurred, before a determined movement on the part of the natives showed that they were not disposed to allow the death of their co-religionist to go unavenged. With frantic yells, and brandishing such weapons as they possessed, they advanced upon the tiny knot of Europeans.

" Fire a volley into the air ! " shouted Maclaren, and obedient to his commands the revolvers rattled forth a message of defiance to the fanatical crowd.

Half-blind with passion though they were, this resolute

attitude on the part of Vansittart's companions made them pause.

Those in the rear were ready enough to urge their friends in the front to advance to the attack; but somebody had to get shot, and the blusterers who saw most likelihood of being selected for this undesirable distinction were not eager to earn immortality. They were, in fact, cowed by the firm front displayed by their opponents; and Maclaren, who was a born leader of men, quickly seized the opportunity.

He stepped forward and sternly ordered them to depart, adding that his men would shoot if his commands were not instantly obeyed.

His words they did not understand; but his actions were unmistakable, and the trembling interpreter mustered up courage enough to come to his side and shout out a forcible translation.

With many a wild curse and muttered threat the infuriated crowd gradually drew off, and Maclaren was at last able to say to Vansittart,—

"We must retire immediately to Gabes. It will be impossible for us to pursue our work until we have a sufficient armed force to protect us. These fellows are wild with rage, and we have unfortunately killed one of the holiest of their religious mendicants."

"Is there no other way out of the difficulty?" said Vansittart.

"Absolutely none. Had it not been for the chance that no disturbance was expected, and they were practically unarmed, not one of us would now have been alive. We shall require a considerable body of troops to protect us, as to-day's events will spread like wildfire throughout the district, and we may easily have a rebellion upon our hands. France is constantly fighting these chaps on the border of the desert, and it will be necessary to teach them a severe lesson once and for all. Otherwise we shall be constantly subjected to similar interruptions."

There was no gainsaying the truth of his conclusions, and that night the whole party were safely lodged on board the *Seafarer* at anchor in the Gulf of Gabes.

Thus was the first step taken in the big enterprise of "Sahara, Limited, and Jerome Vansittart."

CHAPTER XII

THE BATTLE OF EL HEGEF

"THE Departments of War and Marine have placed at the disposal of M. Jerome Vansittart one battery of horse artillery, six machine-guns with a company of Spahi artillerists, one squadron of cavalry, two regiments of infantry, the 67th and 105th of the line, the whole under the command of General Daubisson, and the gunboat *Sphinx*, commanded by Captain Pompier."

Such was the text of an official communication from the French Government received by Vansittart at Algiers, in response to his cabled request for troops to protect his engineers during the initial operations on the Tunisian lakes.

"We shall want far more than that number of men," was Maclaren's comment when he heard the news.

"I should like to have the whole French army," said Vansittart.

"Hardly so many as that," laughed the engineer. "It would cost a bit, would n't it?"

"Yes. It would cost France a great deal."

Vansittart was thinking aloud, as was his habit when in company with those whom he felt intuitively he could trust.

Maclaren glanced at him sharply. The millionnaire puzzled his practical friend exceedingly. Jerome always, by his manner, conveyed the impression that the conquest of the desert was but a means towards an end; and what that end might be, the other could not determine, as the only person in the French Soudan who had a vague inkling of Vansittart's intentions was Arizona Jim, and that worthy was as close as an oyster.

Vansittart suddenly became conscious that his companion was scrutinizing him, and in the same instant he resolved to take him partly, at least, into his confidence.

"Maclaren," he said, fixing his eyes intently upon the keen face of his friend, "I know that you do not understand why I launched myself into this business at the outset. You believe, and rightly, that my actions are not wholly prompted by ambition to accomplish a task in subjugating the desert before which other men might pale. It would not be fair to you, under the circumstances, to say more than this, that I wish to control France; and to control France, one must control the army."

Maclaren returned his gaze with equal frankness. "I guess you're the right sort of man to control anything," he said with smiling confidence, and the subject then dropped.

When they met General Daubisson, they did not immediately exchange views with regard to him. He was short and stout and wheezy,—not exactly the type of soldier for colonial warfare,—and Maclaren was at first inclined to growl at the ministerial choice of a commander for the expedition.

But Vansittart reassured him on this point. "It is more than lucky," he explained, "that our military leader will be likely to break down in front of the hardships of the desert. In such a position, no one can blame me if I direct the troops myself."

The fat general did not belie their expectations. In the Gulf of Gabes he had a sharp attack of fever; and before the expedition had reached the scene of their first exploit, he was so ill from incipient heat apoplexy that he had to be sent for a sea trip forthwith on board the *Seafarer*.

Now, the French Minister of War was not a friend of Vansittart, but he was a nerveless creature; and a cablegram to him soon gave the millionnaire tacit command in the field.

though nominally Captain Pompier, as the officer next in rank to the disabled general, issued all orders.

Vansittart had found a way to Pompier's heart. That gallant officer had shown considerable skill in organizing the commissariat and transport arrangements, which, in common with every French military undertaking known to history, were lamentably deficient.

With the millionnaire's complete approval, he had amplified and perfected the details by extensive purchases at Algiers, and Jerome took the earliest opportunity to congratulate him upon his methods.

"You ought to be a power in the Ministry of Marine rather than commanding a gunboat, Captain Pompier," he said.

The sailor flushed with pleasure, for what Frenchman does not love Paris?

"Such is not my good fortune," he sighed; "I have no influence."

"Perhaps not at this moment," returned Vansittart quietly, "but everything is possible in France."

Pompier did not stop to ask himself what this strange French-American meant. He bowed with gratified courtesy, and there was no further possibility of service etiquette causing a rift in the relations between them.

The troops numbered 2500, all told. They bivouacked in sight of Shott Jerid, and Jerome was amazed to find how amply the prediction made by Maclaren had been fulfilled. Already a tremendous subsidence of the crust had taken place, and it had even spread far to the westward.

The disintegrating influence of the sun had crumbled away the rotten compound, whose surface alone was firm; and it was now quite possible to row a boat over extensive open spaces of the water, the density of which was phenomenal, owing to the quantity of salt held in solution.

An early excursion was made to the island on which reposed the remains of the ill-fated caravan, and a remarkable discovery resulted.

The bodies of men and animals were petrified; and Vansittart's ready wit jumped at the conclusion, that, if he wanted to create a genuine sensation in Paris, he need only send a group of stone Arabs mounted on stone camels for exhibition in a prominent boulevard.

All Paris would gape at the weird spectacle. This project he subsequently carried out, and the sequel was dramatic.

The neighboring country was practically denuded of its nomad inhabitants, but spies soon reported that a large gathering of Arabs and Tuaregs was centred at El Hegef, a town situated some sixty miles from the coast, and close to the great southern bend of Shott Jerid.

A Jehad, or religious war, had been proclaimed, and there could be no doubt that a widespread *émeute* had broken out among these wayward sons of the desert.

A messenger sent to them with pacific and conciliatory words was immediately decapitated: so Vansittart decided that a drastic movement would be the most effective, and, in the long-run, the most humane policy.

He therefore ordered an advance; and in four days, marching by easy stages, the expedition came within sight of the town,—a collection of mud huts, with a few stone houses perched on a rocky eminence which swarmed with swarthy figures.

The white burnous of the Arabs lent animation to the dark hordes of Tuaregs, and it soon became apparent that the rebels were armed with rifles of precision, for dropping shots fell in the midst of the advance guard at a distance of over two miles.

There were no casualties, and as a parley was out of the question, Vansittart bivouacked for the night in a position reasonably safeguarded from attack before sunrise.

The enemy evidently thought their stronghold to be too secure to venture forth from its fastnesses, as day dawned to find them in the same disposition, and a careful reconnaissance made at an early hour convinced both Jerome and the officers of the expedition that the place could be rushed in front only by a considerable expenditure of life, even if the attempt were successful.

Yet on both flanks and towards the rear it appeared to be defended by impregnable precipices. It was certainly a hard nut to crack.

A council of war was held, and it was settled that as a preliminary the artillery and machine-guns should make things lively for the denizens of El Hegef, and a storm of shells and bullets soon beat the wretched little houses into fragments.

But, after the first wild scurrying of the natives before this unpleasant visitation, it was perceived that little damage was inflicted upon them.

"They have their caves and sheltered hollows to retreat to," said an experienced officer of Spahis, who was accustomed to Algerian warfare.

"Is there no way to get at them from the rear?" said Vansittart.

"None that we know of," was the answer.

"*We* do not know, it is true, but some individual in the expedition may be better informed. Let every man be questioned as to his knowledge of the locality."

This novelty in the conduct of warlike operations amused some of the French officers, but in the result Vansittart was shown to be justified in his surmise.

A Spahi was found who had visited El Hegef in his youth, and who quite distinctly remembered driving a flock of goats to an oasis on the plain behind the town by means of a difficult path practicable for two men abreast.

Here, then, was a clew to the solution of the difficulty.

The artillery practice was sustained intermittently, and before the sun went down a cloud of skirmishers feigned a direct attack, but no damage was done by the ineffectual exchange of shots.

Shrouded by the rapidly growing darkness, Captain Pompier and his marines from the *Sphinx*, with the 67th Regiment, guided by the Spahi, moved off on a détour to reach the oasis of which the Algerian soldier had such a fortunate recollection.

Pompier was to begin the assault, if possible, at dawn, and when the sounds of firing reached the main body a general advance of all arms would at once be made.

There was little sleep that night for either officers or men, as it was quite within the bounds of probability that Pompier's movements might be precipitated by events into a surprise at an earlier hour.

And this was exactly what happened.

Precisely at 2 A.M. a brisk fusilade from the direction of El Hegef startled the camp into sudden activity. Within five minutes every man was on the move, and ere the first companies reached the foot of the hill leading to the town they encountered a stream of fugitives bolting wildly down the pathway and scattering over the plain.

A lively but uncertain fight ensued, mostly with the bayonet, and there was more than one severe tussle between the gallant Frenchmen and the maddened rebels before the sharp ring of the Lebel rifle at close quarters warned Vansittart's force that Pompier's troops were close at hand, having passed right through the battered bazaar.

A couple of rockets now spluttered their welcome signal into the sky, and in a little while the two sections of the expedition were congratulating each other upon the excellent result of their ruse.

The French loss was 18 killed and 64 wounded, whilst nearly 500 Arabs and Tuaregs, lying dead or severely injured in the precincts of the place, testified to the severity of the resistance offered to the enemy.

Very few prisoners were made, except women and children, and vast numbers of the tribesmen had escaped during the darkness, cavalry pursuit being impossible under the conditions.

As it happened, Pompier's force had marched rapidly and without check to the oasis, whence the Spahi had easily found the path. This was much shorter than it had appeared to his boyish imagination, and the leading files of the column stumbled unexpectedly upon a small party of Arabs smoking round a fire.

The alarm was at once given, and further concealment was not to be thought of, so Pompier hurried forward with the utmost speed upon the heels of the astounded Arabs.

French troops are always renowned for their dash and *élan*, and their distinctive qualities were never exhibited to a higher degree than upon this occasion. Officers and men were greatly elated by the rapidity and completeness of the victory they had achieved against formidable odds.

It was a new thing for the arms of the Republic to prevail in a Colonial campaign within five days of the arrival of the expedition in the country.

"This comes of having a man at the head of affairs. Sapristi! If Jerome the First could lead us, we should soon see Metz and Strasbourg again," growled the oldest soldier of the 105th, and this view predominated with all ranks.

Vansittart was personally astonished to find that the instinct of the armed conqueror had been so closely hidden away in some mysterious receptacle of his brain that he had never previously suspected its existence.

When he met Pompier he warmly shook hands with him, saying emphatically, "You possess every characteristic of a commander, Captain. I can only express my regret that at present my gratitude can but take the inadequate form of tendering you my hearty thanks, and adding that I shall seize the earliest opportunity of placing 25,000 francs to your credit at your bankers."

He also announced to the troops that he would hand them a year's field allowances, and would see that the relatives of the men killed or wounded in the action were compensated liberally.

These things were telegraphed to France in due course, and the whole nation nearly went mad with delight.

So extravagant were the demonstrations of the army at the tidings of their comrades' prowess in the Soudan that the Berlin Press began to sneer and the French Ministry endeavored to stop the growing enthusiasm.

As well might they seek to turn the tide. They were now irrevocably committed to the Sahara scheme, and although a brisk war of words against England for her prolonged occupation of Egypt succeeded in enlisting the attention of the fickle mob, the army and navy paid no heed.

In every mess, ashore or afloat, the one topic of conversation was the battle of El Hegef, and Vansittart's name was in the mouths of all men. Soldiers and sailors both dubbed him "*L'Empereur!*" and, whilst their officers frowned at the phrase, they used it themselves. It came more easily from French lips than Jerome's Knickerbocker appellation. And it seemed, too, happily to sum up his attributes. By adroit management on the part of Harland and Liancourt, the Paris Press was persuaded to send out special representatives to Shott Jerid for a brief visit, and when they reached the camp near El Hegef they found themselves regarded as the one set of men in existence that Vansittart was particularly anxious to meet.

One night, whilst the leading officers and journalists were assembling in the mess tent, and Vansittart was discussing with them the phenomenal strides Maclaren was making towards opening up the lake, General Daubisson was announced.

It was a ticklish moment.

Jerome went forward to receive him. "Welcome, General," he said. "I am more than pleased to think that so many of your brave comrades should be present to hear me, as the head of the Sahara Company, thank you warmly for the foresight and intelligence of your dispositions, which enabled us to so effectually strike the first blow in the campaign. To you, above all others, our victory is due, and we can only give voice to our deep regret that you were unable to lead us in the field."

General Daubisson was looked upon in high quarters as the future Governor of Paris. By Vansittart's words he was firmly restored to his shaken position.

He became positively balloon-like as he beamed upon the company, and he was thenceforth Jerome's unswerving supporter.

Pompier, who had a note from his banker in his pocket, winked quietly at Maclaren, and the engineer telegraphed an answering signal. These two understood each other.

Events now marched with giant strides.

Great steamers arrived daily at Boca Grande and the Gulf of Gabes from France, England, and America, laden with piers, railways, engines, steam launches, and the thousand and one appliances necessary for the prosecution of the work.

Workmen, too, were coming, but more slowly, as the reality of the undertaking had not yet permeated the laboring classes sufficiently to induce them to leave home and friends for the possible uncertainties of the desert.

But the flaming articles sent to France by the corps of pressmen were insidiously eating their way into the hearts and minds of the people.

The insurrection was steadily gaining force in the interior, and when Mr. Robertson and M. Hézard, the English and French engineers in charge of the Boca Grande section, reported that they had been compelled to suspend their cadastral survey and retire to the coast, Vansittart took advantage of the direction of public sympathies.

He boldly cabled to the Ministry : " The Company requires men who can fight as well as work. Let France send me 50,000 troops whom I can employ in the field and who will also work on the canals. I will pay them the wages of victors."

No one troubled to ask an explanation of this mysterious guerdon. Vansittart said it, and that sufficed.

The Minister of War gave the necessary instructions for the movements of the soldiers, else the political life of the government would not have been worth a moment's purchase. They reflected that the reduction of the army charges to such a considerable amount would produce a flattering budget—the best seen for years—so they yielded to the popular will with ready grace.

And Vansittart wrote to Honorine de Montpensier in a cipher which she and Harland alone could read :

" The shadow is becoming a substance."

CHAPTER XIII

A TOMB IN THE WILDERNESS

AS some weeks must elapse before any forward movement could be practicable in the neighborhood of the great salt lakes, Vansittart decided to run round to Boca Grande in the *Seafarer* and give some personal attention to affairs in that locality.

Maclaren, a man of iron constitution, was nevertheless slightly weakened by the heat of the Sahara, for he had been in the locality for over nine months, and the millionnaire compelled him to accompany him on the trip, as the engineer was very unwilling to leave the scene of his labors even for a brief holiday. But Jerome pointed out that in Pompier they had a master of commissariat detail, and this was the only pressing difficulty that had to be encountered during the next month.

The outbreak among the natives had spread like wildfire. They were in a condition of superstitious fright, and a pretty stiff campaign must be fought and won before work could seriously be entered upon.

All that was possible was to land and house the troops and laborers, and accumulate stores in the vicinity of the Gulf of Gabes, whilst Pompier, in possession of unlimited means and authority, was not only able to undertake this work, but he also guaranteed that by their return a light railway would be laid between the coast and Shott Jerid.

Once they were on board the yacht, Maclaren yielded to the inevitable, and soon came round to the view that it would perhaps be well for him to pay a brief visit to Boca Grande. The position of affairs on the west coast might materially influence subsequent operations from the east.

As the *Seafarer* spun through the Straits of Gibraltar, Maclaren, pointing to the opposite shores of Spain and Africa, said :

"These picturesque cliffs should be an excellent object lesson to us."

"In what sense?" said Vansittart.

"Because there cannot be the slightest doubt that at one time the Atlas Mountains, of which the coast of Morocco is the fringe, were washed by the sea at their base on the south as freely as they are now on the north."

"In other words," said Vansittart, "the whole of Northern Africa was an island."

"Precisely, or a gigantic peninsula, possibly joined by a narrow neck of land on the western confines of Shott Melrhir."

Jerome seemed to be suddenly struck by some thought which interested him greatly, as he was silent for some minutes.

When he spoke it was with a smile. "I have commenced to found an empire," he said, "but I never expected to be also on the way towards restoring a tradition."

"What notion has occurred to you now?" cried the other, who was becoming too accustomed to instances of his friend's penetrating judgment to marvel at any new development.

"Don't you see," said Vansittart, blowing a spiral of smoke from his cigar and darting a number of small rings rapidly through it, "that we are on the verge of discovering the Lost Island of Atlantis?"

Maclaren could only whistle his amazement.

"By Jove!" he cried at last. "You beat everything. What next?"

"But am I not correct?"

"Of course you are; that's the astounding part of it. And it's as plain as the nose on Wellington's face when you only catch on to it. The similarity between the fauna and flora of the Canary Islands and the south Mediterranean littoral are tremendous facts in favor of this assumption. If you want negative arguments on the same side you have only to point to the huge differences found between the plants of North and Central Africa, although the climate is precisely similar. What a sensation this will make among the scientific societies of Europe! And say, Herodotus knew a thing or two, did n't he?"

"He had a fine imagination," laughed Vansittart, "and that goes a long way. However, as you seem to be impressed by the idea, I make you a present of it. It will occupy your spare moments to accumulate proofs in behalf of the contention, and then you can deliver a lecture a yard long before a big gathering of the Royal Geographical Society."

The *Seafarer*, with her average speed of twenty-five knots an hour, made short work of the voyage to Boca Grande. They were surprised on landing to find some preparation made for their arrival, but soon learnt that a cable had been successfully laid from the Canaries, and Harland had apprized Mr. Robertson of their journey. Previously, all telegraphic messages had to be conveyed by steamer to the mainland, and many days of delay often resulted, as there was only one small steam yacht at the disposal of the resident engineers.

"I have extraordinarily good news for you if it can only be trusted," said Robertson, a handsome, well set-up young Englishman. "The natives in these parts heard by some unexplained means of the proceedings in the east, and threatened to be nasty at first. In fact we were, as you know, obliged to retreat precipitately to the coast. But all at once, about a fortnight ago, an elderly sheik, who possesses great influence and poses as a prophet, condemned the growing Jehad, and announced that the ancient dynasty of the Sun was about to be restored. I actually believe that the people are ready to accept you as their deliverer."

"How do you account for the sheik's attitude?" queried Vansittart, who was naturally much interested by this intelligence.

"It seems he has discovered some hieroglyphic inscriptions of great antiquity, and interprets these in some way by the light of your resolve to flood the desert."

"Do you know where the inscriptions are to be found?"

"Yes, at a place named Adsokha, three days' quick ride from here."

"Have you seen the man?"

"Oh, yes. He is quartered in a neighboring temple, half-mosque, half-tomb. I thought he wanted bakshish, but he was in a terrible rage with me when I suggested it."

"Money is good, Mr. Robertson," said Vansittart, "but faith is more powerful. Can I meet this sheik?"

"He will be here in an hour's time, as he is intensely anxious to set eyes upon you."

The arrival of the Mussulman chieftain-priest was eagerly awaited, and, in order to impress him, Maclaren suggested some little display in the shape of a guard, and a liberal exhibition of gaily colored bunting in the large tent set apart for the millionnaire's use.

"There is no harm in your proposal," said Jerome with a quiet smile. "Do as you suggest, by all means, but get me an excellent interpreter, and above all else let there be some writing paper and a pen and ink handy."

Maclaren looked surprised at the nature of the preparations.

"I expect he will open my peepers wider than the sheik's," he said to himself, whilst Arizona Jim shifted his revolver to a handier position.

"I don't like either shakes or moolers," he growled. "It 's as well to be ready to git the drop on 'em."

But when the venerable Mohammedan made his appearance—a tall, stark figure arrayed in snow-white linen, with majestic beard and piercing black eyes darting keen glances from beneath a forehead of great breadth and dignity—Jim Bates was man of the world enough to feel instantly that this time the interview would not end with attempted murder.

In no wise dazzled by the fine parade arranged by Maclaren, and without paying the slightest heed to any other person present, the aged prophet walked firmly toward Vansittart and scrutinized him carefully but without hesitancy.

Vansittart, who mystified his companions by the unwonted air of solemn hauteur he assumed, met the sheik's gaze unflinchingly, and then the old man paid him the greatest act of homage possible in one of his creed.

He bowed reverently, and taking off his plaited turban, laid it at Jerome's feet, murmuring the while a sonorous greeting.

The interpreter would have translated, but the American silenced him with a gesture.

Turning to the table he took the writing materials, drew this sign upon a sheet of paper, and handed the document to the Arab.

The latter no sooner saw the symbol than he fell upon his knees, raised his withered arms aloft whilst he chanted a ringing canticle of praise, and then flung himself prone at Vansittart's feet. From their position Maclaren and Bates alone could see the contents of the paper.

Maclaren kept his wonderment to himself, but Arizona Jim's amazement was such that he whispered loudly:

"It's Injun talk! The totem of the duck an' egg!"

Vansittart heard, and wanted to laugh, but mastered the impulse and gave his henchman such a glance that Jim resolved not to risk his master's anger again.

"He can bore holes in you with a look," explained Bates subsequently to Maclaren.

These unusual proceedings were witnessed not only by the Europeans present, but by a knot of natives gathered at some distance. These easily swayed and emotional people promptly followed the lead given by their religious head and prostrated themselves in similar fashion.

After an effective pause, Jerome told the interpreter to ask the sheik to rise and converse with him.

Slowly obeying, the Arab spoke a few words in awed accents.

"The holy prophet, Sayyid Mohammed ben Izak," explained the interpreter, "gives your lordship humble greeting on your entry into your kingdom. He prays you to accompany him to Adsokha to witness the sacred writing which foretells your arrival."

"Tell him," said Vansittart, "that I will go with him at dawn."

Mohammed ben Izak withdrew with much ceremony and obeisance, and when the Europeans were alone Maclaren said: "What's been going on? The thirty-third degree of Masonry, or what?"

"Something like it," answered Jerome. "But I cannot explain just yet. Wait until the business is ended and then I will gratify your curiosity. So far, I think I am on the right track."

Next day, as the first shafts of light crept over the sand-hills toward the low coast line, Vansittart, Maclaren, and Bates, with a small company of native carriers, rode off with the sheik towards Adsokha. At first the Arab wished the millionnaire to accompany him alone. But the others, including Mr. Robertson and M. Hézard, who feared treachery, were so concerned at this that Jerome yielded the point, though he personally had not the slightest doubt that his aged adherent would give his life to save him from harm.

The journey was uneventful enough, and Maclaren took advantage of the fact that they were practically following the route to be taken by the fresh-water canal to check the observations made by the other engineers, which were noted for his guidance upon a small sketch-map.

He was quite satisfied that the difficulties, though great, were surmountable, and he found, too, that the trend of the irrigation channels was towards the southeast—a logical sequence of the theory of the scheme formulated by Vansittart.

When Adsokha was reached, the ill-suppressed excitement under which Mohammed ben Izak had labored during the few days' travelling obtained complete mastery over him.

The concluding march had been made during the early hours, but the white-bearded prophet would brook no delay. Through the scorching sunlight he hurried the three Americans along a rough path that led into the recesses of a volcanic range of small hills until the party at length stood at the opening to a cave—an opening obviously carved by man's hands into a fair semblance of an Egyptian doorway.

Both Vansittart and Maclaren were surprised to note the style of the workmanship.

How came this quaint device to appear in such a locality, separated as it was by two thousand miles of desert from the Nile, and situated in the midst of a strange tribe of negroes —for the Arabs were, after all, but the military occupiers of the country? That the excavation and its sphinx-like exterior pillars, with their huge superincumbent blocks of stone —such as one may see in dozens of ruined cities along the banks of the Nile—were many centuries old could not be doubted.

The sun had excoriated the figures until they were now almost shapeless, and had they not been cut from the solid rock they would long since have crumbled away into the mould of the desert.

Not much time was given them for noting these dim evidences of a bygone age.

Hastily kicking off his shoes, the aged priest lit a torch which he carried, and invited them by signs to enter. Proceeding in single file through a narrow passage, they found themselves after a few paces in a spacious chamber. When their eyes had become accustomed to the gloom, fitfully illumined by the climbing flames of the resin, they saw that they were standing in a square apartment, singularly lofty and heavy with the odor of bitumen, the substance largely used for preserving mummies.

They perceived that their ancient guide was furious with indignation as he gazed round upon obvious tokens of recent despoilment, as the stone lids of three sarcophagi were displaced, and strips of linen and plaster were scattered on the ground, whilst the aromatic scent showed that the occupants of the coffins had been recently disturbed from their long rest.

The place had clearly been rifled for treasure.

Sayyid Mohammed ben Izak was already aware of the fact, but they did not understand his words, as the interpreter had remained with the other servants.

But his actions were easy enough to follow.

Motioning to Vansittart, he bade him scrutinize a wall-painting, rudely but clearly drawn just above the largest sarcophagus, and he held the torch so that Jerome could examine it.

The millionnaire unhesitatingly stooped to obey his behest, whilst Arizona Jim, although awed by the surroundings, gripped the butt of his revolver, in case of accident, for he had no faith in " niggers." And this is what Vansittart saw :

Beneath, there was a long inscription in smaller hieroglyphic characters, but differing somewhat in style from those reproduced below.

Long and earnestly did Vansittart examine this curious device, and Maclaren, looking over his shoulder, was quick to see that prominent amongst the larger signs was the strange emblem that his companion had handed to the Arab at their first meeting.

This time he could not restrain an ejaculation. "Well, that beats everything," he said, with a gasp.

"What does?" said Vansittart. "Do you understand it?"

"No. Do you?"

"Yes, a little—the drawing represents a sepulchral barge being ferried across water to a tomb. It contains a decorated shrine or canopy, in which a mummy—obviously a person of consequence—is laid, and on the top of the shrine are professional wailing women. The chief line of the inscription reads thus, and he indicated words as follows:

| King of the North and South. (*Title.*) | Nem-ab-Rab. (*Prenomen.*) | Se-Ra. Son of the Sun. (*Title.*) | Nekau. (*Nomen.*) |

"The remainder of the inscription," he continued, "is in the Phœnician character, compounds of certain letters of the Hieratic character, which, again, was a species of written hieroglyphic. I must have it carefully copied and translated at Oxford."

"But how the deuce do you know so much about it?"

Vansittart straightened himself up as he modestly replied:

"During a visit to London once I was vastly attracted by the Egyptian monuments in the British Museum, and spent some time in mastering the rudiments of the hieroglyphics. They are very easy when you have got the key."

"So I should imagine," said Maclaren, dubiously. "And

by that means you were able to paralyze our old friend here with what Bates called the 'duck and egg'?"

"Precisely."

"And have you any theory concerning the business? It leaves me out entirely, I must confess."

"That is because you have been puzzled, but it is really simple enough. Anyone can see that the gentleman interred in this tomb was either a descendant of King Nekau, or was buried here during his reign. The Phœnician inscription will reveal all this. Then, to be brought here he was carried in a boat. *Ergo*, there was water in the locality,—and now there is none—proof positive of our contention that this place was submerged within historic times. Again, this Egyptian potentate was mixed up with the Phœnicians, the great traders and *sailors* of the Mediterranean. When their knowledge of the hieroglyphics gave out they used their own language. Altogether, it is a marvellous find."

"And do you know what is the most marvellous thing about it?" said the engineer.

"No, not exactly."

"Why, your calling yourself Se-Ra at the right moment. You have absolutely stopped the campaign on this side of the Continent. Every native here will work for you for nothing, and be honored in the asking. How on earth did you think of it?"

Vansittart laughed. "To tell the truth," he said, "it was the only sign I could definitely remember at the moment."

When they quitted the cave and obtained the aid of the interpreter, they found that Mohammed ben Izak was acquainted with a prophecy that when the Son of the Sun returned to Adsokha the waters would again flow in the valleys and the land spring into verdure. The news of the American's project had reached him, and he immediately resolved to visit him and ascertain whether or not he was indeed Se-Ra. And had he not given him the sign at the very moment of their meeting ? Allah was Allah, and Mohammed was his prophet !

When the party returned to Boca Grande, Jerome found awaiting him a cable from Harland. It ran :

"De Tournon is stirring up trouble here. Chamber is being influenced against you, and Ministry would withdraw troops if they dared. *Le Soir* is publishing damaging reports from Shott Jerid, written by someone there, and they are steadily gaining credence. Liancourt advises immediate return to Gabes and afterwards visit to Paris to allay public uneasiness. Other matters are curious, but can wait your arrival."

Vansittart re-read the last sentence several times. He cut it from the cablegram form and then handed the rest of the message to Maclaren, saying :

"The curtain is now about to rise upon the second act of our drama."

CHAPTER XIV

VANSITTART RIDES FOR A FALL

"I WONDER which of these gentlemen of the Press it is who writes the articles now appearing in *Le Soir*," said Vansittart to Maclaren and Captain Pompier whilst enjoying an after-dinner cigar and coffee during the march of the troops against the rebels massed at Tugurt.

He had not long returned from Boca Grande and found all in readiness for a forward movement on his arrival.

"None of them is supposed to represent the rag," said Pompier. "They are all too high and mighty to contribute to such a journal."

"The writer, whoever it is, does n't send his pleasant comments to *Le Soir* direct," observed Jerome. "He posts them to an opponent of mine in Paris and the latter has them published in the organ which appeals to the scum of the capital."

"In that case it will indeed be difficult to discover the blackguard," cried Pompier. "If only I knew the rascal I would call him out and pink him in the liver, for he has lied most scandalously about the commissariat."

"I have had inquiries made in Paris," observed Vansittart, "and we may soon be enlightened. Meanwhile, let us amuse ourselves with reading the villain's remarks."

He scanned some copies of the recent issues of *Le Soir* to hand.

Cleverly twisting facts to suit his conclusions, the writer, who signed himself "One of the Deluded," told how many hundreds of thousands of pounds' worth of valuable plant was being buried uselessly in the desert, how trigonometrical signals alone represented the canals (even Maclaren growled at this allusion, as his staff had done marvels in the shape of detailing the operations in sections so that vast bodies of laborers could be employed simultaneously), how the cavalry soldiers were eating their horses (and here Pompier swore fiercely), and how generally the Sahara threatened to be another and a more disastrous Panama.

Vansittart laughed heartily at the description of himself.

"He is a supreme actor, this dangerous lunatic," wrote the correspondent. "He poses superbly. In the midst of obvious privations and losses he comforts himself with tinsel dignity, and reviews the gallant troops of France with the hauteur of a stage emperor. Were he not ruining France, one could tolerate the impostor for his splendid make-believe."

"The rascal has a soft spot in his heart for you after all," commented Maclaren, whose ill-humor speedily vanished.

But Pompier was more fiery.

"These press men," he cried, "grow fat on the menus I give them—I must lessen their diet and teach them manners."

"Not so," cried Vansittart. "You would starve the good to punish the bad. That will never do."

At this moment, an orderly brought the letters. Jerome's quick eye detected one amidst the number and he opened it.

"Now we may have news," he said.

He whistled softly to relieve his feelings when he had mastered its contents. The note was from Folliet. "Listen," he said in a low tone of voice. "It has come with dramatic sequence. I have here undoubted proof that the writer of these attacks is M. Legru, of *La Patrie*."

"*Sacré bleu!*" shrieked Pompier, springing to his feet, "and but to-night I sent him a bottle of Heidsieck '84. Ha! there is a moon. Where is my rapier? I must let some sound wine out of his carcase before it is spoiled!"

"Not so. Pray oblige me, Captain Pompier, as a personal matter, by keeping this affair secret at present. Afterwards, when I have left you for a little while, you can do as you choose. At this moment I desire M. Legru to say his worst."

Vansittart did not add that his Chief of Police had informed him that M. Legru sent his letters to De Tournon, who gave them, type-written, to *Le Soir*.

"By the cross of St. Denis! it was an excellent bottle," howled the French officer in almost comic rage.

"Never mind. Give him another to-morrow. It will inspire him, for his concluding effusions lack point."

"He shall not lack point when I have finished with him," cried Pompier, and he grinned at his pleasant conceit until he had calmed sufficiently to plan out an absolute fattening of the unfortunate Legru for the spit.

.　　.　　.　　.　　.　　.　　.　　.

General Daubisson, at Vansittart's request, had been given the chief command of the now enlarged expedition.

Of the 50,000 troops sent from France, about two fifths were advancing across the desert to Tugurt, where an immense assemblage of the enemy was reported by spies and friendly negroes.

Tugurt, a small town lying at the extreme south of the valley that ran for nearly one hundred miles from the southwest corner of Shott Melrhir, was not only naturally strong but was protected by its fearsome approaches.

On the arid plain lay the bleached bones of thousands of men and animals, relics of generations of trading caravans. These gruesome evidences of the inhospitable climate were more terrifying by night than by day. The moonbeams glinted from their whiteness and created ghostly imageries of malicious gnomes and affrighting demons.

It required all the haphazard nonchalance of the French soldier to endure the tedious horrors of the march; but the success that had attended their first brush with the enemy inspired the men, and each of them was buoyant with the hope that fame and fortune might be wrung from this wild country of sand and rock under the leadership of Jerome.

His wealth and his forethought, applied by Captain Pompier's fertile resourcefulness, had smoothed away many of the hardships that would otherwise have attended the advance.

Every care had been taken by Vansittart for the comfort of the men—little for himself. He shared their meals, their labors, and their amusements. He was ever ready with a kindly word or a kindlier action, and it was no exaggeration to say that by rank and file he was idolized, whilst the officers looked to him in some vague way for promotion and distinction.

Even at that early date every man in the Sahara Expedition was indissolubly bound up in his interests.

As the column neared Tugurt, greater precautions were taken to guard against unexpected attack, and Vansittart communicated to General Daubisson his desire to act personally with the cavalry and guns during the forthcoming battle.

The pompous little commander readily consented.

"I know well your rapidity of thought and action, monsieur," he said. "You are a born leader of horse. But pray be careful. Vast interests are attached to your person. Do not put yourself unnecessarily in harm's way. There are those with us who would magnify even trivial events."

Daubisson meant well by his advice.

"General," replied Jerome, "my power of magnifying events is much greater than that of those against whom you warn me. Above all else, I never forget a friend, and your name is prominent amongst my best well-wishers."

Tugurt was to be assaulted by daylight, and this time there was no guide to help the expedition in the preliminary strategy.

The enemy, too, were strongly posted and obviously better led than at El Hegef.

A cloud of mounted nomads checked and irritated the advance, and their scattered formation prevented the artillery from doing much execution.

The town occupied the usual rocky eminence, and Daubisson resolved to deliver a direct frontal attack by the infantry under cover of the guns, whilst the cavalry were to sweep round immediately by the left to the rear of the town in order to cut off the exodus of flying natives which he assumed would at once take place.

Vansittart doubted the wisdom of the arrangements, but he only asked and obtained the general's permission to slightly delay the movement of the cavalry until the affair had developed to some extent.

The guns galloped ahead and soon made things lively among the rocks on which Tugurt was perched.

As soon as the infantry had deployed, the guns ceased, and it was then seen that the enemy were advantageously disposed behind cover, whilst a rapid and well-aimed fire from arms of precision showed that the opening tussle would be a severe one.

Already many men were hit in the fighting line, and although the advance proceeded most gallantly there was some natural unsteadiness in the formation of the leading regiments.

Whilst this phase of the battle was unfolding itself, Vansittart was neared by the group of newspaper correspondents, amongst whom was Legru, carrying himself bravely on a magnificent Arab. The American was quick to notice that the representative of *La Patrie* had almost encumbered himself with a large haversack and a gigantic water-skin.

"You are prepared for possibilities, monsieur," he said with a smile.

"It is well, monsieur, in the desert," was the jaunty answer.

"That is a fine horse you are riding."

"I have held him in reserve," replied Legru. Then apparently desirous to change the conversation, he went on: "Although a civilian, M. Vansittart, I hear you intend to take part in the action."

"Surely I must participate in my own quarrel. And you?"

"Alas, my profession debars me. I can only observe!"

"I have no keener critic," laughed the other.

M. Legru also seemed pleased, and bowed, but he bit his moustache as he thought:

"Confound him. Does he suspect?"

But a diversion came to his relief. Vansittart had seen a cloud of dust rising from a wady, or depression, on the right, and rode off to call the attention of the officer in command of the cavalry to it.

They watched the moving cloud in silence for some moments, and then Arizona Jim, who never quitted his master's side, said:

"There's spear points in that dust, guv'nor."

His trained vision had discerned this significant apparition long before anybody else, but Vansittart accepted his statement, and counselled a sharp trot in that direction.

The cavalry moved off, and before they had gone half a mile, the right of the fighting line being still well in front, the reason of the dust cloud became quite clear.

A large body of mounted dervishes were advancing at a gallop to take the French infantry in flank, and the nature of the ground would prevent the brigadier in charge of the attack from noting this hostile demonstration until too late to change front.

In a word, General Daubisson had exposed his troops to disaster.

The 6th Dragoons led the cavalry brigade and with them were the 18th Chasseurs and the 9th Hussars.

They now rode hard at the advancing Arabs, and spread

fan-wise, so as to get their full strength at work simultaneously.

It chanced that Jerome accompanied the 18th Chasseurs, whereas M. Legru, in the earliest and most sensational despatch subsequently published in Paris, announced that he headed the 6th Dragoons. The mistake was a trivial one at the time, but it had a highly important bearing upon subsequent events of a very different nature.

When the Frenchmen dashed into the midst of the dervishes an exciting mêlée followed.

Foiled in the object of their attack, and compelled to meet on equal terms three of the finest regiments in the French army, the tribesmen nevertheless made the best of a bad business and offered a desperate resistance.

The fight was of a give-and-take nature, and Vansittart was compelled more than once to hit his hardest at an assailant to prevent the other from cutting him down, whilst on one occasion he owed his life to the smart parry made by a trooper of the Chasseurs to a stroke from an Arab scimitar.

But though his blood coursed madly through his veins with the fierce joy of a cavalry action, he nevertheless felt the constraint of being a non-combatant, and endeavored where possible to use the flat of his sword.

It was otherwise with Arizona Jim. That worthy astounded the French soldiers in the vicinity by the ease with which he emptied saddle after saddle of their occupants by means of his revolver. More than once he safeguarded Vansittart from harm by drilling a hole in some unobserved foe.

Within five minutes the Arabs were thoroughly routed, and the defenders of Tugurt, more conscious than the French infantry of the disastrous nature of the repulse, began to retire before the impetuous onset made upon them.

Hastily gathering his cavalry brigade by bugle-call, the leader sought Jerome's prompt acquiescence in a sharp movement towards the rear of the town, in order to fulfil General

"It was otherwise with Arizona Jim."

Daubisson's first idea, which had been so happily delayed and improved upon.

They trotted off, and whilst passing through some difficult country, broken and intersected by small ravines, a queer notion suddenly possessed Vansittart.

Already dense masses of fugitives were pouring out of the town toward the west, and the French horsemen were breaking into small groups in their eagerness to begin their pursuit, when Jerome said to Bates, speaking in English and in a low tone:

"Follow me closely, and do as I do."

Watching his opportunity, he darted unobserved into an unusually deep nullah, and ten minutes' ride among its tortuous course soon lessened the sounds of conflict almost into nothingness.

"What's the game, guv'nor?" cried Jim, who was genuinely amazed at this singular proceeding.

"The game now is to dismount, loosen our horses' girths, hobble them, have a drink, and smoke a cigar in the shade of a rock."

Bates regarded his master with keen anxiety. "You hev n't been touched up with the sun, hev you?" he cried.

Vansittart laughed heartily at the question. "No, Bates," he said when he had recovered his breath. "Don't think that I am running away from trouble. That fight," pointing towards Tugurt, "is over. By simply resting ourselves here for a little while I am much mistaken if we don't create a vastly bigger row elsewhere. I am only sorry that I cannot relieve Mr. Maclaren's anxiety about us."

"That's just it, sir," urged Bates excitedly. "They'll think you've been knocked on the head, sure, and there will be a tremenjous hullabaloo."

"Exactly what I desire. Come, calm yourself, and light up."

* * * * * * * * *

Two hours later, when the cavalry returned hot and weary from a prolonged pursuit, Vansittart was reported missing.

The news spread like wildfire through the camp, and there were not wanting those who saw him struck down during the fight with the dervishes. Others, however, were positive that he rode with the brigade subsequently, and search parties were sent out to try and find him and his inseparable attendant.

General Daubisson was frantic, Maclaren miserable to the last degree, and reproaching himself for having obeyed Jerome's order to remain with the reserves, and every officer and man in the expedition felt that they had sustained an irreparable loss.

The newspaper correspondents, of course, realized the full significance of Vansittart's possible death, and strove to arrange for camel expresses to reach the coast. But General Daubisson issued imperative orders that his despatches must precede all news telegrams, and refused to allow anyone to leave the camp.

He did not know, then, that M. Legru had already departed, having arranged for stores and fresh camels to meet him at predetermined depots on the march.

Vansittart's death was the one thing he had been waiting for as a rich possibility. He was not going to be balked at the crucial moment by an interfering commander.

At four o'clock one of the search parties, to their great joy, discovered Vansittart, suffering badly from a sprained ankle, and conveyed him to the camp on an improvised stretcher.

Joy now filled the hearts of all ranks, but Maclaren could not understand why, when he hastened to meet his friend, Jerome should press his hand significantly, and murmur in English :

"It's all right. I will explain presently."

General Daubisson was among the first to offer his congratulations. He came personally to Vansittart's tent where Bates was binding up the injured ankle after an approved prairie method, as the millionaire had refused medical assistance.

"My dear sir," cried the General, "I am overjoyed at your safety. I can now write my despatches and expedite them to the utmost, as one of those rascally press men has got away in spite of my orders, and I fear alarmist reports concerning you may be published in Paris."

"General," said Vansittart earnestly, "in the ordinary course of events the staff officer who conveys your despatches would not begin to cross the desert with his escort until the morning."

"That is so, undoubtedly."

"Then let me ask you, as a great favor, not to depart from established custom in this instance."

"But Legru, who is already *en route*, will report you dead."

"In may be so. In that case I shall know my friends by my obituary notices."

The General, who was cute enough in business matters, paused. "You will know your enemies, too," he said at last.

"General Daubisson," replied Jerome, "you are a politician as well as a soldier."

The fat officer smiled with a self-satisfied air.

"The despatches shall not go before sunrise," he cried as he took his leave.

The military surgeons attached to the expedition were much exercised to know the method of Arizona Jim's treatment for sprained ankles, as two days later Vansittart was able to begin the journey to the Gulf of Gabes.

CHAPTER XV

A STORM BREWING

SHORTLY after Vansittart had set out for the Soudan, it was raining and blowing at Paris, and Paris was very wretched.

Some cities have the strange faculty of deriving some fresh aspect of beauty from the inclemencies of weather. Their spirit is akin to melancholy. The solemnity of London becomes awe-inspiring in the rain; the dull, the sombre, become majestic when they are carried to an extremity. So she gains in grandeur, in that imposing appearance of impregnable strength which is her chief virtue. In mist and fog, her hoary buildings and irregular lines of streets become mysterious. Their outlines die away in a rich, vague beauty. The gauntness is lost—only the charm of poetic indistinctness is left. London is then Nature's masterpiece of etching.

But Paris has none of this virtue. She exists for the sun. She is a flower that pines for light and warmth. Let there come wind and rain and she shrinks and quivers beneath them like a sensitive plant struck by a cruel gale. She collapses in a moment. Her smile is gone, her tranquillity, her beauty. There is a pathetic appeal in the aspect of her streets: her great buildings are no longer sprightly, her gardens no more gay; her shops become limp and listless. Even the Arc de Triomphe loses some of its assurance, and the Vendôme Column is not half so truculent. The statue of Strasbourg alone draws its profit from the weather; it becomes more gloomy and more reminiscent than ever.

It is so, too, with the people of Paris.

It is said that on one occasion a French general and an experienced French boulevardier were standing on a portico watching one of these sudden outbursts of popular fury.

" Oh, for a salvo of artillery ! " sighed the general.

" Oh, for a shower of rain ! " groaned the boulevardier.

And the boulevardier was wiser than the general.

In the rain the people of Paris can no longer stroll in the boulevards or sit before the cafés. They are driven from the boats which carry them up and down the Seine. There is nothing to observe in the streets. They have to go right inside their *brasseries* and the windows are all closed. It is not life, that. There is time for grumbling and recollecting evil things.

Sometimes a spell of bad weather will determine a revolution. It is true, the most disastrous riots are those that spring up like thunder in the hot air on a fine summer's day. And there is something to fear when the Parisian hurries gaily to his barricade; but the rainy riot is more frequent, and is not at all to be despised.

Just now there were many mutterings throughout Paris. A skilled observer would have noticed two things—first, that there was every prospect of an outburst, and, secondly, that some skilled hand was piloting it in the way he wanted it to go.

For in Paris there are many volcanic centres and as many formidable parties. There are irreconcilables, whose hand is against authority of all kinds and who are equally dangerous to a republic as to a monarchy. There are democrats who are always suspicious of individuals, for fear of the supremacy of a single ambitious man. There are proletariats whose vague and ignorant theories on Socialism can be directed against any person or any party by a few subtle arguments. There are idlers who can be excited, there are the covetous who can be bought, and there are the pugnacious who love a fight. Paris is, in fact, an instrument of many strings, from which can be extracted the most contrary music. Sometimes the strain may be enchanting and melodious, again it is wild, riotous, and discordant. It is then the prelude to some stormy outbursts of civic fury.

These strings were vibrating to the touch of a master hand. Its victims little knew what skilled player it was that called forth at will their ebullitions.

M. de Tournon knew his instrument well. He made no blunders. His execution was that of an expert.

The first passionate exultations over the great Sahara scheme were naturally followed by a period of calmer criticism. There were some who wondered, some who questioned, some who doubted. But of these last there were not many.

Then came the appalling news of Vansittart's death. There had been a sudden fall in the stock. Paris reeled before the advance of ruin. The croakers opened their lips. Inflammatory speeches, delivered to a stricken public, urged that the scheme never was sound, never could be sound, if it depended on a single man. The report soon proved to be a lie, but shares in the great company were listless. Those who had speculated and lost their money became bitter; the wound still ached.

After this some curious pamphlets made their appearance in every café, and in almost every house. Nobody knew whence they came. The writer, in fierce and virulent language, pointed what he called the moral of the recent slump. France was in the hands of one man.

Who was this Vansittart, to so manage things that the whole fortunes of the Republic depended upon himself? Was it not obvious that he was working for himself—that he did not love or trust France, that *la patrie* was once more to be made the tool of an adventurer? And, finally, was it not clear that, having got the country into his toils, the upstart meditated some daring scheme of personal ambition? The growing mischief was increased by groups of men who moved about inflaming their fellow-citizens, and grumbling and declaiming in every café. They did this at a salary.

Now, there are peculiar and insidious allies of the malicious schemer in Paris. They take the form of newspapers, and their birth is as mysterious as their death is clear to view. The ordinary rules of law would need to be inverted in their case. An inquest should be held upon their birth, and a free certificate granted on their death.

In certain periods of the year, when a damp, heavy atmosphere passes over the meadows, and the night is stifled with moisture, one wakes and finds a miracle. The meadows are filled with mushrooms—they are the creatures of a single day. It is so with these newspapers.

When the air of Paris is laden with omen, there suddenly spring up these ephemeral journals. No one knows how. It does not matter. They do not seek to live. They are created to advocate the fortunes of one man or ruin those of another. The task done, they disappear as suddenly and as mysteriously.

Two points about them are uniform. Their titles betoken incredible honesty and patriotism—their contents display incredible knowledge of the more infamous epithets in the French language.

There were two such journals which came into being at this juncture. One was called *L'Honnête Citoyen;* the other, *Le Bourgeois Patriote.* Both of them attacked Jerome with the most terrible virulence. Paris is not discriminating. She bought and read these papers, and they stirred up the growing sense of uneasiness.

There were doubts cast on Vansittart's descent. *L'Honnête Citoyen* even produced a letter from the true descendant, exposing the pretences of the impostor. It was proved that all this man wanted was to draw France into a second Panama catastrophe, only one much more stupendous, and then involve her in irretrievable ruin.

There were differences of opinion as to the motive. *L'Honnête Citoyen* announced that Vansittart was in the pay of England—it was the new mode of fighting invented by that nation of shopkeepers. *Le Bourgeois Patriote*, which seemed better informed, assured its readers that he was connected with the Royalist party, and that he had bartered his wealth for a dukedom. In proof whereof, the editor pointedly asked who was the lady who was staying at the Grand Hotel, and was undoubtedly a partner in his schemes? Then followed some would-be mysterious but not very impenetrable hints.

Paris is changeable, she is easily persuaded, she becomes quickly excited. The campaign was carried on so skilfully and from so many quarters, that from sheer pressure she began to think, then get restless, then to become roused.

For it must not be forgotten that the Paris which moves and acts in all the turmoils of political strife, which overturns ministries and destroys reputations, is the Paris of the café and the boulevard. That is the volatile, the excitable, the flamboyant Paris. The greater Paris, the phlegmatic, enduring, laboring Paris keeps aloof. It wants peace and good government. When stirring moments come, it shrugs its shoulders, and knows that in a month or two all will be well.

If all is not then well, it raises its great hand and brings it down on boulevard and café, on Assembly and Senate House alike, and there is peace of a different kind. Things begin anew, and much more quietly. That greater Paris knew and believed in Vansittart. But it did its work, ate its black bread, and simply waited.

The weather suited M. de Tournon's mood, as he sat in his office and for a moment dreamily looked out at the dripping façades of a distant street. He knew that there were a hundred agents at work who could catch the Parisian in his angry moments and send the good work along.

"So you have seen him?" he suddenly asked of the Prefect of Police who sat a little way off.

"Yes, monsieur, yesterday. He arrived the day before. When I was assured that it *was* Prince Henri, I hastened there myself. There is no doubt he is back—a dangerous man, that. It is no light matter to jest at proscription."

"He is in the same house?"

"Yes, and in the same disguise. A student of theology. It becomes him."

"You are right, he *is* a dangerous man. He is young, he is handsome, he rides well. His title to the throne is a little too clear for the comfort of our good citizens."

"Monsieur, shall I arrest him?"

M. de Tournon paused a moment. Then, with difficulty, replied:

"No, not that. I have reasons, M. le Prefect. Sometimes it is safer to have the enemy near. Keep a close watch, and, before all, let your guard at the Grand Hotel redouble his vigilance."

The prefect bowed and retired. The minister rubbed his hands. He was evidently much pleased.

"It only needs a meeting!" he chuckled to himself. "My dear friend Vansittart doubtless has a heart. How I grieve to torment it. But women are proverbially fickle; and, after all, the Prince has the first refusal!"

M. de Tournon took up some papers that were on the table and examined them cursorily.

"H'm!" he growled with a grim smile. "My Honest Citizen and my Patriot Bourgeois are expensive gentlemen. That is the worst of virtues. They are never profitable. Bah! It needs only three days more. By that time Vansittart will be a lost man. While he is fasting in the wilderness, I——But stay. There is more than political power to be got out of this little masterpiece of mine. I must write to Bulbère at once."

So saying, he drew out of its case some note-paper, and

proceeded to write a long letter of instructions to his stockbroker. It amounted to this:

The broker was to bear the market for him in Sahara shares. He was to sell £1,000,000 worth of stock at present prices, and he was to buy as soon as the Bourse opened on Thursday—that was in three days' time—and the difference would become payable or due on settling day, which was a week later.

"Admirable!" exclaimed M. de Tournon. "Stock is now at par, £100. I sell 10,000 shares. After I throw out the Sahara Debenture Bill on Wednesday, stock will fall to at least £80. I buy, and thus get a clear gain of £200,000. It lays the foundation of a fortune!"

Which was a most profitable and honorable transaction for a member of a French Ministry!

Having sealed and despatched this document, M. de Tournon put on his coat, summoned his carriage, and went forth to visit M. Ribou of the War Department. M. Ribou received him with every demonstration of delight, and inwardly wondered how he could manage to put his foot on the neck of this powerful and unscrupulous rival.

M. de Tournon soon plunged into the matters he had come to discuss.

"The Sahara Company," he observed gravely, "is not quite well at present. Its ailments are many. But I think the chief is that it suffers from too big a head and too small a body."

Ribou bowed in assent.

"The shares have gone steadily down. They are still fairly high, but they have dropped."

"That is so," assented the other.

"Mr. Vansittart is becoming unpopular. It seems he is not a Frenchman by descent. He is also conspiring with the Royalists. Paris is getting uneasy. I fear an unpleasant reception for our poor friend when he returns."

"Monsieur," replied the other, "you are thinking there is another blow to give."

"True, as patriots, how can we help it? Friendship must yield to devotion to our country."

"Your sentiments, M. de Tournon, are always both wholesome and admirable."

"Well, let us proceed. On Wednesday a motion will be made in the Chamber asking its formal consent to the raising of a fresh debenture stock to the amount of one million of francs. It is a large sum."

"The shareholders can raise it if they choose without our assent."

"Your remark is most judicious, M. Ribou. But, as patrons of the scheme, the directors come to us to give the new proposal our blessing. That is what it means. If we refuse, the public will be alarmed. They will believe that the Government of France no longer trusts the practicability of the Great Sahara scheme."

"That is very true."

"And it will appear that, after all, Mr. Vansittart has been leading us all astray—that, in short, he is burying us in another Gulf of Darien."

"The public will undoubtedly gather that conclusion."

"Now, M. Ribou, the Chamber is getting afraid of the Sahara scheme. Too much money is asked. We are sinking deep in the mire. Progress seems to be almost impossible. If the shareholders care to increase their capital, poof! it is their own concern. But it is something for us to consider—shall we, statesmen of reputation, sanction the raising of a national loan, and risk our position for a project which seems to be an impossible one? No, certainly not. The Chamber does not deny that the scheme may prove to be quite a fine affair. But it is not sufficiently convinced. It cannot commit itself. It is not just that, by the weight of its enormous influence, it should be the means of persuading the people of France to invest all their hard-earned savings in so vast and uncertain a project."

M. Ribou smiled. He knew his colleague's methods thoroughly.

"*Does* the Chamber really think that, monsieur?" he asked.

"Undoubtedly. M. Renouf, M. Poussaint, M. Fourville, leaders of certain active parties, are quite persuaded; so is M. Tanqueville——."

"M. Tanqueville!" cried Ribou in surprise. "Is *he* also convinced? You must be indeed rich, monsieur!"

"Ah, do not misjudge me. I have a clear majority of thirty in the Chamber. You, M. Ribou, will make it thirty-two. Our views are the same. We cannot afford to see this American ruin our country, and if we *have* to deal a blow to his ambitions and to his reputation—shall we hesitate?"

"You need not doubt I am with you, provided you assure me you have the majority."

"Beyond question. There is Liancourt to deal with. I will see him. The more we get, the better. You have friends, M. Ribou. May I count on them?"

The Minister for War smiled in a sphinx-like way. "I will do my best," he said firmly. And the two parted.

Thus, whilst Jerome was hurrying across the sea, and was hastening to the great capital, this cruel plot was hatching to ruin the credit of his company, and of himself—of him who was toiling night and day to give to France another empire!

CHAPTER XVI

A RIVAL PRINCE

ON the following morning, the Comtesse de Fontainebleau, when she went to visit her mistress, was much surprised to find her agitated and distressed.

On the table at her side lay an opened letter. It was clear that this had wrought the mischief. The Comtesse cast a swift look at the handwriting, and a startled look entered her eyes, a look which blended surprise and fear.

"You have heard from him?" she cried, putting her arm around Honorine's neck. "He has written to you? He is in France?"

Honorine sighed.

"You are right, Anita. He has been there over two days, at Fontainebleau, at the old house you must remember so well. He begs of me to come and see him, if only for once. He begs me to come to-day. I suppose, poor fellow, that every moment is dangerous to him. Princes of the royal blood are mere outlaws and vagrants, and in their own country dare not show their faces."

"Prince Henri is very indiscreet, mademoiselle," replied the Comtesse, pursing her lips. "You know he will get you into trouble. And what for? You cannot see him. Surely it would not be fair to Mr. Vansittart. Two years ago things were different. Then you had only yourself to consider. It is, alas, impossible that Prince Henri should help you to——"

"Silence, madame," cried Honorine with great sternness.

"You are forgetting yourself. I need no instruction as to my duty to the man who is restoring the throne of the royal race of France. This young man, who begs me to see him, is also of the same sacred stock. Our interests are in common. Under a happier fate he would have sat on the throne himself. If I visit him, it is as one exiled monarch may visit another."

"I crave pardon, mademoiselle," replied the Comtesse. "I spoke with the freedom of a friend. You must not forget that even kings and queens are men and women, and who can deny that two years ago, when we last met in the woods at Fontainebleau, there was something more than a mere royal conference. You know yourself, Honorine, that Prince Henri loves you. Why deny it? And for you it might have been the same."

"It might have been," said Honorine dreamily. "But was not. Those were pleasant days, Anita. Henri and I were companions in misfortune. He is a brave youth, and would make a brave king. Perhaps I was rash in those days. Perhaps I listened too much to him as we sat in the arbor. But I kept him within limits, did I not? The poor fellow is free to do as he likes. Fate has directed our destinies in widely different paths, and it is no use for you to speak of what might have been."

Honorine trembled as she spoke, and her voice quivered as under the stress of a deep emotion.

"But, Anita, he has come back," she went on slowly. "You know his rashness. He will not depart without seeing me. He might be arrested, imprisoned, who knows what? Now, Anita, I think I see my duty plainly alike to Jerome, to Henri, and to myself. I must put an end at once to any hope that may linger in Henri's mind. I must bid him banish me from his memory. Ah, no! not from his memory, but from his dreams of the future. I must once and for all part from him that he may no more run this terrible risk. I shall give him back a freedom which he has never lost, but only thinks he has lost. He will be under no delusion. His life will be before him to work out as he chooses. As to myself," and here Honorine rose from her chair with dignity, " I shall make the sacrifice of friendship. I shall be true to my word. I shall do so much to help on the cause, even though my heart aches a little."

The Comtesse de Fontainebleau regarded Honorine attentively.

" I feel you are right, mademoiselle," she said, " if you have only strength of mind enough to carry through what you propose. You need not look so imperiously upon me. I know full well that you will sacrifice everything for a sacred purpose like that you have undertaken, but I feel sure that you deceive yourself when you plead that you feel nothing for this brave prince. Nay, what I almost hope is that some spark still lingers in your heart, and that at such a meeting his words—and are they not fiery and eloquent?—may make it burst into flame. I, too, am a woman!"

" I shall not forget myself, Anita," replied Honorine, " nor the word I have given to Mr. Vansittart, nor the dignity of my position, nor the sacred duty of womanhood. Come, we will go this morning, as he desires. It will be well that it should be soon over."

And thus it happened that a little before twelve o'clock these two ladies, closely wrapped up against the inclemency of the weather, were descending the steps of the Grand Hotel in order to drive to the Gare de Lyon.

By what strange coincidence was it that at this moment Jerome made his appearance on the staircase on his return from the wilderness of the Sahara? He had come in quietly by the Southern express, had driven in an ordinary *fiacre* to the hotel, and had been whirled through Paris absolutely unrecognized.

He might have passed the closely veiled ladies without noticing them, had not Honorine given expression to an exclamation of surprise. Vansittart hastened to her, and, in a cheerful tone, begged her for news of herself and of her companion.

Honorine made a hurried reply. The minutes were flying, and trains do not wait. She had not seen this hero of hers for months. He had passed through dangers, had suffered hardships, had encountered terrible risks, all for her sake, and yet here she was, as she bitterly reproached herself, trying to dismiss him the moment she met him.

What is it that makes us so perverse?

Jerome noticed her distraught manner.

"I see you are going out somewhere," he observed. "Is it important? Cannot you postpone it?"

"It is important," replied Honorine. "I am grieved that I must go the instant you return."

"But at least," said Vansittart, "you will have an escort. You will take one of my carriages, and a couple of my footmen."

Honorine shook her head.

"We must go as we are," she said. "We require no assistance."

"I shall see you at dinner?" pursued Jerome.

"I trust so," and Honorine colored, "but please don't rely upon it," and, so saying, the Princess and her companion proceeded on their way.

Jerome looked after them as they drove off, with a troubled look. There was perhaps a little pang of disappointment in his heart, for this was not the reception he had hoped for, and at that moment he seemed to stand so terribly alone. But it was not this feeling that was uppermost in his mind; it was not even jealousy, certainly it was not suspicion.

He muttered to himself as he reached his room, "If she would only trust me! There is something in her life, something that troubles her. Is there not such a thing in every life? I do not want to pry into her secrets, but how much better for us both if she would only have faith in me, and let me help her."

And with a heavier heart than he had borne through all his difficulties in the Sahara, amid the attacks and bitter calumnies directed against him, he sat down to look through the vast accumulations of correspondence which he found upon his study table.

Both he and the two ladies would have been much more uneasy had they observed the curious incident which took place as the carriage was driving off.

A man who had been loitering upon the pavement, idly gazing into the windows of the shops, and affecting to be quite happy with the rain pattering around him, suddenly quickened into unusual animation. Hailing a victoria, he directed the driver to follow the carriage which was conveying Honorine and the Comtesse to the station, and as he settled himself comfortably in the seat, secured from the weather by the drawn hood, a malicious look of anticipated pleasure stole over his face. His expression was not unlike that of a stage villain who is about to have a good time.

Thus the terrible shadow crept on in the wake of the unsuspecting Princess.

Meanwhile Jerome was busily occupied. He merely glanced at the newspapers lying on his table. Some of them were friendly, most neutral; in others he read headings such as "de Tournon, the Savior of France," "Sunk in the Sahara," "The Nation Once More Hoodwinked," "Vansittart Plots against the Republic." He pushed them away with a motion of contempt, and rang the bell.

"Send Mr. Jim Bates and M. Folliet to me."

His Captain of the Guard and the Chief of Police soon stood before him.

"Gentlemen," said Vansittart, in a clear, cold tone. "Our work seems now about to begin. You, M. Folliet, have complained that there is little call for your services. I do not think you will reproach me on that score for a month or so."

Arizona Jim's eyes gleamed. He thought there would be no more "trouble" once they had quitted the Soudan.

"M. Folliet," continued Jerome, addressing himself to the Frenchman. "You know Paris well?"

"Every nook and corner, monsieur."

"Every doubtful house, every harbor of thieves, every dark cellar, every man of bad character?"

"It is so."

"Well, I desire you to find M. de Tournon immediately, and shadow him. I want to know every house and building he visits. Not an act of his must remain unnoticed. Something may occur to change his habits of life, his haunts, and his companions. But you must not leave him. You must find out exactly what he is doing, and keep me constantly informed."

"Monsieur, it is done."

"You shall be munificently rewarded. Those who stand by me now shall stand by me when it will be a favor to come into my presence. You may go, M. Folliet."

"As for you," turning to Jim Bates, "you are in good condition?"

Arizona Jim smiled.

"Bring 'em along, boss, and you'll see."

"How many Frenchmen do you think you are equal to?"

"Frenchmen!" and a look of disgust spread over Jim's face. "Waal, I guess, judging from the sort they keep in Paris, something like ten score!"

Vansittart could not help a faint smile.

"It will be your duty to stand at the head of the staircase outside my door. If visitors call upon me, admit those you know. If you don't know them, treat them with perfect courtesy at first, and if their business seems real, admit them —rich or poor. I don't want any one excluded who comes in a fair spirit. But if you think they are bullies, or seem impertinent, or are likely to cause a disturbance, throw them downstairs. And, remember: no shooting."

Arizona Jim's eyes again gleamed.

"It's a fine, deep staircase," he chuckled to himself as he left the room, "and what the boss says, goes."

Jerome looked at the timepiece. It was one o'clock. On the stroke a visitor was announced. M. Renouf, a distinguished member of the Senate.

The American bowed a little stiffly, and offered his visitor a seat.

"You may guess on what errand I have come, monsieur," began M. Renouf. "I trust you will believe I am one of your friends. You have just arrived. Perhaps you do not know the position of affairs in Paris?"

"I know them quite accurately, M. Renouf," was Jerome's quiet answer.

"Then you know that there has been a storm brewing for some time—a change has come over public opinion—and that it will break to-morrow."

"Precisely."

"In other words, the Request that the Chamber should sanction the issue of new stock will be thrown out?"

"Your summing up of the situation is perfect, M. Renouf."

"Well, monsieur, I come, as I said, as a friend. I cannot stand by and see you ruined. What will be the effect on Paris? Disastrous beyond words. The flame will be sedulously fanned. All France would be up in arms against you and your scheme in a day."

Vansittart smiled.

"It may be so," he said. "We shall see, monsieur."

"Ah, no, that is unwise. It is walking into destruction. I come from influential people, people of high rank, who wish you well. They beg you at least to withdraw the Request."

"Impossible, monsieur," Jerome replied calmly. "That Request has been made according to precedent and proper form, and I absolutely refuse to withdraw it."

"But it is certain of defeat!"

"And if I grant that?"

M. Renouf clutched his hands. What was he to do with this obstinate man who *would* run his head against a stone wall?

"Then do not withdraw, Mr. Vansittart," he continued, "but get your directors together, and raise the stock before the Request comes before the Chamber."

Jerome laughed scornfully.

"M. Renouf," he observed. "You are, I believe, my friend, and you speak honestly. But I assure you it is quite in vain. I will not withdraw the Request. I will not call the directors together.

"Do you understand my position? I have acted throughout this undertaking in and for the interests of France. I have devoted my time and risked my body without asking reward of any sort. The scheme has progressed admirably to the point at which we expected to be at this time.

"Meanwhile there have sprung up enemies of France and of mine who have inflamed the people. I do not inquire into their motives. I merely point to the result, which is, that the deputies are endeavoring to deal what might easily be a death-blow to the noblest and the grandest enterprise that France has ever undertaken. Well, then, if the French people choose to listen to these men, and if the Chamber votes as they dictate to it, upon them be the responsibility. It is no affair of mine.

"You ask me to humiliate myself before these enemies, to let them conquer whilst the evil results of their victory are stayed by my generosity. No, M. Renouf, you forget that I have no interest in the Sahara Scheme, save as an investor. It is undertaken in the name of France. If France withdraws her name, then the scheme collapses—for some other less volatile and changeable nation to take it up.

"But *I!* Am *I* to take the place of France, and act against her will? You say Paris is against me. You say the Chamber is against me. Well, the Chamber represents

France herself. I bow to the decision of France. Let her vote freely. Let her destroy the Sahara scheme or not, as she pleases. I have nothing to do with it. I am indeed already weary of the work—under conditions so harassing.

"If you doubt my sincerity, M. Renouf, I can only assure you I am leaving for the country to-morrow. I shall be amongst green fields when the Chamber votes, and shall be feeling gratitude that the responsibility for the development of the Sahara will thenceforth rest upon the Chamber."

At the close of this spirited reply, M. Renouf rose.

"It is useless to plead further, it is clear," he said. "And, believe me, monsieur, I sympathize with much that you have said."

Jerome was about to dismiss his visitor when a loud noise was heard in the passage, followed by a series of thuds accentuated by muffled curses which became fainter and fainter.

Both men rushed to the door. What they saw was Arizona Jim calmly leaning over the balustrade in the passage, and regarding two tall and powerful Frenchmen who were rolling, entangled and bruised, at the bottom of the staircase.

"What is all this?" demanded Jerome.

"Obeying orders, boss. These two Frenchies came up, sort 'er violent, and asked for M. Vansittart. As you ordered, I began with civility, and in my best French said, '*Vous ne pouvez voir M. Vansittart.*' '*On ne peut entrer?*' cried one. '*Nous le verrons,*' shouted the other, and they both sets at me, and makes for the door. 'Aha, Jim,' sez I, 'it's about time for the other thing.' So I grabbed 'em both by the scruff of the neck, and sent them spinning down these 'ere stone steps. Your orders, sir, and when you sez a thing, it goes!"

Jerome bit his lip.

"You are a trifle too literal, Bates," he said. "However, M. Renouf, you see I am not quite unprepared for my enemies!" And so they parted.

When Vansittart returned to his room, he found Dick Harland awaiting him, having recently arrived from St. Cloud, where he had now taken up quarters.

"It's too bad, old fellow, not telling a chap you'd returned," he complained, after a hearty hand-clasp. "Here I've been fooling about all morning and never knew anything about it, until I met a rascally scoundrel downstairs who was asking for you. And my sister's here, too, old chap. I want you to see her!"

"Your sister!" exclaimed Jerome with interest. "I remember her as pretty and sprightly. I should much like to see her now, Dick, but it's not to be. There's serious trouble on, and I want your sister and you to be off in half an hour."

Dick whistled. "What's up now?" he asked.

"I want you to take train for Leoville at once. I have a country house there I bought before leaving Paris. Everything is in readiness, but I want you to be there beforehand. I shall join you to-morrow, and hey! for a week's rest and ease!"

"Right you are, Jerry," replied Dick, with a merry laugh. "I'm off at once. Good-bye—and don't put your head out of the window!" and he disappeared.

Jerome felt the friendly interest of the last observation, but he winced under it nevertheless. He picked without appetite his *déjeûner*, and then drove in a closed carriage to his broker, with whom he had a long conference.

On his return he felt the bleakness of the day more and more. Some people passing him in the Rue du Quatre Septembre recognized him, stopped, and shouted "Panama! Panama!" at him. Farther along he was met with cries of "*Traître! Vive M. de Tournon!*" Jerome reached home with bitterness in his heart.

Honorine and her companion did not arrive for dinner, and this puzzled and vexed him. He felt solitary once more. He was alone at the crisis of his life.

He went moodily to his room and tried to read. An hour passed.

"Liancourt has not come, though I wired him!" he exclaimed with irritation. "Has he, too, deserted me?"

He looked gloomily out of the window. Paris was black and dull. The Opera House looked like the monstrous tomb of some barbarous monarch. The streets shivered beneath the rain. How altered from the Paris he had left three months back! And how her appearance harmonized with the change that had come over her people during that time! They, too, wore black faces and hearts full of bitterness. Jerome reflected on the mutability of all things human.

He heard some shouts in the distance, away over the Banque de France. He wondered what was happening.

He did not know that some of the "patriots" were engaged in breaking the windows of the offices of Sahara, Limited, and that stones were being thrown at the solemn figures of the Arabs and the camels, standing in stony death on the site of a demolished kiosk outside.

Before turning in, he carelessly glanced at a copy of *Le Soir*, when the following paragraph caught his eye :

"Reuter's agent at Gabes telegraphs that a duel took place this morning between Captain Pompier, of the gunboat *Sphinx*, and M. Legru, of *La Patrie*. The journalist was run through the neck, and died immediately. The cause of the quarrel is unknown."

"Good!" ejaculated Vansittart as he climbed into bed. "Pompier soon trussed his bird."

CHAPTER XVII

THE STORM BURSTS

JEROME rose early, but not earlier than M. Liancourt, who was waiting for him in his room when he entered it.

"My dear Vansittart," cried the Frenchman, extending his arms warmly to his friend, "how delighted I am to see you back safe and sound."

"Yet only last night I was bewailing your desertion," responded Jerome. "I was expecting you all the evening."

"Ah! I was in an awkward position. I had two invitations, and I was bound to choose between them."

"In that case, M. Liancourt, I withdraw all objection. I do not pretend to compete with anyone in hospitality."

"Ah, now you are angry, and you misunderstand me quite," replied Liancourt. "It is true you invited me here. I resolved to come, when behold! A pressing message came from M. de Tournon, begging me to give him the honor of my company to dinner."

"M. de Tournon is an agreeable host," replied Vansittart, coldly.

"My friend, M. de Tournon, was an exceedingly agreeable host last night, and his conversation was most entertaining. He was able to instruct me upon many remarkable matters, more particularly with regard to the Sahara Scheme, and his own distinguished statesmanship.

"He also showed me how money might be made out of the situation, and, in fact, his conversation was so very charming, so full of information, that I really could not leave him until midnight.

"And, if you complain, I can only say that I am not selfish, and that all along I thought to myself during the evening, how delighted I would be to let my friend Vansittart share in the knowledge of these interesting matters. Knowing your keenness for information of every kind, I really thought, my friend, that I was doing you a service."

Jerome's wayward mood had vanished during this speech. A broad smile lit up his face as he extended his hand to the statesman.

"Excuse me, Liancourt," he exclaimed, "you have done me a valuable service, and I was wrong ever to have suspected that you were not away on business of pressing importance like this. So de Tournon has quite made up his mind? The Request is to be thrown out, I suppose?"

"Yes, for in his confidence last night, M. de Tournon showed me how he was building up his reputation as a patriotic statesman. And the people of Paris will bless him. He will become Premier. Indeed, that this is certain, you may realize from the fact that he has already offered me a portfolio! Behold in me, Mr. Vansittart, one who can and will become the Minister for the Interior! My friend, since I heard this delightful news, I am too proud and elated to enjoy life, and I thank Providence hourly for having created so generous and gracious a spirit as that which resides in M. de Tournon's somewhat unattractive figure."

Jerome laughed. "So he has tried to bribe you?"

"He justly claims my support and vote."

"And what did you say in reply?"

"My friend, I ought perhaps to have refused his magnanimous offer at once, but the fact is, I so enjoyed M. de Tournon's remarks, and they became so interesting, I may say so romantic, through the quantity of Château Lafitte he was drinking, that I did not absolutely refuse—indeed, I held out hopes, and I was rewarded.

"For now I understand how it is that you may ally patriotism with personal gain, and may become the savior of your country, and a wealthy man at one and the same time. M. de Tournon is clever. He is an extraordinary genius. He became certain of my friendship, and directed me to follow his example and become rich. And I, being a poor man, have serious thoughts of it.

"It is so simple, my friend. I go to my broker to-day, and bid him sell a parcel of Sahara stock. Stock is at present at par. On Thursday, after the throwing out of the Request, stock, it seems, will fall to eighty. I shall then buy the shares which I have to deliver at the settlement, and thus, you see, monsieur, with a snap of the finger I become possessed of a fortune."

Jerome's brow darkened.

"I guessed as much, and yet I had hoped that de Tournon was not a scoundrel, but only a politician with a diseased ambition. Ah, well, monsieur, we shall see, we shall see. Meanwhile, I have to ask a favor of you. Do you know de Tournon's broker?"

"Undoubtedly. It is M. Bulbère."

"Is he a weak man or a strong man?"

"Well," replied the other with an inscrutable smile, "there are things, perhaps, if I speak firmly to him, I may be able to——"

"Well, my friend," continued Jerome, "what I want you to do is somewhat singular. I desire you to go to M. Bulbère and compel him to sell to you, apparently for yourself, but in reality for me, the shares which M. de Tournon is anxious to dispose of. I will place the necessary funds to your credit. You may require a strong argument to persuade the good man? I will give you one. It can only be a hint. Supposing that shares do not fall but rise, what would become of M. de Tournon's profit? I even fear that both he and the broker might come to grief."

A curious light came into Liancourt's eyes.

"That seems a sound deduction. I will do what you say. But why not confide in me what all this means? Do you distrust my attachment to you? I believe in you, Mr. Vansittart. I believe in your scheme. I, who have belonged to no party, already belong to yours. But am I to remain outside the closest confines of secrecy, or do you conceive it possible that my advice is either worthless or of doubtful faith?"

"No, no," exclaimed Vansittart. "Pardon me, Liancourt, I value your friendship, and trust you with my whole heart, but as yet I must be more or less alone. My projects are leading me into strange paths, they are surrounded by terrible difficulties, and it is because I regard and esteem you that I will not commit you to them as I should wish.

"Were I to take advantage of your kindness, you would become bound, as it were, to a course of action which might be full of the gravest consequences, and which in its full development might not only meet with your disapproval, but even lead to your dishonor and your downfall. So far, you have only been a personal friend of Vansittart. You have been a partner to no secret. You have been advocate of no policy. None can accuse you of being concerned in aught that concerns me.

"Ah, when the time comes that I have to call upon my friends, and ask them boldly to make the line clear between the present and the future, how gladly shall I welcome you, if, in the full light of the knowledge you will then have, you come to my side of your own free will and acting on your own free judgment! You should be, Liancourt, my most honored and my most trusted lieutenant."

Liancourt was visibly moved.

"You are a noble fellow, Vansittart," he said, "and when the times are settled a little, let us speak frankly to one another. If honor bids me withdraw, I will do so as a friend, and I shall respect your confidence."

"Be it so," replied Jerome, "and Heaven grant you may choose to stand with me, and not against me."

"Well," said Liancourt gaily, "I will be off to M. Bulbère. And, by-the-way, would you care for me to speak in defence of the Sahara in the Chamber, if only to break the bubble of that over-grown bladder, de Tournon? It would be a matter of great delight to me."

"No," answered Jerome decisively. "You need not vote for the Refusal, but at least I beg you not to vote or speak against it. I would have de Tournon's victory the more conspicuous, that his downfall may be the more complete. I do not fear, Liancourt. I may be secret, but I am safe. When I have to fight, I fight a decisive battle. I leave nothing to my enemies. It is better than a long, weak series of engagements which harass the spirit, and only lead to a protracted victory shorn of half its value. Well, good-bye. I am away to the country. Let everybody know that Vansittart slumbers whilst his fortunes are trembling."

The two men parted with a warm handshake.

Liancourt left the hotel in a very pleased state of mind. He felt that a dramatic climax was on its way, though he could not guess what form it would take. He smacked his lips, too, at the thought that M. de Tournon was apparently riding as hard as he could for a fall.

He drove to the office of M. Bulbère, and after a long and earnest conversation, in which the broker alternately became flushed with anger and pale with terror, Liancourt gained his point.

"You understand, M. Bulbère," were the statesman's parting words, "I save you from possible ruin, but if I am content on settling day to take at market prices the stock which I have bought previously from you for a smaller sum, it is not done to protect de Tournon. You must clearly understand that. I shall only carry out my word when you have discovered that the Minister for the Interior has not the wherewithal to meet the claim upon him, and becomes, consequently, a ruined and dishonored man. The loss will then fall upon your shoulders, and to save *you* from bankruptcy I will consent to pay for the shares such price as they are quoted at."

On his return, Liancourt passed through some of the great open spaces of Paris, and was mortified to find what a hold, by this time, the agitation against the Sahara Scheme had obtained upon the people.

Excited mobs thronged the streets, and gravely discussed the situation at every corner and at every café.

That evening a vote was to be taken; it was for the Chamber to declare whether the country was once more to be saddled with the burden of a tremendous debt for a venture which they were assured was more mad and impossible than that of Panama.

As the time grew near, the crowd proceeded to demonstrate their feelings and to encourage timid deputies.

Liancourt grew sick at heart to hear the foul rhetoric of mob orators who seized this mood of the Parisian people to sully with every species of vile calumniation the reputation of the great man so lately adored and so loudly applauded as he drove through the streets of the capital.

He was ashamed of his countrymen for their childish weakness, for their volatile character. How superficial it all seemed!

At one moment there was heard the cry, "*Au Grand Hotel!*" They thought that Jerome was still there. There were bright visions of breaking windows, perhaps even the rare felicity of throwing a few stones at the man himself.

By mid-day the police were compelled to form a cordon round the hotel.

The Boulevard des Capucines became alive with the shouts and the screams of the idle, thriftless scamps of Paris.

But Liancourt was cheered by one remarkable spectacle. As he was passing to his house, situated near the Bois, he met a company of soldiers marching down the Avenue des Champs Élysées. Now, the Frenchman is always eager to get the soldiers into his sympathy. He loves disorder much, but he fears the Army more.

It was only when the Royal Guard passed over to the side of the revolutionists and became the National Guard, that the rule of King Louis had really passed away.

This regiment, then, marching peacefully along, was met by a vast crowd of men and women, who, drunk with excitement were actually thinking of marching to St. Cloud and wrecking Vansittart's new house which had risen in matchless grace above the ruins of the old residence.

The motley crowd greeted the soldiers with effusive cries of " Down with Vansittart," " Down with the traitor of the Sahara," " Long live M. de Tournon," " Death to the American," and other similar elegant utterances which they trusted would stir the warm blood of the military.

To their surprise the regiment made no response. There came even a frown upon their faces, their brows puckered up, and their eyes darkened with anger. What did it mean?

Some of the women, after their wont when thus infuriated, ran into the ranks and tugged at the tunics of the soldiers with hoarse shrieks. Usually the French *piou-piou* does not dislike this method of address. He becomes bland and smiling, and easy to persuade.

But, alas! it was noticeable that these fair creatures were rudely disentangled and firmly pushed aside.

Liancourt was almost stupefied. Delight filled his heart, for he knew the meaning of this strange scene. The soldiers were firm in their allegiance to Jerome. They had found him a true man. Many of their brothers had fought under him in the Sahara and had won noble victories, achieved decorations, had smelt the blood of battle, and report came from all that this amateur commander was unparalleled in courage, impartial in favor, generous in reward.

In their eyes, Vansittart was a soldier, a man who could lead, a man under whom honor and glory could be won.

They were not going to cry for M. de Tournon with his great flabby head and his huge ears and his rolling eyes—this gourmet, who spent his time in plotting and eating—in preference to the hero who was now creeping into their dreams and rapidly standing out as the hope of France and of the Army.

And so, when the mob made one more frantic effort to enlist their sympathies, the soldiers suddenly, with one spontaneous impulse, raised their rifles high in air, and shouted, "*Vive Vansittart! Vive l'Empereur!*"

Then, at an angry growl from the colonel, they dropped their arms, and proceeded calmly on their way.

The mob stared aghast, but it did not go to St. Cloud.

Elsewhere things were not satisfactory. Earlier in the morning M. de Tournon had sallied forth in an open carriage, and, on pretence of calling upon supporters in different parts of the city, had contrived to pass through all the principal streets. His was a mean soul that thirsted for inglorious applause.

The shouts of the populace were dear to him. It delighted his heart that wherever he appeared there was always to be found a knot of people to wave their hats, shout his name, and proclaim him the savior of the Republic.

He assumed a look of great gravity, as though the cares and burdens of the state rested heavily upon him, and he took off his hat in gracious response.

He did not know that in all his tortuous meanderings through Paris he was followed by the man who hated him most, the old Prefect of Police, whom he had turned from his office to gratify the preference of a mistress for some relative of her own. Not a movement of de Tournon's escaped the practised eyes of M. Folliet.

He saw him, for instance, enter the office of M. Bulbère, and come out looking singularly well pleased. He had just learnt that the shares had been sold, and that everything was ripe for his financial *coup*.

M. Ribou essayed to glean some of the popular enthusiasm, and came in for the lees of the applause. But it is always so when the principal actor has exhausted the audience; there is little power of demonstration left. Still, M. Ribou, being the most incapable man in France, was always well enough pleased when he was not actually hissed. To cling hard to the portfolio which he knew he would never possess again was the sum of his ambition.

At three o'clock the deputies met. Around the doors a vast crowd assembled, stretching far over the bridge to the Place de la Concorde. Back and forth the multitude of men and women surged in the hope of getting nearer the building, and of seeing something of the spectacle.

It was a terrible ordeal for the poor members. There was not one of whom the French populace had not a pretty shrewd guess as to his policy, and according to their favor or disfavor they cheered or groaned at the newcomer.

The gendarmes with difficulty formed a narrow passage through the dense mass of people from the bridge to the great entrance, and each deputy, as he slowly made his way through this living avenue, became the object of ridicule and abuse, or it might be of encouragement and exhortation. Those who were known to favor the Sahara Scheme had to be conducted into the building by the police.

When de Tournon appeared, a great roar of acclamation rent the sky. He bowed to right and left, and could not bow enough, and he passed into the building with the assurance that he was about to give the final stroke to a gigantic scheme of ambition. He fondly imagined he was going to rule France, at least for the moment.

Never was debate carried on with greater uneasiness. Despite the difficulty of passage, messages were continually brought to the crowd of the progress of the proceedings, who was speaking, what line he was taking, what his arguments were.

And thus it occurred that as each member rose to address

the Chamber his observations were deafened and made indistinct either by uproarious applause, or by the more significant noise of groaning and hissing.

The President gave up the struggle. He did not pretend to listen. De Tournon alone succeeded in bringing off his carefully prepared oration.

He was wise enough to send word personally to the crowd that he was about to address the Chamber, and that his observations were important. He trusted he might call upon the indulgence of his friends and receive the favor of their silence.

The multitude acceded to the request of their most recent idol.

It was in a way a masterly speech. There was great cunning in the careful manner in which the Minister forbore from indulging in any personal attack upon Vansittart. He posed as the distressed friend of the American. He put down his mistake to no other cause than want of good feeling. Perhaps he misjudged, perhaps he was a dreamer, perhaps the task was too much for him.

Anyhow, how was it that this Company, with its boundless wealth, came after six months to demand another million of francs? And how much more would they ask in the next six months? It meant that France was to be drained of her gold.

These arguments were effective only when assisted by the judicious concealment of the real facts, for one of Vansittart's friends was hooted down when he mildly reminded the deputies that this demand was only made in accordance with the expectations formed and duly formulated by the company at the time of its constitution, and that the Sahara Scheme had reached the very point of development anticipated at its inauguration.

When the time came for the vote there was much curiosity to see how the members would go. Some were convinced, many had been bought, most had been terrified by the attitude of Paris. Others were influenced by the advice of Liancourt, and did not vote at all, and thus the Request was refused by the enormous majority of 286, and the House passed to the Order of the Day.

A wild yell of exultation rose from the multitude when they heard this news, and when the Savior of his Country made his appearance, it seemed that words were not equal to the occasion. The only thing left to do was to take the horses from the carriage, and drag him bodily to his residence.

It is not a pleasant way of driving through Paris. The motion is neither easy nor regular, and one sees little of the beauties of the Tuileries or the Champs Élysées when a howling mob is racing on both sides of you. But to M. de Tournon it was the pleasantest ride he had had in his life, and the foul breath of the mob the sweetest odor that had ever entered his nostrils.

Paris, with all her beauty, was not so beautiful as the ragged caps which were flung into the air or the clapped hands which applauded his progress.

When he arrived at the office of the Interior, he mounted the window and made a brief speech.

"Gentlemen," he declared, "France is saved. Her prosperity is assured. Let France rejoice, and let me quietly withdraw into the ordinary routine of my commonplace duties. If I have deserved to-day of your good favor, I am enough rewarded."

The multitude received this speech with another shout of delight, and amid cries of "*Vive le Président! Vive le Président!*" the inflated minister withdrew to his office.

Poor de Tournon—he was the victim of true dramatic irony! He had been carving, inch by inch, the steps which would take him to the pinnacle of his glory, and did not know that each one of these was leading to an abyss of irretrievable misfortune.

The mob passed from one extreme to the next. An orgie of exultation must be succeeded by one of passion.

Vansittart was not in Paris, but his stone Arabs were.

Away rushed the crowd, ropes were procured, and the unoffending effigies from Shott Jerid were torn down from their pedestal and smashed.

The police charged the mob, shots were fired, swords drawn; soon the air resounded with the shrieks of the wounded and the groans of the dying.

Thus, for a third time, did the gaunt relics of the caravan witness with their solemn, staring eyes a scene of bloodshed and death. Ill-luck followed them through the ages.

CHAPTER XVIII

HOW JEROME ENJOYED HIS HOLIDAY

THE little village of Leoville is one of those small jewels which sparkle in the rich diadem of Normandy. It is to-day what it was four centuries back. The same river, the same church, the same parsonage serve it now as served it in days lost to memory.

No impulse from the great world without ever agitates Leoville. The villagers scarcely heed the passage of years. Monarchy, Republic, Empire, these are but vague terms to them. Those who are fortunate enough to discover this beautiful spot are drawn irresistibly into its old-world oblivions, and each century becomes merged in the other.

It would not have surprised one to see D'Artagnan of the Musketeers ride furiously to the hostel door and demand a bottle of wine, a capon, and a fresh horse. If a lumbering coach passed through the little street, and one were told that it was the carriage of Madame de Longueville flying from Mazarin's wrath and on her way to her home in Normandy and to her abandoned husband, there would have appeared no incongruity in the incident.

Time has, in fact, overlooked Leoville, and has left it to dream its dreams undisturbed by the movements of events.

One thing alone had changed. The beautiful Manor House had for years lacked a master. There was no one to rule over Leoville and grind down his tenants to starvation. And this was a pity, for Leoville was conservative at heart, and preferred being ground down to nothing occurring at all.

Judge, then, the delight of the village when it was announced that a great seigneur had bought the Manor House, village and all. There was some chance of tyranny now, and Leoville became excited and cheerful.

In due time strange men entered the place, and extraordinary revolutions occurred in the Manor House. It became a palace. Never was such a wonderful transformation.

Then servants and agents appeared. The Manor House was at last habitable; its grounds became beautiful again as in the days of old. In the end, the name of the new tyrant leaked out. It was Jerome K. Vansittart. The people of Leoville thought it a strange name, and wondered what the K. stood for. They thought it was an eccentricity of the Southern Provinces.

A beautiful home it was, and Jerome became singularly content as he gazed lazily around at the swelling lawns which spread up from the placid river to the house.

He was sitting on the verandah with his hat tilted over his eyes to protect them from the vigorous winter sun. Close to him, snugly ensconced in a basket chair, was Evelyn Harland, her pretty face hidden deep in a wrap. Some distance away reclined Dick, with his head against the root of a vine, an enormous pipe in his mouth, and an air of absolute and inexpugnable indolence.

The silver Seine sparkled at their feet, and through the trees to the right could be seen one of those graceful bridges of chased light stone with which France is proud to decorate her noblest stream.

Jerome had arrived but an hour before. As he was thus peacefully regarding his country house, and drawing deep breaths of relief, M. de Tournon was already entertaining the Assembly, and the rabid mob were cheering to the echo this unscrupulous rival.

A long silence had prevailed. Then, noticing his distraction, Evelyn said:

"Your thoughts are in Paris, Mr. Vansittart, are they not?"

Jerome looked up on hearing the voice, and then, with a smile, replied:

"By no means, Miss Harland. I should be ashamed to tell you of what I was thinking."

Evelyn laughed gaily.

"Then you have descended for a moment from the heroic!" she exclaimed.

"I'm afraid there's little of the hero in me," answered Jerome ruefully.

"Ah, that is not so. Who, but a hero born, would have attempted to carry out such a wonderful enterprise as yours?"

"You forget, Miss Harland. It is not I, but my opportunity that is magnificent. Personally, I am a lazy, good-for-nothing idler, whose existence is not of the faintest consequence to anybody. It is not I, but my wealth that is doing all this Sahara work. Let me misquote Shakespeare:

> ' How oft it is the power to do good deeds
> Makes good deeds done.' "

"How *seldom* you mean," cried Evelyn. "The very possession of means makes men incurably opposed to using them."

"And yet how easy? Suppose a man possessed the seven-league boots, would you regard him as a wonder if he became the champion sprinter of the world?"

"No, but I should if he devoted his boots to the service of international postage!" laughed Evelyn.

"Perhaps you are right," murmured Jerome. "I suppose that most men who had those boots would give exhibitions with them at a dollar a head."

"So that you see you *are* heroic."

"Not at all. A hero is a man who does something exceedingly difficult for the good of others, and not for himself."

"And are you creating this colony for yourself?"

"Not exactly," laughed Jerome, "but I should not grumble if at the end it paid a dividend of cent. per cent. !"

"You mistake yourself," said Evelyn, reproachfully, looking at Jerome with the admiration of a woman who sees in a man the bold unconquerable spirit that stimulates her emotions. "You perhaps are unconscious of your own courage. Perhaps you lack the motive that carries one on to great achievements."

"Indeed!" exclaimed Jerome, now turning full upon the girl, and looking at her with new interest. "And what is this motive?"

"There are several," said Evelyn. "There is ambition."

Jerome shook his head. "I have none!"

"There is love of country. There is self-respect. There is——" Evelyn hesitated and colored.

"Yes!" said Jerome quickly. "Go on! There is——?"

"Love!" Evelyn spoke the words softly. Her cheeks became rosier still.

Jerome gazed upon her with an admiration which seemed to be quite new to him. What a superb creature was this English girl, he thought to himself. How frank and yet how free from the license of speech which in many he had met was often so impertinent and so intrusive. Self-possession and reserve were tempered by a charming candor and an absence of affectation which quite entranced him.

The girl that he was looking at was surely a superb specimen of her race. The delicate brow, the deep lustrous eyes, the fine straight nose, the small mouth with its ruddy, tempting lips, the rounded chin, and the pure complexion which seemed at once delicate yet defiant of wind and weather—these were the marks of a loveliness that was wholly healthy and wholly fascinating.

"Love!" repeated Jerome, after a pause, during which he had gazed so intently upon his companion that she turned her head away. "So that is the great motive?"

"'Love that builds up cities and throws down towers,'" quoted Evelyn. "It is much to a man and all to a woman. And it is the only power left that can work miracles."

"Love!" a second time repeated Jerome.

"Have you not loved?" Evelyn summoned up courage to put this bold question to him.

Jerome started. Had he ever loved? It was the momentous question of his present life. It haunted him, it disturbed his rest, it followed him to his labors, it arose like a spectre at his feasts. Did he really love? Was his feeling for Honorine of this ennobling character that Evelyn had spoken of—something to inspire to heroic deeds and perform miracles? Was there the subtle and elevating change in his being that love brings with it—a passion, an overwhelming instinct of devotion, a constant ever-present feeling that refined, that stimulated, that comforted, that rewarded? He had gallantly done his work. But was it all for Honorine's sake, for the sake of the wife he was to win? Or was it partly from a feeling of excitement in the game; from the honorable resolve to fulfil his promise; perhaps from some feeling of self-pride which carried him through any scheme he had undertaken?

Somehow, as he looked upon this fresh, healthy, charming, educated girl at his side, full of life and hope, he felt that his experience of what is called love was not such as she might have inspired him with. He wondered how far the mere determination to conquer a difficult subject, the mere zest of victory where obstacles seemed superhuman, had entered into his feelings towards Honorine. To the proud Frenchwoman, whose trust in him was so implicit, he would be true to the end. But was it love?

"You do not answer me?" It was Evelyn who interrupted his thoughts.

"Pardon me, Miss Harland. Your question is one of those before which the wisest of us needs to pause a long time and think. Have I ever loved? Do you know, I cannot tell you. I am as much posed as were the poor Greeks by the question of the Sphinx."

Evelyn laughed merrily.

"Then I am afraid the answer is clear as noonday. Some day, Mr. Vansittart, the motive will come into your life and you will do wonders. You are doing them now, but you will not do them quite so languidly and indifferently. Here you are idling away in Leoville and the fate of your Company is being decided in Paris. Fie on you! Have you run away?"

"A pretty hero, after all, am I not?" said Jerome, smiling. "The moment there is danger off I go in a trice and leave the poor directors shivering in their skins. It is shameful."

"Then why are you here?" she asked with a pucker of her pretty brow.

"What!" cried Jerome, in mock dismay. "Has my one believer thrown me up?"

"But you should n't tax your believer's fidelity," she answered.

"Then, O Believer in the true Prophet whose name is Vansittart, hearken unto me and behold! I will reveal to you a mystery——"

"Yes, yes," broke in Evelyn eagerly. "Tell me all."

"Verily I say unto you, wait until 10.15 to-morrow and you shall hear such tidings as shall rehabilitate your fallen prophet and show that he has not neglected to lay snares in the way of his enemies."

Evelyn's voice rang out in a peal of laughter. "You are a thousand times too provoking, Mr. Vansittart. But I will have patience. I have never lost confidence in you. But sometimes pride needs chastening by a pretence of doubt. But, come, tell me now what you were thinking of when I so rudely interrupted you at first?"

Jerome gazed for a moment at a book he had been holding in his hand. "Well, to speak the truth, on this momentous day of all days, I was thinking of the Derby."

"Of the Derby?"

"Certainly. It is my one ambition to win it.

> 'For crowns and empires strive let other folks,
> But let *me* win the Derby or the Oaks!'

"There! My enthusiasm has led me to drop into original poetry! They are my first verses," he added modestly.

"And how are you going to set about it?"

"Very simply. You shall decide it yourself. You see this book? It contains a full list of all the two-year-olds entered. Now I want you to run your eye over it, and pick out a horse whose name strikes your fancy."

Evelyn took the paper and carefully perused it. Suddenly she stopped.

"Here it is! Of course! Victor! Could any name be more appropriate for a horse of yours?"

Vansittart slightly colored.

"Then Victor it shall be. I will send Dick over to buy him, and he shall run next year. And, with you as sponsor, Miss Harland, we shall be sure of the race."

Now, remarkable as it may seem, Dick Harland had been sitting in perfect oblivion of the world, smoking his pipe and puffing great clouds of smoke at the insects on the vine. He had not heard a word of all this conversation. He was too far off if he had tried. And yet is it that when certain subjects to which our whole soul responds are mentioned there comes a miraculous acuteness of ear, or is it from some other deep psychological cause? In any case, at the instant Jerome spoke of the Derby and the Oaks, Dick became alert: when Victor was mentioned, his pipe dropped from his lips: and when his visit to England came on the *tapis*, he suddenly rose and came to his friend.

"Right you are, Jerry, my boy!" he exclaimed jubilantly. "It's better than a thousand of your Saharas. We'll have the finest horse in England, keep him dark, and win a pot of money. I'm off as soon as you like."

"Telegram, sir!" It was a footman who had interrupted. He had entered the closed-in verandah unheard, with a silver tray in his hand. Jerome did not show the faintest sign of emotion as he opened the envelope and took out the message. He mastered its contents in a moment, and then, rising, addressed his companions calmly but seriously:

"You shall hear what my friends in Paris have been doing this afternoon," he said. "'The Request rejected by 286 votes. De Tournon triumphant, and carried home with acclamation. Paris excited and tumultuous. Yet possibility of reaction. Quieter citizens doubtful. A strong move will save all.—LIANCOURT.'

"You hear? That is how France regards this precious scheme which is to add a new glory to her empire!"

Dick clenched his fists, and looked as if he would like to take on the whole Chamber *en masse*. Evelyn glanced at Jerome with a pained expression of sympathy which quite touched his heart. He took her hand gently.

"Do not be troubled, Miss Harland," he said, and the strong, victorious light came into his eyes, whilst all his languor passed away in a flash. "This vote has not shaken the faintest scaffolding of my great undertaking. But it has ruined, irretrievably and for ever, the man who has worked this evil! To-morrow a bomb will fall on Paris which will sweep my enemies into everlasting destruction!"

CHAPTER XIX

DE TOURNON'S DOWNFALL

THE Bourse at Paris is outwardly far too respectable a place for those unseemly scenes which are said to disturb the ordinary progress of stock-broking. It is not unlike a church. An artist would admire it as a Greek temple, and the ordinary excursionist from London frequently mistakes it for the Madeleine. It is a noble building, surrounded by columns, and looks like a great haven of peace and thought and prayer.

Inside, however, it gives rise to no such illusions. The most extraordinary feeling of restlessness prevailed on the morning after M. de Tournon's great political *coup*. Nearly everyone was concerned in the affairs of the Sahara Company, and there was none who could doubt that the effect of yesterday's vote would be to send stock down to a very low point. It would mean ruin to many and financial sickness to all, and therefore there was the utmost concern expressed on the faces of the members of the Bourse as they flocked in at an unusually early hour. Indeed, as soon as the doors were opened, a crowd of members proceeded to discuss the situation. It was calculated that the net loss to investors by the unhappy event would amount to something like twenty millions sterling. It was not only the wealthy who would be affected by this reverse in the fortunes of the Company, but the whole people of France, in every city and every Province.

Agriculturalist, artisan, *ouvrier*—all who had patriotically invested their small earnings in this scheme for the aggrandizement of France would find half their capital swept ruthlessly away and the remainder jeopardized. No member of the Bourse had the hardihood to make a price for the stock. Fluctuations were likely to be too violent and far-reaching.

Much surprise therefore was expressed when it was observed that M. Motteville, who was well known as Vansittart's broker, mounted his rostrum, and, with a curious air of blended importance and grim satisfaction, rapped his desk sharply with a hammer.

A dead silence fell upon 'Change. The impatient audience felt that some announcement of extraordinary importance was about to be made.

"Gentlemen," said M. Motteville, "I have a brief but interesting statement to make. It refers to the vote taken in the Chamber yesterday afternoon. The effect of that vote would, in the common course of events, be to send down the shares of the Sahara Company with a run, and therefore it is imperative that I impart the information I have for you before business is entered upon to-day. The Request made to the Chamber was that an issue of debenture shares should be sanctioned. The deputies have refused that Request. I am directed by Mr. Vansittart to state that he has given to the Company one milliard of francs (forty millions sterling), which will not be repaid until the ordinary stock shows a ten per cent. dividend. For this immense sum he absolutely demands no security. This, gentlemen, he does, because he has no need of mere confidence in the great Sahara Scheme. The first year's work will prove its practicability beyond all doubt. He further hopes by this act to place the Company beyond the reach of political intriguers and the schemes of petty tricksters. I am also authorized to add, not exactly so explicitly as I have hitherto spoken, but still with confidence, that Mr. Vansittart is prepared to make a second advance of a milliard of francs if necessary. In fact, he regards the scheme itself as so absolutely assured that he is ready at any moment, if called upon by the people of France, to take over the entire financial responsibility, and to purchase every share, wheresoever owned, at par. This, of course, he hopes he need not be compelled to do, because he trusts that the Sahara development will remain the scheme of France, and not the scheme of an individual."

The intense silence, which had become almost painful whilst these remarks fell from the lips of M. Motteville, now gave place to a scene of indescribable commotion. It was observed by a very old member of the House that never in his recollection, not even during those terrible days that preceded the Franco-German war, had he seen or heard such excitement, such absolute confusion, such clatter of tongues as upon this occasion.

For Jerome had cleared the air in the masterful way peculiar to himself. He had refused to relieve the situation when the Chamber was asked to express its opinion. He had permitted his enemies to rush into headlong destruction. And now that they were already putting forth their hands to grasp the fruit of victory, by a few outspoken words through the lips of another he had overwhelmed them.

What was the immediate effect of this announcement? Instead of falling to 80, Sahara stock immediately rose to 105. It advanced five points instead of dropping twenty! And, what was more, there seemed every likelihood of a still further advance being made, for it was clear that with such personal undertaking as Jerome had made, there would be a new rush in city and country, at home and abroad, for shares.

There was one man in the Bourse who felt extremely happy. He wore a look of infinite relief. He was wiping with his handkerchief great beads of perspiration that stood out upon his forehead, and his hand shook as he drew to himself a chair and sank helplessly into it. It was M. Bulbère, de Tournon's broker.

For when he had sold the shares which M. de Tournon had instructed him to sell, the deal ran thus: de Tournon sold the £1,000,000 worth of shares at par, 100. He was certain of buying them in at 80. And thus what he sold for £1,000,000 he could deliver for £800,000, with a clear gain of £200,000 to himself, if things had gone as he had hoped and planned. But as the case now stood, he had already lost, in the few minutes since the Bourse opened, £50,000. Nor was this all. How would matters stand at settling day?

From all his experience, M. Bulbère was confident that the stock would go steadily up, and probably at the end of the account, would read something like 120. If so, M. de Tournon would lose nearly £200,000. Could de Tournon pay this enormous sum? Bulbère, who knew his distinguished client well, had watched his progress from poverty to notoriety, from notoriety to Parliament, from Parliament to the Cabinet. He knew that de Tournon was one of those needy politicians who have to live a menial life getting what they can and spending what they get. With his recent expenses, it was doubtful whether de Tournon had 200,000 sous.

And in that case this terrible loss would have fallen upon the shoulders of Bulbère, and this reputable and honorable man, who never took up a responsibility which he could not fulfil, would have paid the money, and in his old age have retired to squalid poverty. Were it not for the extraordinary offer made to him by M. Liancourt, by which Vansittart generously proposed to pay current market rates for the stock, he would have been ruined. He saw it clearly now, and he also still more clearly saw that it would be his duty, nay, his pleasure, to turn in unmitigated wrath against the scoundrel who would have betrayed him. With the terrible weapon that he had in his hand he must ruin M. de Tournon.

The news flew through Paris like wild-fire. "Vansittart has subscribed the money!" shouted some of the people as they raced about. "It's all right with the Company. Hurrah for Vansittart. Long live Jerome the First!" The change was sudden. But how sudden the revelation!

When such indescribable proofs as these were given by Vansittart of his honor, his integrity, and his generosity, how was it possible to harbor those ill-begotten slanders, those miserable lies, those trumped-up stories, which, having no basis, burst bubble-like into fragments as soon as they rubbed up against a solid substance? There was no resisting this great important Fact. The moment he was accused of desiring to drain the life of France, Vansittart had, from his own pocket, subscribed a sum beyond the dreams of shareholders, under conditions that seemed mad in their liberality. If there is one thing that Frenchmen are subject to, it is the emotion of gratitude. And the cleverly worked stratagems of the preceding week only intensified a thousand-fold the feelings which Vansittart's dramatic offer had aroused.

And what still further helped to convert the Parisians was a proclamation Jerome himself made to them. For, about ten o'clock in the morning, those who were walking to and fro in the streets were surprised to see an army of bill-stickers posting in all effective points a huge placard arranged in large type. It was an appeal from Jerome K. Vansittart to the People of France.

It reminded them that the enormous undertaking in the Sahara was solely for the glory of the French people and the extension of their dominions. It was not a scheme of personal aggrandizement. Was there anything in the original proposal which had not been faithfully carried out to the present moment? Nay, was not even the Request, so readily thrown out by the deputies, plainly foreshadowed three months back?

Then Jerome went on:

"Men of France, this project of ours has its enemies at headquarters—enemies who hold high position and seek to make use of it for their own selfish gains and their own political ambition. They have lied, they have deceived, they have bribed, they have tried to seduce you from your loyalty to your own country and its eternal interests; and now they have succeeded in getting your popular representatives to turn against the Sahara Company, to cast a slur upon the Scheme, and to put its fortunes into extreme peril.

"Your new colony is on a fair way to realization, but it has been nearly lost within the last week owing to the dastardly action of some of your statesmen. I call upon you to take the punishment of these men into your own hands, and I ask you to proclaim loudly, once and for all, whether or not your own Government is to fight against your colony, and whether those who are promoting its interests are to be the victims of its spleen and its envy.

"If you make this clearly understood, I promise you that all will go well, and that in a few years' time you will rejoice in a second France in Africa."

There were those afterwards who wondered whether Vansittart was thoroughly acquainted with the characteristics of the people he addressed, when he wrote those last stirring words, and summoned them to take vengeance upon the evil-doers. Such an invitation is never declined in Paris. The natural impulse of the French spirit needs little incitement of such sort to rush into the wildest extravagance of fury.

But Vansittart was true to the word he had spoken. When he struck, he struck hard and true. He was determined to get rid of de Tournon. As the day wore on, the proclamation sank into the hearts of the people, and from far and wide might be observed the growing of the storm, the ominous foreshadowing of a tempest that threatened to overwhelm the whole city.

The instrument of Vansittart's wrath was ready to his hand. Dark masses of men crowded together in angry mood at various points. With that strange unanimity of purpose that seems to grow from chaos, they gathered unconsciously as if in obedience to a common instinct. There soon appeared to be a settled and steady movement towards one locality. Half unknowing what they did, the mob surged in the direction of the offices of the Interior.

De Tournon was in his room. He was sitting before a littered table, his head upon his hand, his eyes wild, his face haggard, and his hair dishevelled. He had the aspect of a man whom ruin of the bitterest sort stares in the face. He was glancing at a note he had received from his broker.

"Curse him! Curse him! Curse him!" he cried a dozen times. "Vansittart has the resources of the devil! There is but a week, and in that time what can I do? A week! and I am ruined, disgraced!"

He covered his face with his hands. This bitter man could have wept. His carefully built structure of ambition was toppling towards irretrievable destruction.

"Will you sell now, or will you wait till settling day?" was the question of his broker, for Sahara stock at 3 P.M. was 105.

Should he get rid of his bargain now, he would lose £50,000, and, with a faint smile of savage cynicism, de Tournon reflected that he could no more clear this sum than he could clear the National Debt of France. Well, should he wait? Aye, and wait for what? For the shares to rise? Was there doubt of that? The American's power was now unbounded, and as the country began to read and hear, what would become of the stock? De Tournon knew not to what fabulous figure it might attain within a week. Yet where a man's case is desperate, even a desperate hope may be clung to. To sell now was to embrace ruin with open arms; to wait was still to cling to some phantom of hope, some faint shadow which might by a miracle become a real thing.

Ruin! Disgrace! Yes, and that not all. For what of his

political position? De Tournon shivered as he thought that this too was gone, that he must resign all his offices to escape the public degradation called forth by the financial intrigue so ruthlessly exposed. Fool that he was, he had struggled with a giant who had played with him as with the feebleness of a child. He found, too late, that the first strong grip of his opponent had choked him. In that supreme moment de Tournon resolved to murder Vansittart.

Thus deep in meditation, he heard nothing of the strange tumult which was growing in ever-increasing gusts of subdued passion along the Rue du Faubourg Saint Honoré. It was like the growl of a coming storm, a terrible, incoherent sound which had nothing human in it; or if there were aught of human, it was of men who had laid aside their humanity and fallen back to the uncontrolled passions of the brute.

This terrible roar is known in Paris. It means death!

It swept along the street, grew into a majestic volume, and were not de Tournon so deeply immersed in his distracting thoughts, his quick sense would have gathered that the Parisians were surrounding the offices of the minister on all available sides.

The staff must have become frightened and fled, for no one approached him. It was only when a loud noise fell upon his ears, as of the bursting of men in wild riot into a corridor hard by, that he started to his feet, and in a moment realized his terrible and unexpected danger.

"It wanted but this," he cried, as he staggered across the room, and with difficulty locked the door.

He paused. Which way would they go? He knew his countrymen too well; they would not be likely to leave open many avenues of escape.

It was fortunate for him that the wild multitude seemed not to be aware of the location of de Tournon's private apartments, or his hesitation might have been fatal. It was enough that he now heard powerful blows against his door.

He turned and fled towards another exit, where for a little time he could not make the key turn in the long disused lock. He had got the door open when a burly *ouvrier* burst into his room, rushed across with savage menace, and, raising a stout cudgel, attempted to brain the helpless minister.

Luckily for his victim, as the man reached the door he slipped on the polished floor. With a cry de Tournon wrested the weapon from his grasp and brought it down with a crash upon his head. The Frenchman sank back stunned. What savage unaccountable instinct was it that made de Tournon strike again and again upon his fallen assailant? Perhaps some symbolic outburst of fury led him thus to express his hatred of all his enemies, for he literally smashed the man's skull to pulp.

With the glistening tokens of fear and horror upon his brow, for a moment he stood, and then a thought struck him. There was one means of escape which he was certain none of the avengers would know. Darting forward, he groped his way through ill-lit rooms and winding passages, getting lower and lower until he gained the cellars of the house, and then, through further tortuous windings, he reached the end of a passage, dug by somebody long years ago, which brought him to a point beneath the garden and to a little grating which the observer would take to be a mere sanitary appliance. Prising this open with difficulty, de Tournon dragged himself into daylight.

Then, after a fearful look round, he slipped into the Rue de Cambacérès.

His difficulties, he knew, had only begun. He must escape detection. He had to cross the busiest part of Paris, and it was folly to think of going to his own house. The day, however, was a dull one, evening was drawing on, and he managed, in an obscure street, to secure a cab, the driver of which was much puzzled by the winding route selected by his fare. De Tournon's sole thought now was to be revenged upon Vansittart, so he resolved, with the calmness of despair, at once to take the first steps towards trapping his victim.

An hour elapsed before he was set down in the Rue d' Allemagne. Dismissing his *voiture*, he waited till it had disappeared. Then he hurried quickly up the street, pushed open the door of a dingy, dirty-looking hovel of a shop which contained nothing that man or beast might want, and disappeared.

De Tournon did not know that the ever-watchful ex-Prefect of Police was still upon his track. M. Folliet was not unacquainted with that dark exit from the minister's office. What was there in Paris he did not know? And he had waited patiently to see his enemy appear.

He was startled when he noted what manner of habitation the minister entered.

"What!" he exclaimed to himself, "you have changed your weapons then! From high finance and political intrigue, you descend to the companionship of String-the-Neck and his crew! I have not yet seen the last of you!"

CHAPTER XX

SOME ROYALTIES—AND OTHERS

THE afternoon had well advanced when Mlle. de Montpensier and her companion arrived at the beautiful forest of Fontainebleau. The sun, slanting through trees which seemed to blend together in such amorous embrace that in many cases they had actually become entwined, struck shafts of light across the path and gave to the beautiful avenues a soft and subdued tone inexpressibly tender. There is no other forest which has been so marked out by Nature as the resting-place of romance. It is as though, flying from the crude tracts of civilization, she had taken refuge here.

But neither of the two ladies paused to contemplate the scene, nor could they be lured by pressing guides or tempted by promises of strange adventures. With their faces closely hidden in their cloaks, they stole along half-frightened and fearful of discovery. Turning from the beaten track, they made their way through a difficult passage barred by bough and rock to an arbor naturally formed by overhanging trees, whose leaves swept down and bore almost to the earth. Within, some enterprising hermit long years ago had built a seat, and so a little grotto was formed which might have served as a wayside temple to one of the dryads of the woods. Here the pious Pagan, on his way to some civic feast, would pause and pray.

When the ladies entered, a young man, slightly built and of the average height, pale, delicate, yet with a certain nobility of face, and eyes that seemed to flash authority when they burned with the passion of a masterful purpose, sprang up and hastened to meet them. He gave a cry of joy, and led them through to the back of the shrine.

"You have come, Honorine. Then you have not forgotten me? What I have heard is false?" he cried, looking at her with eager eyes and still holding her hand within his own, which burned feverishly. Honorine was pale, and she shuddered as she replied:

"You are too rash, Henri; you have no right here. You are in danger. What will happen if they arrest you? You will undo all by your daring, and gain nothing."

"And is this all the welcome you have to give me—you who fill my soul with longing?" replied the other.

"There need be no idle words between us. Our destinies are knit too closely together. But you must go. I have come to tell you that this is not the time for sentimental passages. You will ruin all."

"What? Have you forgotten our compact? Are we no longer allies?" he asked bitterly.

"Allies, yes, dear friend," replied Honorine softly. "But you, Henri, ask more than that. It is not fair. You will ruin France."

"I ask more?" cried Henri.

Honorine took from her pocket a letter. "I wept when I read this to-day. But it was not for joy; it was for sorrow, for I saw that you could not sacrifice your headstrong temper to our great purpose. You speak to me in language you have no right to use. That was not our compact, Henri. I should not have come here. I am in danger, but I have come to tell you that you must not speak like that again—that you dishonor yourself."

"Dishonor!" cried Henri. "Dishonor! You say that to me? I, the heir of France. Nay," he added, drawing himself up to his full height, which was not a great deal, "I may say the King."

Honorine smiled. "Now I like you better, Henri. Yes, the King always, but may I suggest that you should speak and act like a king. You make my duty difficult beyond bearing. You wrong me, you persecute me. Yes, you make my life bitter, for you—you of all men—tremble on the verge of treachery, and in your passion beat down all bonds."

"But I love you, Honorine," cried Henri. "You know it."

"Then," replied Honorine, "keep your secret to yourself, for I can never return your love. You are breaking your whole compact by addressing your vows to me."

"What! exclaimed Henri in consternation and amazement. "You say that you cannot love me! Where is your sacred vow, and what has come to you? Tell me, then, what it was that you have sworn to me—here, in this forest of Fontainebleau?"

"I have sworn," replied Honorine proudly, "to give my hand to the King of France. I can never give it to Henri of Navarre, and when Henri of Navarre presses me with his suit, he dishonors the King of France."

Henri looked upon her with a certain pride. This vehement answer displayed the dignified and noble nature of the woman he loved.

"I, too," went on Honorine, "am working and scheming, wondering and hoping. I, too, am looking forward to the bright day when France will become herself once more. And I, the weak, the impotent—I, who can arm so few, am to be impeded, and baffled, and thwarted by one who says he loves me. You, Henri, have yet to win the throne of France. Till then, you have sworn to be no more than an ally. No word of affection has fallen from my lips, for I love and can love no man but the King of France, and whilst you break your sacred compact, you teach me how easy it is to regard a friend as at last an enemy."

Henri flushed beneath this vigorous attack. He bowed his head.

"Mademoiselle," he said humbly, "I am wrong. I am too reckless, and I do not reflect. But I love you so, and I have felt, as a youth must feel, that love gives strength and makes the battle easy."

"Ah, yes," replied Honorine more gently. "If it is for self we are fighting. But it is that you may become king or that I may become queen that we are struggling. It is that the royal throne of France once more may be occupied by one who has a claim."

"And yet," broke in Henri, "this American, who is your friend—what is he doing? What means this alliance of yours with him? I hear such strange news that my ears can scarce believe it. There is something afoot, Honorine, and you are behind it. Am I, then, to be left in the cold, and to have no share?"

"Henri," replied the other, "we have sworn to trust each other. Will you now begin to suspect me? Whatever there may be afoot, and whatsoever little I may know of it, I have sworn complete and absolute secrecy, and secrecy is essential to its success. Yes, Henri, to tell you even would be a dishonor not to be borne. I take your hand in mine, and I swear as I swore before, that I will give my hand to no one who does not wear the crown of France. But do not forget, Henri, that whoever mounts those sacred steps must have won them himself. Whoever he may be, if he have claimed and deserved it, I will wed him and no other."

Henri raised her hand to his lips and kissed it with reverence. "I can plead no other condition, Honorine, and I am content. We are for the cause and not for ourselves."

"And now," said Honorine, "you must go away. There are strange doings in Paris, and I have come to warn you. You will help France most if you keep from danger. I shall regard you best, Henri, whilst you keep your word. Don't make me unhappy by throwing your head into the noose, and that is what you are doing each time you come like this disguised to France."

Henri pledged himself to leave France immediately. Subdued and thoughtful, he gravely accompanied the two ladies to the pathway. When they had gone out of sight he sat upon a boulder, and a look of infinite sadness came into his eyes.

"Who am I to win a crown?" he cried. "The woman I love will marry him who gains the crown of France, and I, poor, weak, unstable creature, how dare I to raise my eyes to that which powerful kings and warriors would strive for?" He rose and betook himself eastward through the forest.

As he did so two men crept from their place of concealment near the arbor and hastened towards the village.

. . . .

The house into which de Tournon precipitately entered when he escaped from the Paris mob was in one of the dingiest quarters of the city. The shop itself reeked of stale biscuits and of bad brandy. It seemed that no one was ever called upon to attend to customers. The reason was because no customers ever entered. The few relics of a past stock might well have counted their existence since the days of the Revolution, if one were guided by the historical smell which they gave forth.

But de Tournon did not pause to note the peculiarities of the repulsive den. Stamping on a trap door in the corner, and giving certain curious taps, he waited, with such patience as he could summon, for it to be opened.

At last it slowly moved, and a repulsive head made its appearance, a head that might have suited Milton's Comus, or have been evolved from the palette of some degenerate painter of the second period of Greek art. Across the forehead was a scar which had come from a gash so deep that it seemed even now to be a ruddy valley stretching through a dreary morass. The eyes were bloodshot and bleared, and one half of the nose had disappeared, evidently many years ago. To add to the horror of the man's appearance, his mouth had been obligingly split by some antagonist. Its shape would have suited those patrons of the dining-table who find difficulty in consuming all that their hearts desire, for it effected a downward path towards the throat.

To de Tournon the face was evidently familiar, for it did not produce a particular impression upon him, and he slowly put his foot upon the step and followed the guide, who, having recognized him, had held up three fingers, either because the sign signified some secret warning, or because he had not a fourth. The ladder was a long one, the cellar deep, and there at first appeared no light to show to what cavernous depths the two men were descending.

As they reached the bottom the passage took a quick turn, and displayed a large irregularly constructed chamber, which might more accurately be described as a cavern, for it seemed to be hewn out of the earth itself, with no regard to shape. Four huge rough beams supported the roof, and in the corner a small wood fire glimmering forth revealed gaunt walls that were simply damp earth. The floor was uneven, and rendered progress more difficult by reason of a hundred repulsive objects which had been cast away carelessly and never removed.

Close to the fire, sitting before a small table, were three men. Few Parisians had seen them, and yet they were three of the most famous men in France. They were the *doyens* of all that was most depraved, terrible, and bloody in roguery and in crime. Day by day they sat in such unwholesome places prepared to fight for life, should the avenues of escape they had prepared fail them. By night they did their work with such despatch, such secrecy, such certainty, that they became mere living nonentities, shadows, abstractions, which took upon themselves at times the worst powers of human beings.

The one to the right rejoiced in the name of "String-the-Neck," because of a cumbrous but diabolical method of taking human life he had invented, whilst he was still sufficiently unknown to the police to be able to live openly in a little house in Belleville. His victim, lured in, would be plied with drink, and retired to bed for sleep, when String-the-Neck, through a small aperture skilfully concealed in the ceiling, would drop a stout rope. An accomplice, who had crept behind the bed, would tenderly lift the victim's head into the noose, and then, with the help of a windlass, the ingenious murderer would drag by the neck the unhappy being to the ceiling till he was choked. String-the-Neck boasted of thirty who had experienced this novel form of death. This scoundrel's left ear had been cut off close to the skull during some midnight affray.

The man opposite, a dark, heavy-set ruffian, with a most unintelligent look, and eyes that seemed insatiate with blood, was called the Gouger, for reasons which were only too appropriate. He was not content with simple murder. He loved to make it intricate, and when he had slain his victim he would strike out the eyes and rip the body until the mad passion of his bestial thirst for the mutilation of human flesh was cooled by the fear of capture.

The third occupant was sitting with his back to the fire, and he, as de Tournon entered, seemed to be fast asleep, and the occasional twitches of his face appeared to suggest unconscious shuddering at the recollection of a crime.

He was a born leader of villainy. He rarely spoke. His eyes flashed in a manner which none could resist. His form, burly and muscular, was strong as an oak. His great head was like a cannon-ball that had been battered against rocks. The lofty brow might have suggested intellect, were it not pitted with the marks of small-pox; and his figure, though not without some grace of movement, was remarkable for the fact that the left shoulder drooped some four inches below the right. He was the embodiment of animal strength, a silent, inexplicable man, from whom no word came unnecessarily, whom no power had ever turned from his purpose.

He had slain his own family whilst barely a youth—father, mother, brother, and sister—hindrances to the possession of such small property as they owned. Since then his career in murder was unparalleled and incredible. His favorite method was that of the garrote, and, having no consideration for life, and burthened by no sense of remorse, he would garrote a child for a cake if he were hungry. He was even known to turn upon a crippled pauper as though for amusement, and skilfully closing both nose and mouth, he would leave the wretch to die in five minutes in some deserted nook of the great city.

He was feared as no Mahratta chief was feared, and yet he was safe, for his movements were so canny that no evidence could be laid to his charge, nor was he ever detected in a criminal act. If he suspected any of his associates, his days were numbered. They *died swiftly and secretly.* He boasted of hundreds of such victims, and he cared not. To him the taking of life was a form only of recreation, a method of passing the time. Even his companions dreaded him, and never knew when his terrible eye might be turned upon themselves. It might be wondered why they did not strive to rend the man they hated, were it not that their terror of him surpassed their courage. But it was they who had given him his name, and it seemed bitterly true. He was called the Plasterer.

These were the men whom de Tournon had come to visit. They were scoundrels whom he had met in that shady past of his he was so anxious to forget, and which had now rushed back upon him with demoniac swiftness. They were members of the gang he had employed for many purposes, for the Minister of the Interior rested his power upon that low, base, infamous part of the population, not so numerous as audacious, whose very appearance was calculated to produce a strong impression upon a frightened city.

The minister had now joined his accomplices. The two men rose to greet him, but the Plasterer did not rouse himself from his sullen stupor, though he raised his glass to his lips and drained it to the dregs. As de Tournon looked round the chamber, an expression of disgust came into his face.

"I have work for you," he said, "work that will bring you more money than you have yet earned, work which only men like you can do, and for which only men like me can pay. You will be under my direction for three months. I will pay you each week, and you must be ready at a moment's notice to obey me."

He stopped, his nausea overcoming his discretion.

"Why have you moved to this vile hole?" he said, glancing round the reeking, unwholesome place. The Plasterer raised his head, and a sneer came from his lips.

"This is not a fitting spot for gentlemen," he said slowly. "But we don't entertain cabinet ministers too often, you know."

De Tournon turned sharply upon him. "Keep your sneers for your companions, if you please," he cried in a tone of command, "and don't forget that you are my servant. It will please me to hear you speak when you have something of interest to say."

The Plasterer waved his hand and scowled. "I don't speak too often," he said, still in the same slow tones. "Sometimes I act, then no one is my master."

"Come, come," cried the Gouger. "It is but civil to show M. de Tournon our discovery. There is an excellent reason for our removal. Our last quarters were small, and they became known. Besides, they looked mysterious had a visitor come. Come with me, and I will show you something."

De Tournon followed him across the room, and in a corner he saw a passage, hewn out of the earth, extending some thirty feet inwards and narrowing down to a height of about three feet. At the farther end his guide threw aside an impediment that barred the way. They crept through and found themselves suddenly in a frightful place. De Tournon stepped back with a cry of horror.

"It is a sewer!" he exclaimed.

"Yes," calmly replied the other, "it is a short arm of the main sewer. It is visited irregularly, and, anyhow, it is easy to hear the patrol go by. Then, you know, monsieur, it is pleasant to be able to bring a guest here if he be troublesome after a joyous evening, and throw his body downward. Really, it is murder made easy. It is a game for children."

De Tournon frowned. "Let me get out," he cried. "This place makes me faint: to what lengths will your crimes go? You are not men!"

"Men!" cried the Gouger. "Well, well, it is as the times go. Now the purse is lean, and now it is fat. There are bad fortune and success, and we follow the tide of fashion as women do. Just now we are lean enough. It will no doubt cheer even the Plasterer if you were to make some slight advance upon what you promised us."

De Tournon, who by this time felt as though he would faint, promised readily. Sitting down at a table, he drank a small glass of brandy to steady his nerves. Then he carefully discussed a project with his weird associates, and, though details were wanting, it was determined from the outset that the death of Vansittart was the chief object to be aimed at.

CHAPTER XXI

THE RIVALS

SWIFTLY the weeks flew by, and the second gay season of Paris had already opened its winter hospitality to foreign guests. The brilliant salons of the capital were filled with the wit and eloquence of all nations, and having shown how effervescent and beautifully pert she can be in May and June, Paris proudly demonstrated to the world how she could find within herself, despite inclement weather, the resources and the delicacies of refined pleasures. Vansittart was little to be seen in the glittering whirl of society, for he was now away in his palace of Saint Cloud, which had risen like magic over the ruins of this ancient abode of kings.

The large and graceful building, in which splendor blended with domestic comfort, stood proudly serene upon the height that looks down on the park of Saint Cloud and away to the glorious forest of trees which the Parisian *bourgeois* loves so dearly, and where his fêtes seem so much brighter and gayer than elsewhere. There was nothing of the awe-inspiring in its architecture. Dick Harland was heard to say that it might have have been taken for an English country house, "if it had not too much of the feudal castle about it."

Vansittart laughed. "We blend comfort with security," he replied. "It is a home that could be made into a fortress at a moment's notice."

"Just like your American ideas," exclaimed Dick.

"Turn a screw, and you convert a comfortable palace into a grain elevator, or lift a lever, and it becomes a picture gallery, but I must say that it is one of the most delightfully jolly places I have ever stayed at in my life."

A little way to the east was a pretty bijou residence decorated in the French Renaissance style, and surrounded by a garden that was full of flowers; a dainty, delicate structure —a mere bon-bon, as it were—and in this dwelt Mlle. de Montpensier and her companion.

But to-day Vansittart had gathered for that domestic institution which he could not forego, "English afternoon tea," the whole of his "cabinet," as he called them, and the two French ladies had walked through the park to join Jerome, Dick Harland, and his sister in the drawing-room.

When they arrived, Vansittart was gazing contentedly at his surroundings, with a comfortable air, as though he had reached that state of mind which left nothing to be desired.

"I don't know how the old kings stood it," he said. "Saint Cloud could not have been the place of comfort it is now when Louis the Fourteenth used to prowl about dark passages and Louis the Sixteenth tried to keep up vain appearances of strength. Personally, I should not care to be constantly slipping over polished floors, and going to sleep with the courtiers looking on, and eating before a few hundred spectators. That is not to be the rule of Saint Cloud now. Imagine the promiscuity of the kingly life in those days when the monarch could not sneeze without the intervention of a state officer, and when, if he wanted to be absolutely alone, he had to hide himself behind a curtain. How would you like all this formality, mademoiselle?" and he turned to the Princess.

A flush came into her cheeks, and she drew herself up with an air of dignity. "It is a matter of blood, perhaps," she said, "and to some people freedom is not a luxury. If I were queen I would obey the laws of my station. A queen is not a private person."

What!" exclaimed Vansittart. "Is that your notion? L'état c'est moi?"

Honorine smiled. "At least the queen is an order to herself," she replied.

"Ah, yes," retorted Jerome. "How willingly women give of their heart's blood for this terrible ceremony, and endure the dreadful torture of a wearing and ceaseless Court etiquette. What stories the Escorial would relate if its dark corridors could speak, of bright young queens who have entered proudly and pined to death in the suffocating atmosphere of that dreadful prison—who have been choked by the pressure of that grim and terrible state decorum which yields no hope, allows no private authority which checks the manner, the thought, the speech, the dress even, of a king or a queen, and permits no wayward shadow to pass over the cheek unrecognized. Well, those days are past, and yet to-day we have dangers not less to be avoided. The royal state asks the greatest sacrifice a man can give. He must surrender his independence! Surely," he exclaimed, turning to Evelyn, "you don't agree with mademoiselle? How would you care to be a queen?"

"A queen?" she answered. "I? Never! To be a queen, and to do one's duty properly, requires the training of a slave. She must accustom herself to the rigid and unalterable succession of the same tedious routine. What is the difference between the fates of a queen and a slave under such conditions, save in the matter of food and clothes?"

"Well," laughed Vansittart, "there seems to be some difference, that is all. To be supreme—that is the one ambition of the world. But alas! we spend our dearest coin in the struggle, and when we reach the top, behold! our wealth is gone. We are already poor in everything that is worth anything at all."

"Well," put in Dick, "I would not mind trying for a year or two, if only to keep a capital stable. It is said that Royalty has a good chance of winning the Derby now-adays."

There was a general laugh—and Vansittart exclaimed:
"Why, Dick, if you were king, you would hold your court in the mews, and you would appoint your best jockey Prime Minister."

"So you would not be a queen?" he repeated, turning again to Evelyn.

Evelyn colored: "Yes, where best a woman can reign."

"And that is?"

"To rule her husband's heart."

"All very sentimental," exclaimed Dick. "I have often heard of the chatter of afternoon tea, and if this is a sample, I think I had better keep to my whiskey and soda in the study, only I wanted to bring you a letter that had just come, Jerry, and, of course, I forgot it as soon as I entered the room."

Vansittart took it and opened it. He read it carefully twice. "Do you remember the name Beaulieu?" he said turning to Dick.

Dick thought a while. "Why, yes," he answered. "Surely that is the man of whom Bates told us. He knocked an Arab's scimitar aside when he was making for you that last day, you remember?"

"Yes," answered Vansittart thoughtfully, "I remember. I merely wanted corroboration." He looked grave as he spoke, and appeared troubled.

"Anything up?" asked Dick.

"Nothing of any consequence."

Dick's face became clouded also. "I wish you had not sent Folliet away," he said earnestly, and putting his arm affectionately upon his friend's shoulder. "Do you know, old chap, I feel much safer when he is around. The fellow seems to know everything, and you can never tell when the coast is clear."

"Yes," agreed Vansittart almost reluctantly, "but what could I do? There were some matters of the most pressing importance in London, which only a man like Folliet could deal with. Never mind, Dick, cheer up. If the hour has come when Jerome K. Vansittart depends for his career on the presence in Paris of a prefect of police, I think it is about time he retired from the business."

He was going to say more when a strange interruption occurred which threw everything into confusion. The door opened with more violence than was usual, and there entered the room a well-groomed, well-dressed young French gentleman, holding in his hands an immaculate silk hat and a pair of lavender kid gloves. Behind him could be seen the panting form of a footman, whose quick breathing betokened that he must have been pushed aside imperiously, and had followed in vain to announce this singular intruder.

As the new-comer entered, Honorine cast one glance at him, then cried, " Henri, you ! How dare you ? What do you here ? " She rose imperiously to her feet, and gazed at him in the wrath of unutterable dread.

Vansittart had also risen and stood quietly by, for the vehemence of his uninvited guest admitted of no interference.

" I have found you, Honorine," the Prince replied with stifled excitement. " I have searched for days, and none could tell me where you were."

" What ? " and her voice rang scornfully out—" You perjure yourself once more ? You again break your sacred compact ? Away ! Away ! You teach me to hate you."

" No, no," cried Henri impulsively, and made one step in advance. " You wrong me, Honorine. I am free."

" Free ! " exclaimed the Princess.

" My proscription has been withdrawn. I am no longer the hunted outlaw. I can walk the streets of Paris. I have broken no compact."

" But this intrusion," she cried vehemently, " what of that ? What right have you thus to violate the laws of courtesy and civility ? Do you think I would speak to you here ? " and the blood rose to her brow in the fury of her indignation.

Vansittart got his chance. Henri had turned pale. Falling a little back he leant his arm upon the door for support. At this, with perfect suavity, Jerome approached the visitor, and said, "I perceive, sir, that some little emotion on your part has occasioned a slight informality that had better now be removed. I am your host, and will gladly exchange names. I had not the honor of a formal announcement."

Henri looked curiously upon this singularly cool man, whose face betrayed no interest in the strange scene which had occurred, and who approached him with all the dignity and self-possession of a born courtier. This, he knew, was the great Vansittart, and he felt instinctively that this was the man against whom he might have to measure himself. Why, he knew not, but as he gazed upon his host, it was partly with fear, partly with hatred, partly with wonder.

He had paused a little, and then, recovering himself, found it impossible to do anything but bend to the stern will of the American. He said :

"I, monsieur, am Prince Henri de Navarre."

Vansittart bowed. "I am delighted to meet you, monsieur, and to inform you that I am Jerome K. Vansittart, late of New York, and now of Paris. It will be clear to you, sir, that something has occurred to disturb the ladies here, and we will, I think, leave them to recover. Meanwhile, I have some excellent engravings in my study, which I should like to show you, if you care for these trifles in modern art?"

Jerome slipped his arm through that of Henri, and the other, unwilling to go, yet unable to resist the mastership of this strange being, walked gravely out of the room with him.

But they saw no engravings.

When they reached the study, Henri, tearing himself away a little impatiently from his host, walked over to the window, and then turned upon him. "I addressed myself to you, sir, as Henri de Navarre," he said with great hauteur.

Vansittart nodded assent. "Pray sit down," he said.

"But I wish to explain, sir——"

"Come, come," said Jerome, "I must really insist upon a host's privilege, and beg you to sit down." With a scowl Henri obeyed the imperative tone that gave insistence to the request.

"You were about to explain, I think," continued Jerome, "that your name was not Henri de Navarre."

"No, sir," replied the Prince, who flushed slowly; "but I would have you know, for it is necessary in order to explain my intrusion here, that I am heir to the throne of France. Nay, that I may by all proper precedent regard myself as the ruler of this country."

"And a very beautiful country, indeed, it is!" exclaimed Jerome cheerfully. Henri looked sharply at his host. Was there a covert laugh in this remark, but Jerome's face was imperturbable.

"I am indeed honored," he said, "to meet one of your position, so distinguished for his many high virtues. The French throne is not literally occupied at present. I am a French subject myself, and if a new occupant came in my time, I assure you that no one would regard him with more respect, or fight more willingly for his interests, than I."

Henri bowed.

"If, indeed," continued Jerome, "tradition permits you to consider yourself already the King of France, do you require that I shall address you as 'Your Majesty,' or are we to disregard the striking fact for a moment in order that conversation may run smoothly on a more equal plane?"

Henri felt uncomfortable, and scarcely knew why.

"Sir," he answered, "I am content to claim at present nothing but my title, 'the Prince,' and you will understand perhaps how it is that, after a long proscription, on my return to Paris a free man, I have sought the ally of my destiny, the Princesse de Montpensier. She shares with me the unhappy fortune of being of royal blood, and is of standing far above me in regard to the succession were she not of the opposite sex."

"Your search for her," admitted Vansittart, "was natural. It ended successfully, if a little violently. But tell me, if I do not intrude upon your confidence—what caused the French Government thus to give back your liberty?"

"I am utterly puzzled," replied Henri. "The notice of withdrawal of the proscription reached me in England some days ago—a small parchment signed by the name of de Tournon."

"De Tournon!" exclaimed Vansittart. "Why, he has been out of the Cabinet for two months!"

"It is strange," agreed the Prince, "but there can be no doubt—there is no mistake—as I called yesterday upon M. Lacontel, the Minister for the Colonies, and he assured me that this paper was duly signed within the term of office of de Tournon, and if any one questioned it, he would himself present me with another warrant."

"Is that so," said Jerome calmly. "Obviously the change of policy is in the direction of mercy."

He spoke lightly, but his mind was rapidly revolving many things. It seemed clear to him that if this document signed by his enemy, possibly a day or two before his downfall, was permitted to be regarded as valid many weeks after, despite the disgrace of the minister, it must have been so sanctioned by others within the Cabinet who had the same motives as de Tournon. What could these motives be? Above all, who was the minister?

M. Lacontel, the Minister for the Colonies! He, no doubt, being better acquainted with the Sahara Scheme and all its winding operations, was therefore more jealous of one who in his own department outshone him, made him like unto a hired clerk, a mere cipher in the administration of his own office. For the man who was a Minister of the Colonies was as nothing to the man who made them. The motive?—that, too, seemed clear to him. This fiery, hot-headed young Frenchman, with his absurd claim to the throne, might be easily made a thorn in the side of an intruder who was likely to rise to too great a height in the affections of the people.

And his friendship with Honorine? There, again, no doubt lay some so far unrevealed complication which the presence of this young blood in Paris might render dangerous. Jerome looked with interest upon his visitor. His eye gathered in every detail of his features, and sought to enter his mind, in order to weigh every quality and faculty which he possessed. Had Henri of Navarre been the single factor in the struggle the American smiled at the thought that such a rival should have been chosen for him.

At length Vansittart spoke. "You will pardon me, Prince, but there is one point upon which I am sure you are longing to give an explanation. Let it be understood that we are friends, and that my friends may enter my house as they choose. Yet this slight informality to-day in a first visit suggests the existence of some misunderstanding between us, for, surely, you were not refused admittance at the gate?"

"No, monsieur," cried Henri, abashed somewhat by the calm analysis displayed in his host's method of conversation, which had promptly shown him with what folly and recklessness he had acted, "but I did not know definitely of Mlle. de Montpensier's presence, to say nothing of yours. And yet who is not aware that she crossed the Atlantic with you, and since then has been more or less in close connection with you?"

Jerome raised his eyebrows as if in remonstrance. "Prince," he answered, "has mademoiselle no right to choose her friends?"

"That is true," answered the other, flushing again. "But she has cast me off, though we are allies in the great scheme to bring back the monarchy to France."

Vansittart rose and approached his visitor. "M. le Prince," he said, "will you permit me to lay aside formality for a moment, and say something to you, which I think will be of importance? You are younger than I am, and I think you are hastier. It is not well for a man with a burden so heavy as yours to practise intemperance, whether in speech or in deed; and it is, indeed, fatal if he becomes habituated to jump to conclusions without having gravely analyzed everything that bears upon the question. Let us not upon this occasion deal in innuendoes.

"You say that you desire to become King of France. Well, I know that Mlle. de Montpensier will marry no one but the King of France, so I shall re-congratulate you if you succeed in obtaining two such treasures. But mademoiselle is free to do exactly as she pleases. I in no way have the right or desire to interfere. She has the utmost and most entire independence. She may take any course or line of action that she chooses. Unquestionably go to her. Let her decide as to what she desires to do with you, for it is no matter of mine. I value mademoiselle's friendship, but I have no right or desire to influence her in the faintest degree in anything whatsoever. These idle suspicions of yours surely are unworthy of you? Go, M. le Prince, and win your empire. Win it, and I will be the first to bow the knee to you, and I will claim the privilege perhaps of kissing the fingers of the queen. That is all I have to say, and I think it needs no addition."

Henri rose to his feet, still deeply troubled, for he knew not what inscrutable purpose lay in the unfathomable brain of this extraordinary man, who created colonies, and by a wave of the hand brought palaces into existence. There could be no plainer speech than that used in regard to Honorine. Whatever it might be that lay between the Princess and Vansittart, there was nothing that could preclude him from winning her heart if she but willed it, and he had the power.

He held his hand out to his host. "You think, then, there is no reason why I may not visit the Princess."

"As often as you please," replied Jerome with a smile, "but subject, surely you as a gallant must know, to the lady's consent. So far as I am concerned, I shall rejoice the more at the *tête-à-tête* audiences you have the honor to receive."

And thus ended the meeting of these two men, whose thoughts were upon the same goal, and who walked towards it with equipment so vastly different. A strange contrast! Here the strong, indomitable conqueror of men, whose purpose never flinched, whose resources never failed; there the weak, impulsive dreamer, whose purpose bent to his passion, and whose mind knew no steadfastness! If they were rivals, then Nature was in one of her ironical moods.

CHAPTER XXII

A CAPTURED LION

WHEN the Prince had gone, Vansittart drew from his pocket the letter which Harland had given him earlier in the afternoon.

"It is a singular request," he said to himself. The missive ran:

> You may perhaps have forgotten my name, but you cannot have forgotten the slight service I rendered you in the Sahara, in the last desperate fight, when the sword of an Arab Sheik was near making an end of you. You told me then that you would show your gratitude in any way that was possible. I now beg you to fulfil your promise. I am in trouble. I have left the army. Why, I will tell you when we meet, but the causes are just. I dare not show myself in Paris, but I entreat you, in your own interests much more than mine, to come to the little wood at Laudon. The wood is only eight miles from St. Cloud, and here I have got concealment for awhile. If you come to-night it will add to my safety. Walk straight towards the wood from the village and I will meet you. Yours gratefully—F. BEAULIEU.

"It is a request I cannot refuse," mused Vansittart. "Besides, it is likely to be a fine evening. Let me see; if I take a train for a few miles, I shall enjoy a country walk, and be back in time for dinner. I presume he will be on the outlook."

Vansittart was a man of impulse. Whether Beaulieu had nearly saved his life or not mattered little. He was grateful even for attempted service. It needed but the call for help and it came. It was impossible for Jerome to resist the appeal this ex-dragoon had made. A steady walk along a straight country road, in a clear air, and under a serene sky, would do Jerome good after the disturbing events of the day. It was pleasant. He wanted to think, he wanted definitely to realize what meant this new factor in the game which had suddenly sprung up in the guise of the impulsive young gentleman from the South.

"Honorine and he were obviously friends in the old days," he mused as he set out on his short journey.

It was obvious that she had never loved the Prince, or at any rate had never expressed such love—just as certain, he reflected with remorse, that he himself had not a particle of true affection for her. But it was now too late to draw back. Then there was a compact, and what could it be? Vansittart quickly made up his mind on this point. It was the compact she had offered to him. To the amorous youth she had probably replied that she would marry only the King of France, and had perhaps drawn up a kind of alliance which permitted them to help each other, in their efforts, but allowed Prince Henry to hope for no sort of attachment on her part.

And now, free once more to come and go as he pleased, naturally the young Prince had burst in upon the circle at Saint Cloud, seeking his Empress. Too headstrong to perceive that she was in earnest, too little of a diplomat to understand that every dubious step he took rendered his chances of winning her less and less, the Prince had irretrievably damaged his own prospects. Again, the obvious indignation with which she greeted him, had shown that Honorine was true to the bargain, true to the cause. She cared no more for this whipper-snapper than she did for any other person who stood somewhat nearly related to the royal family of France. It was Henri's want of self-control that would have always prevented him from seizing the throne. He was clinging to the fatuous hope that he might shake her resolution. He was one of those who believed that a woman's word, where love was concerned, might never be expected to remain steady. Was he right?

Jerome could not admit that Honorine would allow this madman to repeat his constant protestations of affection in her presence. How, then, receive him, since he could talk of nothing else, since he could not be relied on for a moment's discretion? This was Jerome's analysis of the situation. Whatever affection Honorine had, it was his, and they together were to win the Empire, and rule over it together. He admired this constancy in a woman, and his purpose grew in strength, if strength it needed.

The reasoning was admirable from all points of view but one. Neither Jerome nor Honorine was in love with the other nor with anybody else. When love came, reason would be impotent.

In due course Vansittart reached the little wood of Laudon. It was a deserted spot, and it lay quite out of the reach of the two main roads which came that way, being an uncultivated piece of land neither beautiful nor readily accessible. In itself irregular and wild, it was seldom resorted to, as superstition had invested it with many horrors, and placed there the scene of many strange crimes.

According to popular logic it is impossible that there should be an ugly place unless there be ugly deeds done there, and it was only for the wood of Laudon to lose its good name for it to become untraversable except by the irreverent and the incredulous. The spot was reported to have a brood of adders jumping about in readiness for any wayward passenger.

As Vansittart approached the wood, he looked around, expecting Beaulieu to meet him at the entrance. The soldier was not there, but the course seemed clear; he could but pursue the path that wound its way into the midst of the thicket. In a serene state of mind then, with his thoughts brighter than they had been for many days, Jerome walked on, though the growing darkness caused by the density of the trees, rendered all objects quite indistinct.

He had scrambled into what might be called something of

an open space, and was about to utter a cry or whistle to inform his friend of his arrival, when he heard the rapid approach of feet. They appeared to come from all sides. Glancing quickly in one direction and another, he saw what seemed to him to be the forms of several men, unrecognizable in the gloom, who sprang swiftly upon him, as he stood helpless and unarmed.

Realizing in a second that he was either the victim of a plot or a mistake, he dashed fiercely along the path he had traversed, hoping to burst through this cordon of probable assailants, and then make a bold race for liberty, or perhaps life.

Encountering one man he deliberately closed with him, and the two strained for an instant in deadly embrace. Their muscles tightened like whipcord, and Jerome felt that there was no mistake—a cleverly planned ambuscade was being carried out effectively and unscrupulously. In his rage at the thought he had no mercy. He hugged at his opponent with the grip of a bear until the man lost his balance and leaned back. Then plunging his right foot forward and downwards Vansittart smashed the other's leg above the ankle.

Had he succeeded in getting free that moment he might have escaped. But the frenzied pain of the injury caused the unknown villain instinctively to tighten his hold whilst he yelled a frantic cry for help.

The American at last threw him off, maimed and cursing, but it was too late. Four others had now seized him from behind, and before he could utter a word his head and arms were muffled in a blanket. He was then bound, both hands and feet, the cord fastening his wrists being tightly hitched around his waist.

Some little delay ensued, but after a whispered colloquy Vansittart was carried into a rough hovel, deeply shrouded in the wood, lying apart from the open space, and concealed from human ken beyond a distance of a few feet.

A lantern shone from a rough board over the fireplace, and this, strangely enough, was the only solid piece of furniture of this miserable hovel. It was as though some crazy lunatic had built for himself a squalid kennel and decorated it with a serviceable iron fireplace of the most cumbrous yet useful description.

In the corner of the room were two bags of straw, upon which Jerome was rudely thrown. Now that he was securely tied and unable to move, the covering was taken from his head and shoulders, and he had never set eyes upon such horrible and ghastly creatures as his captors during the whole course of his life.

One of these, the brute who had thrown the blanket over him, was none other than the Plasterer, and two of his companions were String-the-Neck and the Gouger. The five men were, in fact, the chosen spirits of that terrible society of assassins over which Folliet had been keeping such close guard until he was dismissed to England. In their faces was no gleam of hope for the prisoner. Jerome could see there only greed and impatient hate, for the wretch he had injured was calling for his death with frightful imprecations, having been conveyed to the hut by his mates.

Vansittart was bound so tightly that he felt pain, rapidly becoming intolerable, in his arms, waist, and legs. The Plasterer and his crew were evidently afraid of his strength. It was no ordinary rope that they had used, and they had tied it with no ordinary firmness. Yet he lay with his head propped up, looking upon his companions with a smile, which was half-cynical, half-thoughtful. He wondered, not what they would eventually do, but in what order they would do it.

The cut-throats were evidently ill at ease. They had fulfilled their instructions, and there was seemingly a stage wait. They were visibly relieved when footsteps were heard without, and there entered through the narrow door a sixth personage. The new-comer was a man wrapped in a long cloak, whose hat was pressed over his eyes. This latest arrival gazed with deep satisfaction at Vansittart, and the gaze was returned with interest. Suddenly the man turned to the Plasterer:

"Have you injured him?"

"No," was the responsive growl. "But he has cracked Pierre's leg for him."

Vansittart was not surprised when he recognized the voice. He had already guessed from the manner of his capture who the chief conspirator was.

He knew as de Tournon flung his heavy coat off, tossed his hat aside, and sat down upon a log which was put upon end, that his old and unforgiving adversary had stooped to the methods of the highwayman and assassin to obtain his revenge.

The two men gazed at each other for some time, Vansittart perfectly grave, calm, passionless, showing no emotion of any sort, with no tremor of the lips, and no quiver of the eyelids.

De Tournon, weak, frightened by the very measure of his success, was scarcely able to help a change of color and a nervous twitch of the hand, as he saw his victim so fast a prisoner. It seemed to him that now all was over he had done too much for his strength, that the killing or the robbing of this man was hopeless. The perspiration even came to his brow. He had won a victory beyond his capacity. What use was it, he thought.

At length de Tournon broke the silence. "So you see, monsieur, that the game is now in my hands!"

"No," replied Vansittart, "not a game, surely? You are like the impatient player who, when in danger of defeat, clears the chessmen off the board with his hand. Our ancestors played like this, but they did not parade it as a game of intellect, and I have no doubt that they did it very well. But, really, no one is interested in the game now. This sort of thing requires no genius, only the good fortune of having an admirable circle of acquaintances."

"It is easy to say that, Mr. Vansittart," cried de Tournon. "Was it the game when you ruined me in position and pocket?"

"No doubt I had to act in a manner which distressed both of us. Nevertheless, when I placed in the balance the interests of France and those of the Minister of the Interior I was compelled to admit that the former somewhat outweighed the latter. Besides, how could I know that your speeches in the Chamber were made for the purpose of filling your pocket? I have calculated that your patriotic remarks on the last famous occasion were in your opinion worth one thousand francs a word. This, then, I assume, is the new political method which you have happily inaugurated?"

"You may sneer, Mr. Vansittart, but I have the satisfaction of seeing you bound and helpless. It is now my turn to dictate terms."

"Distinctly, M. de Tournon, and surely you need them, since fortune has compelled you to turn forger, footpad—and cut-purse."

"Cut-purse!" cried de Tournon.

"Ah!" apologized Jerome, "that was no doubt a little premature. I should have waited an hour."

"It was you who blundered, Mr. Vansittart. You should have trusted me. As allies we might have carried all before us."

"Nay," replied the other, "I assure you, your abilities shone better as my tool."

De Tournon grew pale with rage, but he constrained himself in retorting: "I am bound to be victorious in the end. When I take up a cause, whatever reverses occur, I carry it through. That is the secret of my statesmanship."

"It is very true," replied Jerome, "and you have good reason to be very proud of the last stroke of what you call your statesmanship. May I inquire whether these gentlemen are the members of your Cabinet? Or, stay—on closer examination, they seem rather to belong to the police department. Your diplomacy, M. de Tournon, is very delicate. You no longer use the parchment but the roller around which it is wrapped. Altogether there is something of novelty—I may say fascination—about the policy which your Cabinet undoubtedly endorses to the full, a policy that consists in alluring your opponent forth by forging the name of an honest soldier, assaulting him with weapons, gagging him, and imprisoning him, and then calmly proceeding to rob and kill him. There is a finish about statesmanship of that sort, M. de Tournon, which, alas! we seldom see in the long drawn-out red-tapeisms of other nations."

"You laugh at these gentlemen," broke out de Tournon with a sneer. "Where are *your* friends, pray? Of what avail are they?"

"My poor de Tournon," replied Jerome, "all France is my friend, and you will find out to your cost that whatever be the outcome of this fine stroke of yours, you will be in a very unhappy position. However, good fortune seems always to hover over you. You have shown so much ingenuity during the last three months in escaping from the persistent bailiff, who, I regret to find, is ever watching for you with a warrant for £200,000, that you are by this time well versed in the shifts of a man who must escape a danger that is always round the corner. But I say no more, monsieur. The conversation is charming, but, as you know, I am always a busy man. I love despatch, and I wish to know without delay precisely what you intend to do."

"You have not yet pleaded for mercy," put in the other in a disappointed tone of voice. He had hoped to see his victim whining before his eyes. He would have enjoyed the spectacle of this man, the greatest he had ever met, humbling himself before him. He was unprepared for the full-faced look of contempt Jerome cast upon him.

"You have discovered one weakness in my armor, M. de Tournon. Nevertheless, though friendship may make me indiscreet, I ask you whether you believe I am also a fool?"

De Tournon moved uneasily. "Then the matter is simple," he replied. "You have not seen an evening paper?"

"No."

"In the later editions to-night of the evening papers in Paris, there appears an interesting paragraph. I supplied it myself. It refers to another caprice on the part of the chairman of the Sahara Company. It states that in order to make a more impressive demonstration of his new scheme, by which he practically gives a milliard of francs to the shareholders, he intends, instead of producing a cheque merely at the meeting of directors to-morrow, to do something more impressive."

De Tournon paused. He hoped to see his enemy wince at this reminder. The chairman of Sahara, Limited, was bound to attend next day's meeting in order to fully explain his latest act of generosity. To be absent would manifest, if even in a small degree, a lack of confidence.

But Jerome, raising his eyebrows, observed: "Pray proceed, M. de Tournon. I assure you, you are not boring me in the least."

"Well, it is stated that instead of writing a cheque to clear up the whole amount, he will, as a first deposit, produce a quarter of a million sterling in bonds and securities. A similar paragraph will probably be repeated in the morning papers."

"I really do not see how the matter interests me at all," replied Jerome. "I have no objection to the Paris newspapers amusing themselves by publishing such ridiculous absurdities."

"Ah," replied the other. "You will see the significance later on. You observe that this information will naturally get to the ears of your banker. When two of your accredited agents go to him to-morrow morning, shortly after the bank opens, presenting a cheque for the two hundred and fifty thousand pounds sterling, duly signed by you, with a note requesting that bonds and securities for that amount shall be handed out for presentation at the impending board meeting, he will not be taken by surprise. These paragraphs will remove any suspicion on the part of the banker, and he will forthwith furnish your agents with these securities."

"It is possible—possible," replied Vansittart. "I only say possible. But you say that my agents are going to present this check."

"Precisely."

"And I still further opine that—well, I scarcely like to offend these members of your cabinet—but I presume that you have gentlemen of less irregular features and of slightly less blemished form under your control. It is a trifle of some moment. You, meanwhile, are about to ask me for a check for that amount; you will secure the money, and then immediately depart with the proceeds?"

"Your calculations, my dear Vansittart, prove your good sense. Those are precisely the facts of the case, though I may still further add that the handing of this check to me is the sole condition on which I will save you from death. If you refuse the check, you understand these gentlemen here will exercise their professional skill upon you. If you are wise, and submit to my condition, why, then, you will remain a prisoner until everything has gone through well and the bonds have been realized, and I have had time to start to other countries beyond your reach. Then you will be set at liberty. I have no doubt that a discreet apology to the directors will satisfy their misgivings, and a quarter of a million to you, my dear sir, is a mere nothing."

Vansittart thought a while. He was in no way deceived as to de Tournon's real intentions! That the subterfuge adopted by these scoundrels for getting the money might very readily succeed he was well aware, because the French were accustomed to strange proceedings on his part. His bank manager would probably not be astonished at the request, but perfectly satisfied by the genuineness of his handwriting, provided that he gave the check.

On the other hand, he knew that de Tournon's promise to release him was pure nonsense. He looked steadily into his face, and saw the soul of the rascal there. The scheme was first to obtain the money safely from the bank, and then to quietly murder him. Was it likely that this miserable villain, having brought him to a spot which no one knew, and having also robbed him of a huge sum, would release an enemy who would be at once upon his track, and in a week or two have him by the heels? Besides, was it only for this trumpery sum that de Tournon had tracked him down, or for a full and complete revenge? Still, to appear to believe this story by giving the check was to gain time. That was the great point, for he felt assured they would not kill him until they had enriched themselves at his expense. So long as he had time, despite the enormous difficulties of the task, and the apparent hopelessness of the position, there was the remote chance that he might make his escape. Finality only came with death.

After a few minutes' silence he answered de Tournon.

"You are a clever rascal. But I am helpless. I have no alternative. Release my hands, and I will not only write the check but a letter to accompany it."

With trembling eagerness, de Tournon did as he was bidden. He produced a pen and ink and a blank check of the Bank of France, in case Vansittart had left his own checkbook behind.

De Tournon shook with gratified cupidity as he carefully perused the written coupon and its covering letter. They were quite in order, and he placed letter and check in an envelope, putting it in a side pocket. Hastily wrapping himself up, he turned to the Plasterer, bade him take good charge of the prisoner, and smiled cynically at Vansittart as he reiterated his instructions.

"Good-bye, M. de Tournon," cried Jerome as the ex-minister was about to pass out into the night. Then, with a malicious tone in his voice, which the blunted senses of the other could not appreciate, he went on, "If all goes well, I should like to be at the directors' meeting to-morrow."

"We will see what we can do," de Tournon observed blandly, as if talking to a child.

"Well, monsieur," retorted Jerome, "there is only one thing I know about this strange matter. I have promised to be in the chair at the directors' meeting to-morrow morning at eleven o'clock, and in that chair I intend to be on the stroke of the hour."

De Tournon laughed, a vulgar, significant laugh, and then went swiftly away.

CHAPTER XXIII

MURDER AS A FINE ART—WITH ILLUSTRATIONS

IN the forest of Fontainebleau shrubs spring from the bare rock ; in Vansittart's helpless case, his solitary shred of hope budded from the fact of de Tournon's absence.

His captors were now reduced to three in number. For the most unfortunate element in rascality is that honor among thieves cannot pass beyond the region of proverb. They never trust each other, so one of the gang was necessarily told off to watch M. de Tournon, and to see that he did not look with too envious eyes on the share which fell to his companions. In so far as this unnamed scoundrel's morality might be weak and open to persuasion, it was still further essential that the Gouger should be sent to follow him in turn.

There were left in the hut the Plasterer, who took possession of the log which de Tournon had quitted, String-the-Neck, and the humbler member of the corporation, who lay, groaning at times with the pain of his broken ankle, in a corner of the dark room.

Jerome carefully surveyed each in turn.

His antagonists, it was clear, might have been a hundred, for all the difference it made to his position, when the two who had come scathless from the contest had the strength of bulls.

Their ingenuity in tying Vansittart was such that any kind of movement was almost impossible, unless he elected to roll along the floor, a form of exercise little likely to relieve his situation.

The lamp began to flicker. It cast extraordinary gleams around the hut, making strange shadows of the uncouth shapes of String-the-Neck and the Plasterer.

Scarce a word had been spoken. The Plasterer sat moodily, now gazing upon his victim with a puzzled look, the nature of which Jerome was not long in guessing, now turning to curse his querulous companion in the corner.

String-the-Neck was restless. He flitted about with the air of a man who is robbed of his night's sleep and of the cognac that he would have lapped up with such satisfaction in his fetid den.

Vansittart did not flinch from the terrible inquiry set before him. Was it possible to escape, and, if so, how?

As he lay there hour after hour, he calculated every chance, however minute, however airy, however ridiculous, which might occur to a mind constantly practised in summing up every element of the most complex problems.

Plans occurred to him such as came to the prisoners in the Bastille. These, to our ears, now appear sublimely ridiculous, even though we know that they were successfully achieved by those who had to suffer the torturing questionings from which they were evolved.

The chief element of difficulty was that by no possibility could he obtain the practical use of any of his limbs. Indeed, if he were left alone, he did not at first see how he could succeed in releasing himself from the bonds so cunningly fixed upon him.

De Tournon's helpmates had experience extending through long years in the art of making their victims helpless. Moreover, if with all his magnificent strength he was able to gain his feet, it would but result, not, it is true, in death—for they would wait at least until they had learned of the check being honored—but in a blow so violent that he would be left incapable of attempting any such rash and impracticable plan as might occur to him again.

He knew that they would kill him. For that consummation he was fully prepared. He even thought, with a sigh of satisfaction, that the Sahara Scheme had now been demonstrated beyond the domain of doubt, and that at least he had not been found wanting in the great task of his life.

He was troubled that he could not fulfil his word to Honorine, but, then, the chances were that she would find herself better equipped at his decease to fight the battle of French royalty than she was when he met her in New York.

His friends would never know his fate, unless—and here he smiled as he thought of Folliet, and of the detective's unbending hatred for M. de Tournon. Yes! that man would guess the truth, and might safely be left to exact a full measure of reparation.

Vansittart was content. To anticipate vengeance is not attractive to one of his healthy organism.

Whilst he had been thinking these things the hideous face of the Plasterer was often stretched slightly forward towards his, with a look of unusual excitement, as of a professor examining a new animal submitted to his knife. He felt the need of speech, so he deigned to honor Vansittart with a question.

"Have you any particular partiality with regard to death?" asked the grotesque.

"To tell you the truth," replied Jerome, "I have not given it much thought. It is a wide region for speculation. There are very many different methods of quitting existence."

"Eh! Ah!" exclaimed the other impatiently, "far many more than you amateurs know about. What can you tell of all the dozen little ways which men of observation learn whilst practising their profession. Dear me! Life would be monotonous if there were only the knife and the revolver."

"I feel assured that you are an expert," replied Jerome in a tone of admiration. "You must have spent a long apprenticeship before you gained renown?"

"Oh, I have killed my share," replied the Plasterer. "But I often regret my early years. I was too fond of garroting then. You see, I was of an easy nature. My inclinations made a sacrifice of art, and I did things simply; but, fortunately, I learned better, and I think I may say it, who shouldn't, that there is hardly another in Europe who would kill his man as variously or with such delicacy of feeling and firmness of execution as I."

"You are a murderer of taste, plainly," murmured Jerome, sympathetically. "Merely to kill is nothing, of course, to one of your education and refinement. You add to it something of the unusual, a spice, perhaps, of the humorous, even a *soupçon* of the tragic, and I suppose that you succeed in obtaining as many gradations of note through the different methods you adopt, as the poet through the varying moods in which he regards nature and man."

The Plasterer eyed the millionnaire sharply. His blunted mind could scarce understand whether he was being laughed at or not.

"Now as to yourself, Mr. Vansittart," he continued blandly, "I should rather like your opinion, for I feel that a gentleman like you should have an end becoming his position, and therefore it would be a pleasure for me and for my companions to feel, whilst we were arranging your affairs, that we were meeting your views and accomplishing everything in the gentlemanly way."

"You are indeed too kind," replied Vansittart, "but really your question opens such a vast field for reflection that you must permit me to give a few hours thought to it. I am a man of simple habit, and although I should appreciate the honor of being despatched in your most artistic manner, for instance in a way which would separate me from the rest of your subjects, and give me the distinction of having had a unique death; yet I don't know whether the greater dignity is attached to the simplicity of throat-cutting or a more time-honored veneration to the blowing out of one's brains. However, I will ponder the matter and let you know in the morning."

The Plasterer appeared to be mollified by the obvious admiration displayed by his victim for an art that he had found not generally so appreciated as it should be. In good humor with the conceit he bade his uninjured companion light in the middle of the room a wood fire. Vansittart then learnt for the first time that the massive iron fireplace was a mere decoration rendered useless by the lack of a chimney, and a hole had consequently been cut in the roof to permit the smoke to escape.

In a few minutes the sharp crackling of dry timber was followed by the ruddy leaping of bright flames, and the wood gave out a white smoke, which, spreading steadily downwards from the roof, tended to obscure the apartment.

"Time for supper," observed the Plasterer to String-the-Neck.

The latter growled acquiescence. Some food was laid upon the floor, and looked upon with disdain by the artist in murder.

"A dry meal this," he observed with an oath. "You might have brought some wine."

String-the-Neck scratched his head.

"You are right, but you know as well as I that it is not impossible to get it. There is a *cabaret* just outside the wood."

"Umph," grumbled the other, "a good two miles on this dark night, with the lamp gone and the way tangled."

Here the sufferer chimed in with a pathetic request for liquor.

"How long do you think it will take you to get a couple of litres?" said the leader of the gang.

"Never you fear, Plasterer," cried his companion. "I will be back in an hour. Supper without wine is not the fare for gentlemen and artists."

With a sigh of satisfaction he stumbled out of the hut into the darkness of the wood.

There were but two left now, but Vansittart was not fool

enough to rejoice. His chance of escape was in no visible way bettered. He would have preferred twelve men more and his limbs free, to being left thus helpless with a single stout and sturdy scoundrel. Besides, he did not leave out of his reckoning the man who lay in the corner. He could do no damage, but his injured state shut out the hope of bribery. One, perhaps, might be tempted, but the two of them would be honest. These scoundrels could as little afford to betray as to trust.

By this time the Plasterer had grown tired of sitting. So he slowly paced backwards and forwards between the fireplace and the fire, showing all his physical defects to the eye of Jerome. He was not a tall man, and Vansittart noted as an idle fact that he was not indeed quite so tall as the iron stove, which was a lofty piece of furniture.

It had been one of Jerome's passions in his youth to study the most difficult and curious problems in mathematics. Tedious and fatiguing work he often now relieved by a return for an hour to the complicated studies of differential calculus.

His eye had consequently become trained to a nicety in observation and to the most accurate comparisons and calculations of space and distance.

He was now employing his time by submitting the Plasterer to a few such fanciful measurements. He found that the garroter would probably stand five inches beneath the mantel-shelf.

He mentally placed him by the side of the great square columns of metal which supported the transverse piece on either hand, their blunt and jagged edges standing out grimly in the flickering light.

Suddenly there came to him a speculative scheme, which he first dismissed as impracticable, but which recurred to his mind constantly and with growing domination.

He began to compare the height of his chief gaoler with the height of the farther column, and to ascertain the precise spot upon the floor on which the Plasterer would need to stand in order that he would dash his head against the corner of this iron support, if violently flung against it from behind.

It was an inquiry which might seem useless, but to one in Vansittart's desperate state it presented a single dim ray of hope. To have the least chance of success, it needed the nicest of calculation, the swiftest of action, and the most heroic physical effort on his own part.

There was a particular moment and a particular spot which occasionally coincided, when the Plasterer stood in direct line between Jerome and the pillar. If by any possibility Vansittart could at the psychological instant attack the garroter, he would hurl him with terrific force against the jagged edge of the iron upright and undoubtedly render him senseless. The other could not help himself, for his hands were deep in his pockets.

Unfortunately, on most occasions when the Plasterer was in a direct line between Jerome and the pillar he was not on the precise spot necessary for the absolute certainty of the experiment, and when he lurched exactly into the proper distance he seemed to be almost invariably out of the line. But both these factors must absolutely coincide.

Nevertheless, they did, very seldom, agree, and Jerome now anxiously asked himself if there was enough nervous energy in his body, enough muscular force in his stiffened limbs, to enable him to spring to his feet, and with one gigantic effort, dash his enemy in the desired direction.

Anyhow, that was what Vansittart determined to try. He silently worked his muscles to free them from cramp, though the experiment caused the numb pain of his bonds to develop into active torture. His hands, which had been freed to enable him to write the check, had been tied again, of course, but they were not now trussed to his waist. Otherwise, all his scheming would have been useless. Ten minutes of fearful agony passed. The whole nervous and physical strength of this extraordinary man were centred in the accomplishment of a single act.

Such things he had read of in records of adventures among savages, and with ready altruism he contrasted his case with the most desperate struggle for life he could recall. And the odds went the wrong way for him.

At length all was ready. Jerome, it must be confessed, watched with unusual interest the perambulations of his gaoler as he walked up and down, all unconscious of the stupendous effort about to be made. The Plasterer's foot was about to fall upon the predetermined spot. Vansittart with silent ease, apparently, rose to his feet. There was needed only a slight bend of the body, but the fierce tension of his muscles, and the veins upon his forehead, swollen as though they were like to burst, showed what the almost superhuman effort cost.

He rose and fell with a tremendous crash upon the Plasterer, whose head was rammed with savage violence against the corner of the column. His skull was fractured by the blow, and with a gurgling groan he collapsed upon the floor.

So far, science, aided by dauntless resolution, had been justified. But there was much yet to be done. String-the-Neck might be back at any moment. Jerome jumped towards the fire, which was now burning fiercely. He sank upon his knees, and withdrawing a half-consumed log, did not spare his wrists whilst he burned through the rope that bound them.

When it fell smouldering from his scorched flesh he made for the Plasterer's knife which lay close at hand, but at that moment he heard a movement on the other side of the hut, and an ominous click warned him of danger. Instinctively he recoiled, there was a sudden glare, a loud report, and through the smoke there came a bullet which grazed him on the cheek, drawing blood. Careless of consequence, and with the rage of a hunted animal, he leaped across the fire though his legs were still untied and fell upon this unexpected assailant, disconcerting a second shot by the rapidity of his action, and clutching the would-be murderer's pistol-arm with his left hand, whilst with the right he grasped his throat as in a vice.

He never afterwards knew what had happened, nor did he strive to remember. But when his senses returned, he again sought the Plasterer's knife and quickly liberated his legs and feet.

He was free.

Free! Yes, but each limb was scarred with wounds, and every atom of strength was spent. Few who had seen Vansittart at that moment would have recognized in him the handsome athlete who had calmly walked forth from his palace a few hours earlier on an imaginary errand of mercy.

He mechanically put on his hat, picked up the revolver with its four undischarged chambers, and then staggered feebly through the door. With uncertain motions he crawled rather than walked through the dark and tangled wood, unable for some time to find the path.

The night air, however, revived him. The exhilaration of gaining this last great victory over his foes brought back much of his mental vigor.

He stumbled laboriously in the direction where he thought St. Cloud lay. Soon he reached a path which seemed to be familiar, and a little farther on conviction grew into certainty. He had hit upon the roadway.

There was one consideration still left to crown his victory. No one must know what had befallen him. He was compelled to walk the whole distance to his residence, for at such an hour there was no train, and to obtain a conveyance was not to be thought of, so he staggered onward through the night, buoyant, even in his weakness, at the knowledge of de Tournon's discomfiture.

When he felt a roll of notes in his breast-pocket, and realized that his assailants had not got a single sou for their pains, he made shift to laugh. But he desisted, for his ribs were sore; he had been sufficiently amused for one evening.

CHAPTER XXIV

THE MEETING OF DIRECTORS

ROBERT OF SICILY, brother of Pope Urbane and of Valmond, Emperor of Allemaine, on one occasion, we are told by Longfellow, found himself benighted and in an unpleasant predicament. This mediæval king,

> Despoiled of his magnificent attire,
> Bare-headed, breathless, and besprent with mire
> With sense of wrong and outrage desperate,
> Strode on and thundered at his palace gate.

And the uncrowned Emperor of France was in even worse plight, save that he had his hat on, and did not expect to find a usurper reigning in his stead when he reached St. Cloud.

His clothes were torn and soiled with blood, he was cut and bruised in many places, his wrists and ankles were stiff and contused with the pressure of the ropes, and when the chill of an early winter day had slightly cooled his feverish excitement, the pain of his burned hands and arms was excruciating.

But he struggled on manfully, and within three hours after he had quitted the ghastly scene of his capture his tired senses quickened into fresh life at the sight of the first beams of the rising sun glinting from the graceful minarets of his abode.

He avoided the lodge and climbed unobserved into the park, whence he hoped to make his way quietly through a small wood of fir-trees into the gardens and thence to his private suite of apartments.

His eyes were dimmed with clotted blood and dirt, and his faltering limbs would scarce bear his weight. It needed the full remnant of his superb will-power to carry him through this final and easiest stage of the adventure.

So reliant was his soul within his weakened frame that he even strove to quicken his pace, but his uncertain steps were suddenly arrested by a woman's scream of terror.

Turning, he saw Evelyn Harland regarding him with affrighted gaze. He smiled to reassure her, and endeavored to bow with his wonted grace whilst he murmured a few words of apology. But the slight jar of her cry of alarm was too much for his exhausted state, and he fell heavily, almost senseless, on the turf beneath the trees.

Evelyn had now recognized him. His mysterious and unaccountable absence from the palace during the preceding evening had caused some inquiry, and Dick could not conceal his anxiety as the night wore on, and there were no tidings of his friend.

Arizona Jim, who regarded Honorine as a sacred curiosity, but whose whole heart went out to the lively English girl, sought Evelyn at a late hour to ascertain if there were any news of his master's whereabouts.

His evident distress at her want of intelligence impressed Evelyn more than her brother's guarded remarks, and she spent a restless night thinking of possible danger to the man whom she regarded in the light of an inspired hero of romance, the first hero of flesh and blood she had encountered in the course of her girl-life.

She had risen with the dawn, ostensibly to sketch on the outskirts of the wood, but really to obtain the earliest information of Vansittart's return.

Tumultuous emotions of joy and fear disturbed her as she ran to the spot where he had fallen. He was alive and safe, apparently, but why so faint, and of what awful scene did he bear the marks?

"Mr. Vansittart," she cried, as she bent over him, "are

you hurt? What has happened? Can you not speak to me? Oh, *do* try and say one word before I go for help."

Jerome opened his eyes, fighting now against an overpowering desire for sleep.

"Stay," he said feebly. "Tell no one, but get me some water."

There was a bottle of water with her palette. She flew for this, and he drank a little. Then with her handkerchief she bathed his face, and the vivifying effect was soon evident. The mist cleared from his brain, his bodily strength returned in some slight degree, and he was able to raise himself until he rested for a moment against the high roots of a fir-tree.

"Miss Harland," he said, speaking with some difficulty, "I want you to help me. Just now I cannot explain. Later, I will tell you everything, for I can at least trust you."

Evelyn's color rose as she listened. "Yes," she cried eagerly, with an unconscious tenderness in her voice that Vansittart afterwards remembered with a pang, "I will do anything you ask me without question, provided that you are not seriously wounded."

"No, I am unhurt, only dead tired. No one must know of my present state, except your brother and Jim Bates. Are they close at hand?"

"My brother has, I feel sure, already gone to Paris to try and learn something of your movements. We hoped that you were staying in the hotel, but, on telephoning there, learnt that it was not so. Bates is in your rooms, I believe."

"Thank you, ever so much. Will you bring Bates to me, and send away any chance gardener on some pretext from the shrubbery opposite my apartments?"

"Yes. I will mount guard myself, once I have found Bates." This with the gleeful laugh of a childish conspirator.

"We are already allies, you see, Miss Harland," said

Jerome with a faint smile. "We have our secret, too. This is what comes from being concerned with men who plot and scheme."

"Well, I will at least be a faithful ally. Wild horses shall not drag my secret from me."

She spoke with such emphasis that she became somewhat confused, so she ran off rapidly to carry out his wishes.

She pretended not to hear the remark with which Arizona Jim expressed his relieved feelings, when told that his master was at home again.

He strode off to find him, and quickly conveyed him to a couch in the dressing-room.

Not a word did he utter until he had succeeded in undressing him, and had helped him into and out of a hot bath. It was then half-past seven o'clock. The meeting of directors was at eleven, but the bank opened at ten.

"Jim," said Vansittart, as a last effort. "Get me up somehow at 9.15. Not a moment later. Get Mr. Harland here to meet me. My carriage—ready—at 9.30. Some wine —something to eat——." He was asleep.

Jim surveyed the exhausted millionnaire with the quiet pride that a father might feel in a precocious son. He carefully covered him up, and then went in for an exhaustive scrutiny of Vansittart's clothing. Every mark, each tear, each spot of blood was examined in turn, and with growing dissatisfaction.

The captured revolver, with its two discharged chambers, particularly aroused his ire.

"Now, who went foolin' round with this pop-gun?" he said aloud. "It must hev' bin either a Frenchman or a Chinaman. No Christian, not even a Dago, would use sich a toy. The chap who had it meant business, though. Guess the boss did n't grab it from him for nuthin'!"

He subsequently took steps to bring Harland back from Paris, and at the appointed hour he awoke his master by bathing his face with cold water. Even this brief rest had greatly restored Vansittart's faculties, and he ate whilst he dressed, for there was no time to be lost.

Jim Bates had a few questions to ask.

"There's bin trouble, boss," he said. "Why did n't you bring me along?"

"Trouble?" cried Vansittart. "Not a bit. These cuts and the rest are mere scratches from thorns and other things."

"Some of 'em, boss, some of 'em. But you 'll allow that I know the graze of a bullet on the cheek when I see it, an' I 've known a man before to-day to burn a rope from his wrists when he wanted to quit in a hurry."

"All right, Jim," laughed Jerome. "I can't bamboozle you. I will tell you all about it later. No one can be more sorry than I that you were left behind. It will not occur again, I promise you."

"Were there many of 'em, guv'nor?"

"Six, I think. Three I will meet later, two I left on their backs, and one of them may be there now for all that I can tell."

"An' where was it?"

"Oh, you will find a note in my clothes that will tell you all about that. I was tied up for some hours in a hut quite close to the spot there indicated. But call Mr. Harland. I expect that some of the scoundrels will be at the bank by ten, and I want to be there before them."

Although pale and feverish, Vansittart had now regained his wonted appearance. The only visible sign of his recent experiences, when his head was covered, was the scar upon his cheek, which was slight enough to escape unusual comment.

Jim betrayed great animation when his master had left the house in company with Harland. He ordered a horse to be saddled immediately, and quitted the park at a fast gallop, rapidly disappearing in the direction of the wood which had so nearly proved to be Vansittart's burial-place.

He had no difficulty in finding the way. Although in the suburbs of Paris the roads were crowded, he drew rein for nothing. He was sworn at by drivers, screamed at by frightened pedestrians, ordered to stop in superb style by furious policemen, but Jim whizzed through them all like a small tornado in a hurry.

At last he reached the quiet woodland pathway, and he hardly slackened his pace until his keen eyes caught the signs of the first struggle between Vansittart and his assailants.

He now dismounted, tied his horse to a tree, and prowled round to pick up the trail. This, again, was a matter of small difficulty to him, and in a few minutes he was peering through the branches at the hut in which the great drama of the previous night had been enacted.

String-the-Neck, it will be remembered, had gone to a distant estaminet for wine, and the spectacle that met his eyes when he returned astounded even that callous villain.

After vainly endeavoring to restore the Plasterer to consciousness, he hurried off to Paris to warn de Tournon and his other associates of Vansittart's escape. But he could not find them, for they had gone to more reputable quarters to prepare for the expected *coup* of the morning, so he retraced his steps to the forest and strove, ere it was too late, to save his insensible comrade.

He was adopting some rough restoratives, when a shadow darkened the door, and he sprang to his feet in amazement —to confront Arizona Jim.

Jim looked him up and down much as he might note the points of some strange animal.

"Well, you are a beauty, an' no mistake," was his leisurely comment.

"*Que veux-tu?*" demanded the startled Frenchman, feeling for his knife, for he realized that this intrusion meant mischief to him and his confederates.

Jim's hand fell to his hip. "Quit that!" he said sternly,

but still String-the-Neck persisted, for he did not understand the other's words. At last he had firmly gripped the handle of his favorite weapon, and he was calculating the distance for an effective spring when Bates growled :

"I shall hev to improve yer hearin'." There was a loud report and an agonized yell from the other, for Bates had shot off the upper portion of his remaining ear.

With the desperation of the trapped panther the ruffian rushed at this new avenger, but that unerring revolver rang out a second time, and the knife dropped from his shattered hand.

He recoiled, livid with pain and terror, whilst Jim again calmly addressed him :

"I shan't give yer any more hints, stranger. If yer don't keep still, I will be obliged to hurt yer."

Heedless of String-the-Neck's appeals for mercy, he proceeded to tie him with Vansittart's discarded bonds, and, this task quickly accomplished, he searched his pockets, appropriating all their contents, except such money as the man possessed.

Letters, in particular, he fastened upon eagerly, and he had a good haul from the inanimate form of the Plasterer. The third man lying in the corner was quiet enough, for the *rigor mortis* had set in, and he owned no document save some scraps of paper.

Jim neglected none of these, however. He even appropriated the pen and ink-bottle that he found on the floor. When quite satisfied that nothing had escaped his observation, he quitted the hut without giving a parting glance at its occupants.

"It's a pity that chap had n't a six-shooter," he mused, as he swung himself into the saddle ; "things might hev bin a bit livelier. But I guess these fixin's will be useful to Folliet. He is a 'cute sort of cuss, is Folliet, even if he *is* a Frenchman."

·   ·   ·   ·   ·   ·   ·   ·

At ten o'clock, sharp, Jerome's carriage drew up at the doors of the bank. Entering, he was met by the manager, who had just that moment arrived, and hastened to greet his distinguished client with effusion.

"Ah! I expected to see you to-day, Mr. Vansittart," he cried. "There are strange reports about that you are going to present bonds to your directors this morning instead of your check. I never like to cross such clients as you, sir, and I will only say that if I am correctly informed we can, I think, manage to hand you the whole sum within half-an-hour."

Jerome laughed. "Don't believe such nonsense. You know me too well to think me mad in anything pertaining to finance. No, monsieur, I shall in the usual way present a check to the directors, and it will be written, of course, at the Board meeting. There are some other matters I wish to speak of to you. May I have a few minutes' private conversation?"

The two men withdrew into the manager's room, where Vansittart hurriedly gave the official some inkling of expected occurrences.

Three minutes had barely elapsed before two gentlemen of gorgeous attire appeared in the bank.

Had M. Folliet been in the locality, he would have noticed that the new-comers shed around the streets a little knot of companions of not too prepossessing appearance, who were apparently watching the doors of the institution very anxiously.

A clerk advanced.

"I wish this check to be cashed at once, if you please," said the spokesman of the pair.

The clerk took it and read it. He even went so far as to violate the rules of official decorum by whistling. "My dear sir," he cried, "you must really give notice for the payment of so large a sum of money."

"My dear sir," replied the other, "do you not recognize the signature?"

"Perfectly."

"You have heard no doubt that it is Mr. Vansittart's intention to present to the directors of Sahara, Limited, bonds instead of a check at their meeting to-day."

"It was so said in the papers."

"Mr. Vansittart has commanded me to present this to you, and to ask for almost immediate payment. I fear that half-an-hour is all the notice I can give you. The meeting is at eleven o'clock."

"Pardon me," replied the clerk. "It is a matter so large that I must consult the manager," and he disappeared. The manager had just left his private room and was speaking with the cashier when the clerk put into his hand Vansittart's check.

He looked closely at the signature.

"Clever!" he said with a smile. "Exceedingly clever." Turning towards the couple fidgeting in front of the pay desk, he continued: "These gentlemen desire this check to be cashed immediately?"

"Yes," cried the spokesman, with a fierce effort to control his nerves.

"I have the misfortune to inform you that this cheque is a forgery," said the manager blandly.

"What, sir!" shouted the other, the blood rushing to his face. "You tell me that you do not accept your client's signature, or"—producing here the letter that Jerome had written—"his handwriting?"

The manager read the note carefully. His smile broadened.

"It is exceedingly clever," he said, "but I still regret to inform you that both of these documents are forgeries. It is my unhappy duty to place the matter in the hands of the police forthwith. I have just been informed by Mr. Vansittart himself that he has not, nor ever had, the intention of demanding bonds and presenting them to the directors, and that he will make out his check at the meeting in the usual course."

"Impossible!" exclaimed de Tournon's agent, now resolved to brazen the matter out. "I left Mr. Vansittart yesterday, and he will be away until long after the meeting has closed."

"But, sir, perhaps, it would be better for you to see Mr. Vansittart?" demanded the manager.

"What do you mean?"

"Mr. Vansittart is at the present moment in my office. This letter and its accompanying check must be accounted for. It will satisfy me the more if you will kindly step this way."

As if he had been attracted by the sound of squabbling, Jerome at this moment appeared at the inner door, and gazed upon the two men.

There was no time for explanations, or, indeed, for anything short of swift movement. The pair darted with extraordinary violence through the folding-doors of the bank, raced along the pavement until they came upon a cab, and then fled as though for their lives.

Their ragged confederates, seeing this miserable outcome of what they hoped to be a magnificent haul, disappeared with remarkable celerity, to the inexpressible glee of Harland, who witnessed the incident from the carriage. There were left only the check and the letter to tell of the strange scene which had just taken place.

"A remarkably clever resemblance, is it not?" observed the manager to Jerome.

"Yes," replied Jerome, "it is indeed a most extraordinary forgery. It is as like my signature as two peas!"

. . . .

As the clock struck eleven, Vansittart entered the boardroom and took this seat at the head of the table. One of the directors rose and congratulated him upon his appearance.

"I was afraid you were not coming," he said. "I called you up on the telephone last night—it must have been about twelve o'clock—on very important business, and learnt that you had gone away without leaving any sort of word to indicate your whereabouts. You are somewhat given to mysterious disappearances."

"Ah, monsieur," replied Jerome, "sometimes in this weary life one requires a little excitement. Last night, I must confess, I filled myself to repletion!"

CHAPTER XXV

HOW THE SAHARA WAS FLOODED

EARLY in the spring Vansittart again journeyed to the desert, accompanied, of course, by the ever-faithful Jim, and this time by Dick Harland, who growled unceasingly when the millionnaire sought to convince him that he should still remain in Paris.

"I would n't care a pin," protested Dick, "if I were any sort of use as a schemer or financier, but I 'm not. Now, there 's Liancourt and Folliet, two chaps to whom that kind of thing comes natural. Let Liancourt do the spoofing and Folliet the watching. Take my tip, you can trust both of them. They are honest right through. And if you want someone to look after the money, why not cable for the old boy in New York?"

"Peter Studevant, you mean?" said Vansittart.

"Yes. From what I saw of him he will not chuck about more millions than are absolutely necessary."

"That 's the soundest proposition you have made for months, Dick. I will have him here within a week."

Hence it was that when the adventurous trio landed at Gabes from the *Seafarer*, their leader felt that all was secure at Paris, and his two associates were satisfied that nothing could go wrong in their absence without the prompt attention of trustworthy deputies.

Jerome certainly possessed the kingly attribute of attaching to himself and his fortunes a band of devoted adherents. Each member of his little "court" was resolved to do or die in the performance of his individual share of the great task undertaken by the chief.

What that task was now remains to be described in some detail.

So far, the flooding of the Sahara has been treated in the course of this tumultuous narrative of strange events as being a definite scheme based upon known data. But to many ears it has sounded more like a wild and incoherent dream. Perhaps this misapprehension may be removed if the full scope of the project be dealt with in proper sequence and with due regard to the different groups of obstacles to be met and encountered.

Scientific proof has already been given, backed up by the names of such men as Sir Charles Lyell, Professors Ramsay and Boyd Dawkins, Herr Escher von der Linth and Captain Roudaire, that the Sahara is a dried-up ocean bed.

It is probable that this North African sea, like the existing Victoria Nyanza, the Caspian Sea, and the great North American lakes, had its normal level above the mean altitude of the Atlantic and Mediterranean.

It lay in a gigantic shallow basin, and was not vivified by vast river systems flowing into it from neighboring highlands. When, in the progress of the ages, the narrow outlets leading into the surrounding oceans became blocked by volcanic upheavals, it was but a question of centuries of steady evaporation under the fierce tropical sun for the whole area to become a parched and arid wilderness.

But the so-called unchanging face of Nature is far more mutable than the deep-rooted characteristics of the human race.

The Arab, born and bred in the desert, makes a first-class sailor. He fearlessly navigates the Persian Gulf and the Indian Ocean in crazy dhows that would daunt the boldest tar in the British navy, whilst he sails under rough-and-ready reckonings that Vasco da Gama would have laughed at as antiquated and unreliable.

The Mid-African negro, unaccustomed for generations to aught save an occasional canoe-journey across a river, rapidly becomes a thoroughly efficient fore-mast hand on a sea-going vessel.

Yet, whoever heard of a Central Asian nomad or a South African Zulu embarking from choice upon the adventurous career of a sailor? Thus, not alone upon the face of each rock in the desert, but upon the apparently transient scroll of humanity itself, is indelibly written the fact that at one time the northern interior of the African Continent was indented with a vast ocean littoral and peopled by a maritime population.

Vansittart's idea, then, was founded upon correct geographical and ethnological deductions. Now for the practical side.

The outer rims of the great central basin were most readily approached at Boca Grande on the west, and Biskra on the east.

At Boca Grande the works for distilling the salt water into fresh, elevating it, and discharging it by an aqueduct into the huge plain that lay beyond the intervening fourteen-mile barrier of volcanic rock, were situated on the verge of the Atlantic Ocean.

At Biskra, on the eastern or Mediterranean side, Maclaren's operations, already detailed, brought the sea through canals and lakes two hundred miles into the interior of the country, providing a splendid passage for vessels of any capacity. Here, again, was encountered the saucer-like edge of the Sahara, and the same method of overcoming the obstacle must be adopted as at Boca Grande.

For France, the chief entrance and exit must be Biskra. For the rest of the world the main avenue of commerce would be at Boca Grande, with its grand situation at the confines of the Atlantic. It was upon this spot that the British Foreign Office kept an observant eye.

With his hordes of workmen and his unlimited supplies

Maclaren had done marvels in the vicinity of the Shotts. There was no waiting for developments. No sooner was one section of the enterprise fairly started than another was mapped out and commenced. The utility for employing troops upon such a task quickly became apparent. Divisions, brigades, regiments, companies, or squads—each and all had their allotted labor, great or small, and an element of rivalry was introduced that resulted in the utmost energy and the maximum of excellence.

Whether in the construction of a dock, a railway, a canal, or the laying out of a temporary town, all hands were busy, and there was work for as many more.

Nearly 200,000 French troops were now on the spot, together with another army of skilled mechanics and artisans. Into every French town and village the word had gone forth that there was room in Africa for all men who were willing to work, and a fortune to be made by those who had brains enough to utilize the chances held forth to them. Consequently the surplus labor of the Republic was absorbed, and in many industries there was actual competition on the part of employers to obtain workers. The immediate corollary was a rise in wages, trade was improved all round, and Vansittart's name was revered by every one. Even at this early date, France was at his feet. The impetus he had given to millions of capital had set in motion the human tide which was to bear him forward to his yet distant goal.

Marseilles was the chief European centre of the Company's operations. Here was situated the principal storehouse for machinery and appliances, and from this port embarked every man who took part in the undertaking.

The Company's labor bureau resembled a government department in its crowded and busy state, whilst the wharves were thronged day and night with men loading and discharging cargoes.

Paris, of course, remained the financial centre, and the Company's offices in the Boulevard des Capucines rapidly became one of the sights of the city. By a wonderfully devised system of accounts the expenditure was kept under daily, almost hourly, control. A staff of engineers and accountants kept record of every foot of work done, and every item of labor and material paid for.

Each morning the immense plans exhibited in front of the offices recorded the previous day's work. The Parisians saw the Sahara Scheme advancing to maturity before their very eyes.

Within, each pound of iron, each square foot of stone, each item of food and clothing was accurately traced from its purchase to its final application.

Thus, whilst the supply was unstinted, there was no waste, and minor contractors who thought they could scamp the performance of a trivial task, soon found to their cost, by sternly pressed actions in the law courts, that Vansittart paid handsomely for honest work, but refused to be victimized.

One wholesale manufacturer of boots, who built up a fortune by supplying the army of Napoleon the Third with foot-gear whose soles consisted of brown paper, thought that a similarly simple enterprise would be successful in the case of Vansittart.

When the whole of his stock was returned to him with each boot destroyed by being cut in two, when he had paid heavy damages, and the cost of expensive legal proceedings, when he surveyed his ordinary business ruined by loss of reputation, he changed his opinion, and blew his brains out.

This final act was sarcastically described by the *Gil Blas* as " giving unnecessary emphasis to a plain fact—the Sahara Scheme is not a swindle."

Vansittart's arrival at Gabes was made the occasion of a local holiday. He left the place a wild and inhospitable sea-shore. He found it a town with electric lights, rows of streets and shops, a steam-car running over some miles of rails, a substantial wooden hotel, and a couple of solidly-built churches rising over the roofs of the smaller buildings.

After the first hearty greetings from Maclaren and Pompier, he naturally inquired as to the progress of affairs.

"Greater than I had ventured to hope," volunteered Maclaren. "There will be no more fighting. Some exaggerated notion of your proceedings at the tomb near Adsokha has percolated even thus far through the desert, and the rebellion has collapsed like a pricked bubble. Hence I have been able to get every man to work. That is all I want. The rest is a matter of time and money."

Pompier was more epigrammatic. "Gabes is now the gate of Africa," he said. "It will soon be a suburb of Paris."

"How so?" queried Jerome.

"It already possesses its Grand Hotel de Sahare, its Grands Magasins de l'Afrique, its Grand Boulevard de la Mer, and its Café St. Cloud—all we want now is a park with a race-course."

"We shall have to wait a little for the park, eh?"

"Not long," exclaimed Pompier proudly. "I have imported 2000 cuttings from lime trees and acacias. The average growth is two inches in ten weeks."

Pompier was inclined to be angry when everybody else laughed at this seeming anti-climax, but Maclaren stopped the others by chiming in: "You may laugh, but it is a marvellous achievement to result from irrigation by undrinkable water from ships' cisterns. Think what it means. It demonstrates the positive truth of our contention that the Sahara is a most fertile land if brought under cultivation once more."

"Those who are successful may well afford to laugh, Captain Pompier," said Vansittart. "It is surely a good sign when we can giggle at difficulties."

"Come, Pompier, produce your profit and loss account, and convince these sceptics!" cried Maclaren.

The gallant sailor, who readily recovered his wonted good humor, triumphantly handed to Vansittart a scrap of paper, which bore the following figures:

Capital expenditure on streets, electric plant, drainage, arboriculture, etc.	450,000 francs.
Weekly receipts from ground rents, less 10 per cent. for administration	8,500 "
Weekly receipts from tramway, less working cost	500 "
Annual yield on present basis	468,000 "

"There," he exclaimed. "The first portion of your property even now pays over one hundred per cent. **per annum!**"

"I fear the rents are high," laughed Vansittart.

"Not a bit," said the delighted Pompier. "An Englishman came here the other day and offered to buy up all existing properties for ten years at an increasing rental of ten per cent. per annum, money down now. But I refused. Albion is perfidious."

"I don't see how Albion can be perfidious when she pays in advance," hazarded Dick Harland.

Pompier swept aside the interruption with a prophecy that in ten years the main street of Gabes would be worth a hundred-fold its present value.

"There is only one thing that troubles me," said Maclaren, when Pompier had exhausted himself in grandiloquent prediction.

"And that is——?" queried Jerome.

"I can see my way quite clear now to the completion of the work at a capital sum which will be a trivial debt upon an extensive and fertile colony. But there is an undoubted rock ahead in the shape of cost of maintenance."

"Why should this be excessive?"

"We propose to do that, in the first instance, which Nature was too exhausted to perform. By continuous irrigation we take the task upon our shoulders, and Nature comes in a good second by delivering an increasing rainfall annually, with resultant storage for the dry season. But when we discontinue our primary operations—that is to say, if ever we find it too costly to pour in some 200,000,000 gallons of fresh water daily, a retrograde influence will be at once established."

"But is there any paramount reason why our efforts should slacken?"

"I cannot yet say definitely, but I must confess that the everlasting cost of distillation appalls me. Distillation is only another name for evaporation, and the mere consumption of coal or petroleum will be enormous. In fact, there is no parallel undertaking in the known world. All the steam engines in existence do not equal it, I should imagine, and every ounce of material must be imported with resultant increase of price. Candidly, this part of the scheme bewilders me by its proportions."

Every one present felt the force of the engineer's remarks. His known strength of character convinced them that he would not have spoken thus if he had not deeply pondered this knotty problem, and failed to find its solution.

Vansittart alone maintained his air of calm, serene confidence. He smiled as he commented: "In other words, Maclaren, you mean to say that although France and I may rescue the Sahara from the destroying sun, you doubt if we can keep it from his clutches?"

"No," cried Maclaren hastily. "I have never doubted, Mr. Vansittart. I believe in you absolutely, but I cannot see the way myself."

The others present vigorously applauded his words, and for a little while Jerome could not conceal the pleasure that such a compliment from such a man afforded him.

"When my own heart failed me at the beginning of our enterprise, Maclaren, your brave words removed my traitorous fears. You then told me that Nature herself was your stoutest ally, and I would ask you to still trust to her. I had not forgotten the difficulty you have now raised, and, subject, of course, to your professional revision, I believe I have solved it."

Dead silence prevailed in the little group. At no other period in the history of Sahara, Limited, had the founder's words been more eagerly awaited by his chosen associates. Even Arizona Jim, who stood near, listened to his announcement with bated breath.

Vansittart himself felt the thrilling influence of the moment. But his wonderful nerve power enabled him to state his case calmly and methodically; he even started with a joke.

"There's no doubt about the supply of salt water, is there?" A sympathetic grin passed round the circle. "Well, we are called upon to resolve an everlasting supply from the ocean into solids, namely salt, some alkalies, and even a little gold, and into liquid in the shape of steam, converted back into distilled water?"

"That's the proposition," assented Maclaren, "though I never thought about the gold."

"Catch the boss forgettin' that," said Jim Bates in a stage whisper which caused a smile all round.

"Let us deal with the solids first, and treat of salt as the staple product. By a little manipulation of existing salt mines we can practically control the salt supply of Europe. Here, at any rate, we have a considerable source of revenue. It will be augmented in the other directions I have indicated."

Again Maclaren nodded agreement.

"There remains the chief element of our scheme, distilled water, which should also be chemically treated to give it the properties of rain water."

"*Diable!*" muttered Pompier. "*C'est magnifique!*"

"This supply," continued Vansittart, gently waving aside the interruption, "must first be raised some six hundred feet to enable it to flow by gravitation into the great central trough, so to speak, of the Sahara. Well, we get it as steam, and steam will rise six hundred feet as easily as six feet, so I overcome one small difficulty without in the slightest degree increasing the working cost."

"A simple method of making water flow uphill!" exclaimed Maclaren.

"Precisely. And now for the motive power. It can be stated in a sentence. If the sun was strong enough to turn the ocean out of the Sahara, he is surely able to turn it in again. We will not use coal or petroleum to heat our boilers, but the sun's rays, focussed in the furnaces by burning glasses. Again, there is no cost beyond the plant. I have already had extensive experiments made in London by a famous firm of astronomical lens makers, and they inform me that under favorable conditions—seldom present in England, but always at command here—they have easily succeeded in creating a heat of 2000 degrees, which burnt a hole through three inches of chilled steel in less than ten minutes."

A sort of cheer came from the excited gathering at this extraordinary statement. In his excitement Maclaren reached out and shook Vansittart's hand vigorously.

"Good old Father Sol!" cried Dick Harland.

"There's spots on him, is there?" yelled Arizona Jim.

Pompier's knowledge of English did not extend to Americanisms. "Vat you say? No spot on de sun?" he shouted.

"No, capting!" replied Jim joyously. "I ain't a blamed astrologer. There's no spots on the boss. What he says, goes."

After some further conversation with Vansittart, Maclaren withdrew and forthwith busied himself with some calculations. They resulted in a long telegram to the engineer in charge of the extreme canal section on the west of Lake Melrhir. Two days later when Vansittart was taken through on the accommodation railway, Maclaren announced that he had arranged a picnic for the following morning on a neighboring height, but observed some reticence as to the reason for the unexpected diversion.

Nearly a dozen persons accompanied Jerome and his chief

engineer to the place selected for an *al fresco* breakfast. It was on the side of a steep hill that overlooked the shallow lake, and the vivid sunlight lit up the moving panorama of men, camels, horses, and engines, that toiled unceasingly in the valley beneath.

At the close of the meal, Maclaren made some flag signals to the occupants of a hut on the verge of the works. The reply he received was obviously satisfactory, for he said cheerfully:

"Come, I will show you a novel spectacle."

They followed, and at a little distance perceived a long iron pipe that climbed up the height from the hut, and ended in a coil embedded in an ice-box.

"All the morning," explained Maclaren to the millionnaire, "my assistants have been generating steam from salt water by means of an improvised set of lenses. They have just turned it into this pipe, and we shall soon see the result."

Not a word was spoken whilst those present watched the mouth of the worm from which Maclaren had withdrawn a plug.

First came a visible tremor in the length of the pipe, which looked like a monstrous snake of vast length but absurdly small girth. Then a drop of moisture appeared at the lip, followed by another, and another, until a small stream placidly flowed forth upon the arid earth.

Stooping down, Maclaren filled a glass with the clear liquid, which he offered to Vansittart. "Come," he cried, "drink to the health of your enterprise."

Jerome sipped it gravely. "It is a sound wine, gentlemen," he said, "somewhat tasteless, I admit, but that is its chief virtue. And it has cost a million sterling for each glass, at the lowest computation."

Naturally there was much discussion of this splendid proof of Vansittart's theory, and the millionnaire warmly thanked Maclaren for his thoughtfulness and skill in providing so convincing a demonstration.

"I am only sorry," said the engineer, "that I did not carry the piping to the crest of the hill, so that our first effort in practical irrigation might flow towards the Sahara, instead of towards France."

Sure enough, a tiny rill was already threading its way down the hillside in a northerly direction.

Vansittart surveyed it quietly before he said, with a smile: "You have made no mistake. It is a good omen. It flows in the right direction."

They all heard him, and the degree of accuracy of their interpretation of his words was measured by the extent of their knowledge of the man and his aims. So there was plenty of scope for difference in their comprehension of his meaning.

CHAPTER XXVI

A COMBAT OF MONARCHS

THE world's Press seized upon Vansittart's suggestion with avidity. News was slack just then. The boom in North Africa had again knocked the bottom out of the South African market—a time-honored operation on the Stock Exchange. The advent of a new American President to power had contributed to keep the United States quiet for a period of three years, and the German Emperor was experimenting in long-distance telephonic communication, as the telegrapth system was slightly out of favor with him. Peace reigned therefore, and peace means dulness for the newspapers.

So Jerome's proposal to turn the sun into a mammoth steam producer came at the right moment.

In England the *Daily Telegraph* found excellent reason in a leading article for comparing him with Archimedes and Galileo. The *Saturday Review* dubbed him the "Jules Verne of finance," whilst the *Daily Mail* was so tickled by his notion that it announced that all future messages from its wondrous Vienna correspondent would be heliographed, weather permitting.

The caustic and always hostile *New York Universe* gave its opinion that Vansittart was already known to be moonstruck—a comparatively harmless ailment—but now that he had succumbed to sunstroke, serious complications might be feared.

In Paris, the *Gil Blas* claimed the discovery as " a French invention," and the *Journal des Débats* solemnly deduced it from the system of sun-baths recommended by a French physician.

Naturally, the latest and most successful toy of the boulevards was a burning-glass that condensed water placed in a small globe of steel, if properly focused.

The millionnaire and his companions found some amusement in reading the various extracts of newspaper criticism collected at the Paris offices and forwarded to them at the headquarters, now situated near Biskra. But progress with the works, exceedingly quick in itself, was not so exciting as to relieve the monotony of life in the desert, where the daily northward advance of the sun was rapidly dissipating all tokens of the winter rains either in atmosphere or natural surroundings.

"There are lions in this neighborhood, are there not?" said Vansittart one day, when his head ached and his eyes were tired with the perusal of drawings and specifications prepared by the unflagging Maclaren.

"Yes, within a couple of days' march; at least, so I have been told."

"Well, let us take a short holiday and arrange a sporting trip."

"Impossible. I cannot afford the time."

"Oh, yes, you can," said Jerome. "For a week at least the chief work in hand is the forwarding of stores from Gabes. Come, you want a change more than any of us."

Maclaren unwillingly yielded, and Pompier was delighted with the idea. Like all Frenchmen, he flattered himself that he was an adept at "*le sport*." But he had never shot lions, so he grounded himself in the principles of the art by reading a book written by an English hunter of wild beasts, who said, "Compared with tiger shooting, the pursuit of the African lion is similar to the killing of a pariah dog prowling about the camp at night in search of refuse." Pompier devoted himself to the slaughter of such wretched curs as ventured within the practicable range of his tent. He did not desist from his " practice " until Maclaren sternly remonstrated with him, pointing out the danger to human life from ricochetting bullets.

Pompier now knew that he could shoot dogs—therefore lions—but he left out of all account the words " compared with tiger shooting."

When the party set out, its chief members were Vansittart, Maclaren, Harland, Jim Bates, Pompier, and Colonel le Breton, chief of the 18th Chasseurs, between whom and Jerome a close friendship subsisted.

It is an axiom of big-game hunting that the quarry is seldom found where expected, but turns up at particularly awkward moments, and under conditions that admit of the least preparation in advance. It was so in this instance. Although the desert was, figuratively speaking, full of lions, during the four days the party never caught sight of one. At night they came near the camp, and frightened the camels and horses by their roaring, but not a shot could be obtained. At last Vansittart heard from some Bedouins that three Englishmen had shot over the same ground a month earlier, so he decided to try another locality, and abandoned all thought of sport for the time. After dinner, on the evening of this decision, the servants commenced to break up camp preparatory to an early start before dawn. There was a bright moon, so Maclaren devoted himself to reading reports from his engineers, Harland started writing a long letter to his sister, and Arizona Jim took the opportunity to thoroughly clean all the rifles.

Vansittart, Pompier, and Colonel le Breton went for a ride to inspect some curious carved rocks they had discovered on the banks of a dried-up river at some little distance. Jerome and the sailor each carried a pair of six-chambered revolvers, but the Colonel of Chasseurs happened to be unharmed. They were well mounted, and Vansittart rode an Arab polo pony. Had he used a larger and less hardy animal, it is probable that this history would have come to an untimely close that night. When they reached the pile of rocks Pompier was slightly in advance, as his horse, a big cavalry trooper, walked faster than the others. The animal neighed and shivered when near the broken ground, but the sailor paid no heed. An instant later he found himself facing a magnificent lion, a huge lioness, and a well-grown cub, which was afterwards found to be nearly nine months old. Of course, what he ought to have done was to wheel his horse, shout to his companions to warn them, and then the trio should have galloped at top speed back to the camp. He did none of these things. Simply yelling, "Here they are, three of them!" he blazed away as quickly as he could. He managed to discharge four chambers before both himself and his steed were knocked sprawling on the ground by a charge from the lion, whose flank had been torn by one of the bullets. Pompier was thrown clear, and the horse, struggling madly to regain his feet, kicked the lion, breaking two of his ribs. In an instant the savage beast pounced upon the charger, fastening on his shoulder with teeth and claws. Vansittart realized what had happened when Pompier began firing. He was barely twenty yards away, but his alert mind soon decided upon a plan of action. His first thought was for his unarmed comrade.

"Ride for your life!" he shouted.

But the gallant Frenchman replied, "I cannot without you. I remain."

Vansittart had already spurred his trembling pony forward. He reached the spot in time to see the lioness spring upon Pompier, who was trying to rise. The mere impact of the huge beast knocked the sailor senseless. A second later she would have torn his head from his shoulders had not Vansittart, reining in his Arab after a splendid jump, bent down in the saddle and discharged his pistol within a couple of inches of her ear. The bullet smashed her skull, and what it lost in shock was made up by the stunning force of the explosion so close at hand.

Her claws clenched convulsively, tearing deep wounds in Pompier's shoulder through his clothing, and she fell dead.

The cub now took part in the fray. Vansittart had barely swung himself back into the saddle, when he caught sight of the youngster crouching for a twenty-foot spring. Instinctively striving to avoid the danger, he fiercely spurred his pony and wheeled him away from the animal. The Arab reared and turned, and as Jerome's body swayed forward and over to retain his seat, he felt rather than saw the lion's leap through space within a few inches of his head. The graceful beast alighted some six feet to the right of Vansittart, and he now fired three times at it as fast as he could relax and bend his trigger finger.

Not until the turmoil was over did he know that two of the missiles were buried in its shoulder, whilst a third had broken its backbone.

The glare of the third shot lit up the vicinity like a lightning flash, and in the same instant Jerome and his Arab were struck with tremendous force from the other side. The pony was spun on to his back as though he were no heavier than a package of wool. Vansittart's superb horsemanship might now have proved fatal to him, for he never relaxed his grip on the saddle, and he consequently lay right beneath the plunging animal. Fortunately, the saddle was a straight one, and he fell on the sand; so, beyond a nasty crushing, he sustained no injuries. It was the full-grown lion who caused this diversion. He had killed Pompier's horse, and forthwith launched himself against the nearest visible opponents.

The frantic struggles of the Arab resulted in the lion receiving another staggering kick, so he sprang to one side in order to gain a better point of attack. As he did so his off fore-paw alighted on Vansittart's arm, thus burying it in the sand, and Jerome's hand closed spasmodically upon what he knew was the butt of a revolver. It was the weapon dropped by Pompier during the first onslaught of the enraged monarch of the desert. Vansittart managed to twist his wrist around and three times pressed the trigger, but only two shots were forthcoming. The second of these reached the lion's heart. He gave a great bound forward, uttering a fearful sob of rage, and fell on his head, lifeless.

During this dramatic scene, Colonel le Breton, who had dismounted from his frightened horse, which at once flew back across the desert towards the camp, stood with folded arms awaiting the end. The brave soldier was helpless from the outset, but he scorned to fly. To ride for assistance was out of the question, for the affair must of necessity be a matter of moments, and he refused to save his life merely to explain how Vansittart and Pompier had met their fate. He remained, therefore, in statuesque pose, watching keenly each phase of the wild struggle between Jerome and the lions. His own doom was nothing to him, compared with the weird fascination of this moonlit fight. When it had ended, and the great chief of this noble band of desert champions had rolled over in the dust, Colonel le Breton's stoicism deserted him. He uttered a cry in which triumph blended with anxiety, for he did not yet know whether or not Vansittart had escaped unhurt. Rushing to the Arab's head, he seized the bridle and pulled the pony off his friend's body.

The millionnaire did not rise immediately. He could not, for all the breath had been squeezed out of him, but in response to Le Breton's eager interrogation he was able to smile reassuringly, whereupon the soldier lifted him to a sitting posture.

"Pompier may be dead," he cried, "but I am sure he still carries some good liquor on him," and he ran towards the sailor's prostrate form. Sure enough, Pompier's water-bottle contained some excellent brandy, but Jerome would not swallow any until he was able to speak.

The first words he said were: "That Arab is worth his weight in gold, though he is heavy enough as it is. Is Pompier alive?"

"I don't know yet. Let us examine him. It was a brave fight. I wish I had taken a hand in it, even if I were lying in Pompier's place."

The Colonel was more excited now than during the actual *mêlée*.

A hasty survey of the fallen sailor revealed that he was alive but unconscious, whilst a huge lump on the left temple, where the lioness's paw had struck him, showed the cause. They opened his jacket and shirt at the neck, and poured small doses of brandy down his throat, with the result that after considerable trouble they restored his senses.

Meanwhile le Breton's riderless and terrified charger had reached the camp, spreading immediate consternation. Hastily arming themselves, Harland and the Americans, followed by a group of orderlies and servants, followed the easily discerned trail of the three missing men, and they reached the scene of the fight just as Pompier opened his eyes. A hurried explanation relieved their anxiety, but Arizona Jim only growled as he listened.

"You'll get into trouble, boss, if you slide off with these Frenchies, an' always leave me behind."

Vansittart felt the justice of this second reproof, and was silent; but history again repeated itself, for Jim, in examining the prostrate lions, discovered that the cub was not yet dead, so he ended its career with promptitude. The cavalcade now returned to camp, with Pompier mounted on the Arab, which had never quitted its master, the lions' carcases being slung on rifles, and carried by the attendants.

"What a lucky chap you are," said Maclaren to Vansittart, when there was a momentary opportunity of not being overheard.

"Yes. It certainly was luck to bowl over three such fine brutes with the revolver."

"I do not mean that, wonderful as it is. But just as things were going slow for you, the French papers will be full of columns about this latest feat."

"But why should that be a stroke of special good fortune?" said Jerome with a laugh.

"I don't know, because you won't tell me, but somehow or other I feel that it is playing your game."

"Well, Maclaren," said the millionnaire after a pause, "the time is at hand when you will know everything. But I don't mind saying that to-night it was a question as to which king killed the other."

"And *you* won!"

"Precisely."

"So you will right through." The two men shook hands silently as they tramped steadily on through the sand of the Sahara.

CHAPTER XXVII

INTROSPECTIVE

"MARRY, come up! Gadzooks! Whom have we here?"

In such merry Elizabethan phrase did Dick Harland apostrophize a package, obviously containing a photograph, that reached him one evening shortly after the party had arrived at their new hunting ground.

Pompier had been hastily despatched to Biskra for proper medical treatment, but Vansittart declared that he, personally, would not return to work until he had met the big game of the desert on more equal terms than obtained at their first encounter. Dick leisurely opened the mysterious parcel, and then found that it contained a handsomely framed portrait of his sister, endorsed "With Evelyn's love," which, in order to surprise him, she had caused to be addressed to him in the shop where she purchased the frame.

"By Jove!" cried Dick, "it's the old girl to a T. Just her sweet face as she looks before she is going to say something desperately in earnest. She is a well-bred 'un, is Evie. Worth fifty thickheads like me. I must show it to Vansittart. He thinks a lot of her, and I wish—ah, well, there's no use in wishing!"

Dick lit a cigarette, read Evelyn's accompanying letter, smiled at her references to Honorine, whom she described as being "quite too dignified for a woman of twenty-three. She would be awfully nice if she forgot occasionally that she was going to be a queen," and then strolled off to Jerome's tent to exhibit the picture. Vansittart was not there. As soon as he had finished dinner, he had gone for a stroll for some little distance, to think quietly over various matters whilst enjoying a cigar.

Dick dropped into a camp-chair, and placed the photograph on a table near a small lamp, intending to await his friend's return. He had not been seated a moment, when Maclaren looked in.

"I was told you were here," he said. "Vansittart has sauntered off into the desert, being apparently anxious to be alone. I don't wonder at it, for he has enough to think about; but he does n't know that Jim Bates is stalking him to see that he runs no risks. Meanwhile, until he returns, will you come and have a smoke in my tent?"

"Delighted."

Dick sprang up, forgetting all about the photograph.

Jerome assuredly had plenty of scope for earnest reflection. His personal affairs were troubling him sorely. Now that the Sahara Scheme was a well-established fact, and the throne of France was no longer a mere imagery, he naturally regarded the question of his union with Mademoiselle de Montpensier from a different point of view. At first it was but the true dramatic sequel to a financial and empire-building fairy tale. The weirdly successful progress of events had changed the fanciful story into actuality. It had left the pages of Hans Andersen to enter the columns of the *Times*, and he was face to face with the fact that within a year at most, he would, in all human probability, marry the charming and high-souled Frenchwoman. And yet he did not love her!

For her sake, apparently, he had conquered odds never yet faced by mythological hero. He had labored like Hercules, but for the same cause—merely to show his strength. Not love, but a vivid consciousness of power, was his inspiration. He had built with surprising magnificence and certainty. The sure foundations were laid for the future edifice. What, then, caused them to tremble? Vansittart himself trembled as his heart gave the answer. Love had come to destroy, not to sustain. He did love, fiercely, passionately, resistlessly, with all the virile intensity of his reliant nature, and he loved a woman who could not be his wife. He was pledged to Honorine de Montpensier by every tie of honor and expediency, yet he hungered for a single blissful instant when he could take Evelyn Harland in his arms and tell her that she was all in the world to him. This terrible knowledge had been forced upon him in slow but torturing conviction. His relations with Dick's sister were only those of a host entertaining one of his numerous friends. Rarely had he met her alone; once only had their conversation touched on other than commonplace topics.

On that morning when they met so strangely in the pine wood at St. Cloud he was deeply touched by her devoted and girlish enthusiasm. Afterwards he bestowed more thought upon her when they chanced to come together in the social life of the house, until one fateful day when he found himself comparing her with the Princess. He had started at the mere thought, and shunned it as unfair and even dangerous, but, like a mocking sprite, it danced before his waking eyes, and grinned at him in his dreams.

"Honorine," it shrieked in his ears, "barters herself for a kingdom. Evelyn will yield for love."

And he groaned at the reflection that whilst a man could be happy in obscurity, he might be miserable in the dazzling radiance of a throne.

Vansittart was neither a moral nor a physical coward. He fought with the fiend out there in the silence of the desert, and believed he had strangled him. Honor, duty, his plighted word, all held him rigidly on the path he had chosen, and he reflected, with a cynical smile at his own wayward fate, that he would bring a clearer judgment to the solution of the many difficulties yet in front than if he were inspired wholly by the grand passion. A lover may be bold; he is seldom judicial. Rapid, far-seeing decisions were now more important than courage in prosecuting his designs.

"I might have been spared this suffering," he mused with bitterness. "It is ill not to love the woman you are about to wed, but it is cruel when the other woman turns up. I wish I had never met Evelyn Harland, and then I should at least have found a negative happiness in my life's work."

He derived some comfort from thus upbraiding fate. In a resolute and unflinching analysis of the situation there was a sustaining element of certainty. The way was clear, at any rate. He had to follow it without murmur or hesitation, and all would be passively well. Indulging in some such delusive settlement of the question—for so he deemed it—he sauntered back to the camp and entered his tent. And the first object his startled eyes fell upon was the pictured presentment of Evelyn Harland herself, with her cheek coquettishly perched upon her clasped hands, and her sweet eyes smiling at him in blissful unconsciousness of the half-hour's torment he had just undergone for her sake.

Vansittart was first astounded and unnerved.

Without asking himself how the portrait had arrived at such an unlikely locality as the midst of a hunting camp in the Sahara, he took it up and kissed it passionately, a proceeding that was witnessed by Arizona Jim, who had strolled towards the tent ostensibly to inquire if the millionnaire wanted anything, but really to assure himself that Jerome was safe within its folds. He now tried to steal away unobserved, but Jerome had heard him, and darted forth to see who it was that had disturbed him.

Bates came to his call somewhat sheepishly, and stuttered over his labored explanation.

"So you witnessed my small act of folly—you saw me kiss Miss Harland's picture?" said Vansittart sternly.

"Well, boss, I guess I did, an' I can't blame yer."

"Why do you say that?"

"It's this way, boss. It ain't for me to pass remarks, but I feel I must plump it out. Miss Harland is worth fifty Frenchwomen, even if you was settin' up as a Turk."

Jerome was constrained to laugh at the reply. In a softer tone he continued:

"I can trust you, Jim. Keep my secret."

"I will, boss, to the finish. But I've hopes as things will come straight yet."

"They cannot. I must choose between an empire and the woman I love."

Jim hesitated a moment before he replied. Then, looking the millionaire straight in the face, he said laconically:

"If I was you I would git both. An' although you know a heap more 'n me, boss, we often think the same way."

Then, well satisfied that he had spoken his mind on a subject very near to his heart, he strode off.

Vansittart re-entered the tent and laid the photograph on the table. He was now in a calmer mood, and smiled as he realized that Harland had evidently brought it to show it to him as a recent arrival. His own letters were lying unopened on one side, and he sat down to peruse them.

The first he scrutinized was from Liancourt. After satisfactory details of the Company's doings in Paris and the growing attitude of certainty on the part of the general public towards the scheme, Liancourt proceeded:

"Ribou and Lacontel are daily becoming more hostile and envenomed. They believe that your success means their downfall, and they are laying their plans. What these may be, I cannot accurately ascertain, but Prince Henri, the Legitimist pretender, is becoming a pawn in their game. General Daubisson, too, is to be detached from you by being offered immediately the Governship of Paris. This has not been definitely decided, but if it would meet your own wishes I could manage it on receipt of a cable. That is to say, I could persuade the passive ministers to help the active ones, and thus allow the latter to triumph with apparent ease."

The only other letter of importance was from M. Folliet.

"De Tournon"—Vansittart smiled at the implacable hate which inspired the man's first thought—"still skulks with his crew of gaol-birds, but he has been in frequent communication with his successor, M. Ribou, who protects and finances him. There will not at present be any further attempt at violence. The next move will be a curious one. An honest and straightforward workingman deputy named Mercier, the chief of the Socialists, together with his friend Hudin, are to be made tools of by the new Minister of the Interior. The propaganda to be adopted is not clear, but it will aim at arousing the people against you. Mercier and Hudin are my friends. They both believe in you and your methods. They consider that you have done more for the working classes in a year than has been accomplished by a century of legislation. You can command them."

Vansittart perused both documents again, whilst an amused but determined expression lit up his face as the subtleties of the situation grew upon his imagination.

One thing he resolved to do at once. He wrote to Mercier briefly, but to the point.

"You are with me, I hear, and those who are with me must share my prosperity. Allow me to send you 100,000 francs towards the furtherance of your cause—this by way of instalment, and as a mere testimony of my good-will. I shall be in Paris shortly, and may want to see you. If so, I will send you as a token a cross, with an initial, and the date. The place will be embossed on the paper."

. . . .

When Vansittart and his companions had hastily returned to Biskra, the millionnaire sought out General Daubisson.

After their first greetings, Jerome came at once to the point with that distinguished soldier. "General," he said, "there is to be no more fighting—here, at any rate."

"If not here, then where else?" queried the fat commander, somewhat surprised at the qualification.

"There are many methods of warfare. The give-and-take combat of the desert may be child's play compared with the social stiletto in Paris."

"If I mistake not, Mr. Vansittart, you are well secured from the most insidious attack. At least so those have found who crossed your path in France."

"Ah, you allude to deceased politicians. True, I have cut off one head, but the dragon has many."

"I wish I could slice off a few for you," said General Daubisson, with great heartiness.

"My friend, you can."

"But how? I shall have to kick up my heels in this— this—well, I don't mean to be unkind, but it *is* a desert yet, is n't it?"

Jerome laughed. "Not so, General. You shall be gazetted Governor of Paris within a week. How will that please you?"

"I?" yelled the delighted soldier. "I, Governor of Paris! It is the desire of my life. But is it possible?"

"It is done, for I have said it. And, General, when the trouble comes, as come it surely will, do not forget the man who gratified your just ambition."

"Mr. Vansittart," cried Daubisson, seizing his hand with effusion, "I can think what I dare not say. But rest assured that if it be in my power, he alone who made me Governor shall unmake me."

"Is that so? Then, believe me, you have a life tenancy of the post."

Vansittart immediately cabled to Liancourt: "Suggestion excellent. Proceed." And the next *Gazette* recalled Daubisson to France to take up the chief military command in the gift of the French Government. The millionnaire did not forget to relieve this valuable ally of financial care in assuming his exalted office, and General Daubisson was courtier enough to smile serenely when assured by M. Ribou that he had obtained the place for him.

CHAPTER XXVIII

ADUMBRATIONS

THERE were strange movements in Paris. Sometimes, before a storm, the leaves of the forest will be full of wide rumors, premonitions; yet, to the onlooker, not a breath accounts for these tremulous agitations. In the early days of July something very similar was taking place in the French capital. One man met another on the Boulevards and said: "What is going to happen?" For answer, the other shrugged. What was going to happen was a summer tempest; some thunder, a tree or two struck by lightning, and it would be over.

M. Ribou, now bearing the Portfolio of the Interior, in place of the disgraced de Tournon, said one day, in an interview with Prince Henri of Navarre:

"Depend upon it, the days of bourgeois rule, monsieur, are nearing their end. The middle class has had its day. It is the top or the bottom which must now rule; or the top *and* the bottom—together."

M. Ribou's deep dark eyes looked keenly at the young man's face; his narrow forehead and high nose were wrinkled into a frown of intense meaning. "What do you mean, monsieur?" said Prince Henri. "Pray be explicit."

"You cannot uproot the instinct of heredity, Monsieur le Prince, from the minds of Frenchmen; nor the *penchant* for kingship. They are like the frogs in the fable. They must have a sovereign, and he must descend from Jupiter."

"But Jupiter sent the frogs *two* sovereigns, and they were equally discontented with both," said Henri.

"Jupiter was unpropitious, monsieur," answered M. Ribou, looking hard at him. "In the first instance, he sent them for a king a log which could do nothing; in the second, he sent them a stork which ate up the frogs. A king resembling neither would be ideal. The people, if they be directed aright, will know where to find him."

Henri's eyes were bright. "But who is to direct them?" he asked.

"Monsieur, we will talk of this later," said Ribou. "Am I right in believing that you attend the reception in the Rue Galilee on Friday, in company with the Comtesse de Fontainebleau?"

"Yes, monsieur."

"We shall meet, then."

"I shall be delighted. But I had a question to ask you. The repeal of my banishment from France was signed by M. de Tournon some weeks before it was handed to me. Do I owe the continuance of its validity to the good offices of his successor?"

Ribou bowed low. "I should have hoped that M. le Prince would have gathered that much from the general tenor of our already long interview."

"I can only say that I owe you a thousand obligations, monsieur," said Henri, rising, "and that in the day of triumph, if it ever come, I am not likely to forget my friends." He went away with flushed brow, in a strange excitement.

An hour later, the Comtesse de Fontainebleau had this whole conversation detailed to her by the enthusiastic Prince. She sat listening, in a small boudoir of the Châlet at St. Cloud, Henri standing with one arm on the mantelpiece. The gleam of hope gave to the young aspirant as much buoyancy as though he had already achieved everything at which he aimed. The Comtesse was silent, but her large bosom heaved with some show of excitement. If Honorine could gain the crown, and the man she loved as well! Such was the thought in her mind. But she only said:

"M. Ribou is a person of considerable shrewdness and tact, I believe. You owe him thanks, Monsieur le Prince."

"And there can be no doubt," said Henri, "that there is something or other in the air. One sees it by many signs; by a certain unrest among the lower orders, by the tone of the public prints, vague hints here and there——"

"And M. Ribou, you think, could control this——?"

"He is Minister of the Interior. He has a thousand agents. In his hands are gathered a thousand threads."

"Above all, he is in our—in your favor."

"Say 'our,' madame. I know that my cause is yours; I have always known it."

"Thank you for saying that," she answered, throwing a glance at his smiling face. "To me the happiness of Honorine is everything. I cannot see her sacrificed to the designs of scheming ambition without a struggle, when a way, of its own accord, opens before me. But, pray, monsieur, do nothing rash. Be sure of your friends before you trust them. Your rival is as nearly omnipotent as man can be. Is M. Ribou your sole ally?"

"He has hinted at many others. In particular, he has mentioned Lacontel."

"The Minister for the Colonies?"

"Yes."

"Well, but that is a powerful—will you excuse me, monsieur? I am all eagerness. I should like to speak with Mademoiselle de Montpensier."

The Comtesse rose, and hurried from the room, accompanied part of the way by Prince Henri. Honorine, under the shade of a wide straw hat, was walking meditatively among the paths of the park, with an open book hanging in her listless fingers.

The Comtesse poured into her ears the whole news of Henri. Honorine listened in silence, with her head slightly inclined sideways to the eager words. When she had heard all, she smiled.

"Henri is a sanguine, amiable boy," she said. "But one expects from the Comtesse de Fontainebleau a certain mental reserve, a greater knowledge of the world."

"Over-caution may ruin lives, Honorine."

"Caution may, rashness will, madame."

"The hopes of Henri, mademoiselle, do not, at first sight, seem so wild as did those of—of—the American."

"But the American is a great man, a man of action."

"Henri also has much spirit, I assure you."

"But no wealth."

"He has friends."

"That remains to be proved."

"At least, he loves you dearly."

She blushed and did not answer.

"And, Honorine, why coerce your own heart, my child? You know that you, also——"

"Pray, let us be loyal, at least in speech," said Honorine.

"I command you to be silent."

At that time M. Lacontel was closeted with M. Ribou in the same office, in the Rue du Faubourg St. Honoré, which Prince Henri had lately left. The two were in fast league. Ribou had voted against the Request in the Chamber of Deputies, the rejection of which had seemed to mean the ruin of the Sahara Scheme. He divined well that there was no pardon for him. That pitiless arm of iron which had struck down his predecessor in the Office of the Interior, might be against him, too—probably would be. As for Lacontel, he looked upon himself as a clerk in his own Office of the Colonies, and as he looked upon himself, so others looked upon him. What is a Minister of Colonies under the august shadow of the Maker of them? He is not a minister; he is an amanuensis. And Vansittart was due in Paris. His next *coup* no one knew. What might such a man not be expected to do to-morrow? It was with the present and poignant consciousness of his expected arrival that both ministers spoke.

"This man's aims are not lower than the very highest," said Ribou, with his narrow, dark head quite near the expansive, pasty countenance of M. Lacoutel.

"You *know* that?" said Lacontel.

"Yes."

"*I* divined it."

"You may know it. De Tournon knew it, and hence, perhaps, his fall."

"But *you* have specific reasons for your view? If so, a hint of them should make Vansittart execrated in France."

"I doubt that," said Ribou ponderingly. "It is a question whether the heart of the French people has that hatred of kings which it is supposed to cherish. Vansittart will be its king, if——"

"What?"

"If we do not take from him, in one *coup*, the foundation stone of his edifice, his motive, and his queen."

"You mean Mademoiselle de Montpensier?"

"She is all that to him, and more."

"Does she know of his designs?"

"Their close association is not only a proof that he has the designs, but that she knows of them, and, in part, approves them."

"You say, 'in part.'"

"Yes—she is by no means an enthusiast in favor of the royal line of Vansittart, I assure you."

"Then, why—— ?"

"I know what I say, M. Lacontel. The Comtesse de Fontainebleau is the lady's dearest friend."

"Well?"

"I have met the Comtesse de Fontainebleau. She, also, is no fanatic in the support of the new dynasty. We have spoken together. She vainly tried to sound *me*, and was herself sounded. We shall speak together again, and again she shall be sounded."

"And you have learned from her——?"

"That Vansittart's schemes are indissolubly bound up with Honorine de Montpensier; that it is in virtue of her royal blood that he hopes to reconcile the people of France and the unbounded insolence of his aims."

"He means to marry her?" questioned Lacontel in some surprise.

"It is clear. Money, popularity, success, he feels, will not avail to win him the crown of an ancient empire. But money *plus* blood will accomplish the conjurer's trick."

"And in the face of such a combination, what can we do?"

Ribou beamed. The man's inborn vanity almost chortled in his throat. He resembled a cock at the instant before it crows. "M. Lacontel," he said, "I never do things by halves. You know me, and you know what I purpose I, in general, accomplish. I have said that I have sounded the Comtesse de Fontainebleau. I have told you that I have got from her Vansittart's object in his association with the female heir to the French crown. But I have not told you all."

"I am all eagerness," said Lacontel.

"All that I have said we might by our native wit have guessed. We did, in fact, divine it without the assistance of the Comtesse de Fontainebleau. But without her assistance, we should not have been aware that Honorine de Montpensier is—in love."

"And not with Vansittart?"

"With Henri de Navarre."

"The female heir in love with the male heir!"

"It is so."

"And he with her?"

"Yes."

"Then why does she countenance the ambitions of Vansittart?"

"Because she believes that Vansittart can do what Henri cannot. He can make her queen. She sacrifices her affection to her ambition."

"In that case we can do nothing."

Again Ribou beamed. "Excuse me—I think we can. We can make the lady believe in the future of Henri de Navarre. We can harmonize affection and ambition. In the eyes of the people we can put in the place of money *plus* blood, a coalition of blood *plus* blood."

"Excellent! if we *can* do it."

"We can do it; at any rate, the first part of it. If we cannot make the people prefer members of its ancient royal family to this upstart, we can at least make the two young people believe that we can."

"And then——?"

"They will marry. They will marry hurriedly, soon. And Vansittart, as far as his great scheme is concerned, will be hopelessly ruined."

"You may count upon me, of course. But I do not see the means."

"The means *I* will make clear. Not an hour ago, I was closeted here with Henri de Navarre. He is a vain and shallow stripling, easily fooled. Our plan will be to delude *his* eyes; and then to make *her* see through them."

"Again I ask 'how?'"

"He shall be cheered publicly in the streets as 'Emperor?' He shall tell her of it with sanguine exaggerations, and she shall believe him."

"But who is to cheer him as 'Emperor?' The people hardly remember his existence."

"Leave that to *me*. The details you shall know hereafter, monsieur."

"Meanwhile, how of this Socialist unrest?"

"It grows. My fingers are on its pulse. There were thirty-five meetings last night. I know what happened at each of them."

"There will be an *émeute?*"

"It is certain. And the result will be disastrous for the American dynasty."

"In what way?"

"Mercier, the heart and soul of the movement is in my power, and——"

"Well?"

"In my pay."

"I do not understand."

"Last night, at one of the meetings, the demagogue, Hudin, said: 'A Socialist Monarchy, that is what we want; away with the rule of the *bourgeois!*' He then, amid loud cheers, referred to the names of Prince Henri and Mademoiselle de Montpensier. You must have seen it in the papers."

"But we ourselves—you and I—represent the rule of the *bourgeois;* we cannot fight against ourselves." Lacontel's cheeks shook with laughter. Ribou frowned.

"This rabble cannot really do away with the rule of any-one," he said, "but they can make a noise; they can create vain hopes; they can unite for us this Henri and this Honor-ine; they can ruin Vansittart. That is why you behold in me, monsieur, for the time being, an ultra-Socialist. He threw himself back in the velveted chair and smiled com-placently.

"But my *rôle* in all this?" queried Lacontel, rising.

"That will unfold itself, monsieur."

They parted. At that hour Vansittart had quietly arrived in Paris. He drove in a close *voiture* to the Grand Hotel. He had come before his time, unrecognized, unannounced. The proprietor gazed in flurried surprise at this swift appari-tion as it hurried past him up the stairs. In half an hour Vansittart was closeted with Folliet.

"And other news?" he said, after a long colloquy.

"Ribou is still holding secret communications with de Tournon," said Folliet, turning the leaves of his little note-book.

"Can you guess why?"

"Yes. I now *know* why. He has had two interviews with Prince Henri of Navarre. He has spoken with the Comtesse de Fontainebleau. He is in fast collusion with Lacontel. There is some understanding between him and the Socialists, Mercier and Hudin. All these relations are directed to the same end as his communications with de Tournon, and all are directed against *you*."

"Undoubtedly. Are the Socialists, then, making a noise?"

"They are about to. All the signs point in that direction."

"Very well, M. Folliet. I congratulate you on your shrewdness, your unfailing skill in affairs. However grateful you may think me, I hope to prove myself better than your anticipations. Will you be good enough to hand this sheet of paper, in person, to M. Mercier."

He put out his hand, took half a sheet of Grand Hotel note-paper, and on it drew a cross. Beneath this hieroglyph, he wrote the letter "V," and a date two days distant.

Vansittart was himself somewhat of a Socialist when it suited his ends.

CHAPTER XXIX

INTRIGUE

VANSITTART'S friends at St. Cloud perceived a strangeness in his conduct in those days. He seemed, after his return, to avoid them. They wondered why, and could not guess that the man was torn asunder by the strength of his will, fighting against a love which had grown, during the later months, into a passion.

His perfect *sang froid* never for an instant forsook him. But he never now chanced to meet Evelyn Harland alone. Even in the presence of others, if she were in the room, he found a pretext to withdraw.

The Comtesse de Fontainebleau was blessed with seeing eyes, and an unerring divination in matters of the heart. What was dark to others, was to her as clear as daylight. At the function five days later in the Rue Galilee, she sank and curved into a profound courtesy before M. Ribou. By her smile, the minister surmised tidings of importance. And these tidings modified his plans.

"I may tell you, madame," said M. Ribou, hanging over her, "that things have taken an unexpectedly upward tendency for your friends—and mine."

They sat in a grotto far down the illuminated gardens. Above their heads swung a Moorish lantern, lit with an electric jet.

"Prince Henri," said the Comtesse, "has mentioned the excursion on which you took him last night, monsieur."

Ribou had taken the Prince *incognito* to one of the noisiest of the Socialist meetings, where it had been previously arranged by the minister that the young man's name should be loudly acclaimed.

"There were, last night, fifty such meetings, madame; some of them secret, but all known to me; and at many of them Prince Henri's name was associated with Mademoiselle de Montpensier's, and with the crown of——"

"Well, monsieur,—is the word too momentous to be uttered?"

"Of France, madame." He glanced round suspiciously. This grotto's wall is of loose, round stones, madame, and between each pair is an open—ear."

"They are eyes, Monsieur le Ministre," she answered laughing. "'Walls have eyes,' the proverb should run. I, at least, have found it so within the last few days."

Ribou's ears were as wide as the wall's in a moment.

"How, madame?"

"A person," she said, "who has persistently been retiring behind a wall on certain occasions in order to screen himself has thereby stood revealed to me. The more the walls which he interposed the clearer was he seen through them."

"Who was the person, if one may ask?"

"The founder of dynasties, monsieur."

"So, madame. And what did he seek to hide?"

"A passion."

"But we already knew that he had it."

"You were deceived. He had it, but it was directed upon an object of which you were not aware."

"And that object is——?"

"Monsieur, our *ménage* consists, in the main, of five persons, Mr. Vansittart, Mademoiselle de Montpensier, myself, an English gentleman called Mr. Harland, and, monsieur— Mr. Harland's sister."

"Ah!" Ribou started.

"Monsieur, since Mr. Vansittart's last return from the

Sahara, he cannot meet Miss Harland with inward composure; he cannot long bear her presence. He either hates her mortally, or he loves her wildly."

"But does Mademoiselle de Montpensier divine this?"

"She may. But I believe not."

"She must be told."

"She shall be told. But, you perceive, monsieur, that to be *told*, is not necessarily to believe."

"Why should she not believe, since you believe?"

"You notice, monsieur, that I said, 'He either hates her mortally, or loves her wildly.' That manner of speaking should be enough to convince you that there is no proof of anything."

"Yet there is sufficient proof to convince *you*?"

"Yes, to give me a moral certainty, both of his love for her, and of her's for him. But if Honorine asked me how I knew, and I then gave her the only reasons I have, she would laugh at me. She would say I was a dreamer. At least, she would not be convinced."

"Mr. Vansittart is not apt to show his emotions, madame?"

"He has a front of adamant, that man! He flames and boils beneath an exterior of Arctic ice. I am sure of it."

"But he has this weak spot, this crack in his armor, this love," said Ribou meditatively. "Madame, I trust your instincts. I do not question the means of your knowledge; I simply believe it, intuitively, to be related to facts. This man is now in our hands."

"But how?"

"Madame, it is clear. We have only two things to do. In the first place, we need to convince Mademoiselle de Montpensier that a man she loves has every chance of shortly ascending the throne of his fathers; this, from what I have already said to you, *you* now know to be true, and you may safely leave it to me to convince Prince Henri, and, through him, mademoiselle, of the fact."

"And our second task, monsieur?"

"We must convince mademoiselle that the love of Mr. Vansittart is not hers, but another's. We must reveal to her her perfect freedom to dispose of herself as she will, in spite of any previous contract with a man whose heart proves faithless to her."

"But there is the very difficulty, monsieur! How are we to do this? We have already referred to Mr. Vansittart's 'front of adamant,' and we have sufficient knowledge of his stern character to be aware that he would sooner die than confess a weakness, than relinquish a scheme."

"Yet, madame," replied Ribou, "you have yourself indicated the means by which Mr. Vansittart may be *forced*, in spite of his adamant front, to confess his weakness."

"I am not aware of it."

"Have you not said that you have seen through the *walls* —that he cannot now bear Miss Harland's presence?"

"That is so. Since his return he has lived mostly at the Grand Hotel, fearing, I am sure, a downbreak of his coldness in her company. But I am still in the dark as to what you would do, monsieur."

"I would make him meet her."

"Ah! Under what circumstances?"

"Privately—unexpectedly—by night—in a long, uninterrupted interview——"

"If it could be done, monsieur?"

Her eyebrows lifted in query.

"It can, madame."

"But who would be any the wiser, if they met privately?"

"Those who saw and heard."

"Mademoiselle de Montpensier is so incredulous of such reports."

"Mademoiselle would herself be a witness of the scene. That is part of my plan. A week later she would be the Princesse de Navarre."

"Monsieur, you overwhelm me. I must think of all this.

I perceive your acumen, I acknowledge your resource. But——"

"I have said it," said Ribou, leaning back with purring vanity—" and it shall be done."

"And when?"

"Within a week."

"And meanwhile —— ?"

"Two things should happen."

"What?"

"Prince Henri and mademoiselle should meet often, alone. You must contrive to throw them together. He must ply her with the news of his sucesses, while they are warm."

"And the other thing?"

"Mademoiselle and Miss Harland must quarrel."

"Oh, monsieur!"

"Yes—it is necessary. Do you not see? They must be made to detest each other. You know your sex, madame. Enmity is with it a strong motive. Miss Harland must be given this added motive for her conduct in the lovers' scene, in which she meets Mr. Vansittart. Honor may be stronger than hate, or than love; it will hardly prove stronger than both together."

"Miss Harland and Honorine already bear each other no superabundance of affection, as it appears," said the Comtesse. "No doubt a hint to mademoiselle of the state of Vansittart's affection, whether I can prove it or not, will not greatly add to her liking for Miss Harland."

"You have said, madame, what I would have tried to say."

M. Ribou bowed; the Comtesse rose; they walked away. M. Ribou then sought out, from amid the throng of the *soirée*, Prince Henri, with whom, in the same grotto, he had a long colloquy, the result of which will appear.

That same night de Tournon sat in the bar parlor of an inn at La Villette. His redundant wealth of buxom chins rested upon his hand; his elbow rested upon the table, and the sleeve between elbow and hand was torn and frayed. He was eyeing some dirty cards on the table, with a languid down-look of the eyes. Around him were gathered a host of yokels, some joining in the game. The white, raftered ceiling was very low—one could touch it with the lifted hand—the room was small, and full of the voices of the village laborers, wearily drinking wine-dregs after the drudging day. The landlord lounged by the bar, and watched the stains of the feet on his white floor of the morning.

"Trumps!" cried de Tournon. And he added, "To-morrow afternoon there will be quite a to-do in the village, I suppose?"

"What about? What about?" said two voices.

"Isn't—what do you call him—the rich American—ah, Vansittart!—going to pass through the village?"

The whole room gathered round him.

"Who says?"

"How do you know?"

"A fine yarn that is!"

"It can't be true!"

"You are nice people, not to know the news of your own little toyshop village! Did n't I see it this morning in a Paris paper?"

"What's he coming for?—since you Paris loungers know everything."

"He is not coming *for* anything. He merely passes through—with the Minister of the Interior."

"In his own carriage?"

"No—the minister's."

"He is a brave one. We will give him a welcoming."

"You should. Do you know how to tickle him?"

"No—how?"

"Call him 'the Emperor.'"

"Yes—one has heard that they do that in Paris. And why not? He deserves it."

"Oh, in Paris, that is his name. When the people call him so, he scatters among them showers of gold."

"The Prince of Wealth! He shall have a welcoming here, and a warm one!"

"Do any of you know his face?"

"I do!"

"I also; I saw him in Paris."

"That all?"

No answer. "Trumps again!" called de Tournon.

Down the street, a hundred yards away, in the "Golden Dragon," Lacontel, in a disguise, also played at cards. And here the same news of the passage of Vansittart was recounted.

And on the next evening, as the shades of night gathered, Ribou's carriage passed through a village street ringing with huzzas. Every soul in the township was here, and from nearly every throat rang the cry, "*Vive l'Empereur!*" But the carriage was a brougham, and closed. Ribou was of opinion that a certain reserved dignity on the part of the Prince would better suit the circumstances of the moment. The Prince sat back in the carriage. Ribou himself looked out and bowed, all smiles. Not ten people saw Prince Henri's face. The carriage passed through the boisterous crowd.

There was, however, a hitch or two which a keen and worldly eye would have noted. One man catching sight of Henri's face, cried aloud, "But—that is not he!" Some others, instead of shouting, "*Vive l'Empereur!*" cried, "*Vive Vansittart!*"

But Prince Henri was in too high a heaven to notice these details of earth. In the royal eye was the scarcely veiled excitement of the conscious conqueror. He did not remain long in Paris. Ribou suggested a lengthy interview, but the Prince was incapable of listening that night. His tongue was envious of his ears, and needed to divulge what they had heard. He set out at once for St. Cloud, and, arrived there, hurried to the Châlet. Was Honorine in? No, she was strolling in the park. Alone? Probably. He went to look. The summer night was still, and full of the sleepy whispers of birds and insects, tired of the long sweet day. Abroad in the heavens sailed the half-moon. He found her after half-an-hour's longings and invocations. He knew her favorite path, and went by it; but she had wandered aside. When he came upon her she was walking, with curved neck, homeward, upon a thick moss beneath the trees, thinking of him. Before he spoke she heard his hurried breath, and stopped. The next moment he was before her.

"Oh, Honorine!"

"Henri!"

"My dear——"

"This is forbidden ground, Henri."

"It cannot last, Honorine. You must listen to me. The Fates fight for us; the stars in their courses are the allies of kings——"

She smiled. Her bosom heaved. A look of tenderest pity came into her eyes.

"Poor Henri!"

"We need no longer pity ourselves or each other, Honorine; and the compact of silence we have made cannot, and must not, be kept."

"But you must allow me to be in private if I choose. You must not be my unrelenting shadow like this, rude boy!"

"Do not suppose that I have come to make love."

"Ah, well, that is some comfort, is it not?"

"You know already how I love——"

"But now you are doing what you did not come to do."

"Your presence is deflecting, as the needle escapes and runs back to the north."

"And I am as cold as the north."

"In the winter of our discontent. But now—surely—Honorine—it is summer with us! Will you not relent?"

"I believe in summer when I see leaves on the trees, and the boughs heavy with fruit. Not before."

"I bring you a basket of peaches—dear; a very cornucopia from the lap of August."

He handed her a card. They had walked to where the moon came pouring on an open space. By its light, she looked at the face of the card, and saw the name of Ribou. On the back, written in pencil, were these words:

"Union is strength."

"I hardly know this man," she said.

"He is a friend."

"With what motive?"

"His heart is pure Royalist."

"Or Ribouist?"

"Undoubtedly that, and Royalist, perhaps, *because* he is that."

"I do not follow you."

"He is a shrewd man. He sees far ahead. He believes it to be in Ribou's interest to be a Royalist. Being a thorough Ribouist, we may be sure of the sincerity of his Royalism."

"Your argument is good, Henri—if your premise be just. Why is it in his interest to be a Royalist?"

"The Comtesse has told you of our excursion to the Socialist meeting?"

"The Comtesse tells too much, perhaps."

"I have just come from La Villette."

"Well?"

"With Ribou."

"Well?"

"We passed down a long street ringing with *vivats* for 'the Emperor.'"

"Is that so, Henri?"

"Yes, Honorine."

"Oh, Henri!"

"Ribou said to me, 'In a month all France will reverberate with that shout of rapture.'"

"Did the people see you, then?"

"Hardly. We were in a brougham. But Ribou had chanced to let out to some journalist fellow that we should pass through, and by means of his paper the news went about the village."

" What paper ? "

" I don't know. Some paper."

" But the cause, Henri, of this sudden enthusiasm ? "

" It is the stars that fight for kings."

" The stars won't do, Henri."

" There is a movement among the people—a hatred for the middle class. Extremes have met and shaken hands. The extreme democracy pines for union with the extreme monocracy ; the extreme modern for union with the extreme ancient. You see in me the hero of—the Socialists."

" It is singular."

" Yet it is so. They have set their hopes upon the marriage of you and me."

" Henri ! " She averted her face.

" Do their wishes coincide with yours ? " he said.

A long sigh came from her parted lips. She struck him with the back of her forefinger on his cheek. " You are a sanguine, charming boy ! I don't know what to do with you ? "

" Honorine ! You will not continue this uphill fight ? Dearest, you will yield to me——"

" Go, Henri—leave me—can the tides fight against the moon ? Can a stone fall upward ? Ah, what am I saying ? —go ! "

His lips were pressed upon her hand. They were just then crossing the lawn, toward the Châlet ; and crossing it also, some distance away, was Evelyn Harland. And she saw them in the vague moonlight.

CHAPTER XXX

TWO WOMEN

FOR three entire days Vansittart had not come near St. Cloud. "Something new is up!" mused Dick Harland. "That Sahara business is a trifle too much for one mortal back to bear, in my opinion."

The Comtesse de Fontainebleau said, "Mr. Vansittart must be more than usually engaged."

She was walking on the terraces amid the flower-beds and fountains with Honorine. It was the morning after the meeting in the wood between Henri and Honorine, when, in the moonshine, Evelyn had seen Henri's lips on her hand. Evelyn and Honorine had not since met. Honorine walked listlessly and dreamfully that morning. Her straw garden-hat swung by the strings in her hand.

She did not answer the Comtesse until the latter said:

"And do you not think it *singular*, Honorine, this absence?"

"I? No. I have not thought of it. He is busy, I imagine."

"Or in love."

"No, that is hardly the inference. His love would make him come to me, not keep away, surely."

"Come to *you*—yes——"

"I do not understand you at all, madame. If you have anything to say, I am willing to hear."

"Mr. Vansittart is a secret and silent man, Honorine. But to me he is as open as a book."

"I should have thought not. And what do you read, madame?"

"Is his absence not due to the fear of meeting Miss—Harland?"

"Miss—the *fear!*—your jest is as poor as possible."

"You are not as old as I, my child."

"Nor, apparently, as erratic."

"I speak to warn you, you know."

"Pray, let the subject drop."

The Comtesse said no more. Honorine was slightly pale. The corners of her mouth curved slightly downward.

They walked leisurely into the palace. On a table were letters on a golden salver. Near it stood Evelyn, reading one. She, too, had just entered, and her fresh face bore its bright morning smile. The letter she read was from a friend in England. But the bow exchanged between her and Honorine was somewhat cold. In the mind of each was a thought, a doubt.

Honorine took some of the letters, and sat to read them. One was from M. Ribou. One was from Henri. The young Prince, after leaving her, had sat up half the night writing it. As she read, she smiled, and the thought that rankled in her mind, for a time, vanished.

Unnoticed, the Comtesse de Fontainebleau had passed from the room. It was large, and oval-shaped. From the domed roof depended three huge chandeliers of the cut glass called *margherita*, whose prismic twinklings filled the upper portion of the apartment with a chaos of rainbows. Into the fleecy carpet, the treasure of some Levantic mart, the whole foot sank. At the four quarters of the room's circumference were heavily curtained doors, and it was behind one of these that the Comtesse passed into the adjoining *salon*. She sat near the tapestry, with ear inclined to whatever sounds the Fates might send, an open book in her lap, at which she did not look.

The Emperors' families, in the days of Rome, thus sat

hidden behind the curtains of the amphitheatre to watch the contests in the arena of the circus. The Comtesse knew that two she-cats could not be left tied up in a small sack with so safe a prediction of clawing, as these two ladies now, in that rich hall, stately with classic chiselling, and the wealth of nations.

"Mr. Vansittart is not here this morning, I suppose?" said Honorine.

"Not that I am aware of," answered Evelyn.

They were both attired in loose morning robes, with wide sleeves and long trains; they were both ladies of stately necks and luxuriant wealth of hair. The difference between Honorine and Evelyn was the difference between a damask rose and a pink.

"Is Mr. Vansittart very busy?" asked Honorine.

Evelyn's fresh pink flushed into a deeper carmine, as she bent over a Benares vase of roses. She answered in carefully calm tones:

"How should I know?"

"I thought you would."

"Why?"

Lower and lower she bent over the roses, with hotter and hotter cheeks. Honorine was reclining backwards in the lap of a luxury of cushions at the couch-head, her clenched right hand supporting her head.

"Do you ask 'why'?" she said, with a little light laugh. "I hardly know. You seem good at business. I always look upon you as Mr. Vansittart's Prime Minister, you know."

"That is quite a high *métier*," said Evelyn; "I should be proud to fill it; but I am afraid no woman could."

"You have a high opinion of the post, evidently."

"Oh, immensely!"

"But you are too open. You betray yourself. You think so much of the post, because you think so much of the giver of it."

"Well, perhaps, as you say, I am too open. It is a characteristic of us English, you know. We hate disguises, falsehood in any form—especially we hate a false woman." She said it with bitter venom. Two little dark red spots flamed out on Honorine's cheeks, and her nostrils began to broaden and pant like a thoroughbred's.

"The English are open, you say? Yes, I have heard that. This quality is no doubt related to their extraordinary genius for affairs!" A long ripple of laughter flowed from her.

"Yes, that is quite so," said Evelyn. "They are essentially practical, faithful to what they undertake, and single-minded."

"*Simple*-minded, did you say?"

"No—single; the word is perhaps too idiomatic for *you* to understand fully. I will explain, if you like."

"Pray, do. You have such a pretty knack of making clear to the dullest eyes that which was hidden."

"I am so glad of that. I may yet hope to do some good, then, even in apparently desperate cases."

"You are too philanthropic. You cannot be a prime minister and a knight-errant, a business man and a missionary all at once."

"Oh, yes. Some missionaries act as traders, you know; some knight-errants were ministers of state. A monarch may unbend to be a lover; a lover may aspire to be a monarch."

"But that is only for the double-minded. *You*, for instance, would never aspire to be a monarch; for you are English, and single-minded, and, no doubt, a lover."

"I do not think you understand the exact meaning of this word 'single-minded,'" said Evelyn, meditatively. "It is, perhaps, a little beyond you, with even your knowledge of English. Its opposite is well expressed in another idiom of ours, 'Having two strings to one's bow.'"

"Precisely; I understand. But suppose a single-minded

English lady who attracted a lover by acting to him in the double capacity of prime minister and missionary, might she not be said to have ' two strings to one bow ? ' She might, at any rate, be said to have one *beau* by two strings."

" Which is, nevertheless, preferable to having two *beaux* by one string."

To and fro flew the cutting, meaningful retort, lashing like whip-cord, the two ladies facing each other with intense eyes and reddened cheeks.

" But to have two *beaux* by any number of strings," darted forth Honorine's answer, " is a venial offence, provided they are both your own. The wretchedness is to have one *beau* who is somebody's else ! "

" It is wretched, certainly—but not criminal."

" It is mean, it is base-spirited."

" It is weak, not wicked. But the other, among the great, honest middle class of my country, is regarded as——"

" Do not mention that class. I have no relation to it, no interest in it. And you—and your brother—by your association with Mr. Vansittart, are now lifted out of it."

The words cut like a knife to Evelyn's inmost, tenderest nerve. She flinched, and shrank. " My brother went to school with Mr. Vansittart," she said, after a second's pain. " There is no question of being *lifted* as regards him or me. Our connection with Mr. Vansittart is not the result of an ambitious scheme. We hope for nothing from his wealth."

Her tongue now was dipped in gall. It was the turn of Honorine to wince. For a moment her face was blanched with rage ; in the next it was aflame. " I cannot but consider your language personal," she said, in a deep guttural.

With these words, the hints, the meanings, suddenly ceased, and there was open war. They were on fire, and fire does not traffic in innuendoes. " It is personal, of course," said Evelyn. " You knew that all along. We might all this time have spoken our minds clearly but for your inveterate lack of candor."

"You are an insolent woman."

"You are not a faithful one."

"You are taking advantage of the absence of Mr. Vansittart."

"*You* are, you mean. You would not have dared to hint the things you have in his presence!"

"*I!*—not *dared* in the presence of the American?"

"No, not in the presence of 'the American,' to whom you happen to owe everything—not in the presence of any gentleman—certainly not in the presence of my brother——"

"Your brother! Ha! ha! He is a—Master of the Horse!"

"But that is something. It proves that he is a real man, at any rate. As you seem fond of the species, you should have him in your court. He is not a silly boy, whom everybody makes fun of."

"Who is everybody?—yourself, the American, and the—Master of the Horse?"

"Especially 'the American.'"

"When I next see the heir to the crown of France, I must tell him that the Master of the Horse of the next dynasty makes 'fun of him!'"

"Surely, you knew before! You should have told him last night, when he was kissing your hand. It might have acted as a damper on the simpleton's ardors."

"You do not, I hope, add to your other delightful functions that of spy to the new dynasty?"

"It is not so much that I am a spy, as that you are hopelessly blinded by folly. The ostrich pokes its head into the bush, and thinks that no one can see his body. If somebody comes along and sees it, and the ostrich chooses to call him a spy, that is because the ostrich is an idiot."

"But there are ostriches and ostriches! All, apparently, have this folly of thinking themselves unseen, when everybody can clearly see, and see into, them. Some, however, are presumptuous. They do not keep to the plain, to their own level. They climb the hills, where they are still more conspicuous. If you have read my secret, others have read yours. And you cannot say that I am presumptuous. I am the equal of Henri of Navarre. In *your* case, there is a difference."

"I do not admit your insinuation. But if it were so, no harm would be done to any one. There is nothing at stake. In the other case, you are fooling a man who is spending his life upon you. Shame!"

There was a tender thrill in Evelyn's voice.

"It is false. I am fooling no one. If any one is being fooled, it is I; and if it is so, *you* know of it——"

At that moment, the Comtesse de Fontainebleau, thinking the fray had served its purpose, sailed into the room. Honorine glanced at a letter which lay on her lap; Evelyn bent once more over the roses. From the cheeks of both the color faded slowly out, leaving a perfect pallor.

A footman appeared, and announced:

"M. Ribou."

And immediately the dapper minister, with a gray topcoat, a gray frock-coat and amber gloves, was bowing before the ladies. He was presented to Evelyn by the Comtesse de Fontainebleau.

"I have already had the honor of a presentation to the brother of Miss Harland," said the minister. "*This* pleasure was not unanticipated."

Honorine, on her side, smiled at him.

"Ah, mademoiselle," said Ribou, "I have had the extreme delight of learning from Prince Henri of Navarre that you will not disdain to attend my *soirée* on Thursday."

"I have indicated my pleasure by letter," said Honorine. "Monsieur's indications of sympathy with the fallen House of France have been neither unknown nor unacceptable to at least one of its descendants."

Ribou and the Comtesse exchanged an anxious glance. This talk was somewhat plain for the ears of Evelyn.

"You, too, madame," said Ribou quickly, "will no doubt be present in company with Mademoiselle de Montpensier?"

"Yes, monsieur."

"And Miss Harland?"

Evelyn had no intention to go. "I am uncertain, M. Ribou," she said. "Invitations of courtesy from dignitaries, personally unknown, are like out-worn ceremonies; they lack intention. Of course, I received your *carte* in common with my friends, and thank you."

"Oh, I beg——" began Ribou, all courtliness.

"Has Mr. Vansittart intimated an intention of being present?" interrupted Honorine, meaningly.

"No, mademoiselle—that is, he *may* be. It is quite uncertain."

"Then I also may be," said Evelyn boldly. It was a retort and a challenge to Honorine. Everybody glanced at everybody else. When Ribou rose, five minutes later, he took Evelyn's hand.

"Then I shall expect, with even poignant anticipation, to see Miss Harland?"

Evelyn smiled. "It would be a pity to balk your *poignant* anticipation, M. Ribou."

"It would certainly." Suddenly he bent to her with lowered voice. "May I write you on a matter of some importance to your friends and mine?"

She looked at him in surprise, and whispered a hurried "Yes."

The Comtesse de Fontainebleau sat nearer the door of entrance. As Ribou parted from her he muttered:

"Vansittart will be present—by special appointment with Lacontel."

Vansittart was pacing from end to end of a long room at the Grand Hotel, while Ribou drove back to Paris. His arms were crossed on his chest, and his head drooped forward and downward. He was alone, and his heart was doing battle with its longings.

A footman entered with a card. It bore the name, "M. Mercier."

"Send him in," said Vansittart.

Mercier was a big man, with a huge head covered with a mane of blue-black hair, which as he spoke, he would shake backward, royally, like a lion's. But he stood lamb-like enough before Vansittart as the latter stopped in his walk and faced him.

"I see by the papers, M. Mercier," he said, "that you have so far followed my suggestions."

"It is so, monsieur. At every meeting the name of Henri has been acclaimed—that is, as far as our friends were able to effect it."

"You had some difficulty, then?"

"Well, naturally. The lad is unknown, or, at any rate, quite ignored by the people. He is not a real factor in the situation at all."

"Is M. Ribou, think you, a genuine Royalist at heart?"

Mercier threw back his lion's mane. "Royalist, no! Wretches of that class are not really anything at heart, monsieur, except supporters of their own interests."

"Why, then, M. Mercier, did he have you, in the first instance, acclaim Prince Henri?"

"I cannot tell you. He put some little money in our funds. It cost us nothing. We acclaimed him."

"Money? Yet I think he is not what might be called extremely rich. And it was a risk—a grave risk. He must have had a motive."

"Undoubtedly. You can perhaps fathom it better than I."

"Perhaps. And since the acclamation of the Prince at *all* the meetings, have you seen aught of M. Ribou?"

"Yes; and of Lacontel, too. It is rather a joke. They only paid me for acclamation at three of the meetings. They were perfectly mystified—even astounded, of course. I told them it was the result of the spontaneous enthusiasm of the people for Prince Henri, which, once aroused, was spreading itself in that way. They seemed amused, and even delighted."

"Good. We shall see. But suppose the people of France were told that two of their ministers were distributing bribes to have an exiled Prince acclaimed all over Paris, what, think you, would be the sudden fate of those ministers?"

Mercier tossed his mane, and roared with laughter. "I would n't give *that* for them," he said, and snapped thumb and finger.

"Very well, Monsieur Mercier. Our opinions coincide. I will say *au revoir*. A further check for a hundred thousand francs will reach you to-morrow."

"*Au revoir*, monsieur——"

"And, Monsieur Mercier! On *Thursday*, in the evening, you may hear from me. I am not sure; but you may. Two crosses, in pencil, or else one. You will know where to strike, and do not spare them. One cross will mean the Interior; two crosses the Interior *and* the Colonies."

Mercier bowed and retired.

CHAPTER XXXI

THE SOIRÉE

"THE rooms are too crowded, monsieur," said Lacontel. "How the throng presses! If you would care to take a turn with me in the gardens——"

"I am entirely at your disposal," said Vansittart, with a smile that was like the smile of an iron mask.

"Or to-morrow, at the Colonial Office?" suggested Lacontel timorously, "or at the Grand Hotel?"

Vansittart considered. "I could see you, then, at either place."

"But—but—it must needs be at a very early hour—for a very short time. . . . I am compelled, monsieur, to leave Paris—to-morrow—our interview would be hurried——"

Vansittart smiled. "And you say that the matter is urgent?"

"Monsieur, it concerns the France in Africa."

"That is enough for me, Monsieur Lacontel. To the gardens by all means, and at once." The breast-pocket of Vansittart's lavender-colored dress-coat bulged somewhat outward. It contained a tiny Venetian revolver of embossed silver. As the two men moved through the thronged vista of rooms, the crowd parting at their advance, he touched the spot with his finger.

For a *soirée* given by the minister of a republic, the reception produced an impression of extravagant display. The mansion had been recently redecorated from top to bottom. On the chimney-pieces, adorned with *ormolu* foliage of the richest sculpture, were placed huge mirrors in superb frames, and on the tables were girandoles of fretted ivory. The tables were Oriental and of alabaster, and the stools gilt and covered with crimson velvet. The apartments received upon their bright delicate summer draperies, and curtains of fine gauze, the strange variegated illumination of innumerable colored lights; and great, swift-darting bluish jets of electric light would, all in a moment, cast pallor over these thousands of other lights, throwing, as it were, the full moon's frosty radiance over faces and bare shoulders, over the whole phantasmagory of feathers, fabrics, bows, and ribbons, crushing each other in the vista, or ranked tier upon tier on the broad staircases. Out in the grounds— half park, half garden—an endless mosaic was wrought among the foliage by Chinese, Moorish, Persian, and Japanese lanterns, some made of perforated tin, cut into ogives like mosque doors, others of colored paper resembling fruits. M. Ribou had sought to set himself up as the rival in magnificence of the millionnaire.

His whole attentions on this gala evening were devoted to a stranger—to Evelyn Harland. The hint of some imminent danger overhanging Vansittart was enough to secure to M. Ribou the friendship of the simple-hearted English girl. Since their first meeting at St. Cloud, this, on the night of the reception, was their third.

A hurried lady came up, touched the sleeve of M. Ribou, and whispered some words.

"I will follow you, immediately, madame," he said.

Then in a low voice to Evelyn: "It is impossible for us, Miss Harland, to speak on such a subject here. I am, you see, called away—always."

"One word," said Evelyn. "Does this scheme of de Tournon's actually include the sacrifice of Mr. Vansittart's *life*—or only——"

"Sh-h-h!" he glanced round in theatrical affright. "Certainly Miss Harland has not learned the truth that everything has ears in such an assembly. If you will do me the honor of an interview—in private—in the grounds——"

"Yes!" she said eagerly.

"Descend, then, the staircase there. You will emerge into a walk of poplars, at the end of which, if you turn to the right, you will enter an avenue of limes. This, I think, you will find deserted. And there, in from twenty minutes to half-an-hour, I will have the honor to lay before you the whole plan."

M. Ribou bowed and hurried away, steering his devious path through the fashionable mob. But he did not make for the lady, whoever she was, who had summoned him. Instead, he passed down one of the staircases leading to the gardens. The avenue of poplars was a triple one, formed by four lines of towering trees, with trunks so near together as to form almost a pallisade. The central avenue was brilliantly variegated with colored lights, but the two flanks, though broad, stretched out in a long gloomy perspective under the crescent moon. Down one of these passed M. Ribou.

Farther away from the house, in another part of the grounds, stood Lacontel and Vansittart. "And now, monsieur," said the maker of colonies to the minister of them, "I think we may here discuss the perils that overhang France in Africa with perfect convenience."

"It is so, monsieur. The point upon which I wish to confer with you, is this——"

But the two men never conferred upon the point. Apparently starting out of the darkness of the shrubberies, a commissionaire stood before them. He bowed and handed to the minister a telegram.

Monsieur Lacontel stood beneath the light of a lantern, and held the telegram before his apparently astonished eyes.

"What!" he exclaimed. "Is this so?" He turned to Vansittart.

"Monsieur, I beg you a thousand pardons. It is absolutely essential that I should be at the Colonial Office at this moment. The message here——"

"Pray do not mention it," said Vansittart. "The Colonies of France are their own excuse. Their minister, monsieur, is above pardon."

"Yet it is essential that I should speak with you."

"I will accompany you."

"Then you are kindness itself. Or would it be more convenient if you await my return?"

"I am entirely at the disposal of the minister for the Colonies."

"You are too good. So then let it be. I shall not be twenty minutes, I think. The night, too, is warm and balmy."

"Very good, monsieur. At the end of that time I await you here."

"Here, then," repeated M. Lacontel. "But stop! Where is 'here?' I declare I do not know at all. We have strolled too far. I have lost myself in M. Ribou's spacious estate. I seriously doubt whether I can find 'here' again."

Vansittart smiled his iron smile.

"There is a staircase," he said, "which leads directly from the central *salon* into the gardens. At the foot of that, let us say, I will await Monsieur le Ministre."

"Good, monsieur—there then. Or, since that spot is likely to be swarming with guests, you might walk up the avenue of poplars which you will find immediately before the staircase, and turning to the right into an avenue of limes, now in blossom, stroll until I come. At that spot we should be perfectly secure."

"I shall not fail to be there, monsieur," said Vansittart, reading keenly every change of expression on Lacontel's face.

"*Au revoir*, then, monsieur."

"*Au revoir*, Monsieur le Ministre."

They parted, the bearer of the telegram following at Lacontel's hurried heels. Vansittart opened the door of one of the lanterns, put a cigar to the flame, and began to smoke.

Evelyn was at the end of the avenue of limes, walking leisurely up and down. It was twenty minutes before the time of her tryst with M. Ribou, but she had left the crowded air of the *salons* immediately after her interview with him for the spiced scent of the night in the gardens.

Lacontel had spoken truly; the avenue of limes was rich with perfume.

In the centre, the spray of a fountain whispered and muttered, like some cold white spirit, weaving, in her far-tossed hair of dew, aureoles of the lunar rainbow. The roots of the trees were thick with growths of moss. But the middle portion of the broad path was of a gray light soil, half earth, half sand. Here and there were rustic seats. Yonder, not far from the fountain, an octagonal kiosk of varnished twigs occupied half the breadth of the avenue of limes. The path was utterly lonely. The chirp of a cicada, piping some song of jubilee from its covert of moss, broke the stillness in a harmony with the serenading fountain.

From end to end of the long avenue walked Evelyn, waiting. This was strange news that she had heard. Could it be that into her hands was about to be given the power of saving him from some evil scheme? That would be the crown of her life—to rescue her king from peril! But why had he kept from her so much of late? Was he secretly hatching some new surprise for civilization? Such thoughts occupied her.

At the end of one of her strolls down the avenue of limes, she entered again the avenue of poplars. A little tired, she sat upon a seat near the angle between the two avenues. Her chin rested on her hands, her elbows on her knees. In this posture she sat for about five minutes, in pensive meditation. A galaxy of lanterns hung just above her head. A longish, crooked twig, fallen from one of the trees, lay at her feet. In her listless mood, she took it up, hardly conscious of the action. She swung it a little in her hand, with the other she wrote a word—still leaning forward in her pensive attitude—in the loose, sandy earth.

The word was "Jerome."

And yonder again the word "Jerome"; and yonder again. She got up presently, and walked back into the avenue of limes. And ever and again, as she went, she stooped a little forward listlessly, and wrote in the loose, sandy earth.

M. Ribou had hastened up the side avenue of poplars.

Half-way, slowly walking, with their backs towards him, were two persons. They were Honorine de Montpensier and the Comtesse de Fontainebleau. It was at the suggestion of the Comtesse that they had taken this walk. Ribou joined them.

"I congratulate you, monsieur," said Honorine, "on the *féerique* glamor of these enchanted grounds. But why have you left this avenue in almost complete darkness?"

"There are minds," said Ribou, "for whom a touch of gloom has more charms than all the bazaars of elfdom, mademoiselle."

"Whither does this path lead?" queried the Comtesse.

"To a side avenue of limes, madame, at right angles with this. Even from this spot the perfume of their summer luxuriance reaches us. If you will permit me——"

Honorine bowed assent.

"Is there a seat, monsieur?" said the Comtesse. "I begin to grow tired."

"There are many, madame. One especially, to which I shall conduct you, stands in an arbor of vines, and will give you sight and sound of a fountain playing in an adjacent avenue."

As the three sat within this arbor, through the interspaces between the trees before them, they saw Evelyn slowly pacing to and fro in the full light. Honorine bit her lip. Upon herself and her companions, as if by mutual consent, silence fell.

The time had come for the appearance of M. Ribou. Evelyn glanced at her watch. She stopped her walk, and stood, waiting. Honorine's heart beat fast. She divined that Evelyn Harland was here for a purpose. But what? An instinct, a presaging voice, whispered to her the name of Vansittart. Was it an assignation? At that moment she thought of Prince Henri with a thrill of passion, and of Vansittart with a pang of jealousy.

Vansittart, at this time, had entered the avenue of poplars. He sauntered to the end, with wary eyes. He sat upon the seat which Evelyn had just left. He touched with his hand the weapon in his pocket. Some plot was brewing, he thought. And he remembered de Tournon's attempt upon him in the woods. Now he was in the middle of Paris. Yet this was a spot as lonely as the depths of the wood. A sudden outburst of brigands upon him would not have surprised him in the least. But this time he was prepared. The danger which threatened him, had he guessed it, was a thousand times more subtle, more terrible to withstand, and more tremendous to overcome than the crude violence of de Tournon's ruffians in the forest. Greater is he that ruleth his spirit than he that taketh a city. He was not even perfectly sure of the existence of a plot against him, though he was *almost* sure. His purpose in coming here at the bidding of those whom he knew to be his enemies was definitely to ascertain that there was a plot, and what it was. Then the thunderbolts of his vengeance would not be slow. He sat leaning forward, waiting, smiling. He touched the weapon in his pocket. Presently, his eyes falling upon the ground, he saw his name written in the sand.

"Jerome."

He sprang up, peering. There it was again, "Jerome." And yonder. And then following the track, "Evelyn." The word "God!" heaved on a pant from his chest. She had been here. He knew—his heart knew—who had written the words. He had had no idea that she was at the reception that night at all! In a moment he forgot all about the suspected plot, about Ribou, and Lacontel, and the world. Evelyn had unconsciously added a thousand aids to the designs of his enemies. The scribbled letters had set his blood aflame. He must see her! To-night! He started at a rapid walk back towards the house; but stopped, and turned again. She might be there—in the other avenue, near him! He went to look, peering again at the marks in the sand. As he strode into the avenue of limes the three watchers in the vine-arbor saw him. Honorine's teeth met with a snap. Evelyn was hidden from him by the summer-house near the fountain. She heard his steps, and thought they were those of M. Ribou. He was quite near to her before he saw her. They stood face to face. Vansittart's visage was as white and tense and stern as the face of a dead man.

"You, Mr. Vansittart!" cried Evelyn.

It was lucky that she spoke first. Her commonplace surprise brought him back a little to the every-day world.

"You are alone?" His voice was somewhat husky.

"I—I was waiting here for Monsieur Ribou—on—on a matter of some importance," she blurted out, with English-girl candor. Honorine, in the arbor, glanced at Ribou in perplexed surprise.

"I am sorry if I intrude," said Vansittart with perfectly cold collectedness. A whole revolution had been wrought in him by one sublime, intense effort of his mighty will. At the name of Ribou, the entire scheme of villainy lay open to his keen eye; and the struggle was over.

"*Do* I intrude?" he said.

"No, you do not intrude," said Evelyn, "only your apparition was sudden."

"May I take you back to the house?"

"I think I will wait for Monsieur Ribou, thank you."

Again Honorine glanced at Ribou.

"I am afraid Monsieur Ribou will not keep his appointment," said Vansittart, smiling.

"No? But why?"

"I fancy he is detained."

"Still, I'd rather stay here for the present."

"Then good-night."

At that moment Honorine stood with them. Her eyes were bright, her cheeks flushed. She held out her hand to Evelyn. "Miss Harland—will you—*will* you forgive me?"

Evelyn took her hand, saying at the same time:

"What for? How strange——"

Honorine turned to Vansittart with extended arm: "Mr. Vansittart—though I should have known you better—I have been guilty of an injustice towards you. Will *you* forgive me?"

"The injustice," said Vansittart, "whatever it was, was forgiven before its commission."

"Will you take me back to the house?"

Vansittart walked with her to the foot of the staircase, and then turned aside to an alley where Arizona Jim, in the dress of a commissionaire, awaited him. He took from a waistcoat pocket a paper marked with two crosses, and handed it to his faithful follower.

"For M. Mercier," he said.

CHAPTER XXXII

A MINISTERIAL PANIC

MM. Ribou and Lacontel had fallen. And with such suddenness, completeness, and ease, that the result had almost the look of magic. As the political prophets had foretold, there was an *émeute*. But it was of no real importance. It occurred on the day following the night on which Vansittart had sent the two crosses on a sheet of paper to Mercier. The next morning a few windows of inoffensive people were broken; three butcher shops rifled; a gunshop stripped, and one man, who had opposed the rioters, shot dead. That was all. This was the Socialist beginning. But the affair did not end with the Socialists. It ended with MM. Ribou and Lacontel.

About noon the feeling of excitement had spread through the whole body of the people. The rumor had got abroad that the acclamation of the Royalists at the Socialist meetings had been due to the bribes of the two ministers. Everyone knew of the fact of these acclamations. And it was here that the skill of Vansittart was magnificently displayed; for it was with the deliberate intention that everyone should know of them that he had caused the acclamations to take place at all the meetings—Ribou's idea, in the first instance, being that they should occur at no more than three.

As the day wore on the storm darkened. It was incredible, this crime, the people cried. It was monstrous; it was the betrayal of France; it was a dastardly blow at their

"It was monstrous. It was the betrayal of France."

idol, Vansittart! The papers were full of it. By evening the Chamber of Deputies had caught the contagion of denunciation; at ten o'clock the swarming streets were howling with anathemas. The next morning MM. Ribou and Lacontel were politicians of the past. They had vanished like mist at the breath of the empire-builder.

It was not at the desire of their fellow-ministers that this thing had happened. The other members of the Government knew full well that the heads of the Interior and Colonial Offices were only using Prince Henri of Navarre as a pawn in the terrible game against the man who was overshadowing all others. But they could not withstand the storm that had burst upon their unfortunate colleagues. Lacontel and Ribou were to be thrown to the wolves to save the entire Cabinet from being devoured. Portfolios are sweet to those who may still hold them, so the hapless pair were sacrificed to the clamor. And the worst part of the business was that Vansittart's position had been immensely strengthened by the incident. In denouncing the ministers, both Press and public were practically unanimous in disclaiming any inherent dislike on their part to one-man rule.

"Why did these puppets resurrect a long-forgotten Prince?" said the *Journal des Débats*. "Had they plotted to place upon the throne the man who had reconstituted France, many would approve their action, whilst the stanchest Republican could at least understand their zeal. But this young gentleman from Navarre! The project would be laughable, were it not criminal."

These were dangerous words. They meant much more than they openly expressed, and they were taken to heart by none more than the remaining occupants of the ministerial posts.

Premier and subordinates alike confessed themselves powerless to decide upon the next step to take. They did not even trust their own judgment as to the selection of new holders of the vacant portfolios, and whilst in this state of dubiety they received an urgent summons to attend a special meeting of the Palais de l'Élysée, convened by the President.

"Gentlemen," said the head of the French Republic, when the responsible officers of State had gathered in ready obedience to his mandate, "I have, in discharge, of my solemn trust, called you together on this occasion to take your counsel upon the highly significant events of recent days. A stranger, a man of wealth, before whom other millionnaires are paupers, has honored France with his residence and devoted labors. I am unable, even had I the desire, to underrate the services rendered to France by Mr. Vansittart. He has created for us a magnificent colony; his enterprise has restored our stricken manufactures; France again stands in the eyes of the world, wholly through his influence, as the pioneer of commercial and industrial progress at the dawn of a new century. Precisely because I do not exaggerate in thus recounting his deeds are we called upon to face a real and active danger to the Republic. Some of us have long foreseen that behind Mr. Vansittart's undoubtedly beneficent work lay an ulterior motive. Even yet I cannot say precisely what that motive may be. It is preposterous to think he would seek to make himself Emperor of the French, but, candidly speaking, I see no other solution of the plans which he has laid with such singular skill. Those of your colleagues who ventured to cross his path or strove to defeat his masterful purposes were swept aside with the vigor of a Napoleon and the finesse of a Mazarin. Unhappily the actions of these ministers could not, by the kindliest interpreter, be called patriotic. They were venal and corrupt; their authors deserved to be cast into the outer darkness; for them there can be no palliation. But the astounding fact remains—it was because they opposed Mr. Vansittart that their fall became more speedy and disastrous. De Tournon, Ribou, Lacontel, not to mention a host of deputies who have been forced to leave the Chamber by the pressure of their constituents, owing to publicly expressed sentiments of hostility to his schemes—these are the outward and visible signs of the man's appalling power. For my own part, I am amazed and alarmed at the extent of his influence. The army, the navy, the public services, the great mass of the electorate, seem to be beneath his sway. In my own family circle I am met with frequent allusions to one whom they flippantly, but with obvious relish, term the 'Emperor.' In this very council of ministers he may have his adherents——"

Here the President was for the first time interrupted by remonstrances, angrily earnest.

"Well, let it pass. I know not, nor care. My duty is plain before me. As head of the Republic, I emphatically state my unalterable conviction. Vansittart must be crushed at once, and with the utmost firmness. Whatever be the real intention behind his acts, whether they relate to Prince Henri of Navarre, or to Mademoiselle de Montpensier, whom we have most unwisely allowed to be domiciled in France under Mr. Vansittart's roof, we must, if we would save our country from a revolution, place him outside our shores."

"Is that all?" cried the Minister for War, in disappointed tones. He expected that the President would have suggested a trial by drum-head court-martial, and a summary execution of the offender.

"All! What more would you have. Do you contemplate restraint or punishment? Even if we could prove any overt deed, which I greatly doubt, are we prepared to face an enraged people, clamoring for the liberation of their hero? Pooh! Our lives would not be worth a moment's purchase. We merely strengthen his power by our folly. Even as it is, by adopting the wisest and least exciting course, we run grave risk."

"What, then, do you propose?" It was the Premier who spoke.

"Nay," said the President. "Let us advance with circumspection. First, has Mr. Vansittart any well-known and powerful supporter?"

"Liancourt!" cried several in a breath.

"Is that possible? Can you give proof of this? Liancourt is surely a disinterested patriot, if ever one lived. I will begin to doubt myself if I am asked to doubt him."

No one answered. The President was clearly in a mood to deal only with facts, not speculations.

"Any one else?" after a pause.

"Folliet, ex-Prefect of Police," replied the Minister for War.

"Ah, a clever man, who, if I remember rightly, was improperly removed from his post by de Tournon. Let him be restored. We can doubtless find a better-paid appointment for the present occupant."

The ministers gazed at each other. This, then, was the President's *modus operandi*.

"It is a good proposal," commented the Premier. "You detach Vansittart's adherents before you deal with him personally. But what is your final —— ?"

"Pardon, monsieur. Let me appeal for orderly progression. From the new basis of accomplished fact we can so much more easily regard the end in view. Now, as to Liancourt. Is it not time he was in the Ministry?"

Again the assembled company sought external comfort from the collective brain. Liancourt, as an unattached politician, might be dangerous. As a member of the Government, his known reputation for personal honor would certainly dissociate him from a plot against the Republic. If he accepted the proffered portfolio, he was free from taint. If he refused, they would know what to think, and whom to fear.

"Excellent!" came the general response.

"The Interior is in bad odor just now," said the Premier with a grim smile. "It will be a pleasant task for Liancourt to revive its former traditions."

Another name, that of a leader of a small party of Opportunists, who had been troublesome of late in the Chamber, was submitted and approved of for the Colonial office, and the Premier at once wrote the three letters of invitation. Ministers separated with lighter hearts. The President clearly had a head on his shoulders. He would save the Republic—and their portfolios. Within the hour Liancourt and Folliet had each received his appointment. The first thought of both men was to hurry off to consult with Vansittart, but their methods of viewing the situation were different.

Liancourt smiled. "My friend will at last be compelled to take me wholly into his confidence," he reflected, as he buttoned his gloves. "I shall be glad to be with him in every sense, and I do not think he will even suggest that I should act dishonorably by conspiring in his favor whilst remaining a member of the very Government he seeks to overthrow."

Folliet groaned; for he, too, had his ambitions. "I would like the post," he thought, "if only to show my enemies that I can survive. But it is impossible. I will never desert the cause of my rescuer, Vansittart, whatever it be."

Yet they were both mistaken. Folliet was the first to reach the Grand Hotel. He was at once shown into Jerome's library, and, without a word of explanation, he handed the Premier's letter to the millionaire. Vansittart read it calmly.

"Let me congratulate you upon this long-delayed reward," he said.

"No," cried the other, "it is no reward; it is treachery. It is a move to detach me from your service. I scorn the proposal."

"True, such is the idea of the giver. But that is only a part of the transaction. When you clinch the bargain you make your own terms."

"What do you mean?" Folliet was a magnificent detective but a poor diplomatist.

"I mean," said Jerome, speaking with the emphasis of conviction, "that much as I value the splendid work you have done for me in your private capacity, its importance is secondary compared with the assistance you may be able to render me as Prefect of Police."

"That settles it, monsieur," cried Folliet, jamming his hat down over his eyes. "I accept the post forthwith; but it is absolutely a compact between us that I do so wholly and solely in your interests."

Liancourt was the next. "There is a climax at hand," were his opening words.

"So I understand," said the millionnaire, turning to light a cigar.

"How so? You surely cannot yet know the object of my visit?"

"I may be wrong, but when my enemies offer Folliet, my chosen protector, the Prefecture, it needs but average wit to guess that a dramatic move against me will shortly be made elsewhere."

"Ah! Your news confirms my own suspicions. Read this"; and he passed over the second letter from the Premier that Vansittart had perused inside of ten minutes.

The American did not speak for a little while after he had returned the document.

He gazed into space, as was his habit when thinking deeply.

"This time," he said at last, "it will be a fight to a finish. Individual opponents gave me but passing trouble. I wonder how I will fare when matched against the Government?"

With a bitter smile he contemplated the chances of the game. His intellect revelled in the prospect of approaching combat, but his heart was careless of its issue. Liancourt watched him closely, even anxiously. Vansittart's character was now well known to him, and he had noted with distress that the erstwhile infectious buoyancy of his friend's spirits had deserted him. In the old days the fascinating glamour of romantic enthusiasm blended with his most clear-sighted and far-reaching words or acts. But now, for some indefinable reason, he was cynical and distrait—vigorous and alert as ever, but a calmly invulnerable mathematician rather than a scientific Aladdin.

"You accept, of course?" Jerome went on, questioningly.

"Perhaps. It depends solely upon your decision."

"On my decision! What can I have to say against it? I have long thought that it was your place to lead, not to criticise."

"My dear Vansittart"—and Liancourt spoke with real emotion—"things have now reached the point where our lives run together or deviate. Out of consideration for myself you have hitherto refused to make me a partner in your projects, however accurately I may have surmised their nature. Your motive does you credit. It is the delicacy of an honorable man. But it no longer obtains. If I refuse this preferment I shall be bracketed with you, and you will not, I am sure, wish me to fight your cause blindfold. If I accept, not even the elasticity of the diplomatic conscience will permit me to serve a government whilst I aid you to overthrow it."

Jerome stood up. His first physical emotion was invariably typical of the mental resolve to throw off difficulties as they presented themselves. If he lost Liancourt, he lost the assistance of a keen intellect, which was specially equipped to cope with the vagaries of French nature, whether political or social. Yet how retain him? He, Vansittart, might fail lamentably and disastrously. Had he any right to involve this noble-minded and gifted politician in his possible ruin? The question had only one answer.

"It is hard," he said, "to say 'good-bye' to such a friend as you. I shall miss you terribly. But there is no other way. You must join the Government."

"What? You cast me off? Am I then so weak that my

alliance is despised?" Liancourt, for the first time in his relations with Vansittart, showed that he had a temper.

"No. Surely you do not misunderstand me. The task I have undertaken cannot be delegated. I must stand alone at the close. Another week, perhaps a day, may determine my fate. As a member of the Government, you cannot, if you would, enter into my schemes, but it is at least better for me that a passive friend rather than an active enemy should occupy the Office of the Interior."

"I would sooner stand at your side in this affair," said Liancourt, convinced, but disappointed.

"And I would prefer to have you as my gaoler than my fellow-prisoner."

"If these are the alternatives, I willingly choose the latter."

"But if there be a third?"

"And that is ——?"

"I may ask you to be my fellow-minister. All things happen in France, you know. But I do appeal to you not to advise the gentlemen who wish to secure your services. I think I can vanquish them single-handed. If you join them in mind as well as in body, I shall begin to doubt."

Liancourt laughed. "If there were no other cause," he said, "if my friendship for you were so easily dissolved, I still have my self-love. The Premier and his colleagues will not have my aid to extricate themselves from their swamp. I will browse complacently on the highlands of art. You forget that the Minister of the Interior is also the official patron of culture."

When the Frenchman had left him, Vansittart at once set to work to destroy all documents and memoranda in his library likely to compromise others, as he might expect a domiciliary visit at any moment. Whilst he was thus engaged he received a note from General Daubisson. It ran:

"In accordance with your wishes, I have effected the exchange of 50,000 fresh troops from Chalons, Lyons, and

Paris, with a similar number stationed in the Sahara. The movement is practically completed. Most of your old comrades are now in the Paris garrison. I throw prudence to the winds, and say, ' The Army is with you.' "

" We shall see," murmured Jerome. " It shall soon be tested."

His precautionary measures ended at the Grand Hotel, he set out, with some degree of ostentation, for St. Cloud.

CHAPTER XXXIII

THE PRESIDENT TAKES ACTION

MADEMOISELLE DE MONTPENSIER had resolutely refused to see Prince Henri of Navarre after she had so narrowly escaped the position of being a mere counter in the stakes played for by Monsieur Ribou. The young prince himself, who, with all his faults, was a gentleman and man of honor, was ashamed of the inglorious part he had been forced to fill, but he felt keenly the rigid fiat against his presence issued by Honorine. He firmly resolved to keep his compact loyally in future. Indeed, in his newborn zeal, he went so far as to ask Jerome's permission to reside permanently at St. Cloud, so that he would be less likely to be tempted by unscrupulous opponents of the man who was now clearly destined to fill the throne of France; if that precarious seat were to be won by anybody. He was anxious to meet Honorine, if only to assure her of his self-reliance.

The Comtesse de Fontainebleau kept her own counsel and hope. Love has a method of picking locks unknown to the most expert burglar. Whilst Evelyn Harland lived the Legitimist cause could not die.

When Vansittart reached St. Cloud he went straight to his private apartments and summoned Dick Harland and Bates. With his own hand he wrote and signed one hundred and eighteen letters, but the task was not a formidable one. Each missive contained the same brief formula:

"I am now President. If you are with me, act."

He placed the notes in envelopes which had been previously addressed, and gave them to Harland, saying :

"Take good care of these. When I give you the word, endorse each letter with the hour and the date. You and Jim Bates, if necessary, must personally see to their delivery, no matter what the hour may be. The first on the list is General Daubisson. The rest are carefully arranged in order of residence. I wish you both, for the next few nights, to sleep in your riding costumes and to have two good horses constantly saddled in the stable. During the day do not leave the house or grounds on any pretext. Everything may depend on promptitude, but, above all, be prepared at night."

Then, as an after thought, he added, "If I should fail, join me in New York."

"You will not fail," said Dick with quiet certainty.

Bates passed no remark, but left the room. He returned in five minutes, and the ring of his spurs as he re-entered showed what his errand had been.

"You have not been long in taking me at my word, Jim," exclaimed Jerome.

"No, boss, an' I ain't rigged out for a sea-trip, either."

Vansittart laughed with something of his old merriment. "Really," he cried, "this confidence is encouraging. But, believe me, boys, the way is dark ahead, for the next move cannot be mine; it must come from the enemy."

The "enemy," as it proved, was at that identical moment preparing the final blow. The President had summoned another meeting of the Cabinet, and the joyful news was made known that Liancourt and Folliet had been readily detached from Vansittart's cause, if they had ever espoused it.

The Premier asked what was the next step proposed by the President.

"To-morrow, gentlemen," he replied, "I will, at an early hour, smooth down any possible international complications.

We meet here at ten o'clock in the evening precisely. Monsieur Liancourt will, of course, be summoned in his new capacity. You"—addressing the War Minister—"must see to it that General Daubisson is in attendance. I am sure you will pardon me for not carrying my proposals farther to-night."

There was some grumbling at this want of confidence; but the President was master of the situation, and he was obviously disinclined to reveal his final plan of action, though its general nature was sufficiently indicated.

Next day Vansittart was at lunch when a note reached him from the British Embassy. It was from a sporting military *attaché*, and read:

"Just now (mid-day) I was talking to His Excellency about your horse, Victor, entered for the Derby next week. He has a good outside chance, and I am backing him. His Excellency said, 'Write to Mr. Vansittart at once, and advise him strongly, from me, to start to-day for London, and see after the final preparation of his horse for the race.' I don't exactly know what His Excellency means by this, as he is no racing man, but I am carrying out his wishes. He seems to be rather anxious about it."

Almost at the same moment a letter came from the U. S. Ambassador. Mr. Van Regen wrote, "Have you seen India or Siberia? If not, take a trip to either place, or both. Don't ask me why, but quit."

Jerome passed the documents to Harland, saying, "Glance at those, and then set a match to them."

Dick could only express his feelings by a slang phrase.

"Now we shan't be"—Jerome reached for a heavy water-bottle—"a great while," he said, with a grin, a remark somewhat on a par with Mr. Cecil Rhodes's famous decision to "face the music."

Men on the eve of a desperate enterprise seldom resort to epigram. Even Vansittart was commonplace.

"There are lots of things I ought to place in order," he

said nonchalantly. "But let them go to Jericho. I am sick of affairs. Come and play snooker."

So it came to pass that whilst the millionaire's magnificent scheme of empire was rushing towards the fateful hour when it must see success or failure, he spent the afternoon in a keen struggle to get the better of his chosen friend and Prince Henri in a game of pool for half-franc points.

There was no pretence of carelessness or ennui on his part. He was simply waiting for action by others, and he was fixed in his determination to deal with events as they arrived, not to anticipate them. He was positively happy at the thought that finality was at hand, and his smiling self-possession deceived even the ladies when they came to tea in the billiard-room. At dinner the whole party were in high spirits. If the sword of Damocles hung over the host's head, it was well hidden. After a pleasant evening they separated, apparently to retire for the night, but Vansittart and Harland simply changed their clothes, and they were joined in the millionnaire's study by Arizona Jim.

By ten o'clock the rulers of France were gathered in a spacious inner chamber of the Palais de l'Élysée. Liancourt was present. He received the congratulations of his colleagues courteously but coldly, for he was ill at ease. General Daubisson, too, was much preoccupied. This late and unexpected assembly puzzled and distressed him.

The President lost no time in stating his project.

"We are now called upon, gentlemen, to save the Republic," he said. "I have already informed the representatives of the United States and England of my unalterable decision to deport Mr. Vansittart this night from our shores. It surprised them, but they could urge no tangible cause for delay. This is the supreme step towards the accomplishment of our difficult and responsible task."

General Daubisson started and became pallid. What if his note to Jerome were discovered among the papers that would surely be seized? Did the Government suspect?

Cold drops of perspiration glistened upon his brow. But no one paid any heed to him. All eyes were fixed on Liancourt. The statesman stood it grandly. Not a muscle betrayed his agitation. He even smiled as he said icily, addressing the President:

"Is the Sahara a myth, then?"

The President took up the challenge. "No, France will at last have a colony. She will not rob this American. He shall be paid in full. But he must not rob France."

"Kindly explain."

"Mr. Vansittart would wrest from France her most cherished possession. He would strangle the Republic. It is our duty to save the Republic by strangling him."

"I thought you said you were going to deport him?"

The President flushed with anger. "This is no fit season for playing with words," he cried. "We will act with firmness and constitutionally. He will be sent to his own country in a French man-of-war from Cherbourg. He will not be allowed to return. Upon our shoulders will rest the grave duty of restoring public order should it unhappily be disturbed."

"His own country?" continued Liancourt. "Is he not a Frenchman by special act of Chamber and Senate?"

"Monsieur, I will discuss details with you afterwards. General Daubisson, I command you to send for a regiment of cavalry, to whose colonel I will give sealed instructions. Meanwhile, no one must leave this room."

A murmur of applause buzzed through the chamber. The Cabinet approved of the President's bold attitude.

Liancourt never lost his wonderful self-possession for a moment. Daubisson sat next to him. As the General nervously rose to obey the President's order he murmured, so that Daubisson alone could hear, "The 18th Chasseurs!" In the same instant he cried to the President, "You are juggling with edged tools. I warn you, for I doubt your skill."

"As a member of the Government, you would surely save the Republic," sneered the Premier.

"I would prefer to save France. The people will not tolerate your action."

"The people must be taught reason."

"You may change your views, monsieur. I will honor your convictions if you say those words to-morrow in the Chamber." It was a bitter cut, for the head of the Ministry was a notorious time-server.

The President now interposed to explain his project *in extenso*. They would send for Vansittart, and await his arrival. He would be examined by the Council, and, if his answers were not satisfactory, deported by special train from the Gare de l'Ouest. If, as could not be expected, he gave his word of honor that his designs were not hostile to the Republic, and would consent to the immediate banishment of Mademoiselle Honorine de Montpensier, then the incident ended. Mr. Vansittart would be free to attend to the concerns of his Company.

Liancourt smiled at the suggestion. "Again I ask you to pause before it is too late," he said. "Mr. Vansittart is a man of action. You cannot treat him as a naughty child."

But his remonstrances were unheeded. Daubisson returned, having telephoned for the troops.

"What regiment have you sent for?" inquired the Minister for War.

"The 18th Chasseurs, commanded by Colonel le Breton."

"But were they not engaged with this upstart in the Soudan?"

The Governor of Paris had now regained his composure. He fenced blandly with the question. "Ah, you are thinking of the 6th Dragoons," he replied. "The men of that regiment were reported by the Press to be personally attached to the American, for he is a brave man, monsieur."

"You are assured, General, of the loyalty of the 18th?"

"Quite assured, monsieur."

Liancourt did not even look at Daubisson. These two, alone in that company, knew that the Press had been mistaken in the identity of the regiment so closely associated with Vansittart.

The Palais de l'Élysée faces the Champs Élysées, but a long garden intervenes between the front of the building and that popular thoroughfare. Ordinarily, entrance is gained to the official residence of the President from the Rue St. Honoré, or from either of the two side streets, the Avenue Marigny, and the Rue de l'Élysée. By the President's orders, however, the great gates at the end of the garden had been thrown open, so that the passage of a regiment through the narrower and more crowded thoroughfares should not attract public attention. The Council sat in a room overlooking the grounds, and shortly after eleven o'clock the clanking of accoutrements outside warned those present that the Chasseurs were at hand.

Colonel le Breton was announced. He entered and saluted, standing with soldierly uprightness near the door, amazement struggling with military *sang-froid* in his face at this unexected summons before so distinguished a conclave.

The President wrote the following letter:

"COLONEL LE BRETON:—You are commanded to bring Mr. Jerome K. Vansittart, unarmed and unattended, save by you and your men, to the Palais de l'Élysée at once, to meet the President and Ministers of the French Republic, on a matter of grave and urgent public importance."

The President signed and sealed the paper, enclosing it in an envelope, which he handed to the officer with these words:

"You will proceed rapidly with your regiment to St. Cloud. You will halt your men in front of Mr. Vansittart's house, and you will personally demand Mr. Vansittart's private attention. In his presence, when alone, you will open and read this letter. See to it that both he and you obey the instructions there given."

The soldier saluted, took the mysterious missive, and the Council listened in silence to the clang of his brass scabbard on the marble steps as he strode down-stairs to fulfil his mission. Liancourt was the first to speak. "Monsieur le President," he said with a pleasant laugh, "I would suggest some light refreshments. None of us know when or where we may breakfast."

. . . . .

On the stroke of midnight Jerome was helping himself and his companions to a fresh cigar, when suddenly Arizona Jim went to an open window and looked out. He listened intently for a moment, and then peered earnestly across the moonlit lawn to the point where the road to the Paris gate of the park lost itself among the deep shadows of the trees. He was soon satisfied. "Boss," he said, turning to Vansittart, "there is a regiment of cavalry coming to the house, and they've just broken from a trot to a walk."

"Cavalry? Capital! I feared it would have been police. No. There must be no violence. I insist that you remain here until I personally send for you. Bates, I cannot give my orders twice."

Both Harland and Arizona Jim had seized revolvers and cartridge belts, and Bates was clearly unwilling to fall in with his master's instructions. But Vansittart's tone left no room for further protest, and with a parting handshake he quitted them. There were two windows in the room. Harland occupied one and Bates the other. They watched the approaching cavalcade, and neither spoke. They could not, for the tears were in their eyes, and each man feared lest the other should learn of his weakness.

As Jerome descended to the entrance-hall, deserted save for one attendant, whom he at once sent to the rear of the house, he felt a buoyant sense of expectancy. Sir Walter Scott has told us in stirring verse of the "stern joy that warriors feel in foemen worthy of their steel," and the blood now coursed through Vansittart's veins with a fierce tumult that presaged the utmost mental and physical activity. His hands were clinched, and his feet seemed to grip the ground as he walked. Truly, if ever political adventurer were ready for the fray, he was at that moment. As to eventualities, he cared not a straw. He would deal with events as they came, and would either mould them to suit his desperate fortunes, or be broken himself in the effort.

There was no doubt, no hesitation, no torture of useless questioning. Calm and *débonnaire* as ever, with a smile on his handsome and intellectual face, he waited near the door the advent of his enemies' emissaries. And so he would have continued had he been only called upon to face armed men. But there were others who waited and watched in St. Cloud that night.

Evelyn Harland and Prince Henri occupied rooms in the front of the building. They were each striving to drown thought by reading when the tramp of the horses' feet and the jingle of bit and sabre fell upon their ears. Evelyn was the first to catch the ominous sound. For a moment she looked, spellbound, at the soldiers; then, with a wild rush of fear in her heart, she knew that their presence boded no good to Jerome. His bold plot had been discovered. They were come to arrest him. Perhaps his life was in danger. He might resist them and be wounded. Whatever the pain, no matter what the cost to herself, she must learn the truth, for suspense would kill her.

She ran from the room, along a wide corridor, and reached the head of the staircase to see Vansittart standing in the hall, quietly tapping his right boot with a riding-whip. He had not heard her footsteps on the heavy carpet, and she positively startled him by saying, "Oh, Mr. Vansittart, why are these soldiers coming here?"

He wheeled rapidly. "Do not be alarmed, Miss Harland. I expected them."

She darted down the stairs and took him by the arm.

"Yes," she half-whispered, whilst a strange light shone

in her eyes. "You may have expected them. But they will harm you. They will imprison you. Let me entreat you to save yourself. Trust me, I will be calm. I will lie to them. I will delay them. I will tell them you are in Paris."

"Miss Harland, Evelyn, I pray you leave me. All will be well. Believe me that if I fail now, I can only be banished from France."

Evelyn looked into his stern face, and she mistook its agonized fixity for mere strength of purpose. She recoiled a step, the tears welled forth, and she wailed, "Ah, no, no, no! They will kill you! I know they will!"

As she spoke they heard the sharp words of command that brought the troops to a halt, and the grating of the horses' hoofs on the gravel outside suddenly ceased.

Convulsive sobs shook the girl's frame, and Vansittart did what he would not have done before the levelled rifles of a company of infantry—he yielded.

In a second he was at Evelyn's side, his arms were around her, he raised her tear-stained face, and kissed her passionately.

"Evelyn, my love, my love!" he cried, and for one blissful instant those two forgot all other considerations in the frenzied delight of knowing that their secret was a secret no longer. They loved and were beloved.

But their happiness was more fleeting than a dream.

By mutual instinct they read in each other's eyes what the tongue was loth to utter. Evelyn was the first to speak. Gently disengaging herself, she said slowly, but with exceeding firmness, whilst a vivid blush suffused her forehead and cheeks: "Mr. Vansittart, you honor me, but I cannot dishonor you. My happiness is as nothing to your duty. Go! I pray heaven that you may succeed, and that the love of another may be worthier than mine. If we meet again, we meet as friends and well-wishers only. Meanwhile, I will pray that you may be safeguarded from all peril."

In the anguish of the moment Evelyn placed her left hand across her eyes, and Jerome took the other in his and bent to kiss it. A tear reached it before his lips. And neither knew that Colonel le Breton, standing in the open doorway, and Prince Henri of Navarre, leaning over the balustrade of the entresol, had heard and witnessed all that had passed between them.

CHAPTER XXXIV

VANSITTART MEETS THE CABINET

PRINCE HENRI quietly effaced himself; Colonel le Breton advanced. His footsteps on the tessellated pavement aroused Vansittart.

"This is hardly an unexpected pleasure, Colonel." The words were clear, but his voice was forced and unnatural, even to his own senses.

"I am glad to hear it," replied the gallant officer, with a bow to the lady, "for I do not know myself why I am here."

"Is that possible? Have you not been sent by the Government?"

"My faith, yes, by the President and every big-wig in Paris. I hope they have not asked me to do anything unpleasant or unworthy of the Army, for my men have been growling all the way from the Palais."

"But have you no instructions?"

"Yes, this letter, which I am to open in your presence alone." Vansittart glanced at Evelyn, who met his gaze with a look of such mute entreaty that he said smilingly, "Your orders could hardly contemplate the presence of a lady at this late hour. Proceed, I beg you."

Colonel le Breton forthwith opened the President's letter, and read it aloud. As he proceeded his bronzed skin grew swarthy with indignation and the veins on his brow swelled visibly. But he persisted to the end, and then threw the document on the floor.

"A thousand thunders!" he hissed. "This is an arrest!"

"So it would seem."

"Is there no regiment in Paris but the 18th to do their dirty work? Is it for this that we fought with you in Africa? My men may carry out the rascally order if they like, but their Colonel will not."

In his rage he drew his sword, and would have broken it across his knee had not the millionnaire prevented him.

"Not so, my friend," he said. "We met lions once when you were unarmed. There may be wild beasts in Paris to-night, and I want your help."

"But I cannot fight against the Government?"

"You shall not. Unless I am mistaken, you will fight for it, if there be the need, which I doubt."

"Yet, what can we do, Mr. Vansittart? The Cabinet even now await you."

"I will come. But tell me, Colonel, I may greet my old comrades?"

"Assuredly. They will be right glad to see you."

Vansittart picked up the fallen letter, and passed out on to the verandah into the full light of the moonbeams. He was followed by le Breton, and by Evelyn, who remained in the shade of a pillar. When the Chasseurs caught sight of Jerome, a great shout of delight went up from all ranks. With a common impulse, they drew their swords and saluted. There could be no mistaking the feelings of the army for the man whom they always called "the Emperor."

"Messieurs," said Vansittart, "I am glad to meet you again. I have missed your cheerful company since affairs recalled me to Paris. I trust we shall not be readily parted again."

Another hearty cheer expressed their sentiments, to be succeeded by eager, but subdued comments.

"He is a rare one, eh?"

"What's he up to now?"

"Going to stick to us. That's good!"

And then a single stentorian voice, "*Vive l'Empereur!*"

The cry was taken up with vigor. Startled sleepers in the Château were now flinging wide their shutters to learn what strange proceedings were taking place on the lawn. There came another yell from an upper window, this time in solid Anglo-Saxon:

"Go it, my bucks. *You're* all right!"

All eyes were turned upwards, and the Chasseurs hailed Arizona Jim with a friendly shout of recognition. At last silence was restored, for the soldiers realized that something dramatic must happen.

Vansittart at once addressed them in clear ringing tones:
"Officers and men of the 18th Chasseurs. The President of the French Republic, with the consent and connivance of the members of the Government, has sent your colonel and yourselves here to-night to arrest me, so that I may be packed out of the country like a felon. Lest you may imagine that there has been some mistake, I will read you the letter of instruction given to Colonel le Breton by the President." And he forthwith placed his hearers in possession of its contents.

Had a dozen live bombs been thrown into the midst of the Chasseurs, the missiles would not have created such furious consternation as this remarkable document. The regiment was dumb with indignation. Taking a quick advantage of the general inability to say anything suitable to the moment, Jerome continued:

"Of what crime am I accused? My enemies are silent on this point; but I will tell you. I—and you—have conspired to raise the fortunes of France. We have given our blood and our treasure to lift her supreme among the nations. We have fought and toiled in the desert that France may possess a colony equal in riches and superior in position to the most favored territories of other lands. This is my crime, and you are my abettors. You know full well how I have been thwarted and annoyed and maligned by the self-seekers who usurp the high places in the councils of this great country. The Ministers of France have descended to the most petty and ignoble shifts to injure my projects and delay their accomplishment. But they have failed thus far because the Army upheld me, and the vast body of the people believed in me. Now, as a last resort, before they vanish into everlasting nothingness, they strain the resources of authority, and hope to imprison me or deport me to exile whilst they wreck the fair prospect which I have held out before you. Will you permit it?"

Eight hundred voices bellowed a thunderous "No."

"I believe you. I never doubted you for one instant. Friendships made as ours, in the storm and stress of battle, cannot be dissolved at the breath of any place-hunting politician. For what are these men who dare to cross my path? Three of them I have unmasked already. De Tournon, Ribou, Lacontel—you know them. They would sacrifice France, as they slandered her army, for their own selfish ends. And the others? I will tell you why they hate me. I am not one who will sell the Cross of the Legion of Honor to any huckstering knave who bids the highest price. Under my code, the Cross, your Cross, could be bought only by a brave deed in the midst of peril. I will not pay the bribes of another Panama. I will not tolerate laws written on the counterfoils of a check-book. I refuse to recognize men who barter their political faith for a salary. These are my crimes, and I now go to answer for them before my self-constituted judges. Do I go as your leader or your prisoner?"

A fierce roar of acclamation gave him no uncertain or faltering reply. And again rang out the tremendous shout, "*Vive l'Empereur!*" The 18th Chasseurs were ready to follow him anywhere, and do anything at his bidding.

Turning to le Breton, Vansittart said: "Do you come with me, Colonel?"

"On my life! As well be shot to-night as at daybreak?"

"There will be no shooting. Do you know where General Daubisson is?"

"With the Council."

Jerome now approached Evelyn. "Will you go to your brother and Bates in my study," he said, "and tell them to ride off at once on my errand, but to omit Daubisson, and go straight to Folliet?"

"Yes. And even as I obey you, let me be the first to call you ' my Emperor. ' "

He came nearer, but she ran into the house, and the soldiers, mistaking her for Honorine de Montpensier, of whom they had all heard, cried, "Long live the Empress!"

Five minutes later, having left a troop to guard St. Cloud during his absence, Vansittart rode off to Paris at the head of the Chasseurs, but the dust was already settling down where it had been disturbed by the rapid gallop of Dick Harland and Bates. No quicker delivery of letters ever took place in Paris than the distribution effected by those two that night.

. . . .

In the room of the Palais de l'Élysée the President and ministers sat, thoughtful but confident, to await the return of the Chasseurs. Liancourt, after a little reflection, determined to resign forthwith, as he was now powerless to help Vansittart. He wrote a formal letter to the Premier to that effect, but the head of the Ministry refused to accept it. It did not suit his plans to permit Liancourt to wriggle out of his share of official responsibility for that evening's deeds. Liancourt adhered to his resolution, and the letter lay on the table.

There was much animated conversation in the gathering, and the flow of wine, provided by the President, tended to raise the depressed spirits of politicians who had not felt secure in possession of their portfolios since the departments of the Colonies and the Interior had been so suddenly beheaded. Curiosity blended with hope to render feverish their anticipation of the coming dramatic scene, and furtive glances at the clock showed a burning anxiety as time progressed, and the soldiers did not arrive. At last even the President lost patience. He despatched a messenger to see if there were any signs of the Chasseurs, and a thrill ran through the company when the man returned, about 1.15 A.M., to announce that the cavalry were now coming at a trot down the broad avenue of the Champs Élysées.

As the attendant quitted the room, the listening Council heard the first sound of the approaching horses. A minute later the clamp of many feet on the staircase heralded Vansittart's approach. The folding doors were flung wide, and the millionnaire, accompanied by Colonel le Breton and a dozen officers, entered. The soldiers stood near the door, and did not salute. Vansittart advanced alone. His quick eye caught the signs of festivity on the table.

"Good evening, gentlemen," he said with an affable smile. "A late supper? I am delighted to join you, though the manner of your invitation was somewhat unusual."

The President rose, slightly nonplussed. He ignored Vansittart's words. "Colonel le Breton, you and your officers may retire. Kindly await instructions with your regiment."

The plain-spoken Chasseur was no coiner of elegant phrases.

"I am obeying orders," he growled. "My orders are to remain here."

"Your orders!" shouted the President. "Whose orders?"

"Mr. Vansittart's."

The assembly more than paled at this strange reply. It blanched. It visibly shrunk. In mere avoirdupois it lessened materially.

Jerome's glance chanced to fall upon General Daubisson, and he was hard-set to keep from laughing at that warrior's miserable aspect. He was livid with frightful uncertainty, for he was quite unable to decide how the cat was going to jump.

In the midst of an awed hush Liancourt struck a match with a loud noise, and lit a cigarette.

The President choked with rage.

"You scoundrel!" he roared. "You insulting dog. You dare to tell me. You dare——" and he spluttered incoherently.

Le Breton's visage was aflame. "You are an old man," he cried. "Else would I run you through the liver. It is not I who presume; it is you."

The President found his voice again: "I will have your epaulettes torn from your shoulders by the public executioner. I——"

But Vansittart broke in.

"Silence!" he said sternly. "This unseemly brawl ill agrees with your age, monsieur. I would have you, and all here, know that Colonel le Breton acts with my authority. Keep your temper, I pray you, and imitate my example. Let us toast each other."

With apologetic politeness he leaned over the Premier's shoulder, and helped himself to a glass of champagne, which he drank at a draught, observing, "The dust rises when one rides hard. I was quite thirsty."

By a violent effort the President regained some degree of self-control. With tolerable firmness he said:

"This outrage shall cost you dear, Mr. Vansittart. You are summoned here to-night to answer a charge of conspiring against the Republic. I, for one, hoped that you might have answered it to our satisfaction. But the attitude of yourself and your associates proves that our suspicions were well founded. It is not befitting my dignity to discuss the matter under present conditions. I will deal with you at a later hour."

"No, monsieur. You shall deal with me now. I require your immediate resignation."

"My resignation! Insolence!"

"Possibly. So far I have striven to be courteous, but explicit."

"And if I refuse?"

"You remain a prisoner, as you now are, subject to my directions."

"By what extraordinary right do you make this astounding proposition?"

"By virtue of the fact that I am President of France."

"Since when?"

"Since you and your councillors resolved to use unconstitutional methods to attain our ends."

"Our ends, monsieur, were to save France from your clutches."

"You are not France. France shall decide. I shall abide by her decision."

The President sat down, dumfounded at the amazing turn taken by events.

Vansittart coolly continued: "Perhaps you require time for thought. Reflect, by all means. I have the fullest trust in your good sense."

Then he turned to Liancourt. "My friend. Do you leave this ministry that loves you not?"

Liancourt pointed to his letter. "I resigned an hour ago."

"I am more than delighted. At last I can speak to you openly. Will you take in hand the formation of a new ministry to meet the Chamber this afternoon?"

"With the utmost pleasure—and confidence."

"And *you*, General Daubisson? Do you retain the command of the army?"

"So long as I retain the good-will of the President." Daubisson was now square upon his feet. The cat had jumped unmistakably.

Vansittart gave to the Premier and his colleagues the alternative offered to the President. They were utterly nonplussed, and knew not how to act.

Apparently this magician had every force in France at his back. They had not the slightest doubt of the result of a popular plebiscite. Vansittart would be acclaimed by the people; they would be in a minority of ten compared with forty millions.

And Liancourt was forming a Cabinet!

Perhaps——

The Minister for War spoke first: "I resign," he said, "and at the same time regret that a mere difference of opinion should have brought about this disagreeable rupture."

"And I!"

"And I!"

Including the Premier, they all followed suit.

"Thank you, messieurs," said Vansittart. "You are free to depart. Colonel le Breton, kindly see that these gentlemen are escorted to their private residences."

The Minister for War muttered an oath. "I wish first to visit my bureau," he snarled. There were incriminating letters there from de Tournon and Ribou.

Jerome was suavity itself. "For private documents, no doubt. They shall be carefully preserved and sent to you."

"But——"

"Monsieur, I have much to attend to. Your escort waits."

Utterly disheartened, cowed, browbeaten, disgusted, and disappointed, the ex-ministers of the Republic passed out into the night. Their only solace was to rail extensively at the stolid Chasseurs who accompanied them to their homes, and permitted conversation with no one.

The President had noted their actions with bitter scorn. When the last of their number had quitted the room he rose: "You are apparently master of the situation, M. Vansittart," he said. "I, too, resign, but not with the hope of retaining office. I am an old man, more than twice your age, and it is possible that you can see into the future more clearly than I do. I hope, with the utmost sincerity, that your actions may be justified by results. Certainly, France has not lost much in the persons of her chief citizens. But I beseech you, let there be no bloodshed. In these cases it is too often the poor and weak who suffer."

Vansittart was touched by the honesty of purpose revealed by these words.

"If I can prevent it, monsieur, I shall not climb to power by the loss of a single life. Meanwhile, though the Palais must perforce become my official residence at once, I beg of you to regard it as wholly at your service for as long as you choose to remain."

The old gentleman bowed, and slowly went out. He was stunned in body and mind. He cared not for the issue of events. He did not make the slightest effort to communicate with anybody save his own family, and with them he was reticent. Thenceforth he learned the progress of affairs through the newspapers, and marvelled that he should ever have thought of crossing swords with Vansittart.

Yet he had his consolations. "It was I who gave him his chance, my dear," he would say confidentially to his wife. "If I had not been an addle-headed old ass, and acted as I did, he would have lacked the opportunity. Still, it has all turned out very well, and I was growing tired of the Presidency. Why, I never knew from one day to another who was in office. In one month we had four distinct cabinets."

CHAPTER XXXV

A BLOODLESS REVOLUTION

VANSITTART had given to Liancourt a bare summary of events, with a view towards seeking his advice as to further action, when a pistol shot rang through the external lobby, coming apparently from the entrance hall. Colonel le Breton, followed by Jerome, hastened forth to inquire into this threatening circumstance. They were met on the stairs by Folliet, laughing heartily, Arizona Jim leisurely mounting the steps behind him, and fitting a fresh cartridge into an empty chamber of his revolver.

"Bates," said Vansittart, and this time he was genuinely angry, for he meant at all hazards to stop unnecessary violence, "how dare you shoot at any one when I have forbidden you!"

"I did n't, boss. I did n't even singe his whiskers."

Folliet was clearly much tickled by some occurrence, for he continued to laugh immoderately.

"What do you mean by disobeying my orders, you—you —I am tempted to call you a horse thief."

"Well, don't, boss; there ain't no 'casion. Folliet said you might happen to want me, so I left Mr. Harland to do the letter-carryin', as he knows Paris a heap better 'n me. I comes along with his nibs, and when we hops inter the hall he sees a jay in the telephone box, and hears him shout a number. 'Mon Jew!' cries Folliet, 'that 's the number of the Invalides barracks, and that scoundrel is one of Ribou's agents. He will alarm the troops with false news.' It struck me hard, boss, that there was n't no time to be lost, so I just plugs a bullet into the talkee part. I guess that machine wants repairs, an', holy smoke, did n't that chap quit? It was more fun nor a box of monkeys to see him skip!"

Folliet's unrestrained mirth was contagious. Vansittart was forced to follow his example, to be joined by Liancourt and the Chasseurs when the incident was explained. Surely never before was conspiracy to seize a state so jovial at the hour of its birth.

"Well," said Jerome at length, "I am glad you are here, Jim. I had forgotten one thing, and that most important. Ride back to St. Cloud with this note."

Sitting in the Council chamber, in the President's chair, he seized pen and paper, but hesitated a moment over the first word. Then he wrote:

To EVELYN:—All is well so far. I have succeeded, I think, without a blow.—JEROME.

He crumpled it up in an envelope and handed it to Bates, saying, "That is for Miss Harland. She will be anxious for news, so I suppose, I need not tell you to hurry."

Bates made no reply, but in ten seconds he gave the Chasseurs on the lawn a fine lesson in the art of mounting a horse that has already jumped off into a gallop. It is five miles of pigeon-flight from the Élysée to St. Cloud, but Arizona Jim, who rode a superb bay hunter, threw himself from off his foam-bathed steed eighteen minutes after receiving the note, and strode up to the main entrance to ring for an attendant. The doors were wide open, and within, standing in an anxious group, were Evelyn, Honorine, the Comtesse de Fontainebleau, and Prince Henri. Arizona Jim was no fool. He knew exactly how certain it was that the delivery of a message from Vansittart to the English girl at such a juncture would be misconstrued by the others.

He did not hesitate a moment. "The boss don't know his own mind," he ruminated, "but I do. Jehosh! A wad of lead in a telephone is nothin' to *this* bee in a bonnet-box."

They all saw him, and ran to him questioning. "Ah! a letter!" cried Honorine. "From Mr. Vansittart? Give it to me."

"It's not for you, miss," he said quietly, advancing towards Evelyn.

Evelyn blushed furiously, but opened the note and read it aloud after one hasty glance.

"He wrote to me," she added, "because he knew that I had seen my brother and the others go away. Otherwise, he would have sent the first message to you," with a glance at Honorine.

It was a magnanimous utterance, and showed the honesty of her heart. The other woman, a queen in all but name, was equal to the situation, though she felt its bitterness.

"Of course," she said, swallowing the pill with a smile. "He naturally thinks I am still sleeping. Come, Bates, supplement Mr. Vansittart's brief intelligence. Where is he? What has happened?"

In the Palais by this time all was bustle and animation. General Daubisson had summoned the leading officers of the Paris garrison, and they unanimously congratulated Vansittart on the bold but necessary step he had taken. In response to the laconic information left by Dick Harland, politicians, permanent heads of departments, and well-known members of society hurried to the Élysée, and Vansittart already felt assured that he had in no way underrated the extent of public sympathy in his favor.

One of Liancourt's first cares was to send to the newspaper offices a full and authentic account of the night's events, and also a statement of Vansittart's intentions, thus leaving no room for panic or sensational rumor. Placards to the same effect were posted throughout Paris, and when the City of

Light poured her citizens into the streets, there was no lack of food for gossip in the early hours of the day.

The millionnaire described in simple language the nature of his dramatic act, and the causes that had led up to it. He promised that the Provisional Government would make a statement to the Chamber that day, announcing a general appeal to the constituencies at the earliest possible date, when the issue before the people would be a plain one—did they, or did they not approve of his determination to make an end of the class of ministers who had, in his opinion, so long mismanaged the affairs of France? If they were with him, and elected a Chamber pledged to nominate him as President, he would do his best for the country. But if the electors believed that the old *régime* was better for France, then he would at once retire, and await prosecution at the bar of a legal tribunal. Meanwhile, during the interregnum, he would conduct the public business on constitutional and non-committal lines, for he would take no step that did not command and obtain the good-will of the people.

Paris read the newspapers and the proclamation. It talked with exceeding quickness and gesticulated with unusual animation. It gathered in groups, big and little, to discuss matters, and not a policeman interfered with it. Whereat Paris marvelled, for such a thing was unprecedented. Then Paris grew hungry. It was time for *déjeûner*. So it went to its favorite eating-house, and was invited by the proprietor "to take lunch with Mr. Vansittart."

Every restaurant in the city had received *carte blanche* to feed its customers that day at the expense of the Provisional President.

A knot of communists talked of a barricade in the Faubourg St. Martin. A police commissiary appeared and announced the free meals, of which the redshirts were previously ignorant, and there was no barricade. In a word, Paris lunched well and extensively.

After it had done full justice to the varying menu, there

was no talk of business. Paris drove, or ran, or hobbled, it even staggered, to the Chamber of Deputies, and, if any patriotic Republican member doubted the expediency of Vansittart's jump over the barrier of law, he had no doubt as to the expediency of keeping his doubts to himself. For the deputies passed to the Chamber through a vociferous but orderly mob, which was for the millionnaire down to the last man, woman, and child.

"This is a new sort of July Revolution," said one member to another. "What do you think of it?"

"I don't try to think; I observe."

"And what is the outcome of your observation?"

"That when the people have made up their mind in this fashion, the sooner we make up ours on the same lines, the better it will be for us."

"But it is outrageous, this *coup d'état!*"

"It is nevertheless a fact. I am more concerned with to-morrow than with yesterday."

When Liancourt rose in the Chamber there was an unwonted hush. All the ousted ministers were present in their capacities as deputies. They were now resentful, and ready to make a scene. He had hardly uttered three sentences before they violently interrupted, backed up by a few shortsighted partisans.

But even as Liancourt was speaking, there came through the open window a roar of exultation that momentarily grew in volume until it rendered impossible any further debate in the House. The great shout swelled into frenzy. There is no sound like that of tens of thousands of human voices united in the same cry. Concerning its nature there speedily was no ambiguity. The people were yelling "*Vive Vansittart!*" with extraordinary power and unanimity. Was it mere exuberance of sentiment, this cry, or was there an exciting cause?

An official entered, and the news quickly buzzed through the Chamber that the man upon whom all thoughts were centred, was riding alone towards the building, and that the crowd, unguided, had prepared his triumphal path.

This move by Jerome was an absolute stroke of genius.

What better proof of his unbounded confidence in the people than that he should pass through their midst in such manner, and trust himself, unarmed and unattended, within the precincts of the parliament that might conceivably be hostile to him.

"Will he, single-handed, arrest us all?" laughed a deputy. The joke was an uneasy one. Whilst it ridiculed, it admitted his power.

Vansittart was seemingly in no belligerent mood. Having patiently extricated himself from the crowd, he gave his horse to a janitor, and sought a place in the visitors' gallery. Not knowing how to deal with him, the attendants ushered him into the section reserved for distinguished strangers. Now, this happened to be the spot whence Napoleon the Third would at times watch the debates of a Chamber that helped him to his ruin. Republican usage had broken the tradition, but it could not banish the memory. All eyes were fixed upon him, and he bowed low to the assembled deputies, whereat there burst forth an approving cheer.

Then the chairman's bell rang out sharply, and Liancourt concluded his speech. Others followed, but they all agreed that the wisest course was to appeal immediately to the country, and thus obtain the unequivocal opinion of the electorate upon the strange occurrences of the preceding night. Before they well knew what they were doing, the Chamber had passed the necessary credits to enable the Provisional Government to administer public business until the general election was over, and the sitting concluded. This important fact was telegraphed to provincial prefects and mayors, and all France went to its evening meal profoundly astonished, but wonderfully well pleased. The national complaisance may be readily explained by the phenomenal hold that Vansittart now possessed over the affections and imaginations of every adult in the country.

But London and New York were stupefied.

Notwithstanding the *Daily Telegraph's* Paris article and the *New York Clarion's* extensive references to his deeds, none in either country regarded him as other than an amiable and clever man, who found delight in applying his unprecedented riches to utilitarian ends.

When French opinion saw in him a possible Emperor, the superior Saxon smiled at the conceit. That which is a political faith in France may be scoffed at in England or the United States.

True, the Governments of both countries were better informed. But in neither case did ministers discover ground for alarm in such a consummation. There was, however, an unmistakable flow of popular sympathy towards his cause, and every steamer from both countries conveyed to France crowds of idlers and pressmen, anxious to witness and describe the stirring scenes expected.

It was left for Germany to consolidate Vansittart's position, if he needed any such extraneous help.

The Kaiser was naturally agitated by the incidents in Paris. Of course he sent a telegram—to the wrong man. He wired a message of condolence with the fallen President, but the latter, one of the soldiers of 1870, bitterly and publicly resented it. There was some bluster in the Press, so William II. moved a couple of army corps nearer the Rhine. Vansittart sent a civil inquiry as to the reason for this display of energy, and the answer was curtly unsatisfactory. The Emperor of Finance smiled when he received this retort from the Emperor of Bounce. After a short consultation with Peter Studevant, he administered a severe rattling to the Berlin Bourse, and ordered the whole French Army to assemble for the autumn manœuvres in the neighborhood of Belfort.

This was sufficient. The Kaiser realized that he had met

an opponent who was versed in the first principles of poker, and knew enough to raise the hair off his head at the earliest opportunity. The German army corps were recalled, the Berlin Bourse was allowed to breathe again, and the French troops were directed to indulge in territorial training, as the Belfort mobilization would be too expensive.

The Paris Press wept for joy, and the statue of Strasbourg, in the Place de la Concorde, was for once decked with a garland of roses. "At last," shrieked the *Gil Blas*, "the lost provinces are seen again, after being shrouded for a generation in the midst of bitter regrets," whilst a semi-official communication to the St. Petersburg papers declared that "Russia is regarding the phase through which France is passing with a curious but friendly eye."

Liancourt arranged for the election to take place a fortnight after the dissolution. It was to be conducted on the *scrutin de liste* basis—that is to say, the entire population of a department voted for candidates *en bloc*. Thus, if the people supported Vansittart, there would be no minority representation. When all that human ingenuity could do had been done to insure his success, the volatile goddess of chance stepped in to help. Jerome's horse, Victor, won the Derby, and was backed by the "French Division" with that thoroughness and liberality which on other occasions make them so popular with "the ring."

And to crown all, the day before the election, Maclaren sent a definite description of the opening of the Gabes Canal, with the other waterways connecting the lakes, thus permitting Captain Pompier successfully to navigate the *Sphinx* and the *Seafarer* to the western shore of Lake Melrhir.

Under these conditions, Vansittart calmly awaited the verdict of the polls. It came in splendid style. Every deputy was pledged to elect him President, and to support him in all his undertakings.

A superb spectacle was arranged for the eventful day when the Senate and Chamber of Deputies foregathered at

Versailles to carry out this pleasant duty, and Vansittart's triumphal return to Paris was unanimously declared to be the record display of the capital since the collapse of the Third Empire.

Late that night, thoroughly worn out with the fatigue of the brilliant pageant, President Jerome Vansittart smoked a peaceful pipe in the sanctuary of his friend Dick. Both had been silent for some moments. Harland was the first to speak.

"The next thing, Jerry, is Notre Dame and a coronation, to be immediately succeeded by your marriage with——"

"For heaven's sake, Dick, talk about something else. Sufficient for this day, at any rate, is the ceremony thereof."

Harland was surprised at this testiness, but he only said :

"I can't see any harm in such a simple bit of speculation after all the wildly impossible things you have already turned into realities."

"No, no, I quite appreciate your words, old chap, but the prospect ahead worries me."

"In the name of goodness, why ? "

Jerome hardly knew how to frame his answer, when he chanced to think of a note he had received after dinner. This would serve to change the conversation, and cover his own petulance. He handed it to Dick. "My keenest enemy is still at work," he said.

It was but a plain sheet of notepaper, and it bore the words : "Hail, President. All goes well so far, but there are those who know how to wait."

"Who wrote it ? " inquired Harland.

"De Tournon."

CHAPTER XXXVI

THE PRINCESS MARCHESI

A WEEK after Vansittart's election, the Princess Marchesi, his aunt, arrived in Paris. Previously, it has been stated that she was once known as *la belle Américaine* in the American colony at Rome. She showed signs of being *belle* still, but was also *usée*, and shrivelled. She painted thickly, in a loud carmine; her hair should have been gray or white, but was brown. In her preoccupation with herself, she did not stop to remember that girlhood is more than a dye, that youth is not a confection of *poudre de riz*.

Wishing to be young again, she looked about her for an enchanter to work this marvel, and had the shortsightedness to pitch upon the *parfumeur*, the druggist, the dentist, and the manicure. They succeeded in effecting a rejuvenescence in her hair, but could not alter the texture of her skin. She became a patchwork of youth and age. Her nose was young, but when she smiled the corners of her eyes wrinkled up into a very chaos of age. In the evening she was half a century younger than she had been in the morning. And even in the evening, a little tuft of fine gray hairs grew out of her ears. There were a few also on her chin. Her food she ate with the teeth of a woman long since dead.

But in her heart, in her manner, was youth. She was a little, erect, pert lady, with a quick bird-like perk of the head, full of vivacity, of sprightliness, of resource. One could not but be captured by her inborn good-nature, her gossipy officiousness, her childlike simplicity of temperament.

And she was wonderfully fond of her nephew, Jerome K. Vansittart. "Jerome," she would say, "is a prince of men, my dear. That is the view I have *always* taken of him, and always shall take. A prince of men."

She came down in force upon St. Cloud, with an army of servants and a pyramid of luggage, and pitched her camp there. Vansittart had now filled the entire area of civilization with the *bruit* of his name. New York could no longer contain the Princess Marchesi. She came to Paris to see and to hear.

"Jerome," she said a few days after, in one of the palatial *salons* of St. Cloud, "you owe me thanks for this visit, sir. I am no longer as young as I look, or at least as I have been. And all this way I have come solely to see you."

Jerome, with his elbow on an alabaster mantelpiece, stood regarding her with a half-tolerant smile.

"I acknowledge my obligation, aunt," he said. "Had you warned me of your intention to cross the ocean you should have been convoyed by a fleet."

"Yes, I know—you are making fun of a poor old woman. But I can afford to laugh at you, Mr. Jerome. It is through *my* prophecy that you are what you are to-day. I always believed in you. I always said that Jerome K. Vansittart had something in him. Only don't get spoiled by success, Jerome."

He laughed, and in a moment was grave. "There is little fear of that."

"There is, sir. You are not happy."

He winced. "But to be unhappy is a different thing to being 'spoiled.'"

"Yes. But unhappiness often comes through one's being spoiled."

"Explain yourself."

"No. That is asking too much of me, surely. I have only suspicions to go upon, and even if I had not, one cannot always speak with perfect plainness."

"Not even an aunt."

"Not even an aunt—to her President nephew."

"Then I retort that your suspicions must be unfounded."

"*My* suspicions unfounded ? Why Jerome, what do you take me for ? I am no longer a chicken ! I have been about the world. A young man's heart is no secret to me, at this time of day."

"A young man's *heart*, aunt ? You surprise me. I did not know that I had one."

"Yes, yes, you have one, and you know it, and you will not listen to it, I am afraid."

"Really, madame, you speak in enigmas."

"What shall it profit a man, Jerome, if he gain the whole world and lose his own soul ?"

"I see. For 'soul' read 'heart,' and one arrives at my aunt's philosophy-of-life for 'a young man.'"

"I am surprised that you should take the trouble to be sarcastic to *me*, Jerome," said the old lady, looking at him examiningly, with a perk of her quick head. "Sarcasm is lost upon me. I merely say that the presidentship of France has not made you so happy as you thought it would."

"I never thought that it would make me happy."

"But you were happy before — you were happy in America."

"Possibly."

"Then you should be now ! And if you are not, then there is something——"

Jerome began to find that incessant tongue like a needle in his side.

"Pray excuse me. I must leave you——"

"There is something, I tell you ; something which you will not admit to yourself. And that is what I mean when I say : don't get spoiled. With all your wealth you were always a simple-hearted, natural fellow. Don't ruin your life by becoming artificial, hard-hearted, over ambitious——"

"Really, madame——"

"Oh, I can see a change in you! Don't think these eyes are dim. Let me look at you—you look taller, for one thing, and stouter. Pray, do not develop a paunch, Jerome." She had to raise her voice to make the last sentence heard. Vansittart had fled.

She and the Comtesse de Fontainebleau soon became boon companions. The little lady found it necessary to perk her head high when walking in conversation with the large-bodied Comtesse. But they had much in common, and were generally to be seen together.

"That, surely, is a dear child!" said the Princess one day, after a visit of ceremony paid her by Evelyn and Dick Harland.

"Personally, I like her," replied the Comtesse coldly.

"Why does she not *live* here now?"

"The pretence is, madame, that Mr. Harland has to reside in Paris, in order, for some reason or another, to be in close proximity with the Sahara Offices. His sister, of course, accompanies him. They only went a short time ago, a couple of days after Mr. Vansittart's *coup d'état*."

"You say '*the pretence*'?"

"Of course that was not the real reason. It is the sister who persuaded the brother to go."

"What for?"

"Miss Harland and Honorine were not the best of friends." The Princess's eyes winked fast. She saw a secret opening before her.

"Madame," she said, "say no more. You have told me the whole history. I divine all."

"The history is perhaps more complicated than you think, madame," said the Comtesse with a sweet smile. The enjoyment of this talk to the two ladies was intense. To the Princess it was the joy which the hungry have in eating; to the Comtesse it was the joy of one who feeds the hungry, in slow doles, lest they over-gorge themselves, and choke.

"So, madame, the history is complicated, then?" said the Princess. "Well! Well! Tell me the whole." Their voices were low, though no one was near. They spoke in intense whisperings, with heads close together.

"Jealousy was not the chief reason of the quarrel between the girls," said the Comtesse.

"There was a *quarrel?*"

"Oh, quite a regular stand-up battle; you should have been there to hear it—you would have *died* with excitement. They lashed each other with pitiless venom, as one lashes convicts in the galleys with the cat.

"Now, you don't say that! Did you ever, now!"

"It is quite true. I am not exaggerating one little bit. Both girls locked themselves in their rooms for an hour soon after it, and wept bitterly for rage and shame. I saw it by their eyes."

"Well, this is a revelation. But the motive, you say, was not jealousy——"

"Not wholly. To tell you the truth, Honorine does not care sufficiently for Mr. Vansittart to be violently jealous of him——"

"Not care for Jerome K. Vansittart?" queried the Princess in surprise. This was indeed a shock.

"That is so, madame. And there is no love lost between them, really. It is only paying him out in his own coin, if she loves another."

"And that other?"

The Comtesse smiled. "Madame la Princesse, in her acquaintance with the world of Society, must often have met the heir to the crown of France."

"Henri of Navarre?" The Comtesse bowed.

"Well! This is of all surprises the greatest. And Jerome, on his part, has something on his mind, I know. He is in love. I divined it at once. And I saw that Mademoiselle de Montpensier was not the object of his affections. So it is this Miss——"

"Harland."

"Can't we do anything?"

"What can we do?"

"We should do *something*—come now! It would be too hard to sit down calmly and see these four lives ruined and spoiled on account of some absurd provision in the Salic Law, you know."

"It would, yes. But we can do nothing. I confess that for the other three my head does not greatly ache; but I do feel for Honorine."

"I am in the same position, Comtesse. For the other three I cannot be expected to be bowed down by sorrow. But the interests of Jerome K. Vansittart do closely touch me."

"I am rather sorry for Prince Henri, too," said the Comtesse.

"And that Miss Harland is really a sweet girl, you know," answered the Princess.

"But it is of no use talking of it now; the die is cast. I may tell you that there was an attempt made to throw Mr. Vansittart and Miss Harland together. But it failed. You have a nephew, Madame la Princesse, of superhuman will. What can one do with such a man?"

"To throw them together, you say? And why?"

"He won't meet her, you see. He avoids her like the plague. If they could be got together, all might be well. When she was here, he generally managed to keep clear of St. Cloud. Now that she is gone, you see he is here, though he ought, for official reasons, to spend more time at the Élysée."

"I see. And your attempt failed."

"Yes; Mr. Vansittart was adamant. Honorine was carried away with admiration. There was a general shaking of hands; and everybody's mind was reconciled to letting things remain as they were. So it appeared at least on the surface. Inwardly, I know, they are all groaning and travailing, and straining at their strings like chained lions. And the end is near now. Mr. Vansittart is within measurable distance of attaining his ambition, and then—the marriage. To Honorine, I assure you, I can see signs that the situation is becoming intolerable."

"It *is* intolerable," said the Princess.

"Well, but if *they* are reconciled to it——"

"But *I* am not reconciled to it, madame! I will not bear to sit still and see it!" The Princess grasped the arms of her chair, and turned round upon the Comtesse with a busy alertness.

"Madame, what can two feeble women do?" asked the Comtesse.

"We shall see!" cried the Princess.

At this hour of the day, in the heat of the afternoon, a neat French *bonne* was looking down into a deepish well, just a little beyond the point where the dense forest began to mingle with the park of St. Cloud. The well was deserted but for the girl, and, to judge by the way in which it was embosomed in jungle, had long been unused; but the wheel was still there intact, and the axle, and a frayed old rope, and the bucket. And deep down, watching her pretty brown face reflected in the gloomy pool below, looked the girl with motionless gravity, as though she were stone.

She had come to St. Cloud in the train of the Princess, and in her way was a Princess, too, and a tyrant. Three times had her pay been raised, lest she should depart and leave Madame desolate. For no fingers in the wide world could insinuate themselves with so sweet and sleepy a touch into Madame's brown-hued tresses as those of Lisette. She was a lady of leisure, was Lisette. If her day's work, all told, lasted more than an hour, a threat came from her. She would go—it was too much—it was killing her, by degrees. The menace would frighten the little Princess into momentary silence; then she would implore Lisette to go out and take the air. Lisette had strolled forth into solitude this afternoon, admiring Nature. The bit of Nature which she most admired, though she only half-admitted it to herself, was Man. To talk to a man,—that, at present, was to Lisette the tip-top and sum of her languid existence. But that bit of Nature which consisted of her own face was charming, too. She leant over, studying it in the well. Yet how solitary, how mateless it was! Suddenly she started. There was a mate—a man, a face—down yonder, beside hers, in the deep water. She straightened herself, vexed.

"You porpoise! to frighten me like that——"

That male face, nevertheless, was a nice one. By the side of Lisette's, it looked companionable. It was more captivating still when it grinned and said: "Beg pardon. Not likely I would frighten you for the purpose."

Lisette looked at him. His countenance was a wicked one, though handsome. It was known, and not admired, at the Paris Prefecture and in Scotland Yard. Vansittart had seen it at the Bank of France when the attempt to cash his check failed. But it had this advantage for Lisette—it belonged to a man. And when she compared it with Arizona Jim's, who was the only male creature within the precincts of St. Cloud that, so far, seemed conscious of her charms, she somehow gave the preference to the face before her. Jim, it must be confessed, was not the *beau idéal* of the penny novelette; and he was absent—which, in a lover, is a crime.

"It is of no consequence," said Lisette. "I am just going away."

"No, don't go away; stay and chat," said the male.

"You 're joking, ain't you? I don't know you."

This was unanswerable. The male twirled his moustache. "It don't matter," he said. "I admit it. But I 'm all right. I don't mean to hurt you."

"Oh, I 'm glad you don't mean to *hurt* me," said Lisette. "You 're a funny man, are n't you?"

"Well, p'raps I am. Flop you down—here on the well."

"Well, suppose I do. Now let's hear what you've got to say for yourself."

"Are you from——?" He jerked his thumb in the direction of the palace.

"Yes. What about it?"

"Nothing. What you doing out here?"

"I'm come to take the air. It's a constitutional, if you want to know."

"I see. You're pretty high and mighty, ain't you?" She pouted.

"I expect you think yourself too good to marry, don't you?"

"I should just think I did!" she said.

"Well, I don't think that folks ought to be stuck up. If *I* like you, you ought to hold out your hand and say, 'It's a bargain.'"

"Yes, I should like to see myself! I should want to be sure, first of all, that you *did* like me."

"Can't help liking a smart one like you."

"Thanks. I'm elsewhere engaged. But have n't you any work to go and do, except sitting here?"

"I'm looking for work, you see."

"What are you?"

"Me? I am a—well—I'm a variety of things. I am a carpenter, a locksmith, a valet——" He began to chuckle. It was an odd combination of trades. "What do you call yourself? You are nice company, ain't you?"

"You're a fool. Good day."

"When am I to see you again?"

"Not at all."

"I shall! I shall go to the palace, and ask for you." He jerked with his thumb.

"You dare!" she cried.

"I shall! I like you! I mean to keep you altogether."

"You! I would n't have your betters!"

"You shall! I must see you to-morrow."

"Well, I sometimes take a stroll to the well about this hour."

"*Au revoir*, then. Take care of yourself!"

She walked royally away, without looking back; and they parted—to meet again, many times. And this talk, and these meetings, had an intimate relation with the talks and consultations of Madame la Comtesse and Madame la Princesse in the grand *salons* of the big house beyond the wood.

The pair were unnoticed, for the Park of St. Cloud, where the fountains are, are public property, open during the day to visitors, and lovers, and children from the neighborhood. Only a small portion of the estate around Vansittart's house had been enclosed to secure privacy. Lisette's admirer was an ex-clerk from the Office of the Interior; a clever scoundrel, who had been sent to penal servitude by Folliet during his first term as prefect, but released from the galleys by de Tournon because he knew too much about that precious minister's affairs.

CHAPTER XXXVII

THE CONSPIRATORS

AT this time Vansittart well knew that his life was not worth an hour's purchase. The gloom on his brow, the unrest of the man's life, which the Princess Marchesi had noted in him, was not all caused by the pain of his hopeless love. He lived on a volcano. But to live on a volcano is tolerable. It is to be haunted by a Shadow that no man can bear. He knew that as he walked the streets, or drove, or lay in bed at midnight, the blow might fall. The Sword hung over him. And his annoyance was caused by the fact that he could not see the Sword. He did not know where or when, or how manifold, or in what form, was the Peril which tracked him. But he was sure of the Peril itself. In consultation with his colleagues, at the opera, at a soirée, in his library, he felt the proximity of the Spectre.

One morning he received by post an envelope, which, when he opened it, he found to contain a half-sheet of paper with a death's head and crossbones roughly drawn upon it. Underneath was written the one word, "*Bientôt*" (soon). He was not a man to be frightened by threats; but the next day when he entered a kiosk in his own grounds, and at the threshold met a real death's head with real crossbones, and near it, on the floor, the word "Soon," he growled something like an imprecation.

Everything grew into a suggestion of death for him. Were it not for his strong nature, the entire world would have become to his fancy a place of tombs, and worms, and epitaphs.

As it was, he could not banish thought. The air was sickly with death. How many were leagued against him? To judge from the signs, it must be thousands. Once, as he was entering the office of Sahara, Limited, he slipped on the step and bruised his shin. It was found that the step had been smeared with slime of some sort. It was Vansittart's private entrance, and hardly ever used by any other person. Ten minutes before, Dick Harland had walked up those steps, and they had not been turned into a death-trap. His enemies seemed to foreknow his movements.

They seemed to be delaying his death only in order to make him live in what they hoped would prove to be a Torture of Fear. Once, as he passed in his carriage through a street loud with the huzzas of the crowd, a large nail was thrown at him. It struck him on the arm. To it was tied an oblong parchment ticket, on which was written the word, "Soon!"

They were bold and sure enough. Why were they not bolder? It was easy, for instance, to shoot him. Vansittart had divined their reason well; they wished to torture him. But there was another. They knew that, for the man who had been found to do harm to Jerome Vansittart, the people of France would invent a death more hellish than any which ever entered the dream of buccaneer or Inquisitor. They did not, it was clear, mean to be martyrs. In thrusting him over the precipice, they had no idea of being themselves dragged in. It was their design that, in falling, he should hear their laugh on the brink above.

One night he started from a troubled slumber, hearing a sound. He was always a light sleeper, and the sound which awoke him was faint. It resembled a slow scratching on the woodwork outside, near a window. He rose, crept stealthily toward the spot, a pistol in his hand. He pushed up the window suddenly, looked out, and saw—nothing.

But the next morning a ladder in an outhouse was found to have been mysteriously moved from its place, and into one of the uprights a letter had been carved—the capital letter "B." To others this was an enigma. Vansittart alone knew that "B" meant "*Bientôt!*" That day he was much engaged in thought. He sent for the architect of the new Palace at St. Cloud; and in the afternoon an army of carpenters were busy effecting certain alterations in his vast bedroom. About the same time he had a long consultation with Folliet at the Élysée.

"One thing is certain," said Folliet. "For the future you ought to live almost entirely here."

"Why?"

"Because here you can be safeguarded more thoroughly than at St. Cloud."

"If there were no other reason for my preference, I should still reside at St. Cloud. I want to meet these scoundrels, and have done with them once and for all."

"Why not let me meet them? They can all be transported."

"No! It is my quarrel. What is the extent of the plot? Have you discovered any more accomplices?"

"Yes, but they are only remotely connected with it."

"In what way?"

"They act as spies upon you. They play tricks. They are amateurs. They are rabid Republicans, who merely dislike you for political reasons."

"They need not be feared?"

"No. They have no personal, morbid rancor against you. Their hatred of you is a hobby. They detest you as a pastime. If they heard that you were murdered, they would cry 'Bravo.' If you went to their door in need, they would give you food, and their softest bed."

"They are the mere skirmishers of the army?"

"Yes, and the army itself is wonderfully small. In *my* opinion—as far as the minutest search can guide me—it consists of positively no more than five men."

"Led, of course, by——"

"De Tournon."

"We must strike down the leaders."

"Yes; but I want you to understand one thing. The situation has changed. De Tournon is no longer the briber of needy assassins, ready for any job. He is now only the first among equals. He leads an army not less eager than himself."

"How is that?"

Folliet smiled. "I see you do not understand the nature of the Paris brigand. He is not accustomed to resistance from his victims. His rôle is to kill; he is resentful of being killed. When you outwitted and damaged the Plasterer, String-the-Neck, and the Gouger in the hut of the forest, you created yourself three foes, whose designs can only end with their death—or yours. To de Tournon your life is an anticipated *bonne bouche*—the sweetest morsel of his life—to his three friends it is all this, and more—it is a point of honor. They are fanatics. Your life is their object. They have a religion which you inspire."

"Who is the fifth?"

"An ex-convict, named le Grand, known to his mates as "Le Fongeur,"—the blotter, a skilful rogue, who is a notable forger and desperado."

"But why is he in league against me?"

"From pure love of villainy. He is also an old-time associate of de Tournon's."

"What of Ribou? Of Lacontel?"

"Neither Ribou nor Lacontel is a prime mover in the matter, though they know of it, and give it their countenance. Ribou is a vain simpleton; Lacontel is a weathercock. Remove the others, and they disappear. Their revenge for their fall would hardly extend to personal assassination. They are not men of desperate character. They do not spring from the lowest criminal class—like de Tournon."

"I see. And what are the recent movements of our five friends?"

"On the 13th, the Plasterer bought a new knife at a shop in the Rue de Savon; on the 15th, it was sharpened by a knife-grinder in a wood at Marly."

"Proceed."

"On the 16th, de Tournon and the Gouger met in an inn at La Vilette, and conversed for two hours; later, the same day, the Gouger and String-the-Neck bought at two separate shops in the Rue Dupin a file and ten yards of rope; still later, on the same day, the Fongeur attended the *Théâtre des Variétés* with an unknown girl. He parted from her at the corner of the Rue de Madeleine and the Rue des Hermies, she afterwards taking train for St. Cloud."

"The Fongeur is a gallant, then?"

"He appears to have an extraordinary influence upon girls of a certain class."

"You saw them yourself?"

"No—one of my men. Unfortunately, my spy had to leave the girl, after finding her destination, in order to overtake the Fongeur again."

"How many men have you in your service?"

"Seventy-three."

"And what is your view of the whole matter?"

"On the 17th, all the five men met in the forest yonder, not far from the palace. They are afraid of the streets; they avoid Paris; they shun the day. My idea is that we should be careful of the palace and of night."

"But I am secretly well guarded. To any one entering, there is certain capture or death."

"There are the windows of the upper floor," replied Folliet.

"After to-day there will be no windows to my bedroom."

"Yet I mistrust, I fear. These men are no amateurs in the art of entering a house. You may be sure that they know that we are on the watch, and will anticipate all our possible precautions. I propose that I sleep here every night from henceforth that you are in the house; and that a room next to mine be set apart for Mr. Jim Bates."

"Certainly—if you desire it."

"And you should not sleep twice in the same bed until whatever arrangements you are making in your bedroom are complete."

"I had thought of that. But now, M. Folliet, the question with me, I assure you, is not so much how to escape these men, as how to brush them from the world. I have the police of France at my disposal—I have you. Let us end these men."

"Let me arrest them, then, and guillotine them in due course of law. I will arrange it."

"We must *not* arrest them, M. Folliet! I repeat it to you. We must *not* guillotine them in due course of law! If I die, we must not. These men have declared private, personal war against *me*. In this case, vengeance is *mine;* I will repay."

Folliet's eyes flashed. "Good, sir!" he cried. "Good, sir!"

"Ah, I see I touch a cord in your bosom, M. Folliet! You entertain much the same sentiments with respect to M. de Tournon, I think, as I have just expressed with regard to him and his gang."

Folliet was pale, trembling with excitement. In his eyes gleamed a deadly hate. "Mr. Vansittart," he said; "with all due deference to you, sir, de Tournon is not yours. He is mine. Ah, if ever the day comes——"

"Very well, M. Folliet. I respect your sensibilities in this matter. If ever the day comes, you may depend upon me to yield M. de Tournon to you. Meanwhile, watch well to balk them—and, above all, to ensnare them."

On that day the Princess Marchesi was absent from St. Cloud. She was paying a visit to the Grand Hotel, where Evelyn Harland was staying. This call of hers was the fifth within a week. Often she sat, with her skinny face perked judicially sideways, watching the movements of Evelyn. She would say: "What a charming child you are! I am in love with you. Men are so impossible! If *I* were a man——"

When she was putting on her bonnet to go, she said: "Very well, if you have the heart to make an old woman like me come rushing up every day to this dreadful hotel to see you, I will do it. But that is not pretty, Evelyn."

"What can one do?" cooed Evelyn demurely.

"I may call you 'Evelyn,' may n't I?" Evelyn kissed her. "Then come and stay with me, and don't be an absurd child! Where can the eyes of the men be to let a prize like you stay like that? The men are degenerate. In my time, you would have been snapped up like ripe apples."

Evelyn laughed. "I wait to be picked!" she cried.

"If you do not fall to the ground beforehand! But you have to come, Evelyn, if only for a week. Why, child, I have nobody to talk to all day! I shall be dumb in a month, like what 's-his-name on the desert island."

"There is Mademoiselle de Montpensier."

"She is impossible and unhuman. I dislike her."

"There is the Comtesse."

"Yes, but the Comtesse is getting old. The toilsome heave of her large bosom annoys me; and she objects to snuff. You must come, Evelyn."

"There is Mr. Vansittart."

"He thinks me a bore; and he is nearly always away."

"Still?"

"Yes. You must come. I must have a breath of fresh youth about me; I begin to recognize my absolute need of that. That is why I can't part from that Lisette. Say next week, then."

"There is Dick to be thought of."

"Dick is out of the question. I do not recognize Dick— I do not admit him. You have got to come, so you may as well say 'Yes' at once. It would be shocking to make me come tearing up to Paris every day like a *grisette*. And I am in love with you—I cannot do without you. If you say 'No' again, I shall kiss you with my rouged lips!"

"Only for two days, then," said Evelyn.

"No—a week."

"Three days!"

"I insist upon a week."

"Very well—but no longer, remember. You are incorrigible!"

They kissed, and parted.

CHAPTER XXXVIII

THE SIEGE OF ST. CLOUD

A DESPERATE siege was laid to St. Cloud by de Tournon and his brigands, the first object being to discover the exact position and place of Vansittart's bed. One day an old woman was found skulking in a lonely part of the upper floor. She was bent double with apparent age, and, when asked to account for her presence in the house, seemed daft. It was thought that she had merely strayed inside in her aimless wanderings, till she was brought before Vansittart, who said:

"Take that wig off his head."

Jim Bates gave a tug at a tangled mass of gray locks, and the smooth hair of a boy of sixteen stood revealed. He had failed, however, in the object of his quest: he had not discovered the bed of Vansittart. This determined, the assassins had the means in their hand and head to effect, without fail, the destruction of the millionnaire. The problem was to determine it.

Vansittart, perhaps, was at this time more or less foolhardy. He might have invested himself, sleeping and waking, with cordons of thousands of soldiers. But to this he would not stoop. His pride was stubbornly set upon the personal annihilation of these men. He would owe no unfair advantage over them to his official powers. He waited, patiently bearing their manœuvres, not helping them, not hindering them, trusting to chance, and his own wit, and the cunning watch of Folliet.

"Then we must burn the house down," said de Tournon. "We must hunt the rat out of his hole."

"I should n't trouble," said the Plasterer, rather scornfully. "The nights are warm enough."

"What 'd be the good?" the less sarcastic Gouger wanted to know. "You don't suppose he 's going to get burned to death, a man like him, do you? And next day, he 'd have fifty other houses, just as big, to live in."

"There must be a plan of the house somewhere at the architect's," suggested String-the-Neck, whose right hand had been amputated at the wrist.

"Pin your lips, you!" cried the Fongeur. "As if that was going to help us in what we want!"

He got up, climbed the stairs of the cellar in which they lounged, and in an hour's time was waiting at the well at St. Cloud. He was considerably better dressed than on the occasion of his first introduction to Lisette. He wore a fine tie, and carried a handkerchief made of the most exquisite Indian silk. They had once been worn by Vansittart, and were presents from Lisette.

"Here, you!" he said when she appeared; "what do you mean by being late?" The Fongeur had begun to speak with rather guttural sternness to his *grisette*.

"I come just when it suits me," said Lisette, pinning some wood-violets in her bosom.

"We 'll see about that later, my lady," he mused. "But what about this affair?"

"What affair?"

"Oh, come now! You know. Were n't we talking about having a look round Vansittart's room together, to see what we could fish?"

"*You* were talking of it; *we* were n't. How disagreeable you are of late."

"But you love your husband, Lisette? You love your husband, confound you, don't you?"

"Such as he is," said Lisette, looking down, and patting

her violets. Then she gave le Grand a little swift, fond slap on the cheek. "But you must n't think, because I 'm married to you, that I 'm going to do everything you want."

"You 're going to do this, though, I 'm thinking, because it 's *got* to be done, you see."

"But what 's the matter with you? Are you a thief?" said Lisette gravely. "Don't let me think that of you! Look here, you see that stone there. You might just as well ask that."

His brow darkened ominously.

"Now, look you," he said, "stop it. I 'm not a man accustomed to that sort of thing. What I say must be done. I 've got a fondness for you, with your airs and graces. Don't let me do you an injury."

"An injury!" exclaimed the wife of five days.

"I don't want to do you one, I say."

"I see. You are a *beautiful* husband, *you* are! But I shan't give you the chance. *Adieu.*" She rose with the grace of a princess. He had her by the arm.

"Here, are you going to do what I tell you? What d' you think I married you for?"

"I won't do it!"

"You shall!"

"I shan't!"

Down came the cruel blow, smack on her face. In the next moment Lisette had her arm wrenched free, and was flying down the path, he after her. But she was young, and light, and swift. He stopped within sight of the entrance lodge, hopelessly distanced.

The next day, at the appointed time, he came to the well, and the next, but there was no sweet Lisette there. She was trembling in the palace, thinking of him, fearing that he might come and claim her, and reveal all. She did not know that the Fongeur could not show his face within the palace grounds. And he dared not write. Lisette was the hope of the besiegers of the palace. When she vanished, they began to approach desperation. But de Tournon only smiled, his fleshy, firm, cruel lips curving into scorn.

"If you are balked by a servant girl, I am sorry for you!" he said. "Look here, I am going to crush that man between my hands like *that*. And I know how."

"How?" queried the Gouger.

"I am going to enter his house in the middle of the night, and strangle him in his sleep with my two hands, *so*." His goggle eyes glared as he brought his fingers together.

"Ah, yes!" said the Plasterer, "but how, you grampus?"

"It's no use trying to get into the house from outside. We must get into it from *beneath*."

"Dig a tunnel, you mean?"

"Aye."

"It 'll take us a year. Tie up your mouth."

"If it takes us fifty years. But it won't. We 've got friends enough."

"But we are watched. Our tunnel 's sure to be squinted long before we 're half-way through."

"You 're a fool. Not if we begin it in the right place." And the next day the tunnel was begun—in the right place.

The right place was beneath the seldom-used trap-door that gave access to the works of the fountains in the park. These were rusty with desuetude, and not a workman had been engaged on their repair for years. There was a spacious chamber, roughly flagged, beneath the level of the ground. Its sides were boarded, and de Tournon's plan was to take out some of these boards—sufficient only to permit of easy access, and then dig far enough to permit the boards to be replaced, and their tools hidden before their operations could, by even remote chance, be discovered.

To slip unseen through the outer grating at dusk was an easy matter. To observe them Folliet would need to closely watch the suspected spot itself. Anyhow, they made the experiment, and, to their surprise, succeeded. They found the earth behind the boards wonderfully loose and light. The ground required hardly any effort on their part to be shovelled away; and there was not a single stone. In two hours a square opening had been dug almost equal to the area of a doorway. They continued to dig by the light of lanterns. The removed mould they placed on one side, to be taken away hurriedly and simultaneously by all of them together at dawn, thus eluding the chance of detection. Anyone passing over the pathway that led from the palace to the fountains would not dream that beneath it were men sweating with toil.

But the next evening, when they descended to their labor, their presence in the place was known. They had been spied as they entered. Folliet ran unannounced into Vansittart's presence, followed by Arizona Jim.

"We have them!" he cried joyfully, "and in a beautiful spot! They are in the accommodation room at the base of the fountains in the park—the whole five of them!"

"Very good, M. Folliet," said Vansittart, pushing away a pile of correspondence. "Happily, I have dined. I am entirely at your disposal." He took in his hand a heavy-headed oak walking-stick from a corner, and from an escritoire a small silver revolver. He put on a wide, soft felt hat.

"They are five," said Folliet, "we are only three."

"But three is a lucky number, M. Folliet. We will be generous foes to these men. Let us do them the honor to consider each of them as three fifths of a man, and then we shall be three to three. Their majority of two will thus be only apparent."

They set out. On the way through the full-leafed woods M. Folliet said, "It may interest you to know, sir, that the Fongeur, le Grand, has lately entered into the holy bonds of matrimony."

"Ah!" I felicitate the lady," said Vansittart. "Who is she?"

"We don't know yet, but shall soon. She lives somewhere in or near St. Cloud, apart from him. This, to my knowledge, is his sixth wife; and four of the others, I strongly suspect, are still alive."

They parted at a little distance from the manhole, crept near it from different directions, and then, with a rush, were beside it. They flung it open and peered down. The room was empty. They descended the iron ladder, and the workers in the excavation, having heard the clang of the trap-door, ceased their digging, and quickly put out their lanterns. On the floor was not a particle of brown mould and earthy *débris*, to indicate the labor of the men beyond. Every trace of their undertaking had been carefully removed on the night before. The plank wall was held in its place with the old irregular naturalness by a transom-piece screwed within. The three men looked at one another.

"This is a rum go!" said Jim.

"They've gone," said Folliet.

"Better luck next time, monsieur," said Vansittart.

They ascended, and Folliet blew a shrill whistle three times. A man who seemed to drop from the clouds, or come from the land of Nowhere, came running.

"They've gone, then?" said Folliet.

"I'll swear they're not," answered the spy.

"Why, you blind eyes, of course they are! Be sure never to come near *me* again, if you please." The man stood in wide-eyed astonishment. The conspirators breathed again as they heard the trap-door bang behind Jim, who was the last to mount the stairs, and resumed operations.

In an hour the five men were twelve feet farther advanced. It was incredibly swift work. They questioned themselves with strange hopes. What was the meaning of it? A bevy of some twenty-five helpers were to come later in the evening. But de Tournon now sent the Gouger forth to tell them not to risk it yet. Their presence might excite suspicion, and there was no need for them. The reason of the looseness of the earth was now known. A wonderful discovery had been made. Whilst they were delving persistently ahead, a mass of earth suddenly dropped down before them, and they stumbled into a vault.

The tunnel to St. Cloud which they intended, with infinite labor, to make, stood ready made for them, and had so stood for five hundred years. The lanterns shone luridly upon their leering, grimy faces, upon their sweating brows, and lit up there a joy hideous as the laughter of demons. These secret passages and escapes were the commonplaces of the days of ancient tyranny. The old kings knew both how to govern their subjects, and how to fly from them. If things grew too hot for them, they called upon the earth to swallow them. The earth swallowed them, and vomited them again some distance away, at a convenient spot.

Resurrection is an Art; and so is self-crucifixion. The great cardinals, the Richelieus and Mazarins, the high ministers of state, the king's favorites, the king himself, had, all and each, these happy underground exits for the day of stormy winds and stress of weather. The back-door of the great was—a tunnel.

The passage upon which de Tournon had hit led from the old vaults of St. Cloud, upon which the present palace and its predecessor were built, to a hidden exit near the site of the existing fountains, since the times of Barbarossa and the Hohenstaufens.

"The thing is done," said de Tournon. "If there be no other means, we must employ dynamite to remove St. Cloud."

It was not quite done, however. Much labor remained to be accomplished. An attempt had been made, probably long ago, to destroy the tunnel as a means of escape, even for those who might know of its existence. It had been walled up transversely in several places. And though the stones of these walls were soft and disintegrating, they were cemented together by a mortar grown hard as granite. Two fell before the earnest picks of the underground toilers that night; but in the small hours, advancing about a hundred yards, they were faced by yet another. The walls were thick; to break down one was the work of hours. And they were still only half-way between the exit and the palace; there remained other walls for them to attack and to demolish.

"Let us get this one down before we leave!" said de Tournon, mopping his dripping face near the new obstruction.

"Not I!" said the Plasterer. "A galley-toad like you may. But I am leaking through every pore. To-morrow's good enough for me." He tossed down his pick, and slouched back in the direction of the exit.

Le Grand, the Gouger, and String-the-Neck followed him. But de Tournon remained. He began to toil at the wall with slow, resolute strokes. With every blow and heave a hollow "humph!" sounded from his chest through the darkness of the long, vaulted corridor. Far into the growing day, in his ghoulish vigil he stood, with the dim beam of the lantern about him, with earth-bedabbled clothes, all alone, heaving and toiling, like a maniac against the stubborn rock. Every stroke was a stroke nearer the heart of Vansittart. All the night he had labored, and still, as he mined more and more into the stone, he was unconscious of fatigue. About seven A.M. his intensity grew into a very paroxysm of frenzy. "Down you come!" he cried, as his heavy body heaved forward to the impact.

"Down!" he panted at the next stroke; and "down!" at every succeeding stroke came laboring forth upon the "humph!" of his gasping chest, while the foam of his fury went flying in a white spray from his deathly, distorted lips. At last he dropped panting upon the wall, catching his breath in sobs and spasms. He had accomplished his task.

Early the next evening the conspirators, with elaborate secrecy, arrived, one by one, at the shed; de Tournon first, in spite of his long agony and sweat in the tunnel the night before. Ten men this time descended into the excavation, determined to bring their labors to a close. But some of the new-comers brought with them pickaxes, and in an hour Folliet knew of this fact. He had been puzzled—now his mind was clear. The impossibility of the men being able to leave the chamber on the previous day, without being seen by his spy, had more and more forced itself upon his mind. He said to himself, "They were there, they must have been there, if evidence is worth anything. But there in a state of invisibility? Dissolved into air? Swallowed by the earth? When he heard of the pickaxes, he snapped thumb and finger, and called himself a fool. The truth stood revealed to him, or something like the truth; they were digging a tunnel somewhere.

He hurried to Vansittart with the news.

"By all means, let us inspect their operations, monsieur," said Jerome.

Followed by Jim Bates, they once more proceeded to the underground room, well armed. This time a careful scrutiny of the floor revealed the fresh scratches of hob-nailed boots leading to one part of the timbered wall. It needed slight effort to reveal the tunnel.

"They have done a wonderful deal in the time," whispered Folliet, astonished at the great gap he beheld. "This is very strange. Where can they have placed the earth?"

He stepped forward into the darkness. When he had reached the point where the rough-hewn passage met the roof of the tunnel, he stopped, bending down and peeping. Far yonder in the distance he saw the glimmer of the lanterns, saw the moving shadows, heard the faint echoes of the picks. He ran quickly back.

"Sir," he said, "they have discovered an ancient tunnel leading, most probably, to the vaults of St. Cloud. These ruffians are fiends!"

"Not at all, monsieur," said Vansittart, "they are merely

determined men. They are probably, then, from your report, now in my palace."

"No. I don't think so. They are using tools down there. They have met a wall of some sort, I think. At any rate, we have them. They are so self-sure that they have set no watch. They do not suspect our presence. Within a quarter of an hour, I can have a dozen men here to knock them on the head like rats. They shall never come out alive."

Vansittart's brows were knit; he was thinking.

"Yes, they shall come out alive, Monsieur Folliet," he said. "Let us hasten gently, as the proverb says. They do not take away their tools by day, I think?"

"No, sir."

"Very good. We will permit them to prosecute their labors in peace for the present."

"What! and leave their ladder for them to mount again?"

"Yes, we will leave them their ladder." Vansittart was smiling his mysterious iron smile.

"How many of them are there?" he asked.

"Ten, to-day, I think."

"When the tenth man leaves in the morning, pray let me know. Do you happen to have with you—a tape?"

Folliet produced a tape from his pocket, and Vansittart handed it to Jim. "Oblige me by taking the measurements of the area of the doorway," he said. When this was done, they walked quietly away to the palace.

At the palace, Folliet at once descended underground into the old vaults of St. Cloud. His lamp showed him a vast intricacy of dungeons, made of unhewn rock, damp with antiquity, black as night. After an exhaustive search he came to the conclusion that the conspirators when they reached this end, would have work enough for their picks in order to enter the palace. The entrance to the tunnel on this side had been blocked up with solid masonry somewhere about the end of the seventeenth century.

At three o'clock next morning, the subterranean workers came upon another transverse mass of masonry. Their food during the night had been scanty; their frames were worn with the long siege upon the blinding, splintering stone; their spirits flagged. Even de Tournon thought of a bed with longing. They rightly guessed that this was the last cross-section of masonry to be conquered. They dropped their tools simultaneously, and hurried, with parching throats, and languid limbs, to the upper air.

At five, Vansittart, Folliet, and Jim Bates were down in the tunnel about a hundred yards from its commencement at the chamber. There, near the block of walls, lay the tools of the men, white with dust, where they had dropped them. Burdened with these, the three men returned to the opening and ascended by the ladder, having carefully replaced the boards.

The tools they bore to a thick growth of tamarisk trees near by, surrounded by stubble, in the centre of which already stood two thin square slabs of iron, leaning against a tree, and made in haste in the village of St. Cloud, from the measurements taken by Jim Bates of the entrance to the tunnel. The slabs were pierced by four lines of holes, in each of which holes now loosely lay a screw. The tools taken from below were flung down in the thicket, and the three men walked homeward.

Vansittart was about to strike.

. . . .

Lisette's hands were, a few hours later, busied with the Princess Marchesi's hair. What a touch of the fingers had Lisette in the deeps and thicknesses of one's hair! All the drowsy syrups of the world were not worth comparison with Lisette's gentle seduction of hand.

" Lisette, you are a narcotic in yourself," said the Princess, whose eyes were closed in trance before the mirror.

" Lisette, did you undo Miss Harland's hair, as I told you last night?" she said presently.

" Yes, madame."

"Did she enjoy your touch, Lisette?"

"She did not say, madame." There was delicious silence.

Then, again, presently: "Lisette, do you know what I want?"

"No, madame."

"I want a locksmith, Lisette."

"A locksmith, madame?" Lisette's heart gave a little bound.

"Yes, Lisette."

"When, madame?"

"To-morrow."

"You can easily get one, madame."

"Could *you* manage to get one for me, Lisette?"

Lisette was pale and excited. "I dare say, madame."

"All right, then. Pray do."

"You want him to come into the house to you, madame?"

"Yes."

"What time?"

"Oh, after dinner. Say nine o'clock in the evening."

"Where shall I bring him to you?"

"Take him to my dressing-room, and then call me."

Lisette did not answer. She was very pale. When she went out of the room, she was flurried, uncertain, nervous. She stood still, thinking for some time. But at last, she ran below stairs, and wrote a letter. She said in it:

"I will meet you at the well this evening, at 8.30."

Among his other pursuits, her husband was, as he had told her, a locksmith. And it was now absolutely necessary that she should see him. Her terror of his coming to claim her had grown too strong to be any longer borne. And here was a way to end their quarrel about bringing him into the house, a way proposed by the Princess Marchesi herself.

"Everything always comes out right in the end," meditated Lisette, as she re-entered the palace.

CHAPTER XXXIX

THE CONSPIRACY ENDS

THE Princess Marchesi, in her amiable diplomacy, did not act alone. She had won the acquiescence of the Comtesse de Fontainebleau. For days the two women's heads had been going together in earnest, whispered confabulations, in low, sibilant, busy interviews, secret as the grave. This was during the week that Evelyn was staying at St. Cloud by the request of the Princess.

"It can be done, Comtesse! It can, and it *should* be done!" the Princess had said.

"It can, undoubtedly, Princess. But there is the risk. What if Mr. Vansittart be angry?"

"Jerome angry with *me?* Well, let him! So long as we effect our purpose, what do we care about the anger of a boy? But men never notice anything, Comtesse! Fifty to one, when it is all over, he will know nothing whatever about the matter!"

The *boudoir* of Evelyn had been appointed by the diplomacy of the Princess to be immediately next to Vansittart's library. Only an arched cedar door separated the two apartments. But this door was locked, and some one or another—Vansittart himself, in fact, though the ladies did not know it—had removed the key. The scheme was to restore communication between the two suites of rooms by the removal or unfastening of the lock.

"But suppose, after all our trouble, nothing happens?" suggested the Comtesse.

"My dear, you lack adventure," said the Princess; "you are unfamiliar with the Law of Probabilities. Love will pass through any opening larger than a keyhole. If nothing happens in a week, something will happen in two; failing that, you may be certain of results in a month."

"But Miss Harland returns to Paris in a few days."

"Not if *I* know it. Miss Harland is in safe hands now. I have already devised the means by which she shall be compelled to remain with me at St. Cloud for at least a month." And so, on the morning after the third night's labor in the tunnel, Lisette was instructed to procure the services of a locksmith.

The fourth evening came. By nine o'clock, the last of the conspirators who were to aid in that day's work had descended the iron ladder and adjusted the boarded door behind them. At ten minutes past nine, Folliet and Jim Bates were jerkily urging screws through the slabs of iron, with a screw-driver, fastening them to the firm and undisturbed planking of the wall. Could the men beyond have heard it, that commonplace sound would have thrilled them with a wilder terror than the crack of doom itself. They were imprisoned in a living tomb, from which, though they had the cunning of fiends, and the strength of Behemoth, they could never extricate their lives. For at that moment they stood at the spot where their tools had been. With pallid awe they stared into the blanched visages of one another, and then raced back to the exit, to find that it firmly resisted all efforts to open it.

There are moments in life so horrid, that the mind cannot contemplate them. The thing which these men now saw in each other's eyes was—Madness. After a day or two of hunger, they knew that they would be galloping about their den, and tearing each other's flesh with their teeth, like wild horses in the midst of a flame. De Tournon felt in his hurrying heart how stern was the vengeance of his tremendous foe; how long his arm; how dreadful his frown.

Vansittart had struck. The men did not need to ask what had happened to them. They knew. And there was not a tool among them. A man cannot tear the world to pieces with his nails.

The food they had would hardly last them a day. Their lanterns would soon burn out. Madness, and blackness, and the tongue that lolled dry from the mouth, and the rush of frenzy through the long and rayless vault, and the short howl of rabies, and the drawn-out wail of the damned. Was, this, then, their doom? Was it so the Emperor took vengeance upon his enemies?

It was so. But this time Vansittart failed. He had reckoned well. But he was unaware of the existence of Lisette. It is not unusual for the simplest to bring to nought the counsels of the mightiest. The schemes of the man who was in the mouth of all the world were balked by the love affairs of a little servant girl. And Lisette did not suspect a word of the matter. The Fongeur received her letter that day, and, having to meet her, did not descend into the tunnel with his mates.

"Well, you wretched little winkle," he said, as Lisette, half-frightened, made her appearance at the well. "So you turn up at last, do you? But I don't want you any more, you see."

"What have you come for, then?" said Lisette coquettishly.

"Well, you're not a bad sort, you know. But I'll bruise that pretty face of yours if you play me any more tricks, I tell you."

"A lady wants you."

"Wants who?"

"Wants you."

"What are you talking about?"

"It's true. The Princess Marchesi. You've got to go and do something to a lock."

Le Grand's face wore a look of puzzlement. "Who is it you're talking to?" he said.

"I'm talking to you."

"The Princess who?"

"Marchesi."

"Where does she want me to go?"

"To her room in the palace."

He whistled. "I'm too fly."

"Too what?"

"Too fly. It's only a trick to get hold of me."

Lisette laughed. "Why, you must be mad! The Princess Marchesi get hold of *you!* She does n't dream that there is such a brute as you in the world."

"How does she know I can mend locks?"

"I tell you you are mad! She does n't know that *you* can mend locks, or anything about you. She asked me to get a locksmith for her, and as—as—you said you wanted to—to—see Mr. Vansittart's room, I thought you would like to get near it, at any rate."

"I'm not going, all the same."

"Very well. Good-bye."

"I say—kiss me."

"You may go, and—drown yourself. You don't kiss *me!*"

"Kiss me, I tell you!" He jumped from his seat, caught her, and kissed her.

"You have n't asked my pardon for striking me yet," said Lisette, content, at any time, to be kissed.

"Asked pardon! Nonsense. But I say—you would n't betray me, would you?"

"I don't know what you 're talking about," she answered, "but I would n't—not for anything."

"Well, is it honor bright about that lock?"

"Of course it is. I have told you."

"All right. I'll go."

"It's to-morrow evening, then, about half-past eight. Come round to the back, and ask for Mademoiselle Cibras—that's me, you know." She looked up, slyly smiling, into his face.

"No, that won't do," said the Fongeur. "Look here—it's like this. There's a little matter in dispute between me and Vansittart, you see? He must n't catch me anywhere in his grounds at that hour. Is n't there some little side entrance to the house on the park side, where I could slip in without anybody seeing?"

"Y-e-s," said Lisette, meditating; "there is a postern on that side just opposite a summer-house, which nobody ever uses."

"That's the place for me! I'll lurk behind the house or thereabouts, and you come to the door and call when there's nobody about." This was agreed, and Lisette, unbruised and pleased, took her departure in a run.

He hastened to apprise de Tournon of his good luck, and was astounded to find his way barred by the handiwork of Follict and Jim Bates.

He laughed as he examined this death-trap.

"Lucky for me, and for them, that I'm not with them on the other side," he muttered. But there was a shudder in the thought, and he vowed to take no risks with Vansittart if possible. He always carried a burglar's bit and brace with him. These were useful in removing the screws, and he made a dramatic appearance among the doomed men. He was as if crowned with light in their eyes, for he brought life. And he also brought the sweetest news to de Tournon. No need now to toil in the depths. Surely it would be easy to enter St. Cloud with their victim's aunt conspiring to help them.

The following evening, at a few minutes after nine, le Grand stood secure in Vansittart's library. With him was the Princess Marchesi.

They had entered from the passage. On one side lay the suite of rooms occupied by Evelyn Harland, on the other the dressing-room and bedroom of Vansittart, these latter connecting with the library, and all with doors into the corridor. In the right-hand wall of the library, as you faced the doors from the passage, was the cedar door which divided Evelyn and Vansittart.

"Will it be necessary to remove the lock?" asked the Princess.

"No, madame, I think not," said le Grand.

"Very good. Then set to work."

"But madame sees that I have brought no tools?"

"And what on earth is the good of you without tools? Did you ever!"

"I merely came to examine the lock, madame."

"But why not bring tools with you?"

"I was given to understand that there was some amount of secrecy in the matter, madame. This is Mr. Vansittart's library."

"Well?"

"May I examine the locks in the other rooms? If, as I expect, they are all of one class, it will help me to judge this one correctly." Suiting his action to his words, he walked through the dressing-room into the bedroom, followed by the Princess, and bent to examine the fastenings.

The chamber was a very large one, consisting of two rooms thrown into one. Lately, by Vansittart's instructions, it had been divided into two portions by a partition of wood, containing a high-arched opening in the centre. It was too wide for a doorway and seemed to be a mere embellishment, or was intended, perhaps, to render the room cosier. Two doors communicated with the corridor, one on each side of the partition.

"We are now in the President's bedroom?" said the Fongeur, still busy with the lock.

"Yes. What of it?"

"I see no bed."

"The bed is on the other side of the partition, and is a small one. He does not love luxuries. Sometimes he sleeps in that part of the room; sometimes in this. But what has all this got to do with your task, workman?"

"Suppose Mr. Vansittart were to come in here now?"

"He won't; but it matters not."

"I have no authority from him to touch the lock."

"You are insolent, workman!"

"No, madame; but I am timid. At what hour does M. Vansittart dine?"

"At eight."

"Well, would n't it be better, madame, for me to come just before, or just after, or during dinner? It is only a bit of a job, and I should soon polish it off if I felt all right. There's a little side-door down below near the summer-house where you could meet me without any of the servants being the wiser—say at 8.30. No doubt madame would make an excuse to the gentlemen beforehand for being absent from dinner."

"That stupid Lisette!" said the Princess—"to get me a workman who trembles at shadows!" Then she thought that if she were absent from dinner—if she said, for instance, that she was going over to the Châlet, Evelyn and Jerome would probably have the meal all to themselves, and this decided her. She said: "Very well! that will do. Bring your tools at eight-thirty to-morrow. But you should be bold, workman!—you should have pluck!—you should be a man!"

The Fongeur grinned demurely. He noted the way carefully from Vansittart's room to the side-postern. The first thing he did, on emerging from the palace, was to purchase a screw-driver and a chisel. He calculated that he would need to show his implements for a moment or two to the Princess when he first entered the palace next night, and therefore provided himself with these at once.

When the Princess Marchesi stood at the postern the following evening at eight-thirty, the Fongeur, slipping from behind the summer-house, walked towards her, ostentatiously showing his chisel and turn-screw. Near the Princess was the Comtesse de Fontainebleau in a flutter of happiness at all the charming secrecy and mystery of the affair. The two ladies were glad that they had been born. The Comtesse looked upon the Princess as the very Goddess of Intrigue.

Before the Princess was well gagged, the Plasterer and String-the-Neck swiftly, but quite coolly, performed a similar feat upon the Comtesse. There was, opening on a narrow passage, a small, empty room, which the Fongeur had noted in the day. Into this they threw the ladies, tied hands and feet. The Fongeur now took his leave. He had done his share of the work, he said, and would await his friends at their customary meeting-place. He was lucky, this scamp.

De Tournon, the Plasterer, String-the-Neck, and the Gouger, taking with them a plan of the premises prepared by le Grand, entered the small room and locked the door. They waited five hours. At the end of that time the house was wrapped in perfect silence. One servant only in the kitchens sat sleepily waiting for the return of the Princess from her announced visit to the châlet. One servant at the châlet sat sleepily waiting the return of the Comtesse from her announced visit to the palace. The Comtesse and the Princess lay on their backs, more silent than they had been for some years. Even in her sleep the Princess was wont to talk. At present, however, she did not say anything. She was tongue-tied.

The four men ascended warily to the passage before Vansittart's room. The house was utterly black, yet they made hardly a sound. The Plasterer went first; two others clung to his sleeves; de Tournon to the sleeve of one of these.

Into which of the two doors should they go? They did not know, for the Princess had told le Grand that the bed was moved from room to room. And this was the fact. The millionnaire slept on a narrow iron bedstead, without any pretensions to luxury, and his bed was rather hard. Into which of the doors, then? The assassins cut the knot of doubt by entering both, two by one door, two by the other, the keys prepared by le Grand readily fitting the locks. De Tournon and the Gouger passed in on the left; the Plasterer and String-the-Neck on the right.

Vansittart had been asleep. But when they entered the room, he knew it.

He lay still—listening. He did not move.

He was immensely puzzled, because he believed that his active enemies were imprisoned in the tunnel. It was no part of his vengeance to let them starve there, but only to let them suffer the torture of imagining this to be their fate. On the third morning he proposed to free them, or such as were alive, as they would probably murder each other in their rage, in the belief that the terrible lesson would be sufficient to keep them quiet in the future. Under the conditions, even the vigilance of Folliet had relaxed somewhat.

Now, when the keys turned stealthily in the locks of his bedroom door he was naturally at a loss to know how his assailants had got there. But though puzzled, he was not alarmed. In fact, he was perfectly safe.

The partition lately set up, which divided his room into two, was not a fixed partition, but ran on minute wheels concealed in the depth of the flooring. The last thing that Vansittart did every night before lying down, was to shift the position of his bed, one night pushing it hard up against the right wall, near the locked and bolted door of his dressing-room; the next against the left wall opposite. In either case, he would then touch a button, and the partition would move across the room till it nearly touched the side of his bed. And in the narrow space between wall and partition he slept. No one in the house had any suspicion of this ingenious mechanism; not even Folliet or Jim Bates.

When the partition had moved across the room near to the bed, two people entering by the two doors, and expecting to enter two different rooms, would be infinitely bewildered to find themselves in one and the same room.

They would question the truthfulness of their senses. They would be amazed beyond human utterance. They would be abashed, and stricken, and crushed by the miracle. When, in addition, utter darkness was about them, their confusion would be turned into inanity. An element of wildness, a touch of frenzy, would enter their dismay. They would be routed without hope, undone beyond expression. They would be dazzled by blindness, lost in an abyss of mystery. They would roll and tumble together, tearing each other in a rage of incredulity.

And that is what really happened to the four men. By the left door de Tournon and the Gouger had entered; by the right, String-the-Neck and the Plasterer. To the left of de Tournon stood the running partition, and to the left of the partition lay Vansittart, listening. As the two left assassins groped about, they encountered the two right assassins groping about. As each two believed that they were alone in the room, each two supposed that they had secured Vansittart trying to make his escape. They struck. The Gouger was stabbed to the heart by the Plasterer; String-the-Neck was stabbed in the throat by de Tournon—and fell dead.

De Tournon and the Plasterer were left. They met. But each supposed that he had already killed Vansittart. Who, then, was this? The question was like a madness. It grew into a rabies. They clutched, they struggled together. They were in a Babel, or a Bedlam. Confusion and distraction had fallen upon them. In their close grip, neither could make the deadly stroke, though both were wounded. They wrestled each with a phantasm.

Suddenly they saw each other's faces with dazzling distinctness. A white, bright flood of light filled the room. Vansittart had stretched out his hand, and turned on the electric current. Previously he had touched the electric button which communicated with the rooms of Folliet and Jim Bates. As de Tournon and the Plasterer stared at each other with eyes wide open in awe and wonder, a bullet from Jim Bates's revolver entered the brain of the Plasterer.

It was Folliet who saved de Tournon. He leapt upon him pinning him to the floor by the throat, crying, "a rope!"

Jim did not understand this move. Why not kill the man, and be done? He stared, till Vansittart stood in the arch of the partition in his pajamas, and said: "Why stare? Do quickly as M. Folliet directs. And be speedy in removing these corpses from my presence."

De Tournon was hustled, five minutes later, into one of the most noisome of the dungeons of old St. Cloud, deep down in the earth, between Jim Bates and Folliet. Here, bound hand and foot, he was left.

In an hour the house was again in quietude. The servant who sat up for the Princess had retired, supposing that her mistress was remaining for the night at the châlet. Vansittart was sound asleep. Jim was snoring loudly. But Folliet lay awake. When he was certain that all was still, he rose softly, took a lantern, and descended to de Tournon's dungeon. It was a small, square apartment, unfloored, of rough stones. De Tournon lay in a bundle in one corner.

Folliet deposited his lantern in another corner, and without a word undid the cords which bound the prisoner's hands and feet. The portal of the room he had secured on his entrance. De Tournon's dagger, which had been taken from him, he threw at the wretch's head; another, of similar length, was in his own hands.

"Now, de Tournon!" was all he said.

The hate of years was concentrated in Folliet's face. For this hour he had prayed to God and to the devil in hell, and it had come. The two men, from opposite corners, looked at each other in the red glow of the lantern. But their faces were hardly like the faces of men.

It was a long fight.

In the first ages of the world, when man was but little

removed from the beast, and the instinct of the use of implements had not arisen strongly within him, the fiercest fights were fought out with hands only. The weapons of Nature—the nails—were the weapons chosen by the first of our race. And to this primary stage of life had those two now reverted in their brutal malice. The instinct to use the *hands*, to slay with the nails, to squeeze with the fingers arose in them. Half-way through the fight, when they were bleeding from many stabs, the daggers were discarded. They took to the weapon of the tiger.

See them crouched in opposite corners, panting in a rest, with side-way glare of the maddened eye, with murderous grin of the lower jaw, ready to spring ! Then flying, as with the wings of demons, through the air, then rolling and wallowing together with a cat-o'-mountain fury ! It lasted long. But the *dénouement* was unexpected.

Folliet resolved to make an end of the business, and picked up his knife again, but even in his frenzy he was amazed to hear de Tournon shrieking with laughter, and feebly attempting an insane dance. This final strain had snapped the man's intelligence. He was a hopeless maniac, gibbering over the grave of his dead intellect. Folliet was hardly able to stagger out and bolt the door. He somehow gained the ground floor of the palace, where he fell fainting, and was discovered in the early morning about the same hour as the gagged Comtesse and the Princess.

All three remained many days in bed before they ventured out again, and meanwhile de Tournon had been removed to the asylum at Charenton, whence he never emerged alive.

He was not violent, but he had, nevertheless, to be placed under forcible restraint, as he was always striving to dig a tunnel, whether through earth or solid wall, it mattered not. The only way to stop him was to tie his hands behind his back, and the paroxysms of rage he suffered under this physical drawback gradually weakened him until the end came—and others dug.

CHAPTER XL

ARIZONA JIM SPEAKS HIS MIND

IT may be readily surmised that the Princess Marchesi and the Comtesse de Fontainebleau were not in good heart to engage in further intrigue for a considerable period after they had again recovered the use of their tongues and their crippled limbs. Lisette, too, had fled from the palace to join her precious husband, and that rascal himself was, for once, frightened into submission. When Folliet had thoroughly investigated the circumstances that led to the disastrous attack upon Vansittart, he gave Monsieur and Madame le Grand one day's notice to leave France forever. They promptly availed themselves of the opportunity to seek redemption and an honest living in a new world.

With the destruction of de Tournon's gang, Jerome's last active enemy disappeared. Politically, of course, he had opponents, but their numbers rather decreased than otherwise, as his rigidly honest and straightforward methods of government gained public knowledge and appreciation.

Although he put in force many reforms calculated to improve, whilst cheapening, the national services, not an official, from the highest to the lowest, was dismissed from office. If posts were abolished, their occupants were bought out, retired on a pension, or provided with employment elsewhere. Dishonesty, bribery, peculation of every sort, received no countenance. In six weeks the revenues showed a visible improvement, whilst a marked alteration for the better had taken place in the army and navy.

In a word, Vansittart moulded France to his will, and France liked it.

For once there was fixity of purpose in the national councils, and the newspapers openly amused themselves and their readers by predictions as to the date when "Jerome I." would nominally as well as in reality occupy the throne. Such was the temper of the people that had he asked for a dictatorship in place of a constitutional sovereignty, his demands would have been readily acceded to.

In Liancourt he found an admirable coadjutor, and Pompier was taken from the active list of the navy to occupy a high position as Comptroller of Stores for both services—a reform which was much criticised by naval and military experts at first, but which, in efficiency and economy, soon proved its excellence.

The Sahara was booming. Already the rents received from private trading enterprises paid the interest upon the first issue of capital, and such a speedy financial outcome of the Scheme tended to raise the price of stock materially. No one now doubted that, from a monetary point of view alone, "Sahara, Limited, and Jerome K. Vansittart" was destined to rank as the most successful enterprise the world had ever seen. Even Peter Studevant was convinced.

One day, after much examination of accounts, he arrived at a decision.

He sought his chief, and said:

"I want to hand you a check for a million sterling, together with £40,400, being the accumulated interest at two per cent. for two years on the money."

"I am much obliged for this windfall," laughed Jerome, "but where on earth does it come from?"

"From my own banking account. I stole the money from you, and I can only throw myself on your mercy, pleading the best of intentions."

"What on earth are you talking about, my old friend?"

"I am telling you the naked truth. When you embarked

in this tremendous undertaking, I thought you would be ruined, so I appropriated this sum from the gross amount of your realizations. I appointed trustees, and made an irrevocable will in your favor in case of accidents. You see, I wanted to save something for you out of the expected wreck. You can have proofs of all this if you——"

"For goodness' sake, shut up, Peter, you dear old cautious soul. I'll take the million, but I'll see you hanged before I touch the interest."

"But——"

"The million down, or I send for the police!"

So when Peter Studevant made up his mind that his self-imposed task was no longer necessary, it may be taken for granted that the Company was secure enough.

In one matter the new President encountered an unforeseen difficulty. It will be remembered that the Boca Grande, or western, approach to the Sahara ran through Spanish territory, which was practically valueless before the inception of the scheme to flood the Sahara. Spain's rights must, of course, be respected in the matter, but it now leaked out that England had, years ago, acquired a preemption to this strip of coast at a fixed price, and that she had called upon Spain to complete the bargain, which that impoverished country was very ready to do.

There was some growling in France about this move by perfidious Albion, but Vansittart soon made terms with the British Cabinet. The capital expenditure upon the works within the disputed area was agreed upon, and Great Britain undertook to buy the Company's interest in this section at one hundred per cent. premium within five years, meanwhile paying three per cent. interest annually on the amount of capital thus absorbed. The Company would work the canals, etc., and levy equal charges upon all vessels of whatever nationality using the Boca Grande approach.

The deal gave general satisfaction. Sahara shares took another jump on the strength of it, and when the time came for England to pay up, the property she thus had acquired was worth much more in the open market. Which explains the mysterious wink at a subordinate indulged in by the British Permanent Under-Secretary for Foreign Affairs, and noted in an earlier page of this record of marvellous events.

The President had seemingly but little spare time to devote to his own affairs, yet they were ever uppermost in his thoughts.

Prince Henri of Navarre, whose character had borrowed some degree of strength and manliness from his association with Vansittart, had lately assumed an elder-brother attitude towards Honorine de Montpensier. He more than once respectfully but plainly urged Jerome to carry his projects out to their full extent, and the latter could only plead the urgency of state affairs as an excuse for delay.

The Frenchwoman, with that delightful uncertainty that marks her sex, somewhat resented this fraternal solicitude on the part of the young Prince, and severely tested his honesty of purpose by treating him with marked coldness and regretful confidence by fits and starts.

Evelyn Harland took to riding desperately after the staghounds of Fontainebleau, and astounded French huntingmen by the manner in which she risked her neck.

The whole four were desperately unhappy, and in this deadlock Princess Marchesi again began to plot. But this time she found a new ally, and went to work on more direct lines. Of all people in the world, she selected Arizona Jim as her confidant.

"Jim," she said one day in the park at St. Cloud, "why don't you tell your master what he ought to do?"

"Me, ma'am!" cried Bates. "Why, he 'd hoof me out of the place. I did hev a go at him once, an' he kicked hard."

"I don't quite understand your methods of expressing yourself, Jim, but I do say that you are the one person privileged to talk to him as you like, and you ought to tell him he is ruining, not only his own life, but many others."

"Well, ma'am, I'll think it over. There'll be an awful row, you'll see. If you want to stir a man up bad, tell him the truth. An honest knock-down fact is wuss nor a squib in a wasp's nest."

Bates was a perfect Napoleon in act when he was resolved. The next time Vansittart came to St. Cloud, Jim followed him to the library, and, having entered, locked the door and put the key in his pocket.

Jerome looked at him with amazement.

"What's the matter?" he cried. "Another revolution, or what?"

"Somethin' like it, boss. I've got a few remarks to fire off, and I want to make sure you don't chuck me out until I've sung my little song."

"Why, Jim, do you wish to leave me? Is life too quiet for you under these new conditions? Or, stay. Jim, you're going to get married?"

"Not me. But it's a wedding I've come to talk about, all the same."

"Whose wedding?"

"Yours."

Jerome's face grew stern. "Bates," he said, "you are the last man I wish to quarrel with, but you must not speak to me in this manner. Do you understand? Never again, or we part."

"That's just it, boss. That's why I locked the door. I'm going to hev my say, if I'm forced to hold you on the floor whilst I'm coughin' it up. I ain't a-goin' to see you start on the wrong tack without tellin' you what I think before I quit for Nevada ag'in."

Jerome was silent for a moment, and he looked his faithful henchman straight in the face before he spoke. He saw there a bull-headed determination to go through with the business, whatever it was, and he well guessed its nature, but he resolved to try one last appeal.

"Bates, you are, I firmly believe, the most devoted friend

I possess in the world. Do not pain me in this way, but leave me, or talk about something else."

Arizona Jim came closer to him, and it was evident that some powerful emotion shook his stalwart frame. He almost whimpered as he replied: "Boss, it hurts me wuss nor you. But it's heavy on my chest, an' I can't quit unless I tell you."

Jerome clinched his teeth. "Very well, confound you. Say what you want to say, and don't come near me again for a week."

In view of this compromise, Bates was in a worse mental plight than ever. Hitherto he had been buoyed up by heroic resolve. But now he had to find words to express himself, and he could see none in the depths of his hat, or outlined in the frescoes of the ceiling.

"Well," said Vansittart, "can't you go on?"

Jim had nearly prepared what he thought was a nice sentence, but the question drove it from his mind. He blurted out:

"It's like this. You're goin' to marry the wrong gal."

"I know that better than you can tell me. Why torture me, man, by talking about it?"

"That's just the trouble, boss. If you'd talk about it, everything 'ud come out all square. Everybody else is talkin' about it, an' they can fix it right away. A pair of silly old women talk about it, an' kin see through the hull business, yet you can't. It's sickenin'."

"Why, you idiot, what can I do? I have pledged my word. It is impossible to draw back, even if I would."

"Nobody wants you to draw back, boss. It strikes me that, if you start in on the right lines, you'll pull things through in style."

"What would you have me do?"

"Kin I ax you a few questions?"

"Yes."

"In the fust place, boss, you don't want to be no emperor?"

"Not a bit."

"An' you air kinder gone on Miss Harland?"

"Yes, you scoundrel."

"Well, boss, I guess it's about time you knew that Mam'selle what's-her-name 'ud sooner marry the Frenchman than forty derned emperors. But she's like you; she is too proud to own up the fax of the case."

Vansittart sprang from his chair and grasped Bates by the shoulder, a wild excitement in every tone and feature.

"Bates," he shouted, "prove to me that what you say is true, and you shall have any sum you choose to ask for within the hour."

"I don't want no money, boss. All I wants is ter see you hitched to the finest woman in the world, an' her name ain't Honorine. What I tells you is as true as the Gospel. You stand on me."

"But why have I not been told this long ago? What conspiracy of silence has kept me from knowing it sooner?"

"How could anybody say a word? Neither you nor the Frenchwoman would own up if either of you was dyin'. Miss Evelyn knew all about the other two gallivantin' together, but *she* could n't tell you. An' her brother was n't likely to do what he would n't consider the square thing. The little Prince is n't a bad sort of chap, an' he tried to go straight for the sake of the woman. So he kep' his mouth shut. The Princess Marchesi might hev spoke, but she was kinder scared. When she tried to fix things, she nearly got the whole crowd scalped. No, sirree, there was nuthin' left but for me ter lock the door and argy to a finish."

Vansittart was deeply moved. His face was flushed and excited. He seemed to have become ten years younger in the last five minutes. A telephone on his library table called him up from Paris, but he seized the instrument, and shouted into it, "I am having my first holiday for twelve months—leave me alone," and then threw the apparatus down with a bang. Turning to Jim Bates, he said:

"Jim, I owe you my life many times. Now I owe you my happiness. Leave me. All will go right, but I must think. My thanks to you cannot find expression in words."

The doubts and difficulties of his existence had been dispersed as a mist by a strong wind. True, there were awkward situations ahead, but these were nothing to Vansittart, restored as he was to hope and cheerful determination. Long did he pace to and fro in the library before he had thought out a definite line of action. He had almost decided upon the course to be adopted, when the reflection came with a smile that there were others to be consulted besides himself. He must see Mademoiselle de Montpensier at once, and obtain full confirmation of Bates's news, together with her consent for the amazing development which had suggested itself to his alert mind.

Ah, if he could only meet Evelyn for one instant, and tell her, as he had long pined to do, that he was free to offer her his heart, and that she was free to accept it. At any rate, he would see her that evening. He hastily wrote a telegram to Harland, bidding him not to fail to bring his sister to dinner, and then he set out for Honorine's residence at the other side of the park.

A short cut lay through the wood, and he was walking slowly through the shaded path with bent head and eyes seeking inspiration in the pebbles, when a fresh clear voice rang out merrily:

"Why so preoccupied, Mr. Vansittart? Is it politics, or a new Sahara Scheme?"

Jerome was genuinely startled, for Evelyn Harland herself stood before him, looking gracefully neat in a walking dress, and rosy red at this unexpected meeting. She had visited the French ladies at the cottage, and was now on her way to call upon the Princess Marchesi at the château. She was quite close to him, and he neither hesitated nor answered, but took her in his arms and kissed her.

If Evelyn was red before, she was crimson now. She

struggled to disengage herself, crying vehemently, "Mr. Vansittart, is this fair? Is it——?"

"It is quite fair, my darling," he said, looking her steadily in the eyes. "I am at last able to tell you, honorably and openly, that I love you, and shall go on loving you whilst life lasts."

She still resisted him, but with less vigor, and the color rushed from her cheeks as rapidly as it came. She, too, began to hope, wildly, desperately.

"But how? What has happened?" she said.

"Everything has happened. Prince Henri of Navarre will marry Honorine de Montpensier, and I will marry you, if you will take me."

Whereupon Evelyn placed her hands round his neck, and began to cry. But tears of joy are more precious than diamonds; they are rarer. They sparkle with the dewdrop lustre of the rainbow, for there is sunshine behind the shower, and the smile on the girl's face, as she raised it to his, conveyed the most eloquent message that Vansittart had ever received in his life.

How long they stood there they knew not, until Evelyn suddenly became aware that some one was looking at them. She ran off towards the palace, and Vansittart advanced to meet Prince Henri.

The young Frenchman was white with rage.

"Monsieur," he growled beneath his teeth, "this is too much. I have long borne with you, but this insult to a lady I revere can only be met by your death or mine. Will you be good enough to appoint——"

"What?" shouted Jerome gleefully. "You don't want to marry Evelyn, too?"

"Evelyn! Miss Harland! What is she to me? I allude to the woman you are so grossly deceiving, Mademoiselle de Montpensier."

"Surely I am not deceiving her by kissing another girl!"

"Monsieur, this is no matter for jest. I refuse to discuss it. Name your second, and my friend shall wait on him within the hour."

"Prince, I like to see your spirit; but bottle it up—you and I won't fight. At least, not about Honorine. Come with me to her. I shall not wait many minutes, and then you can settle matters with her yourself."

"Discuss your perfidy in Mademoiselle's presence? Never!"

"Oh, yes, you will. You see, Prince, we are not going to arrange the date for a duel, but the date of your marriage."

"My marriage! With whom?"

"With the lady who will shortly be Queen of France. I have been blind for a long time, my friend, but my sight has been restored with astounding effect. I will explain to you as we walk to the cottage." Thereupon they walked off, arm in arm, to visit Honorine de Montpensier.

CHAPTER XLI

THE CORONATION

VANSITTART was called upon, at this stage of his career, to face the most difficult task of his life. Although he had in the past, accomplished undertakings that were seemingly superhuman, he always had the advantage of asking his fellow-men to accept something achieved. This sort of evidence cannot be refused. He first created by his intellect, and then carried out by his money and intelligence, until the point was reached when all might see the clear path leading to the attainment of his project. But in the final development that occupied his every waking moment there was a fresh element of resistance which threatened, at the slightest hitch, to bring him up against an impassible barrier.

In every previous step of his progress in France he had magnetized the majority of men into full belief in him. The public accorded ready acquiescence to his plans; his friends gave unquestioning support. Now, the attitude of the public might be dubious when they were taken into his confidence, whilst that of his friends would be actively and bitterly hostile. Worse than all, he was compelled to act a highly melodramatic part, which was in itself utterly distasteful to him.

The object that he aimed at was definite enough. He had vowed that he would place Honorine de Montpensier on the throne, and at the same time leave himself free to marry Evelyn Harland. How to reconcile this dual proposition

—that was the question. When he first broached the matter to Prime Minister Liancourt, that shrewd and unimpassioned man of the world laughed at the claims of Honorine.

"Pay her a pension, my dear boy," he cried. "Let her marry the Prince, and live in graceful dignity. You have won the empire without her aid—nay, somewhat hampered by a Quixotic alliance—surely you can choose your own wife, when neither you nor the so-called legitimate heiress is in love with the other."

Liancourt was a Frenchman. His ideas of the relations between the sexes were not those of the Anglo-Saxon, so Vansittart did not lose his temper at the suggestion. He simply repeated his arguments with the utmost patience and determination, until at last the level-headed statesman, seeing that the other was quite in earnest, agreed to support him, as being the best way out of a disagreeable situation.

After Liancourt came the chief ministers, financiers, senators, and deputies, leaders of society, soldiers, diplomats, and representatives of various sections of the people—an unending stream of friends who began by protesting, but who finally resolved to show the reality of their friendship by promising to help him.

Gradually strange rumors crept into the newspapers, but they were all inspired. Vansittart was about to give one more sublime proof of his disinterestedness. He wanted nothing for himself, this wonder-worker, he was all for France. His name would pass through the ages untarnished by the faintest breath of self-seeking; he would be the model revolutionist of all time.

When, in due course, he received the unanimous invitation of Senate and Chamber to assume the royal style and prerogatives, he accepted the request on the plainly expressed understanding that he would be empowered to resign at any time he should think fit, and to designate his successor, provided his nominee were acceptable to the people of France.

There was much marvelling at this stipulation. Every one knew that it foreshadowed some unexpected move on his part, but the popular confidence in his integrity was at such a pitch that nothing he asked for could be refused.

France had good reason for this unbounded trust. Vansittart had concentrated the national life, and practically doubled the national resources. Commerce had never been so good, the government never so strong, the working classes never so contented, as during the millionnaire's *régime*. People were so busy making money that they ceased to worry about the usually too delicate French susceptibilities in other directions, with the immediate result that the influence of France among the nations had increased tenfold. Neither Press nor politicians had any longer the incentive to plunge the country into difficulties with Germany or England. They were both utterly subjugated by Vansittart's all-powerful domination, and in Parliament or Bourse they were helpless and voiceless. Truth to tell, Jerome obtained no inconsiderable slice of support in his subsequent proceedings from these free-lances of French public life. There were many who would be glad to see his commanding personality removed from the arena. With the giant gone, there were chances for the pigmies.

Perhaps the chief element in his favor was that most potent popular force—curiosity.

Vansittart had so often astounded France that she was eager to be astounded again. It suited her humor. She had waxed fat and prosperous under this showman's rule. Each successive *tableau vivant* was more piquant than its predecessor, and had meant more money. Pray heaven the American might keep it up!

All this time his tact was unfailing and inimitable. Having impressed Mademoiselle and Prince Henri with the necessity of leaving matters entirely in his hands, he gave a series of superb entertainments, at which he contrived to make them the chief figures. They became *connu* once more in society, and France learnt again, to her amazement, that she not only possessed some notable scions of her past monarchies, but that they were on the most friendly terms with "The Emperor." Prince Henri of Navarre set up a magnificent establishment at Versailles, and Mademoiselle de Montpensier was formally installed in the Château of St. Cloud.

The Princess Marchesi and the Comtesse de Fontainebleau moved in an earthly paradise. There was intrigue on foot, and they were allowed to be behind the scenes whilst the principal actor was leading his audience up to the thrilling *dénouement* of the last act. And the curtain was about to rise upon it.

Vansittart was formally declared Emperor by both Houses of Representatives. By his own special desire, however, he continued to be officially recognized as President until the date of the coronation ceremony at Notre Dame, which was fixed to take place at the earliest possible moment.

And now he commenced to hurry things. He published a proclamation to the effect that what France wanted, above all else, was a responsible and lasting government, to enable her to consolidate her position and economize her improving finances. Again he asked the people to trust him as they had done before, and to demonstrate their trust by promptly approving the steps he should take to achieve the end he had in view.

The Chamber of Deputies responded by a hearty vote of confidence, for already there was ample indication of his intentions. Even England and the other Great Powers, some of whom had looked askance at the rapid climb of this adventurer to the pinnacle of Empire, took a friendly interest in his scheme. This was shown by the fact that they all accepted his official invitation to attend the coronation ceremony.

When at last the great day itself arrived, Paris, indeed all

France, was ablaze with color, and quivering with pleasurable excitement.

A noteworthy item in the official programme read as follows :

"The Emperor-Elect, accompanied by Prince Henri of Navarre and the Princesse de Montpensier, will proceed from the Palais de l'Élysée to Notre Dame in a State carriage," whilst at the foot of the processional programme it was stated that the *cortège* would return to the Palais " in the same order as it departed." Each phrase in this notification suggested question and provoked analysis.

It would be a pleasant task to chronicle the glories of this unique display, were it not that the mere fopperies of existence can find but trivial place in the life record of such a man as Vansittart.

Paris is the most beautiful city in the world. On this memorable occasion she decked herself as a bride for the wedding day. And she was serious withal, for the sway of this strong man, who had moulded her fortunes to suit a whim grown to a passion, had influenced her character and taught her a decorous philosophy. Vansittart sought to espouse France to happiness and quiet development, and, in yielding to his desires, a volatile and fickle people had suddenly become politically domesticated. These unsuspected virtues shone in the conduct of the millions who came to gaze at the brilliant spectacle. They shouted themselves hoarse in greeting a conqueror who offered them peace instead of war, colonial extension in place of foreign aggression, lands smiling with cultivation rather than provinces deluged with blood.

No wonder the people cheered, or that they were content to believe that what Vansittart did was right. Had the French workman understood the quaint language of Jim Bates, he would have agreed with that worthy fire-eater's oft-repeated truism, "What the boss says, goes."

Within the spacious cathedral of Notre Dame a notable

company had gathered, and before the royal procession arrived it was remarked, with some degree of astonishment, that two crowns reposed on fauteuils in front of the golden altar—a guard of honor, consisting of the colonels of every cavalry regiment in France, lining the sanctuary behind the altar and on both sides of the choir.

A subdued murmur of excitement also greeted the appearance of Vansittart, who, in the simple evening dress worn for ceremonial purposes in France, advanced alone to the rails, and stood on one side.

He was followed by M. Liancourt, who supported on his arm Mademoiselle Honorine de Montpensier, attired in an exquisite wedding-dress, with a veil that had graced the brows of Marie Antoinette.

Prince Henri, attended by an Austrian Grand Duke, came quickly behind them, and at the same moment the Archbishop of Paris, accompanied by a bevy of high dignitaries of the Church, entered the chancel.

Before the assembly had quite grasped the significance of what was happening, Prince Henri and Honorine were wedded, and Jerome was the first witness to sign the register, which was produced by an attendant for the purpose. Unknown to any save a few, the civil marriage had taken place earlier in the day. Every one present was definitely aware of the nature of Vansittart's contemplated action, but its manner was novel and highly dramatic.

The newly made husband and wife entered the chancel, and seated themselves under a canopy, whilst Vansittart quietly stood with his hand upon the rail of the sanctuary, facing the body of the church, but slightly inclined towards the Prince and Princess of Navarre.

It was evident that he was about to address the vast congregation, and a deep hush swayed it into silence like a breath of wind through a forest on a still summer's day. He had prepared a careful address, but he now realized that the selected words of judicial reasoning are seldom applicable to the major moments of existence. So he stated his case simply and candidly, with an entire absence of effort that went to the hearts of his auditors.

"My friends," he said, and the homely phrase penetrated even the diplomatic bosom, "I have to ask your kindly interest in a personal statement.

"Three years ago, inspired by the twofold motive of a keen interest in the fortunes of the gracious lady you have now seen happily married, and a strong desire to use beneficially the wealth with which Providence had been pleased to endow me, I set out from my home in America to win an empire in France.

"I make no secret of my object, and all the world to-day knows that I have succeeded. I offer no excuse. This part of my scheme was entirely a personal one. In the same breath, I state my conviction that the people of France, whom I love, have not had cause to complain of my methods of conquest.

"But with success has come experience. I have learnt that my true reward lay in my work, and since that work has practically passed from my hands, being in an administrative and almost completed stage, there has come the conviction that it will be better for the people of France if I should strive to restore and remodel old and well established institutions rather than wholly create a new system of government.

"At best, a man can only be an humble instrument in the hands of Providence. I firmly believe I am doing right in the eyes of the Deity and of my fellow-men when I forthwith renounce the position which the citizens of France have seen fit in their generosity to confer upon me. In thus abdicating, I also wish to exercise the further power they have entrusted me with, and I now nominate Prince Henri of Navarre as King of France in my stead, whilst in the same breath I wish their Majesties, the King and Queen, long life and happiness for themselves and their most excellent subjects."

A lady fainted from excitement in the nave of the cathedral, and the incident gave all present a momentary relief from the extreme tension created by Vansittart's magnificent renunciation.

When he resumed his address he wisely adopted an impersonal strain.

"The Cabinets of Europe have been consulted with regard to the accession to the throne of His Majesty Henry V. and Her Majesty the Queen, who both take the honored titles of their race. Without exception the Great Powers have given unqualified approval to the proposition. A special session of the Senate and Chamber of Deputies held this morning has conferred constitutional sanction upon the coronation ceremony which will now take place, and His Majesty the King will subsequently confirm all existing Ministers in their appointments. It only remains for me to ask you to join me, in all sincerity and good feeling, when I say, 'Long live their Majesties the King and Queen of France.'"

Amidst the clang of sabres and scabbards, as every officer present drew his sword, and held it high in air, a great shout of wonderment and approval rang through the vaulted aisles.

Vansittart stepped down from the elevated platform of the chancel, and as he did so, his quick glance sought one figure in all that brilliant company. His eyes met those of Evelyn Harland, and she smiled at him through her tears.

Meanwhile some inkling of events within the cathedral had been communicated to the crowd without. Indeed, through the whole of Paris the newspapers had made known the fact that the Senate and Chamber had approved of Vansittart's resolve to abdicate in favor of the Legitimist heir to the throne. But in the same issues they contained a signed statement from Vansittart announcing that he would still continue to serve France in an unofficial capacity.

"I am a French citizen," he wrote, "and I will retain that honorable distinction until I die."

He thus cleverly answered the first question that would arise in the public mind—France was assured of his unabated interest and support.

Yet, when the royal party, with whom was Jerome, emerged from the great doors of Notre Dame, it was a ticklish moment.

Things *might* go wrong. The people *might* resent Vansittart's action, and if they became possessed by this notion, there would be disturbance in Paris that night. But the mere sight of the millionnaire standing on the left of the Queen, with his confident smile and his pleasant greeting to the crowd, at once banished such thoughts if they ever existed. A roar of exultation met him. Although the courtiers among the people shouted, "*Vive le Roi*," and "*Vive la Reine*," the vast voice of the multitude yelled, "Long live the Emperor."

Vansittart was "the Emperor" for them, and would be "the Emperor" as long as the breath remained in their bodies.

"It is well," he said to Honorine as he took a seat facing her in the royal carriage. "The more they cheer me the better it is for you."

For answer she bent forward, took his hand, and would have kissed it, but he was quick to anticipate her, and his lips met her fingers instead.

The young King sat silent and preoccupied until Jerome addressed him.

"Your Majesty already feels the weight of the crown!" he said.

Henri smiled seriously.

"Please don't call me 'Your Majesty' just yet," he cried. "It sounds ridiculous from *you*. I have been thinking what I can say or do to thank you. But I am unequal to the duty; I can only resolve to try and live up to the splendid example you have given me."

It was late that night before Jerome could get a single

moment alone with Evelyn. When he did he took her in his arms and whispered:

"I felt quite sorry for those two to-day. They must live in the midst of wearisome Court ceremonies, everlastingly the same. I was bored before the thing commenced. Now, you and I——"

And their lips met.

CHAPTER XLII

"SAHARA, LIMITED," WOUND UP

JEROME and Evelyn were married quietly, a month later, in the English Church in Paris. There were six witnesses—the King and Queen of France, Dick Harland, Liancourt, Arizona Jim, and Peter Studevant, who was officially present as a trustee under the marriage settlement. That is to say, six were present by invitation, but there was a seventh guest who invited himself, and who was none the less welcome when he appeared.

For what happened in Paris that M. Folliet did not know? He was now Minister of Police under the restored monarchy, but in his private means he was independent of his office, as the millionnaire had rewarded his devoted services with a liberality that astounded even one who was well acquainted with his generous nature.

When he came forward to tender his congratulations, Vansittart reproached himself for having momentarily forgotten him, but Folliet settled the matter with ready wit.

"Monsieur," he said, in his best Prefecture manner, "the mere fixing of the date was an invitation to the Chief of Police." Then, turning to the newly made bride, he added: "I ask your kindly acceptance of a small memento of this notable day. When your distinguished husband came to Paris, I chanced to be the first citizen to exchange words with him. He gave me a ring which has in very truth been a talisman to me. But my destiny is determined; yours but dawns upon you. The ring is here, intact, but in form more suitable to a lady, and I trust you will honor me by accepting it."

He produced a superb bracelet, studded with diamonds, the central object being Vansittart's gift, cunningly refashioned to suggest in relief its original shape. Evelyn could not resist a cry of delight at the beauty of the ornament no less than the motive of the giver.

"It is indeed a symbol of good luck," she said, "and you have taken care, Monsieur Folliet, that it shall not be wanting in appearance to back its promise."

Folliet was greatly pleased by her appreciation.

"There is a diamond to mark each month that I have had the honor of knowing your husband, madame," he explained.

"I think, monsieur," cried Honorine, with a merry laugh, "that you might hand a similar token to me, as I also am fortunate in Mr. Vansittart's advent to Paris."

"Not so," interrupted the King. "M. Folliet would be ruined by the deed; he would require to purchase a diamond for every hour."

"In truth, yes," said the Queen. "I withdraw my request, monsieur, for it is I and not you who should make the presentation."

"At any rate, I may offer your Majesties my life-long service and devotion," said the Minister of Police with a deep bow.

"Then believe me," cried Vansittart, "there are no jewels equal to such a gift. Had I a dozen lives I should have lost them all were it not for you, monsieur."

At the informal breakfast that followed, the King broached a subject close to his heart.

"When may we expect you back in Paris from your wedding tour, Vansittart?"

"There will be no wedding tour, in the ordinary sense of the word," answered Vansittart with a quiet smile at Evelyn. "We do not leave France for a few days, and then we will visit America for a prolonged sight-seeing trip. I am anxious to show my wife the glories of the New World."

"After I have seen the Sahara," chimed in Evelyn.

"Yes, we take that *en route*."

"But, look here. This is not fair," said Henri, whose sudden anxiety made him pale. "I cannot do without you. It is impossible, this journey, at least for months, if not years. I am too inexperienced, too impulsive, too prone to act rashly. Even when you are near me, I am at times bewildered by the pressure of State affairs. You must not go. It is not to be thought of; is it, Honorine? And you, Liancourt; say that it cannot be."

Honorine was silent, but looked with a grave face from the King to Vansittart. Liancourt gazed into his plate.

"Bear with me a moment, whilst I place matters in a different light," said Vansittart, the earnestness of his words carrying conviction to the ears of the perplexed monarch as he listened.

"There is every reason why I should leave France, if not forever, at least for a lengthened period. You are now firmly placed on a constitutional throne. You are surrounded by devoted and able ministers, headed by my most trusted friend and councillor, Liancourt, who, I can see, is already disposed to favor my views. Your people are contented and prosperous. Keep them so, and you cannot do wrong. Forget ancient shibboleths concerning the divine right of kings, and remember that you are only the chief citizen of France. You cannot be removed from your high position, but the knowledge of the fact should render you only more anxious to act in accordance with the wishes of those whom you govern.

"So long as I remain in France, you will never fill your true place. Surely I do not need to urge this view upon you. But when I am gone my name and deeds will soon be a memory, a pleasant and notable one, I trust, but nevertheless a personality ever becoming more dim and legendary. You are the King, and as fresh events take new ground in the public mind, you will be the King in tangible and ever present reality.

"I am not wholly consulting the desires of my wife and myself in thus quitting France, the glorious scene of my life's work. But destiny has shaped our ends very different to that which was visible to our mortal eyes three years ago. We are all, I am sure, well content. Providence has guided us more truly than our own puny intelligences. And it would be injuring, nay, almost imperilling the fair structure we have erected were not the course adopted that I now recommend."

The King offered no word when Jerome concluded. Henri was, as he himself said, rash and impulsive, but he was clearly learning the art of self-control.

"Vansittart is right," said Liancourt.

"Mr. Vansittart is always right," said the Queen.

"But what of the Sahara? How will your Scheme fare if you are thousands of miles away?" The King was even becoming business-like.

"Naturally, I have not forgotten that. The Sahara is now an accomplished fact. A week ago Maclaren cabled that fifty million gallons of distilled water were daily flowing into the desert from both sections, and barely a quarter of the plant is yet at work. The development and control of the irrigation is a mere question of time and ordinary skill. Mr. Studevant agrees with me that the right course to take now is for France to nationalize the undertaking. This can be done by issuing Government stock at a little over the present market value of the shares. There will be no dissatisfaction at this course, and no call upon the finances of the kingdom. It is a mere paper transaction, and will render the Sahara an integral portion of French territory. For convenience, it will be advisable to retain the organization of the Company, and I strongly advise you to keep Mr.

Maclaren in chief control so long as he lives. You will never regret the transaction in any sense."

"Is it really such a simple matter?" Henri was even yet astounded by Jerome's ease in dealing with financial problems of phenomenal scope.

"There is no difficulty; it can be settled in a day by the Chambers. 'Sahara, Limited,' must go into liquidation as a formal affair, but you will find your creditors highly complaisant. Some may want their money, and that is a momentary question of selling sufficient stock to pay them. I, as the largest shareholder, and the vast majority of others, will gladly accept French bonds at 2½ per cent. for our property, as it will be acquired by the State at 100 per cent. premium. On the other hand, a sixty-years sinking fund will probably clear France of this great increase to her national debt, and she will have the finest colony in the world for nothing."

The King was convinced, but still desirous to stop Vansittart's departure.

"This is a splendid project, and quite worthy of you; but surely you will remain to see it through?"

"What? Put in a year's clerical work, which Studevant and the Bank of France can perform better without me? Not I ! We want our honeymoon, don't we, Evelyn?"

"Most certainly," cried Evelyn. "I can't spare you at an office all day. Besides, you deserve a long holiday. You 've not had one since—since——"

"Since I first met you," laughed Jerome.

When the party broke up a little later, Evelyn confided to him that she was personally delighted at the proposal that they should leave France, as she felt somewhat constrained at meeting Honorine so constantly.

Vansittart chuckled at the confession.

"My little girl is not jealous, is she?" he cried.

"I jealous! No, indeed. I can afford to pity her for her poor taste."

"Well, what is the other reason?"

"There is no *other* reason. Just one, but that is sufficient. One day at St. Cloud, we had—well, there—we had an awful row."

"You and Honorine?"

"Yes."

"What about?"

"About you!"

"About me! For goodness' sake, why did you quarrel about me?"

"Oh, I don't know how it commenced. But she knew that I was fond of you, and she taunted me with it. I said some terribly nasty things to her about Prince Henri, and we both wept for hours afterwards. Now, Jerry, don't! How ridiculous we would look if a servant came in. There! My hair is all disarranged, and I cannot look Suzanne in the face, for she is *sure* to know. Oh, well. It does n't matter *now*, as I *must* put it straight in *any* case. But I'm so glad we're going."

The *Seafarer* bore a small but happy company from Marseilles to the Gulf of Gabes.

Vansittart and his wife were accompanied by the inseparable pair, Dick Harland and Jim Bates, no longer the Master of the Horse and the Captain of the Guard, but rejoicing in the less sonorous and equally lucrative posts of Private Secretary and Chief of the Luggage Department.

Maclaren met them at Gabes, and conveyed them by special train to the well remembered scenes of former difficulties and dangers. Wheat was growing on the battle-ground of El Hegef, and a tolerable stream flowed through the gully where Vansittart and Arizona Jim remained in hiding after the affair at Tugurt.

But the Sahara sun was powerful, and Evelyn began to pale beneath his ardent rays, so Vansittart hurried her back to Gabes and on board his palatial yacht. The word now was "Home," and on the evening of the second day after they left Gabes the Highlands of Morocco were fast sinking into the horizon as the *Seafarer* sped gallantly on her path across the Atlantic.

Vansittart, Evelyn, and Dick were sitting in the saloon, when they were startled by a noise like a pistol shot. They rushed on deck to find Jim Bates leaning over the after taffrail and gazing at the African coast as though he saw a vision.

"What's the matter now, you Sioux?" shouted Vansittart, realizing in an instant that there was no cause for alarm.

"Nuthin'. I did n't allow you 'd hear me, an' I hope you was n't frightened, mam, or I 'd never forgive myself."

"But why did you fire, anyway?" said Jerome.

"Well, boss, I kinder felt I oughter fire a last shot as a salute. I was thinkin' of the times we had together over yonder, an' it seemed as if the hills nodded 'Good-bye; see you soon,' friendly like."

There was a far-away look in Jim's eyes, and an unconscious pathos in his voice. Vansittart understood his mood and joined him at the taffrail.

"I guess they 'll want you ag'in, boss," said Bates, after a pause.

"Why do you think so, Jim?"

"Well, you see, they 're helpless critters, the French. They kin fight when they 're set on, an' they can cook bully, but their blamed heads are like feathers. They just go as the wind puffs. They 'll want you ag'in, or my name ain't Arizona Jim."

"Perhaps you are right, my friend," said Vansittart, as he too looked steadfastly at the blue outline of the coast. "But whether they do or not, I am mighty glad that I am returning to America as I left it, and that my name is nothing more or less than plain Jerome K. Vansittart."

THE END.

www.ingramcontent.com/pod-product-compliance
Lightning Source LLC
Chambersburg PA
CBHW051723300426
44115CB00007B/441